STATE LEGISLATURES TODAY

POLITICS UNDER THE DOMES

THIRD EDITION

PEVERILL SQUIRE

University of Missouri

GARY MONCRIEF

Boise State University

ROWMAN & LITTLEFIELD

Lanham • Boulder • New York • London

Executive Editor: Traci Crowell
Editorial Assistant: Deni Remsberg
Senior Marketing Manager: Amy Whitaker
Interior Designer: Ilze Lemesis

Credits and acknowledgments for material borrowed from other sources, and reproduced with permission, appear on the appropriate page within the text.

Published by Rowman & Littlefield
An imprint of The Rowman & Littlefield Publishing Group, Inc.
4501 Forbes Boulevard, Suite 200, Lanham, Maryland 20706
www.rowman.com

6 Tinworth Street, London SE11 5AL, United Kingdom

British Library Cataloguing in Publication Information Available

Library of Congress Cataloging-in-Publication Data
Names: Moncrief, Gary F., author. | Squire, Peverill author. | Squire, Peverill State legislatures today.
Title: State legislatures today : politics under the domes / Gary Moncrief, Boise State University, Peverill Squire, University of Missouri.
Description: Third Edition. | Lanham : Rowman & Littlefield, [2019] | "Second edition 2015"—T.p. verso. | Principal author of second edition: Peverill Squire. | Includes bibliographical references and index.
Identifiers: LCCN 2019013295 (print) | LCCN 2019013336 (ebook) | ISBN 9781538123379 (electronic) | ISBN 9781538123355 | ISBN 9781538123355 (cloth : alk. paper) | ISBN 9781538123362 (paper : alk. paper)
Subjects: LCSH: Legislative bodies—United States—States. | U.S. states—Politics and government.
Classification: LCC JK2488 (ebook) | LCC JK2488 .S695 2019 (print) | DDC 328.73—dc23
LC record available at https://lccn.loc.gov/2019013295

Contents

Preface

While we were writing this third edition of *State Legislatures Today*, the 2018 elections took place. Although most of the national media's attention focused on what the returns meant for the federal government, an equally important story was unfolding at the state government level. Democrats picked up a substantial number of seats and took charge of several legislatures, putting a dent into the control of state governments Republicans have enjoyed since the 2010 elections. But, more importantly, while the election created divided government at the federal level, it left a substantial number of states operating under unified government. Thus, while gridlock is likely in Washington, D.C., at the state level those governments under GOP control will be passing conservative policies while those being run by the Democrats will be putting liberal policies into place. All of this means that much of the policymaking action in American politics will be taking place in the legislative institutions found in Sacramento, Albany, Austin, and Tallahassee, as well as in Boise, Jefferson City, and Pierre. As we have emphasized starting with the first edition of this book, understanding how state legislatures operate is essential for a full understanding of how American politics operates and that continues to be the case.

Because the governing environment in the fifty state capitols is dynamic, we have had to address a number of new topics in this edition. Thus, we examine the #MeToo movement, increasing membership diversity, the changing relationship between the states and the federal government and the states and their local governments, changing redistricting rules and procedures, and how lawmakers make use of social media. And, as always, we have worked to integrate recent scholarly findings into our analysis.

We are grateful for the comments our colleagues who have used the book have offered, as well as Julia M. Hellwege (University of South Dakota). We think they have helped improve it. As always, we are grateful for the support we have gotten from Jon Sisk, Traci Crowell, and their colleagues at Rowman & Littlefield.

Peverill Squire
Gary Moncrief

Chapter 1

Ninety-Nine Chambers and Why They Matter

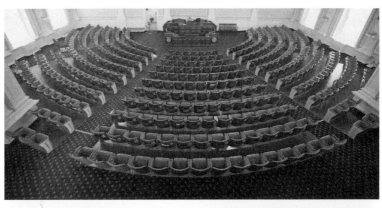

The large and small of state legislative chambers: The New Hampshire House of Representatives (top) has four hundred members and the Alaska Senate (bottom) has twenty members. © iStock / P_Wei; AP Photo/Becky Bohrer.

On June 1, 2018, Missouri governor Eric Greitens resigned. Beset by multiple scandals, Greitens was forced out of office in large part because of the efforts of a special legislative committee established by the Missouri House of Representatives to investigate the accusations leveled against him. What was particularly noteworthy about this episode was that it involved a Republican governor being brought down by the actions of a legislature in which the GOP enjoyed a supermajority in each house. The information compiled and made public by the committee and the prospect that the full House might use it to start impeachment proceedings put Governor Greitens in a politically untenable position.[1]

As might be expected given its sometimes sordid details, the governor's saga dominated the state's news media. Consequently, for many Missourians the drama surrounding the governor's political demise may be all they know or recall about the 2018 legislative session. Yet any assumption that legislators had focused all of their time and effort on the governor's problems would be misguided. By the end of its five-month session, the legislature had actually accomplished a great deal. Lawmakers had adopted a $28 billion balanced budget containing full funding for K–12 education for the first time in many years. Bills to reduce the corporate state income tax rate and to reform individual state income taxes had passed. The way the state structures utility rates was changed. Legislation revising the state's prevailing wage law for public construction projects passed, as did a "paycheck protection" measure that forces public employee unions to get permission from their members annually to withhold dues for partisan political purposes. Revenge porn was outlawed, and the minimum age to marry was raised to sixteen.[2] All of this legislation was important to the lives of Missourians.

Missouri's situation is not unusual. Every state legislature suffers from a lack of public attention. Constituents often take note of their activities only when something dramatic or frivolous gains media attention. Yet the decisions made by state legislators impact every aspect of Americans' daily lives, including the taxes they pay, the education they receive, the roads they drive, and the health and safety of their communities. Despite the centrality of the policies they make, Americans know remarkably little about their state legislatures or legislators.

This book is an effort to remedy this deficiency by examining state legislatures and state lawmakers in depth. In this chapter we begin by placing state legislatures in their proper historical context, demonstrating that although the original state legislatures and the U.S. Congress had much in common when they were first established, they have evolved over the past two centuries to become different kinds of legislative organizations. We then provide a primer on the fifty state legislatures today, highlighting their variety of institutional sizes and structures, again to emphasize the point that they are not copies of Congress. In the final section we provide an outline for the rest of the book.

State Legislatures in Historical Context

State legislatures as a group have a longer history than does the U.S. Congress. By the time Congress first met in 1789, the original state legislatures had already been in existence for thirteen years. But the age discrepancy is actually greater than that because the original state legislatures evolved directly from their colonial predecessors.[3] In the case of Virginia, its colonial assembly first met in 1619, meaning the legislature enjoyed a 157-year history even before American independence was declared.

This history is important to appreciate because it means that state legislatures are not simple imitations of Congress. Indeed, in several notable regards, the evolutionary relationship actually runs the other way. The design of the Congress created by the Constitution owes much more to the original state legislatures than it does to its predecessor Congress under the Articles of Confederation.[4] That the founders drew on the state legislative experience in writing the Constitution should not be surprising because, of the thirty-nine men who signed that document, eighteen had served in colonial assemblies and thirty-two had served in state legislatures.[5] Yet the similarity between the Congress and the original state legislatures is ironic because many of the men who wrote the Constitution, most notably James Madison and George Mason, distrusted the state bodies because they thought they wielded too much power.[6]

The most obvious similarity between the first state legislatures and Congress was the number of houses. Like eleven of the original thirteen state legislatures—Georgia and Pennsylvania were the exceptions—the Constitutional Congress was created as a bicameral body. In contrast, the Congress under the Articles had been unicameral. The two houses of Congress were also given the names most commonly used in the states.

There were other similarities. The U.S. Senate was given longer terms than the U.S. House; upper houses in four states had longer terms than their lower houses.[7] U.S. senators were given six-year terms, longer than any upper house terms in the states. The Senate's terms, however, were three times longer than those for the lower house, as were those in Delaware. And although all but one state legislature had either six-month or one-year terms for the members of their lower houses—the Congress under the Articles also had one-year terms—South Carolina gave its representatives the same two-year term that members of the U.S. House were later granted.

Other significant provisions of the U.S. Constitution regarding Congress appear in earlier manifestations in the original state constitutions. While separation of powers among the legislature, executive, and judiciary appeared in each state constitution and the U.S. Constitution, these institutions had been fused under the Articles. In the U.S. Constitution, individual members of Congress were each given an equally weighted vote, just like their state legislative counterparts. In the Congress under the Articles, each state, not each lawmaker, got a vote. Other noteworthy resemblances were the provisions allowing each house to adopt its own rules and to select its own leaders, powers that enhance legislative independence from other governmental entities. State legislatures were given explicit authority to select their own leaders in ten constitutions and to devise their own rules in five constitutions. Thus, the leadership selection and rule-making provisions put in the U.S. Constitution are similar to those that appeared in many of the first state constitutions.

Another important provision in the U.S. Constitution involves the power to originate tax legislation. The idea that *money bills*, as they were called, should originate in the lower house was well rooted in American history; colonial assemblies successfully claimed exclusive origination privileges early in many of their histories. The majority of the original state constitutions continued the tradition by granting the lower house exclusive rights to initiate tax legislation. Most state constitutions forbade the upper house from amending tax bills. The Constitutional Convention, however, opted for the process established in Delaware and Massachusetts, in which tax bills originated in the lower house but the upper house could amend them.

Finally, although most state constitutions did not grant their governors a veto power, three did: South Carolina, New York, and Massachusetts. The veto power given to the president in the Constitution is the same as that granted the governor of Massachusetts. Indeed, the language used in the Constitution is lifted almost verbatim from the Massachusetts Constitution.

Congress, then, initially started out looking like the state legislatures rather than the other way around. Moreover, at the beginning, Congress was not seen as being more important or powerful than the state legislatures. For instance, although Jonathan Dayton was elected to serve as a member of the U.S. House from New Jersey in 1788, he declined the office to serve instead as speaker of the New Jersey Assembly. Even into the early nineteenth century, it was not unusual for a member of Congress to give up his seat to take a state-level post: over the first three decades under the U.S. Constitution, roughly a third of all departing members of Congress later took state legislative seats.[8]

Once the Congress under the Constitution was established, however, it began to exert influence on state legislative organization. When Georgia adopted its second constitution in 1789, for example, the legislature was made bicameral, largely to emulate the new federal structure, and Pennsylvania quickly followed suit in 1790.[9] Over the next century, however, Congress and the state legislatures generally began following separate and distinct evolutionary paths.[10]

The Lineage of the State Legislatures

As shown in table 1.1, the original thirteen state legislatures emerged from their colonial predecessors. The other thirty-seven state legislatures have different lineages.[11] A total of thirty-one state legislatures came directly out of the thirty territorial legislatures that preceded them (upon statehood, Dakota Territory was split into North Dakota and South Dakota). The U.S. Congress created territorial legislatures as part of the governing structure it put in place when territories were established. The territorial legislatures were important because their rules, committee structures, and occasionally personnel transferred over to the state legislatures that eventually supplanted them.

Other legislative bodies preceded several of the territorial legislatures, and they also played important roles in the territorial legislature's institutional evolution. In Oregon there were several iterations of a provisional legislature that made laws while the United States and Great Britain competed for political control of

TABLE 1.1 The Lineage of American State Legislatures

State	Year State Legislature First Convened[a]	Predecessor Legislature(s) (Years Met)
Connecticut	1776	colonial assembly (1637–1776)
Delaware	1776	colonial assembly (1704–1775)
Massachusetts	1776	colonial assembly (1634–1777)
New Hampshire	1776	colonial assembly (1680–1775)
New Jersey	1776	colonial assembly (1668–1776; split into separate East Jersey and West Jersey assemblies from 1676 to 1702)
Pennsylvania	1776	colonial assembly (1682–1776)
Rhode Island	1776	colonial assembly (1647–1776)
South Carolina	1776	colonial assembly (1671–1775)
Virginia	1776	colonial assembly (1619–1775)
Georgia	1777	colonial assembly (1755–1776)
Maryland	1777	colonial assembly (1637 or 1638–1774)
New York	1777	colonial assembly (1683–1775)
North Carolina	1777	colonial assembly (1671–1775)
Vermont	1791	Vermont General Assembly (1778–1791)
Kentucky	1792	none, earlier represented in Virginia General Assembly
Tennessee	1796	Southwest territorial legislature (1794–1795), earlier represented in North Carolina General Assembly
Ohio	1803	Northwest territorial legislature (1799–1801)
Louisiana	1812	Orleans territorial legislature (1804–1811)
Indiana	1816	territorial legislature (1805–1816)
Mississippi	1817	territorial legislature (1800–1817)
Illinois	1818	territorial legislature (1812–1818)
Alabama	1819	territorial legislature (1818)
Maine	1820	none, earlier represented in Massachusetts General Court
Missouri	1820	territorial legislature (1812–1820)
Michigan	1835	territorial legislature (1824–1835)
Arkansas	1836	territorial legislature (1820–1835)
Florida	1845	territorial legislature (1822–1845)
Iowa	1846	territorial legislature (1838–1846)
Texas	1846	Congress of the Republic of Texas (1836–1845)

(Continued)

State	Year State Legislature First Convened[a]	Predecessor Legislature(s) (Years Met)
Wisconsin	1848	territorial legislature (1836–1848)
California	1849	none
Minnesota	1857	territorial legislature (1849–1857)
Oregon	1859	provisional legislatures (1843–1849) territorial legislature (1849–1859)
Kansas	1861	territorial legislature (1855–1861) and Free State Legislature (1856–1857)
West Virginia	1863	none, earlier represented in Virginia General Assembly
Nevada	1864	territorial legislature (1861–1864)
Nebraska	1866	territorial legislature (1855–1867)
Colorado	1876	territorial legislature (1861–1876)
Montana	1889	territorial legislature (1864–1889)
North Dakota	1889	Dakota territorial legislature (1862–1889)
Washington	1889	territorial legislature (1854–1888)
South Dakota	1890	Dakota territorial legislature (1862–1889)
Idaho	1890	territorial legislature (1863–1889)
Wyoming	1890	territorial legislature (1869–1890)
Utah	1896	General Assembly of Deseret (1849–1851) territorial legislature (1854–1895)
Oklahoma	1907	territorial legislature (1890–1905)
Arizona	1912	territorial legislature (1864–1909)
New Mexico	1912	territorial legislature (1851–1909)
Alaska	1959	territorial legislature (1913–1958)
Hawaii	1959	Kingdom of Hawaii legislatures (1840–1892) Republic of Hawaii legislature (1894–1898) territorial legislature (1901–1959)

[a]   State legislatures in some states met prior to the state being admitted to the union.
Sources: Peverill Squire, *The Evolution of American Legislatures: Colonies, Territories and States, 1619–2009* (Ann Arbor: University of Michigan Press, 2012) and Peverill Squire, *The Rise of the Representative: Lawmakers and Constituents in Colonial America* (Ann Arbor: University of Michigan Press, 2017).

the area. Prior to the creation of Utah Territory, Mormons founded the State of Deseret with an elected general assembly. In Hawaii, the territorial legislature was preceded by several legislatures of the Kingdom of Hawaii and a legislature established under the Republic of Hawaii. Finally, in Kansas an unofficial Free State Legislature arose to not only challenge the pro-slavery territorial legislature but also eventually displace it in the state legislature's evolutionary line.

There were six state legislatures that did not have either a colonial or a territorial predecessor. Both Vermont and Kentucky were admitted as states before Congress created the territorial system. Maine and West Virginia were split off from Massachusetts and Virginia, respectively; Maine's new legislature looked much like its parent, but West Virginia's drew on a number of different models. The Congress of the Texas Republic, which had been modeled on the U.S. Congress and several state legislatures, preceded the legislature in Texas. Finally, California became a state before any civilian territorial government was established, leaving it to have to create its legislature from scratch.

State Legislative Evolution in the Nineteenth Century

During the nineteenth century, state legislatures experienced two significant evolutionary trends. One was that existing legislatures underwent extensive organizational transformations. Many of these changes were pushed by disaffected political elites and voters who were disgusted by the perceived (and in many cases, real) abuses of power on the part of state legislatures. Thus, as state constitutions were revised or replaced, provisions were adopted that greatly constrained the power of legislatures in the policymaking process.[12]

The other trend was that the number of American state legislatures increased markedly, with twenty-nine of them being created between 1803 and 1896 as new states were admitted to the union. All of the new legislatures were established as bicameral bodies because it was thought that a second house prevented, or at least slowed down, the passage of bad legislation.[13] (Vermont's unicameral assembly was transformed into a bicameral legislature in 1836.) Most importantly, new state legislatures were created to look like existing state legislatures.[14]

Although modeled on established bodies, these fledgling institutions were often rowdy and difficult to manage. For instance, during a legislative debate in the inaugural session of the Arkansas House in 1837, Speaker John Wilson and Representative Joseph Anthony became so angry with each other that Wilson left the speaker's chair and lunged for Anthony on the House floor. In the ensuing fight, both men drew hunting knives and Wilson stabbed Anthony to death.[15] Such outrageous behavior was not unusual. The first session of the California legislature in 1849 was labeled the "Legislature of a Thousand Drinks" because, at the end of each session, one senator would encourage his colleagues to adjourn to the whisky kegs he kept stashed just outside the meeting hall, saying, "Well, boys, let's go and take a thousand drinks."[16] Reputedly, California's initial lawmakers "appeared in the legislative halls with revolvers and bowie knives fastened to their belts and were drinking, rioting, and swearing nearly all the time."[17]

But even with primitive facilities and boorish members, organizationally, the new legislatures were anything but rudimentary because they were closely modeled after their existing peer institutions. The generational impact of older state legislatures on newer ones is clearly seen in two areas: committee systems and rules of procedure.

The first thirteen state legislatures made limited use of standing committees—committees that continue to exist from session to session—to process their work. In Massachusetts, for example, standing committees appeared in 1777, and a "fairly elaborate system had developed by 1790."[18] Thus, in the first legislatures, standing committee systems evolved over time. By 1819 every legislature had at least a few standing committees—Connecticut had only two and the mean was seven—while several had a good number of them—Massachusetts used seventeen. Seven decades later, the mean number of standing committees had exploded to thirty-three, with Delaware using only fourteen and Iowa and Michigan each naming fifty-three. Importantly, by the end of the nineteenth century standing committees played a central role in the legislative process in every state, with most enjoying gatekeeping powers allowing them to kill legislation.

The pedigree of legislative rules and procedures is more complicated to trace. An examination of the rules in the early Indiana legislature, for example, reveals, "The first general assemblies drew their rules from those adopted by the House of Representatives during the first territorial assembly in Indiana in 1805. These were in turn based upon rules adopted by the first session of the House of Representatives of the Northwest Territory in 1799."[19] The rules of the Northwest Territory House were directly descended from the rules developed during the first session of the U.S. House. Similar inheritance patterns were evidenced in other state legislatures.[20]

More generally, these legislative rules became more sophisticated and complex over time. Over the course of the nineteenth century, lower houses greatly increased the total number of rules under which they operated. In 1819, the mean number of rules across the states was thirty-seven, with Delaware using the fewest at sixteen and Massachusetts using the most at fifty-eight. By 1889, the mean number of rules had increased to sixty-four, again with Delaware using the fewest at twenty-six and Massachusetts the most at 102. More important, toward the end of the century most rules focused on managing the complexities of the legislative process rather than controlling member behavior.

Thus, state legislatures were well-developed institutions by the end of the nineteenth century. They had adopted standing committee systems and sophisticated rules and procedures. In that sense, they looked much like Congress. But while state constitutions were rewritten to rein in legislative powers, the U.S. Constitution was left untouched in regard to congressional organization, and the Thirteenth, Fourteenth, and Fifteenth amendments, which were added to it in the aftermath of the Civil War, expanded congressional powers (although it was decades before these new powers were exploited). Toward the end of the century, Congress also began to professionalize, greatly increasing its informational resources and, in turn, its impact on the policymaking process. Thus, during the course of the nineteenth century, the power of state legislatures waned while Congress was becoming a more powerful institution.

State Legislative Evolution in the Twentieth Century

It was only in the twentieth century that state legislatures began to view Congress as a model to be emulated. This was not necessarily because Congress was deemed more visible or important but because Congress became a more professional organization that was better equipped to meet the policy challenges it faced. The story of state legislative evolution became one of a lagging effort to effect similar organizational improvements.

As we will discuss in greater depth in chapter 3, legislatures that are deemed professional meet in unlimited sessions, provide superior staff resources, and pay members well enough to allow them to pursue service as their vocation. The evolution of state legislatures in the twentieth century is a story of professionalization. At the start of the twentieth century, the vast majority of state legislatures were similar to one another. They paid their members little, met for relatively few days, and had almost no staff. Over the following century, substantial differences emerged across the states.[21] Legislatures in a few states, all with large populations, became well-paid, full-time bodies, with large staffs, much like the U.S. Congress. Many of the remaining legislatures improved their lot, at least a little. Some, however, failed to change much at all.[22] Thus, by the beginning of the twenty-first century, state legislatures varied greatly from one another, as well as from Congress.

State Legislatures Today

The basic characteristics of state legislatures today are given in table A.1 in the appendix. None of them is referred to as *Congress*. Just over half of the states call their lawmaking body the *Legislature*. Most of the rest are referred to as the *General Assembly*. North Dakota and Oregon blend the two names with the *Legislative Assembly*, the title given to the territorial legislatures. Finally, Massachusetts and New Hampshire use the archaic name *General Court*. This label was applied in the colonial era and was grounded in the fact that lawmaking bodies at that time performed both legislative and judicial functions. Indeed, the separation between the two branches actually sharpened only in the twentieth century. Divorces, for example, were granted by many legislatures until the mid-nineteenth century, and in a few states even into the early decades of the twentieth century.[23]

Number of Houses

Perhaps the most fundamental question about the structure of a legislature is how many houses it has. Bicameral legislatures are a fixture at the state level; every legislature today, save for Nebraska, has two houses. Importantly, like the two houses in Congress, both houses in the forty-nine bicameral state legislatures are powerful because both must pass bills for them to become law.

(Bicameral legislatures in other countries often have one house that is dominant, as in Canada, Great Britain, and Japan.) As noted previously, one reason for the prevalence of bicameral bodies was the calculation that two houses allow for greater reflection in the policymaking process. Legislation that passes one house must still pass the other house, inevitably slowing down the lawmaking process by requiring a second chamber of legislators, elected independently from the members in the first chamber, to render judgment on a measure's merits. Thus, having two houses makes it more difficult for bills to become law because it increases the number of obstacles any proposal must overcome.

This can be a source of considerable frustration for supporters of a bill that passes one house but fails to make it out of the other house. As a speaker of the California Assembly told newly elected members of his chamber from both parties, "You may think the Republicans or the Democrats are your enemy, but your enemy is the Senate."[24] Indeed, having two chambers creates opportunities for political games. One chamber can attempt to jam the other. For example, in 2018 the GOP controlled both houses of the New Hampshire state legislature. During a special session called to consider an internet sales-tax bill, the Senate passed the measure on a unanimous vote. But to everyone's surprise, the House quickly defeated the Senate bill, save for one provision to create a state commission to study the issues that they had stripped out of it. The House then adjourned, thereby leaving the Senate a choice to either accept the House version that now only created a state study commission or to vote it down, which would leave both houses with nothing to show for the special session. Despite the potential political embarrassment, an angry Senate unanimously voted to reject the bill as the House had amended it.[25]

Having two houses also allows each to shift blame. A leading Republican in the North Carolina Senate, for example, candidly complained about the GOP-controlled House passing a measure that he opposed, claiming the other body was "a bunch of [expletive]. . . . They got political heat. They said we can no longer sit on this [bill]. We know the Senate will not pass it because it is a piece of crap, so we will send it to them and they will take the heat." The senator went on to tell his audience, "Ladies and gentlemen, that is politics 101."[26] Each house can also point to the other house for a legislature's failure to pass important legislation. When the Pennsylvania legislature failed to pass a bill to establish a citizens' redistricting commission, the GOP leaders in each house blamed the other body. The House speaker claimed "Many of us are open to a commission. . . . The Senate chose to include judicial lines" which the House did not want included. In turn the Senate majority leader said "We want to do it. We think it's the right thing to do. Doesn't mean the House believes that."[27] Bicameral legislatures make it possible for lawmakers to evade accountability for their decisions.

The existence of two houses that must each consider legislation also requires the creation of rules to manage that dual consideration. Rules can dictate the sequencing of bill consideration and voting, such as the constitutional provisions currently found in twenty states that require the lower house to originate all revenue or tax bills.[28] There also are rules governing how conflicts between two houses are to be resolved, with, for example, several states making little or no use of conference committees with members from both houses while other states rely heavily on them.[29]

There is another aspect of bicameralism that merits mention. Typically, the two houses evolve contrasting cultures. Sometimes it surfaces in humorous ways. A standing joke in the Idaho House of Representatives is that when a member leaves to move to the Senate, it is said that "Both chambers have been greatly improved." But there are also real behavioral differences. A Missouri lawmaker who has served in both of his state's houses explains the difference between them to visiting students in this way; "Think of the House as your school cafeteria and think of the Senate as your school library."[30] Lower houses have more members and they tend to be boisterous, while state senates have fewer members and are inclined to be sedate. In the Missouri House members refer to each other as the "gentleman" or "lady," while in the Senate each member is referred to as "senator." Indeed, senates can be somewhat stuffy about decorum. North Dakota's Senate does not allow members to wear jeans in the chamber. When the state's governor appeared on the floor wearing blue jeans, the Senate's sergeant-at-arms escorted him out.[31]

The Nebraska Exception

Nebraska's unicameral legislature is the great exception among current state legislatures. When the state entered the union in 1867, its legislature was a bicameral body, like every other legislature at the time. Indeed, the current state capitol, designed in 1920 and completed in 1932, has two chambers. But in 1934, Nebraska voters passed an initiative to change their bicameral legislature to a unicameral body. The idea had been pushed for years by U.S. senator George W. Norris (R-NE), who railed against what he saw as the corruption promoted by the actions of conference committees in bicameral legislatures. Other unicameral supporters, however, backed the idea because they thought one house would be more economical, a powerful appeal at a time when the country was in the grip of the Great Depression.[32] The unicameral legislature first met in 1937 with forty-three members, a considerable reduction from the 133 members in its bicameral predecessor.

Voters hoped the switch would reduce the cost of running the legislature and make the legislative process more efficient. It is not clear, however, that the unicameral functions more economically, efficiently, or effectively than other state legislatures.[33] For example, the unicameral costs more to run per citizen than the larger two-house state legislature next door in Iowa. Still, in recent years, proponents of unicameral legislatures have promoted the idea in California, Connecticut, Hawaii, Iowa, Maine, Michigan, Minnesota, New York, Ohio, Oregon, Pennsylvania, South Carolina, South Dakota, and Virginia, albeit unsuccessfully.[34]

But the Nebraska legislature is exceptional for a second reason as well. When unicameralism was adopted, the legislature was also changed to become a nonpartisan body, meaning that party labels do not appear on the ballot attached to candidate names. (Nonpartisan elections are usually associated with contests for local offices or judgeships. Minnesota's legislature also was nonpartisan from 1914 to 1973, but during that time its members caucused as "liberals" and "conservatives.")[35] Although most Nebraska voters know which candidate for the unicameral is a Republican and which is a Democrat, after they are elected to office members have tended to downplay partisanship. There are, for example, no party caucuses in the legislature; instead, groups are organized regionally, with members assigned to the Omaha, Lincoln, or West caucuses based on the district they represent. Moreover, Democrats have occasionally been elected as committee chairs and speaker even though they were in the minority. But partisan polarization appears to have infected recent sessions, with party affiliation explaining how Nebraska legislators vote on bills to a greater degree than in the past.[36] Still, it appears that being nonpartisan has a greater impact on the behavior of Nebraska legislators than the fact that they operate in a single house.

House Name

Almost every state now calls its lower house the *House of Representatives*. This name was used by many of the original states, but a few of them took other names before switching to it. North Carolina, for example, referred to its lower house as the *House of Commons* until 1868.[37] A few states continue to use other names. California, Nevada, New York, and Wisconsin call their lower houses the *Assembly*, while the lower house in New Jersey is called the *General Assembly*. Both New Jersey and New York kept the Assembly name from their colonial assemblies; the name spread to the other states because of the use of an older state's constitution as a model in the development of a new state's constitution—New York's in Wisconsin and California and California's in Nevada.[38] Finally, Maryland, Virginia, and West Virginia refer to their lower houses as the *House of Delegates*. Maryland used the name for its colonial body and kept it in its first constitution. Virginia switched the name of its assembly to House of Delegates from the *House of Burgesses* when it wrote its initial constitution in 1776. West Virginia held on to the name when it split from Virginia during the Civil War.

Every upper house today is called the *Senate*. Thomas Jefferson first suggested the name in his proposed draft of Virginia's first constitution.[39] Although a few states initially referred to their upper house as the *Council*, the name often used in the colonial era, they eventually switched to calling it the Senate as well.[40]

Membership Size

Currently, state legislative chambers range in size from very small (20 members in the Alaska Senate) to very large (400 members in the New Hampshire House, down from 443 members as recently as 1942). As has always been the case, in each state the lower house has more members than the upper house. But none of the lower houses today is as large as the 435-member U.S. House. And none of the fifty senates is as large as the one-hundred-member U.S. Senate; the largest is Minnesota's, with sixty-seven members. Indeed, only twenty-two of the lower houses in the states are larger than the U.S. Senate. Surprisingly, there is no statistically significant relationship between state population size and the number of lawmakers.[41] California, with 39 million residents, for example, has 120 legislators, while New Hampshire, with just over a million residents, has 424 legislators.

Typically, membership size is established in the state constitution. Some constitutions, such as Alaska's (Article 2, Section 1), are specific: "The legislative power of the State is vested in a legislature consisting of a senate with a membership of twenty and a house of representatives with a membership of forty." Other state constitutions allow somewhat more flexibility. Arguably the most flexible is Nevada, where the constitution imposes no limit on the number of lawmakers, leaving that decision to the legislature itself (Constitution of the State of Nevada, Article 4, Section 5): "It shall be the mandatory duty of the legislature at its first session after the taking of the decennial census of the United States . . . to fix by law the number of senators and assemblymen." The only constitutional restriction is "the number of senators shall not be less than one-third nor more than one-half of that of the members of the assembly."

Given that many state constitutions make it relatively easy to change the number of legislators, it is not surprising that a majority of legislatures either increased or decreased their number of seats during the past half century.[42] In contrast, both houses of the U.S. Congress remained the same size during this period. A number of legislatures changed membership sizes in the aftermath of the Supreme Court's 1964 decision *Reynolds v. Sims*, which, as will be discussed in chapter 2, forced a number of states to alter the way they apportioned one or both houses.[43] Later, alterations in a few states were pursued to make legislatures smaller, and, it was hoped, less costly and more efficient. In 1979, the number of seats in the Massachusetts House was reduced to 160 from 240, and in 1983, the Illinois House experienced a one-third cut in the number of seats, to 118 from 177. More recently, in 2003, Rhode Island downsized both chambers of its legislature by 25 percent as mandated by the voters several years earlier.[44] Finally, a handful of states (notably Nevada, New York, North Dakota, and Wyoming) often tinker with the number of members in their legislature after each decennial census.[45]

Adding or reducing the number of seats in a legislature involves an implicit trade-off between efficiency and representation, as Politics under the Domes 1.1 discusses. But there is a practical consideration in setting the number of seats in each house that is often ignored. Of the ninety-nine state legislative houses, sixty are currently configured with an even number of seats, and in twenty-one states both houses have an even number. Given a two-party system, an even number of seats enhances the possibility of a potential complication—a tied house. This occurs more frequently than one might anticipate. Between 1966 and 2017, forty-two chambers were tied at some point, creating organizational challenges.[46] Problems with managing the Washington House, which has been tied three different times in the past three decades, have prompted so far unsuccessful calls for adding another seat to make an odd number.[47] Although we might assume that a tie would be avoided in the thirty-nine houses that have an odd number of seats, the problem can still arise. In 2001, the thirty-five-member Maine Senate found itself tied with seventeen Democrats, seventeen Republicans, and an independent that forced a power-sharing agreement with the two parties.[48]

What difference does membership size make? It appears that the number of members influences organizational structures and rules. A study of decision-making in the ninety-nine state legislative chambers found that party caucuses are more important in smaller chambers and party leaders more important in larger chambers.[49] Size also influences the way members interact with one another, with political parties structuring relationships to a greater degree in larger chambers.[50] More generally:

> Size has its effects on the following: the atmosphere, with more confusion and impersonality in larger bodies and friendlier relationships in smaller ones; hierarchy, with more elaborate and orderly rules and procedures and greater leadership authority in larger bodies and informality and collegial authority in smaller ones; the conduct of business, with a more efficient flow and less debate in larger bodies and more leisurely deliberation and greater fluidity in smaller ones; the internal distribution of power, with more concentrated pockets possible in larger bodies and greater dispersion of power in smaller ones.[51]

Congressional scholars frequently cite differences in membership size to explain why the larger House developed much more rigid rules and procedures than the smaller Senate.[52] An examination of national legislatures around the world reached a similar conclusion.[53] But this relationship does not appear to apply to state legislatures. If size alone matters in explaining the evolution of legislature rules and procedures, then most state legislative houses should operate with less rigid rules, like the similarly sized U.S. Senate, and only a handful of the really large bodies should be regimented along the lines of the U.S. House. In fact, as will be discussed in chapters 5 and 6, more state legislative chambers organize and proceed like the U.S. House than like the U.S. Senate, regardless of membership size.

POLITICS UNDER THE DOMES

The Representation and Efficiency Trade-Off

In recent years, John Cox, a wealthy San Diego businessman (and 2018 GOP nominee for governor of California), has promoted a novel if impractical reform. He calls for increasing the size of the California legislature to 12,000 members from its current 120 members. Under Cox's plan, each lawmaker in the lower house would be elected from a "neighborhood" district of 5,000 people, while upper house members would be elected from districts of 10,000 people. A total of 100 lawmakers would be elected in each of the current 120 legislative districts. Each district's

100 members would meet locally—where is not specified—to elect one member to go to Sacramento, thus composing a 120-member executive council to draft legislation. Any legislative proposals the executive council put forth would have to be passed by the full 12,000-member legislature to become law.

The notion behind the proposal is that smaller constituencies would cause lawmakers to have a closer connection with their constituents. According to Cox, "We are converting campaigns for the Legislature from huge, mass-media efforts to little neighborhood efforts." Although his idea has received a fair amount of media attention, it has failed to generate enough support to be put on the ballot.

The notion of tinkering with the size of a state legislature is not new, and changes in the number of members occasionally occur. In 2003, for example, the Rhode Island House was reduced to seventy-five seats from one hundred seats, and the Senate to thirty-eight seats from fifty seats. The chair of the Rhode Island commission that recommended creating a smaller legislature stated, "The goal of the downsizing was to increase responsibility and give individual legislators an opportunity to influence decisions and be more effective in representing their constituents." Embedded in this rationale is an inherent but often unrecognized trade-off, fundamental to all proposals to alter the size of a legislature: Having fewer members in a chamber gives each lawmaker greater opportunity to influence legislative decisions. That is, being one of seventy-five legislators is better than being one of one hundred legislators. At the same time, however, reducing the number of seats means that each lawmaker will necessarily represent more constituents. In the case of the Rhode Island House, the reduction increased the average district size to roughly 14,000 people from 10,500 people. Consequently, in the smaller house, each legislator would be able to exercise greater power but would do so on behalf of more constituents.

One side or the other of this trade-off is often acknowledged in debates over changes in membership size. A different proponent of increasing the number of legislative seats in California touted the perceived benefits of representing fewer people: "Smaller districts would mean candidates could conceivably . . . meet more voters face to face. It would also mean voters could stay in touch with their constituencies better." On the flip side a Pennsylvania state representative who supports decreasing the number of seats in his House claims representing more constituents would not really change much: "Currently, each House member represents approximately 62,000 constituents. Under this downsizing plan, that would increase to 84,000. I believe serving 84,000 constituents is very reasonable and would not have an adverse effect on service to Pennsylvanians." Other supporters assert that "modern-day representatives can more easily serve larger numbers of people in an age of cellphones, emails and other instant communication."

Some people in these debates focus on the anticipated impact of a change in membership size on legislative dynamics. Speaking in support of a measure to reduce the size of the Pennsylvania House, the Speaker noted, "We may not always agree but I believe we will do a better job if there is a smaller number of us because we will have a better understanding of what the other person's problems are, what their constituent views are." Rarely, however, is the trade-off between seats and district size explicitly recognized.

Moreover, practical concerns rather than theoretical ones often drive support for or opposition to proposed changes in membership size. Many times, proposals for increasing the number of legislative seats are opposed because of the additional costs in salaries, staff, and equipment. When in 2010 Alaska voters rejected a measure to add six seats to their legislature, a Republican pointed to the prevailing Tea Party–inspired political mood: "Now is not the time to go to the voters and say 'let's increase the size of government.'" Those pushing for a smaller legislature, of course, highlight the claim that it will cost the state less money to run. Such claims need to be put into proper perspective. As two Pennsylvania skeptics note, the forecasted annual savings of $10 million to $15 million (out of the state's $66 billion operating budget) amount to roughly $1.17 per taxpayer.

But in many cases, there is more than just a concern with costs. It is not unusual for there to be a desire to reduce the number of legislators as a way of limiting the number of officials who can abuse their positions. As a cynical letter to the editor supporting the reduction in the size of the Rhode Island legislature put it, "Fewer legislators means fewer brothers-in-law that have to be found state jobs." A California editorial writer who backs proposals to increase the number of legislators in that state acknowledges that Californians likely harbor similar reservations; "I know: You may be thinking we need more politicians roaming around Sacramento like we need a plague of locusts."

Others evaluate proposed alterations from a purely political perspective. A Republican representative who opposes reducing the size of the Pennsylvania legislature observed, "I do see this as a rural legislator as a step to consolidate power in the hands of a few. . . . I believe this piece of legislation does take away the voices of rural Pennsylvania, which is why the (Pennsylvania) Farm Bureau opposes this." A Nebraska lawmaker advocates reverting back to a bicameral legislature for much the same reason; a larger legislature would allow for at least a few more lawmakers to be elected from rural parts of the state and as a consequence there would be "more voices speaking for the Sandhills."

It is not clear that reducing the number of legislators actually produces a lower-cost legislature or a more efficient legislative process. A decade after a dramatic reduction in the size of the Illinois House, administrative costs had actually increased rather than decreased, and the number of bills introduced had stayed about the same. One analysis attributed this outcome to the fact that the legislature's workload was driven by the size and diversity of the state, not by the size of the legislature. Consequently, it may be that in the case of legislatures, size does not matter.

Sources: Tom Barnes, "Lawmaker Cuts Still in Committee; Attempt to Fast-Track Bill Fails," *Pittsburgh Post-Gazette*, October 16, 2007; Tom Barnes, "Time at Hand to Downsize State Legislature?" *Pittsburgh Post-Gazette*, January 18, 2006; Senator Tom Brewer, "Nebraska Should Abandon Unicameral System," *Chadron Record*, April 15, 2018; Alan Ehrenhalt, "'Rightsizing' the Legislature," *Governing*, July 2001, 6; David H. Everson, "The Cutback at 10: Illinois House without Cumulative Voting and 59 Members," *Illinois Issues* 17, no. 7 (July 1991): 13–15; Edward Fitzpatrick, "The Incredible Shrinking Legislature," *State Legislatures* 28, no. 7 (July/August 2002): 51–54; Pat Forgey, "Rural Alaska in a Fight for Its Voice," *Juneau Empire*, April 26, 2010; Karen Langley, "Another Push Begins to Shrink Pennsylvania Legislature," *Pittsburgh Post-Gazette*, August 20, 2013; Patrick McGreevy, "Proposal Seeks to Expand California Legislature from 120 to 12,000," *Los Angeles Times*, December 19, 2013; Jan Murphy, "Pa. House Takes Historic Step toward Shrinking Size of General Assembly," Harrisburg *Patriot-News*, December 17, 2013; Representative Steve Mentzer, "Time to Reduce the Size of the State Legislature," LancasterOnline, November

20, 2017; https://lancasteronline.com/opinion/colu
mnists/time-to-reduce-the-size-of-the-state-legisl
ature/article_63c38534-cbbf-11e7-89a3-2bdebc9
de263.html; John Myers, Political Road Map:
There's a Simple Reason Some Say It's Time for a
Larger California Legislature," *Los Angeles Times*,
August 20, 2017; Foon Rhee, "Think California's
Legislature Doesn't Represent You? Here's a
Fix for That," *Sacramento Bee*, June 26, 2017;
Karen Shuey, "Can Reform Make Headway in
Pennsylvania?" *Reading Eagle*, June 25, 2018;
State of Rhode Island and Providence Plantations,
Journal of the House of Representatives, May 31,
2000; Charles Thompson, "Shrinking Size of Pa.
State House Takes a Hit from Lawmakers who
Demand a Smaller Senate as Well," pennlive.
com, September 25, 2018, https://articles.pen
nlive.com/news/2018/09/game_of_chicken_over_
shrinking.amp; Berwood A. Yost and Matthew
M. Schousen, "Legislatures Aren't Supposed to
Be Efficient; Keep Pa. General Assembly Large,"
Philadelphia Inquirer, April 2, 2018; and Steve
Wiegand, "His Master Plan: More Legislators,"
Sacramento Bee, November 30, 2006.

Bicameral Size Differences

Perhaps the most underappreciated contrast between the two houses in bicameral legislatures is the difference in membership sizes. Size differences between the two houses may affect their relationship because of disparities in their relative capacities to gather and digest information. A house with far more members than its companion house enjoys considerably lower information acquisition costs, thereby conferring policymaking advantages on it.[54] Additionally, differences in membership size affect legislative productivity, with upper houses that are small in comparison to their lower houses, creating legislative bottlenecks.[55] Finally, as the ratio of lower house seats to upper house seats increases, state expenditures decrease.[56] But, perversely, the imposition of supermajority voting rules may reverse that relationship.[57]

There is another aspect of bicameral ratios that deserves attention. Some state legislatures require that certain actions be taken in a joint session. Article 2, section 16 of the Alaska constitution, for example, requires that the legislature meet in joint session to override gubernatorial vetoes. In such a joint session, the 40-member House enjoys twice the voting power of the 20-member Senate. Where joint legislative committees are used they run the risk of the same sort of disparity problem. In 2015, the Massachusetts General Court was roiled by a dispute between the 40-member Senate and the 160-member House of Representatives. Although both houses were dominated by the Democrats, senators felt that representatives used their superior numbers on joint committees to throttle the Senate's policy preferences in favor of their own.[58] Despite the disagreement, the General Court continues to use joint committees, but during the 2017–2018 session most joint committees had six senators and eleven representatives while a few had seven senators and thirteen representatives—both ratios being far smaller than the one senator to every four representatives found at the full-membership level.

The most common ratio between upper and lower house memberships in the states is one senator for every two lower house members, which is found in sixteen states. But the ratios range from a low of one senator for every1.67 representatives in New Mexico to a high of one senator for every 16.7 representatives in New Hampshire and four state legislatures have higher ratios than the one senator to 4.35 house members found in Congress.

Terms of Office

Term length is thought to influence member behavior, with longer terms giving legislators greater freedom from electoral pressures and shorter terms providing less freedom. Terms for state legislators have changed over time. In general, they were lengthened over the course of the nineteenth century.[59] In most states, lower house terms were extended from one year to two years—New Jersey was the final state to make that change, waiting until 1947 to do so. Typically, upper house terms were extended as well, although the number of years adopted occasionally bounced around. Georgia, for example, kept changing the term of office for its upper house: "Her first senators, provided for in 1789, were to be elected every third year. Annual election was substituted in 1795; this was changed to biennial in 1840 with the adoption of the biennial system; in 1868 the four-year term was substituted; and in 1877 return was made to the two-year term."[60]

Terms continued to change over the past century. Today, thirty states have two-year terms in the lower house and four-year terms in the upper house. Members of both houses are given two-year terms in twelve states, and in five states both houses get four-year terms. Nebraska legislators are given four-year terms. And in Illinois and New Jersey, senators have shifting terms, with one two-year term and two four-year terms to accommodate redistricting every ten years. (A variety of mechanisms are used to accommodate the required decennial redistricting in the other thirty-seven states that have staggered four-year electoral terms.)[61]

Proposals to lengthen legislative terms have surfaced in several states in recent years. The arguments advanced by lawmakers in favor of longer terms revolve around the electoral stress imposed by two-year terms. A New York senator pushing for a four-year term observed that with a two-year term, "Legislators have basically one year in office before they have to run for reelection over and over again. Once the campaign year begins, they are anxious to get back to their districts and are often reluctant to deal with controversial issues fearing voter reactions."[62] Other lawmakers see advantages in two-year terms. A West Virginia legislator argued that shorter terms "make us closer to the people we represent," adding, "I do think the more often we run, the more responsible we are."[63] Analyses of state legislative elections reveal that lawmakers with two-year terms enjoy higher reelection rates than their colleagues with four-year terms, probably because less frequent election cycles draw better challengers to a race.[64] But in practice there appear to be few differences in the election contests themselves between states with two-year terms and states with four-year terms.[65] There also is evidence suggesting that term length does not impact legislative behavior in terms of member legislative output.[66] Although legislators occasionally contemplate pushing for changes in their term lengths— usually longer terms—no state has done so since 1996, when North Dakota increased its lower house term to four years from two years.

A critical question that has to be addressed by any state that gives its legislators four-year terms is whether those terms should be staggered. Having a staggered four-year term means that half of a chamber's seats are scheduled to come up for election every two years. A non-staggered term means that every

TABLE 1.2 **State Legislative Chambers with Non-Staggered Four-Year Terms**

Chamber	States
State Senate	AL, KS, LA, MD, MI, MN, MS, NJ, NM, SC, VA
Lower House	AL, LA, MD, MS

seat is scheduled to come up for election at the same time every four years. The difference between the two revolves around responsiveness. With staggered four-year terms—used, for example, in Nebraska and both houses in North Dakota—only half of the membership is vulnerable to being replaced each election. Non-staggered four-year terms politically insulate the full membership for an extended period, but then every four years every member is at risk of being replaced. Table 1.2 lists the state legislative chambers with non-staggered four-year terms.

Term Limits

Limits on the number of terms a legislator may legally serve are not a recent idea. They were first imposed on the Pennsylvania legislature by the state's 1776 constitution; members could only serve four one-year terms over any seven-year period.[67] These limits were, however, dispensed with when the state adopted its second constitution in 1790. But the notion of limiting legislative service still held in various places around the nation. Often called *rotation*, lawmakers in some districts during the nineteenth century were expected to serve only one or two terms and then step aside so that someone else, usually from another county, could hold the seat. This political norm constituted an informal term limitation. By the twentieth century, rotation agreements were found only in a few legislatures, almost all in the one-party South. The U.S. Supreme Court's reapportionment decisions in the early 1960s effectively ended such pacts.[68]

Term limits were not seriously debated again until the late 1980s, and then they were adopted in twenty-one states with amazing speed.[69] In 1990, voters in Colorado, Oklahoma, and California were the first to impose term limits on their legislators. Two years later, term-limit measures passed in all twelve states in which they appeared on the ballot, and they were adopted in six more states by 1995. There were, however, some bumps along the way. Nebraska voters had to pass term limits three times—in 1992, 1994, and 2000—because the Nebraska Supreme Court tossed out the first two versions on legal technicalities. State supreme courts overturned term-limit laws passed by the voters in Massachusetts in 1997, Washington in 1998, Oregon in 2002, and Wyoming in 2004.

Voters pushed the term-limit movement, not legislators. Only in Utah and Louisiana did lawmakers place limits on themselves, and in Utah they were pressured to do so by the threat that voters would pass a ballot measure imposing more stringent limitations. In every other state that adopted term limits, voters, not legislators, made the decision.

The term-limit movement has slowed in recent years. Other than Nebraska, no state has adopted term limits since 1995. Mississippi voters rejected term limits in both 1995 and 1999; North Dakota voters did likewise in 1996. In 2002, the heavily Republican legislature in Idaho repealed the term limits voters had imposed eight years earlier (a repeal option is afforded to legislatures in only a few states).[70] In the general elections that fall, Idaho voters upheld the legislators' decision to remove term limits, albeit by the thinnest of margins. Utah's Republican-controlled legislature repealed term limits in 2003 without much dissent from the public.

Term limits, however, still appear to have political appeal in the states that have them. Ballot measures to soften or eliminate them were rejected by voters in California in 2002 and 2008, Arkansas and Montana in 2004, Maine in 2007, South Dakota in 2008, and Nebraska in 2012. California voters did agree to alter term limits in 2012, in this case by removing chamber-specific term limits holding members to six years in the lower house and eight years in the upper house and instead allowing members first elected in 2012 and after to spend a total of twelve years in the legislature, split in any fashion between service in the two houses. In 2014, Arkansas voters passed a similar measure, allowing legislators to spend up to sixteen years total in the legislature. (A constitutional amendment to reimpose shorter term limits was tossed off the 2018 ballot at the last minute by the Arkansas Supreme Court.)

Currently, while fifteen states impose term limitations, their limits vary substantially in specifics, as table 1.3 shows. The main differences revolve around the number of terms a legislator may serve and whether those term limits are lifetime bans or simply limits on the number of consecutive terms. For example, Louisiana and Nevada have twelve-year limits in each house, while Michigan has a much more stringent limit of six years in the lower house and eight years in the upper house. Both Ohio and Missouri have eight-year limits in each house, but Missouri's is a lifetime limit while Ohio's is simply a consecutive term limit. Therefore, in Ohio, a termed-out legislator is eligible to hold office again after sitting out for four years. In Missouri, after a legislator reaches the term limit, his or her career in that house is over.

Assessing the effects of term limits is a complicated enterprise, partly because the nature of the term-limit laws are not the same everywhere and partly because of the differences in the various legislatures before term limits went into effect. In other words, not all legislatures were the same before term limits, and therefore the precise effect of their imposition will not be the same.[71] Nonetheless, careful studies of term limits have identified some clear consequences.[72] The most obvious is greater turnover in most term-limited legislatures.[73] And this, in turn, has led to instability in standing committee systems. As will be discussed in chapter 5, committees are a crucial element in the lawmaking process. The upshot is that "the informational, deliberative and gatekeeping roles of the committees are undermined by term limits."[74] Term-limited lawmakers also invest less time and effort in learning about proposed policies.[75] Furthermore, strong evidence suggests that term limits put legislatures at a disadvantage in their relations with the executive branch.[76] Indeed, it appears that legislatures with term limits are even less interested in monitoring bureaucratic agency activities than they were before they were imposed.[77] At the same time, it is worth noting that term limits do not appear to have any impact on state spending levels.[78] But there also is some evidence that states with term limits have lower bond ratings, leading one scholar to conclude that they have a "negative effect on the ability of legislatures to set effective fiscal policy."[79]

TABLE 1.3 State Legislative Term Limits with Year of Adoption and Year Limits Took Effect[a]

Term Limit	Consecutive Service	Lifetime Ban
6 years lower house		Arkansas (1992, 2000)[b,c]
8 years upper house		California (1990, 1996 H, 1998 S)[c]
		Michigan (1992, 1998 H, 2002 S)
8 years total	Nebraska (2000, 2006)[d]	
8 years lower house	Arizona (1992, 2000)	Missouri (1992, 2002)
8 years upper house	Colorado (1990, 1998)	
	Florida (1992, 2000)	
	Maine (1993, 1996)	
	Montana (1992, 2000)	
	Ohio (1992, 2000)	
	South Dakota (1992, 2000)	
12 years combined in either one house or both houses		Oklahoma (1990, 2004) California (2012, 2014)[c]
12 years lower house	Louisiana (1995, 2007)	Nevada (1996, 2008)
12 years upper house		
16 years combined in either one house or both houses		Arkansas (2014)[c]

[a] State courts in Massachusetts, Oregon, Washington, and Wyoming tossed out term-limit measures passed by their voters. State legislators repealed term limits in Idaho and Utah.

[b] The first number in parentheses is the year term limits were adopted. The second number is the year term limits went into effect. The year they went into effect for different houses is designated by H for the lower house and S for senate.

[c] California voters passed Proposition 28 in June 2012 limiting lawmakers elected from that point on to twelve years of service but allowing them to serve those years in one chamber. Arkansas voters passed Issue 3 in 2014, allowing legislators to serve sixteen total years in the legislature.

[d] Voters in Nebraska passed term-limit measures in 1992 and 1994, but both were ruled unconstitutional by the state supreme court.

Source: Data from National Conference of State Legislatures.

Finally, it warrants mention that restructuring the constraints imposed by term limits in the manner recently done by Arkansas and California can impact the way a legislature operates. In 2019, the California Assembly experienced its lowest level of membership turnover in thirty years. That happened because Assembly members who had served for six years were no longer forced to leave; they now had the option to continue serving in that chamber. As a result, the Assembly enjoyed a more experienced membership than it had in a generation. This development was thought to have two consequences. First, it was expected that the Assembly would be a stronger policymaking competitor with the state Senate because it no longer lost so many veteran lawmakers to that body. Second, there were indications that with their longer time horizons many Assembly members were now more willing to invest their time in tackling thorny political issues such as housing and criminal justice that might take years to resolve.[80]

Constituency Size

Since the U.S. Supreme Court handed down *Reynolds v. Sims* in 1964, all state legislative houses must be apportioned on the basis of population, meaning that all districts in a chamber in a state must have roughly the same population per legislator elected. States, however, vary greatly in population and in the number of lawmakers in their legislatures. Thus, it is not surprising that the range of constituency sizes across the fifty state legislatures is extraordinary (see appendix, table A.2). At one extreme, the forty California senators each represent 958,313 people, an impressive number when put into context: it is 230,000 more constituents than the average member of the U.S. House represents and more constituents than U.S. senators from Alaska, Delaware, North Dakota, South Dakota, Vermont, or Wyoming represent. Members of the Texas Senate, with 853,168 constituents each, also have districts larger than the average U.S. House district. At the other extreme, many New Hampshire representatives have districts with as few as 3,309 people in them. Overall, state legislative districts in five houses have fewer than ten thousand people, and twelve houses have districts with more than two hundred thousand constituents.

What difference does constituency size make? At the extremes, being a California senator is markedly different from being a New Hampshire representative for many reasons. Obviously, relations with constituents differ between the two. As a representative in New Hampshire observed about his connection with the people in his district, "You personally knew them. I knew 60 percent of the people in my district."[81] To make the same claim, a California senator would have to personally know almost 600,000 people in his or her district!

Constituency size also matters because as the number of constituents (and, we would assume, the number of organizations and distinct interests) in a district increases, more demands are made on a legislator. An increasingly important and time-consuming part of a lawmaker's job is helping constituents with problems. This is known as *casework* or *constituent service*. Casework involves everything from fielding complaints about potholes in the street to intervening on behalf of a constituent in a dispute with a state agency. Obviously, the constituent service workload increases with the district population. The way a legislator interacts with his or her constituents also changes; for example, contacts with lawmakers per constituent decline as district size increases, suggesting that voters may feel less connected to their legislators as the size of the legislative district increases.[82]

Geographic Size

There is another way of thinking about district size. State legislative districts come in every geographic size and shape imaginable. The variation can be astounding. Take, for example, the maximum size difference. At one extreme, Alaska Senate District T is only a bit smaller than the state of Texas. Its 35,000 residents are strewn across a vast expanse in ninety communities that range from as large as 4,400 people to as small as 5 people. At the other extreme, districts in smaller, more densely populated states may cover remarkably little territory. New York Assembly District 76, for instance, contains 133,000 residents but only goes from East 61st Street up to East 92nd Street and is four to five blocks wide—not much more than a square mile or two—taking up just a sliver of Manhattan.

Obviously, the geographic setting of a district can have significant implications for representation. Sparsely populated areas combined with inaccessible topography can conspire to make effective representation challenging. One Alaska senator with a huge district tried to visit each of its towns—travel was by car, airplane, and ferry—but after having been gone from home for three months, she managed to only get to about 75 percent of them.[83] Idaho's District 8 covers five rural counties that stretch from the Bitterroot Mountain Range that marks the Montana boundary westward across the state almost to the Oregon border. It encompasses 15,600 square miles, about the size of Massachusetts and Connecticut combined. Most of the district is rugged mountains and deep river canyons, and it includes the massive Frank Church–River of No Return Wilderness Area. There are no paved roads across the district from east to west, and as a consequence District 8 is referred to locally as "The Helicopter District."[84] In contrast, the Rhode Island House has tiny districts in terms of landmass, so small that one representative could say that, "I learn by listening and I listen to my voters over the fence, at the swimming pool. . . . My office is a shopping cart on Sunday afternoon at Stop & Shop."[85] Her western counterparts with geographically gigantic districts would find the notion of running into most of their constituents at a local grocery store or neighborhood swimming pool to be unfathomable.

Multimember Districts

Today, the vast majority of state legislators are elected from single-member districts (SMDs). This has not always been the case. Earlier in American history, multimember districts (MMDs) were the norm. MMDs and at-large districts were used to elect some members of the U.S. House as recently as the 1960s.[86] At the state level, the use of MMDs was even more pronounced. In 1962, multimember districts were used in forty-one lower houses and thirty upper houses.[87] Over the following decades, however, the use of MMDs declined precipitously, partly because of concerns that they made it more difficult for minority candidates to win office.[88] By 2013, MMDs were found in just ten lower houses and two upper houses, as shown in table 1.4. At least 90 percent of all legislators are

TABLE 1.4 States Using Multimember Legislative Districts in 2018

State	Chamber	Percent of Members Elected from Multimember Districts	Number of Multimember Districts	Number of Members Elected per Multimember District (Range)	Type of Multimember District System
Arizona	Lower house	100.0	30	2	Plurality[a]
Idaho	Lower house	100.0	35	2	Post or Place[b]
Maryland	Lower house	85.1	47[c]	2–3	Plurality
New Hampshire	Lower house	73.8	99	2–11	Plurality
New Jersey	Lower house	100.0	40	2	Plurality
North Dakota	Lower house	100.0	47	2	Plurality[d]
South Dakota	Lower house	94.3	33	2	Plurality
Vermont	Lower house	61.3	46	2	Plurality
Vermont	Upper house	90.0	10	2–6	Plurality
Washington	Lower house	100.0	49	2	Post or Place
West Virginia	Lower house	53.0	20	2–5	Plurality
West Virginia	Upper house	100.0	17	2	Plurality

a   For example, if voters may vote for five candidates, then the top five vote getters are declared the winners.

b   Voters cast more than one vote but only one for each place, position, or post on the ballot.

c   Maryland has forty-seven electoral districts, all of which send three members to the House of Delegates. Voters in thirty-two districts cast three votes for three delegates from their district. The remaining districts are divided geographically into subdistricts. In twenty-one of these subdistricts, a voter casts a single vote to elect a single delegate. In twelve of these subdistricts, voters cast two votes to elect two delegates.

d   Members of the North Dakota House of Representatives are elected to four-year terms. Each district elects two members using a plurality rule. District elections are staggered; odd-numbered districts are contested in one election, and even-numbered districts are contested two years later.

elected from MMDs in eight of these twelve chambers; the figure is greater than 50 percent in the other four chambers. All told, 19 percent of lower house members and 3 percent of state senators across the nation are elected from MMDs.

The number of members representing a district influences how lawmakers behave. Legislators in MMDs are more likely than their SMD counterparts to think of themselves as being *trustees*, or representatives elected to act in the broader interests of their constituents, rather than as *delegates* simply reflecting their preferences.[89] Lawmakers from MMDs claim to spend more time providing constituent services.[90] MMD legislators use their shared constituency as the basis for collaboration on legislative issues.[91] But they are less successful in getting bills through the process than their SMD colleagues, suggesting that MMD lawmakers pursue actions that require little legislative effort while still attracting public attention.[92] At the same time, however, they appear to bring home more government dollars to their constituents.[93] There may be institutional effects as well. Political parties in the Illinois House, for example, were ideologically more diverse when the chamber was elected using MMDs than when SMD elections were used.[94]

Further Explorations of State Legislatures

Clearly, state legislatures come in all shapes and sizes, and none exactly mirrors the size and shape of Congress. Their histories differ as well. Even the facilities they occupy differ, as discussed in Politics under the Domes 1.2. Thus, understanding Congress is not sufficient for understanding state legislatures. State legislatures merit separate study.

POLITICS UNDER THE DOMES

Where Legislatures Meet

State legislatures are often thought to be smaller versions of Congress. As argued in this chapter and throughout the rest of the book, that notion is untrue. Along these same lines, while many Americans think of state capitols as being smaller versions of the U.S. Capitol, the reality is that they too vary in significant ways.

Along with skyscrapers, capitol buildings are an American architectural innovation. The colonial assemblies first met in whatever local facilities were large enough to contain them. Consequently, they assembled in churches, taverns, schoolhouses, and even private homes. But over time it became apparent that they required facilities dedicated to their use. As a result, the original capitol buildings were constructed during the colonial era. Indeed, the word "Capitol," derived from Capitoline Hill in Rome, was first applied to a government building by a Virginia colonial governor.

Most of the pre-independence capitols have long disappeared from the scene, replaced by a series of newer buildings. (The most notable exception is Independence Hall in Philadelphia, which was constructed as the Pennsylvania State House.) Still, several of the current state capitols predate the U.S. Capitol; Maryland's, which was under construction at the outbreak of the Revolution, is the oldest capitol building in current use. Most in use today, however, were constructed after the U.S. Capitol took shape and many of them were clearly influenced by its architectural style. Thus the similarities between the U.S. Capitol and state capitols in Arkansas, California, Colorado, Idaho, Kentucky, Michigan, Minnesota, Missouri, Oklahoma, Pennsylvania, Texas, Utah, Washington, West Virginia, Wisconsin, and Wyoming are easy to see because they are all are some variant of the same American Renaissance architectural style.

Other state capitols, however, exhibit obvious stylistic differences. The Virginia capitol, for example, is in the neoclassic style, the Massachusetts capitol is Classical Revival, the Ohio capitol is Greek Revival, the Iowa capitol is Beaux Arts, the Illinois capitol is Italianate, the Connecticut capitol is Victorian Gothic, and the New York capitol is Second Empire. More recently constructed state capitols are, if anything, even more distinctive. Louisiana, Nebraska and Oregon all have Art Deco capitols built in the 1930s. North Dakota's International Style "Skyscraper on the Prairie," capitol (with an Art Deco interior) is of the same vintage. The New Mexico capitol, built in the 1960s, is a circular design intended to form the Zia, or Pueblo Indian sun sign. Hawaii's capitol, also constructed in the 1960s, is done in the International Style; inspired by the islands, it has an open center atrium surrounded by upward sloping roof, suggestive of a volcano. None of these capitols would be confused with the U.S. Capitol. But perhaps the most unusual capitol is Alaska's. It differs from its all of its counterparts because it is a converted federal

office building rather than a structure originally designed as a capitol.

It is also important to note that several state legislatures do not meet in their state capitols. The North Carolina and Nevada legislatures have their own buildings. Constructed in the 1960s and 1970s, both are done in modern styles. Arizona's capitol is flanked by buildings housing the Senate and the House that opened in 1960. Alabama's legislature was exiled from the state capitol at the beginning of a major restoration project in the mid-1980s and, as it turned out, permanently relocated to a state highway department building that was transformed to meet its needs. That building has since been renamed the Alabama State House.

The vast majority of buildings in which the state legislatures meet—forty-one of them—have a dome. Most of them are evocative of the U.S. Capitol dome. But a few are strikingly different. The Ohio and Oregon capitols have flat domes. The Nevada Legislative Building has only a small, token dome. And, state legislators in Alaska, Delaware, Hawaii, Louisiana, New Mexico, New York, North Dakota, Tennessee, and Virginia assemble in buildings without any dome.

While there are substantial differences in the facades of the buildings where state legislatures meet, their interiors share many commonalities. Bicameralism figures prominently in these features. Typically, for example, the lower and upper house chambers are on the same floor, physically separated by some distance, and opposite each other (although in some buildings, among them Colorado, Massachusetts, Minnesota, Vermont, and Wisconsin, the two chambers are perpendicular to each other, in Montana the House chamber is down a hallway behind the Senate chamber and in Alabama the chambers are separated by two floors).

More importantly, however, the chambers are comparable, if not in size, than in accommodations and trappings, befitting institutions of equal stature. And in almost every capitol which they occupy the legislature is the dominant institution, given more space and greater prominence than the other branches of government.

Sources: Charles T. Goodsell, *The American Statehouse* (Lawrence: University Press of Kansas, 2001); Henry-Russell Hitchcock and William Seale, *Temples of Democracy* (New York: Harcourt, Brace Jovanovich, 1976), and Peverill Squire, *The Evolution of American Legislatures: Colonies, Territories and States, 1619–2009* (Ann Arbor: University of Michigan Press, 2012). The website *Cupolas of Capitalism* also was helpful: http://www.cupola.com/html/bldgstru/statecap/cap01.htm.

Having come to understand how state legislatures as organizations evolved and what they look like today, the rest of this book is devoted to exploring important aspects of state legislative life in greater depth. Chapter 2 investigates state legislative elections, examining what it takes to get to the legislature and what it takes to stay there. Among the topics covered are how legislative district lines get drawn, candidate recruitment, the emergence of women and minority candidates, competition for state legislative office, campaign finance, the power of incumbency, and the nature of campaigning for the legislature in different states. The chapter also explores the recent increase in party competition for chamber control in much of the nation and assesses the evidence of party realignment at the state legislative level.

Chapter 3 details the changing job description of state legislators and examines the substantial variation across the states in the sorts of legislative careers lawmakers pursue. The chapter begins by exploring the concept of legislative professionalization. In doing so, we look at the roles that pay, time demands, and staff and facilities play in legislative career decisions, and how term limits change career patterns in the states where they are in effect. We document how the face of the legislature has changed significantly over time and explain what difference these occupational and demographic changes make. Problems surrounding ethics are investigated as well. Finally, the concept of legislative career opportunity structures is introduced.

Chapter 4 focuses on state legislatures as organizations. We analyze the roles of political parties, legislative leaders, committees, and staff in structuring legislative decision-making. Links are drawn between member careers and the ways legislatures are organized. One point highlighted in this chapter is that the structures found in Congress do not exhaust the organizational configurations of American legislatures. The diverse organizational forms found across state legislatures have strengths and weaknesses that merit examination.

The convoluted and often messy process by which legislation gets produced is described in chapter 5. We begin with a discussion of where ideas for bills originate, explore how ideas get turned into proposals and how different legislatures process legislation, and conclude with an explanation of how members decide how to vote on bills. Major emphases of this chapter are the differences in legislative rules and procedures across the states and analyses of the policy consequences of those differences.

The main goal of chapter 6 is to understand how legislators are influenced by a multitude of forces as they consider legislation. Topics covered are relations with the governor, executive agencies, interest groups, courts, and voters through the initiative and referendum processes. We discuss legislative oversight of the executive branch and the rise of legislative independence in policymaking. We examine how initiatives and referenda influence the legislative process by either forcing legislatures to act or allowing them to pass the buck to the voters. Particular attention is paid to the effects of voter-passed tax-and-expenditure limits.

Finally, chapter 7 tackles the question of how state legislatures today are to be judged. We look at different ways of measuring how the public assesses its legislators and the institutions in which they serve. That is followed by an exploration of the sorts of information voters have about the legislature. We finish with thoughts on how well state legislatures perform as representative institutions.

Chapter 2

State Legislative Campaigns and Elections

California Assembly member Sharon Quirk-Silva, center, campaigns in Anaheim in 2018. Like most incumbents, Quirk-Silva won reelection. AP Photo/Amy Taxin.

Steven Glass is a ceramics artist who holds the position of Resident Potter at the Virginia Museum of Fine Arts in Richmond. For a few moments in early January 2018, one of his artistic creations held center stage in Virginia politics. Described as "a decorative blue bowl," Mr. Glass's creation was lent to the Virginia State Board of Elections to help determine which party would control the Virginia House of Delegates following the 2017 state legislative contests.[1]

The events leading up to that moment are complicated, but they highlight many of the important features of state legislative elections. There are four states that elect their state legislators in odd-numbered years, and Virginia is one of those states. In November 2017—one year after Donald Trump was elected President—Virginia held elections for statewide offices such as governor and lieutenant governor, and for the Virginia House of Delegates. There are 100 seats in the House of Delegates and they all are contested every two years. Democrats, seeking to regain some momentum after the 2016 national elections, hoped to cut into the substantial Republican majority (66–34) in the Virginia House by challenging GOP incumbents.[2] Women were especially energized; fifty-two of them—mostly Democrats—appeared on the general election ballot, the largest number to ever run in the state.

Democrats contested many more districts than in the previous election. They had run a candidate in fewer than thirty districts in 2015. In 2017 they fielded candidates in sixty races. The increase in competition was reflected in campaign finance reports; $39 million was spent on the state legislative races in 2017. One contest (District 12) saw over $2 million spent and over $1 million was spent in each of ten other districts. All of these districts shifted to the Democrats.

Because of Virginia's unrestrictive campaign finance laws, independent groups can contribute as much money as they want, and they can coordinate their campaigns with the candidates. Consequently, quite a few super PACs and 527 organizations associated with one or the other political parties spent money in the Virginia House elections. Much of the increased spending was aimed at energizing the party faithful and getting out the vote; turnout across the state increased by an average of almost 20 percent over the 2013 election. And in the districts that switched party control, turnout increased by an average of more than 25 percent.

After the votes were counted, the Democrats had flipped fifteen seats from Republican to Democrat. It was the biggest electoral shift in favor of Virginia Democrats in a single election in over one hundred years. Suddenly, the party distribution went from 66–34 in favor of the Republicans to 50–49 in their favor. Only one race, District 94, remained undecided. Ultimately, in that last contest it was determined that the Republican incumbent, David Yancey, had received 11,608 votes and the Democratic challenger Shelly Simonds had also received 11,608 votes. The election that would determine control of the Virginia House was a tie. If the Democrat ultimately were to be declared the winner, the chamber would be tied 50 to 50.

Finally, in January 2018, after several recounts and only a few days before the legislature was set to convene for the new session, the State Board of Elections held a drawing to determine the District 94 winner. The names of the two contestants—Simonds and Yancey—were written on separate slips of paper and placed inside two small containers, which were then placed inside the decorative blue bowl crafted by Steven Glass. An official from the State Board of Elections drew one of the containers from the bowl and opened it. Written on the enclosed piece of paper was the name of the Republican incumbent, David

Yancey. He was declared the winner of the District 94 election and the Republicans retained majority control of the Virginia House.

While the Republicans were pleased with the outcome, the Democrats still had reason to be happy with the elections. They had gained fifteen House seats and set what they hoped would be a precedent for 2018 state legislative contests across the country. Eleven of the fifteen seats that flipped from Republican to Democratic control were won by women candidates. The number of women serving in the Virginia House jumped from seventeen to twenty-eight (twenty-three Democrats, five Republicans). Among the Democrats who had won were Kathy Tran, the first Asian American woman elected to the Virginia House and Danica Roem, the nation's first transgender state legislator.

The story of the 2017 Virginia House elections highlights several points we will examine in this chapter, including (1) the variation in campaign costs across states; (2) the relationship between campaign expenditures and voter turnout; (3) an increase in the number of women candidates; (4) the rise of independent spending in state legislative elections; and (5) the impact of political polarization on state races. And, of course, (6) the importance of voting; a single additional vote could have changed the outcome of the District 94 election, which, in turn, would have changed who controlled the chamber.

Differences in State Legislative Campaign Costs

Some state legislative races can be expensive. Often this is because both parties see a legitimate opportunity to win control of the chamber. But even when this is the case, not all legislative districts in the state will be competitive. Some districts will be safe for one party and spending tends to be much lower in such districts. About 40 percent of state legislative races nationwide are uncontested. In many states, another 40 percent of the districts might be contested but not genuinely competitive—one party almost always wins the district without having to invest a great deal of campaign money. In other words, in many states there will be little money spent in most races, but a large amount spent in the few truly competitive districts. As one veteran campaign consultant in Texas observes, "At the end of the day, how expensive your race is is a function of how competitive your race is."[3]

The most expensive state legislative race in 2016 was in the Chicago suburbs, the 20th District of the Illinois House. More than $4 million dollars was spent between the two sides.[4] A 2017 New Jersey State Senate contest approached $20 million in expenditures. This was an unusual situation, in which the New Jersey teachers' union was seeking to defeat the leader of the Senate Democrats. Much of the money spent came in the form of independent expenditures made by labor groups. Races with such fantastic amounts tend to be the exception. As previously mentioned, while there were eleven Virginia House races that each exceeded $1 million in campaign expenditures in 2017, there were also thirty-five districts where total spending was less than $100,000.[5] Keep in mind, the population of Virginia House districts is much larger (about 85,000 people per district) than the median state house population (about 45,000 people per district). Campaign spending in states with smaller district populations is usually lower.

In Texas, where House districts are also large (about 180,000 people) but many districts are safe for one party, the amount spent by the winning candidate in contested races in 2016 ranged from under $10,000 in one uncompetitive contest (District 66) to $450,000 in a more competitive race (District 41). The median expenditure was $65,000—much less than one might forecast was needed to win.[6] But, of course, a winning candidate does not have to raise or spend large sums of money if the district tilts heavily to his or her party—what is referred to as a "safe seat."

Where state legislative campaign spending is high, it is often driven by the cost of television advertising. Few state legislative districts match up well with television media markets; therefore a candidate is often paying to reach many people who actually live outside the candidate's district. It is an expensive campaign communications technique and often inefficient. Most candidates are likely to rely on direct-mail advertising, which may cost only a few thousand dollars to produce and distribute to targeted households in the district. Radio is another more cost-effective campaign tool.

Increasingly, legislative candidates are turning to advertising on the internet (known as digital marketing). As one Maryland newspaper reported recently, "Online ads are playing an ever-growing role in U.S. political campaigns. They are especially useful for candidates in down-ballot races such as for state delegate, for whom the costs of television or radio can be prohibitive."[7] Campaign advertising on digital media platforms was projected to be about 18 percent of total campaign spending in state legislative races in 2018, and we can anticipate that figure will grow rapidly over the next few electoral cycles.[8]

Many state legislative races, however, are still traditional "retail" campaigns. These are "old-school" contests involving face-to-face, door-to-door, one-voter-at-a-time contacts. They do not cost a lot of money. But they typically do require a large investment of a candidate's time and energy. Good examples are the campaigns of Ellie Boldman Hill (now Hill-Smith), who served four terms in the Montana House until she was term-limited out in January 2019. Campaigning in a district in Helena, Hill-Smith raised an average of $6,500 in each of her four successful elections. Legislative districts in Montana are small in population, averaging about 10,000 residents. Such a district is not likely to contain more than six thousand potential voters, so expensive broadcast communications are unthinkable. Almost all of the money Hill-Smith's campaign spent was on direct-mail and door-to-door literature drops. As she noted, "I had to win on the ground with grassroots volunteers and support. My first election cycle, I knocked on nearly every door in my district, at least twice. It took me the better part of four months to do, knocking on doors daily. I also had teams of volunteers doing literature drops when I could no longer afford direct mail."[9] Smith-Hill's story is typical of Montana legislative races; in 2016, the average general election candidate received less than $10,000 in contributions.[10]

One recent study estimated the amount of money a candidate needed to raise in order to have a good chance of winning a competitive race, one where both candidates had adequate financial resources.[11] In the 2016 electoral cycle, the amount a candidate needed to raise to have a legitimate chance of winning in such a race was over $1 million in California and Illinois. In Missouri and North Carolina, the figure was closer to $200,000. But in most states, the cost to win was much less—around $80,000 in Arizona, Arkansas, Colorado, and Mississippi, and roughly $50,000 or less in a dozen states.

Obviously, campaign finance expenditures vary by state, by chamber, and by political context. One study identified "low cost" states as Maine, Montana, New Hampshire, North Dakota, Vermont, and Wyoming—all states with small-population districts and part-time legislatures. "High cost" states included California, Illinois, Missouri, New Jersey, New York, Ohio, Pennsylvania, and Texas—all states with large-population Senate districts and (with the exceptions of Missouri and Texas) more professionalized legislatures.[12]

Differences in Electoral Rules

Cost are not the only variable in state legislative races. Most of the laws pertaining to elections in the United States are determined at the state—not national—level, and because states created their electoral systems at different times and under different circumstances, election procedures often vary. Indeed, people are frequently surprised to find out just how much electoral structures and procedures diverge from state to state. Legislative elections may differ on district size, district magnitude, redistricting practices, campaign finance laws, rules to determine winners, when elections are held, who is eligible to vote, and who is eligible to run for office.

Thus the rules governing state legislative elections are not the same across the states. This means that the electoral context differs. We use the term *electoral context* in a broad sense—to refer to the recruitment, nomination, campaign, and electoral phases of the process by which private citizens become elected officials. Used in this way, the electoral context depends on the particular electoral rules of a state; on whether candidates are incumbents, challengers, or open-seat contestants; and on the processes by which candidates are recruited to run. A primary goal of this section is to examine how the electoral context shapes the nature of legislative campaigns.[13] A secondary goal is to discuss how legislative campaigns are run. All of this matters, because how lawmakers gain office has implications for how the legislature operates and how legislators behave in office.

As mentioned earlier, some of the sources of campaign variation are related to dissimilarities in electoral rules from one state to another. One political analyst puts it this way, "[E]lectoral politics aren't just about the issues, but are also about the rules the candidates run under."[14] State rules may differ in at least the ways discussed below.

District Magnitude

District magnitude refers to the number of representatives being elected in a given legislative district. The most common case in U.S. politics is to elect one representative per district—known as a single-member district (SMD). All 435 U.S. House districts, for example, are SMDs. But, as noted in chapter 1, ten states use at least some multimember districts (MMDs) for one or both of their state legislative houses. In almost all cases, these MMDs are simply two-member districts where two lawmakers are elected in each district. But a few states have some larger MMDs. Maryland, for example, has many three-member districts, along with some two-member districts and SMDs. The most prolific user of large MMDs is New Hampshire. It has about one hundred SMDs, but there are numerous other districts that elect anywhere from between two and ten Representatives. The largest MMD, Hillsborough District 37, elects eleven members.

In chapter 1, we noted that there are some differences in the way legislators from MMDs behave compared with legislators from SMDs. But there are also electoral consequences to the choice of SMDs versus MMDs. For example, the incumbency advantage appears to be somewhat less in MMDs, meaning that MMD incumbents have a somewhat more difficult time winning reelection.[15] There is a tendency for "team campaigns" in MMDs—that is, campaigns in which all the candidates from one party pool their resources and urge the electorate to "bloc vote" (e.g., "Vote for the Republican team in District 5!"). And MMD candidates are more likely to seek new and more diverse donors to their campaigns.[16] Historically, MMDs made it more difficult for minority candidates to get elected, and for this reason they are no longer used in many states.[17]

Candidate Qualification Rules

For potential candidates, among the most important obstacles they face are the rules for establishing candidacy. These rules vary by state.[18] The first qualification is U.S. citizenship, and it is required everywhere. In most cases the citizenship standard is explicitly stated in the state constitution, in others it is implicit given a requirement that a candidate be a qualified voter in the state or be a state citizen.[19] Still, citizenship became an issue in several state legislative elections in 2018. In Georgia, a Democratic candidate who had been born in Mexico was removed from the ballot because although she had lived in the state for nine years, she had only become a U.S. citizen in 2017 and Georgia's constitution requires a candidate to be a state citizen—and therefore by inference a U.S. citizen—for two years before he or she can run for the legislature.[20] In Hawaii, a Republican candidate was disqualified because as a citizen of American Samoa she is considered a U.S. national and not a U.S. citizen with voting rights and, by extension under the Hawaii state constitution, the right to run for state office.[21] Following the election, a Latina who had won a seat in the Arizona House had a lawsuit filed to prevent her from taking office on the grounds that she was not a U.S. citizen. But she had been born in Arizona, and the case challenging her right to citizenship under the U.S. Constitution's Fourteenth Amendment was dismissed by a state judge.[22]

A qualification that does vary by state is that age at which one is eligible to serve in the legislature. As shown in table 2.1, there are substantial differences in terms of the minimum age at which one can be elected. In fourteen states (among them California, Massachusetts, New York, and Wisconsin) the minimum age for a legislator for either house is eighteen years old. In five states (Kentucky, Missouri, New Hampshire, New Jersey, and Tennessee) the minimum age for service in the upper house is set at thirty years. In New Hampshire, a person can serve in the House at eighteen, but cannot serve in the Senate until age thirty. Notably, no state uses the exact same set of age qualifications that the U.S. Constitution imposes for serving in Congress.

Residency requirements vary as well, as documented in tables 2.2 and 2.3. The U.S. Constitution sets weak residency requirements for members of Congress; those elected only have to be residents of the state on the day of the election. No state is as lax. There are eight states where one has only to be a resident of the state on the day of the election, but he or she must also be a resident of the district. (There is no constitutional requirement for U.S. representatives to live in the district they represent, only that they live in the state.) The most stringent residency requirement is in New Hampshire, where one must be a state resident for seven years before filing for a state Senate seat. When he ran as the Republican nominee for a U.S. Senate seat from New Hampshire in 2014, Scott Brown had only recently reestablished his residency in the state, but under the U.S. Constitution he would have been qualified to represent the state had he won. However, under the New Hampshire state constitution he would not be eligible to serve in the state Senate until 2021.

The cost of filing to run for the state legislature varies too; in about half the states there is no filing fee at all, and in most other states the fee is less

TABLE 2.1 Age Qualifications for Election to State Legislatures and US Congress

		Minimum Age for Election in Lower House			
		18 Years	**21 Years**	**24 Years**	**25 Years**
Minimum Age in Upper House	18 Years	CA, CT, HI, KS, LA, MA, MT, NY, ND, OH, RI, VT, WA, WI			
	21 Years		FL, ID, IL, MI, MN, NE, NV, OR, SD, VA		
	25 Years	WV	AL, AK, AR, GA, IN, IA, ME, MD, MS, NC, NM, OK, PA, SC, WY		AZ, CO, UT
	26 Years		TX		
	27 Years			DE	
	30 Years	NH	NJ, TN	KY, MO	US

Source: Compiled by the authors from National Conference of State Legislatures, state legislature and state elections websites and state constitutions.

TABLE 2.2 Residency Requirements—Lower Houses

State Residency Requirement	District Residency Requirement	State Lower House
Resident	Resident	CT, KS, MI, NM, OK, SC, VA, WA
Resident	6 months	OK
Resident	1 year	ID, MA, NC, OR, WY
Resident	2 years	IL
30 days	30 days	RI
30 days	1 year	OH
1 year	Resident	WI
1 year	30 days	NV, ND,
1 year	60 days	IA
1 year	3 month	ME
1 year	6 months	MD, MN, MT
1 year	1 year	CO, WV
2 years	Resident	FL, NH, SD
2 years	1 year	AR, GA, IN, KY, LA, MO, NJ, TX, VT
3 years	Resident	HI
3 years	6 months	UT
3 years	1 year	AL, AK, AZ, CA, DE, TN
4 years	1 year	PA
4 years	2 years	MS
5 years	1 year	NY, WV

Source: Compiled by the authors from National Conference of State Legislatures, state legislatures and state elections websites and state constitutions.

than $200. Although there is no filing fee in Illinois, candidates are required to submit petitions with valid signatures of registered voters in support of the candidate. For the Senate, the figure is one thousand signatures. In Texas, the fee to file is $1,250. Arkansas has a unique system. Each party sets the fee for their candidates. For Democrats, it costs $3,000 to file for a House seat and $4,500 for Senate seat. For Republicans, House candidates are charged $3,000 and Senate candidates are assessed $7,500. The parties use these fees to cover party advertising and campaign costs. Obviously, costly filing fees potentially exclude a significant segment of the population from becoming candidates; as one lawmaker observes; "I think the fee absolutely discourages low-income Arkansans from running for the state legislature, 57% of Americans don't have $500 to cover for an emergency and we're asking them to pay thousands of dollars in order to run for office."[23]

TABLE 2.3 Residency Requirements—Upper Houses

State Residency Requirement	District Residency Requirement	State Upper House
Resident	Resident	CT, KS, MI, NM, OK, SC, VA, WA
Resident	1 year	ID, NE, OR, WY
Resident	2 years	IL
30 days	30 days	RI
30 days	1 year	OH
1 year	Resident	WI
1 year	30 days	NV, ND,
1 year	60 days	IA
1 year	3 months	ME
1 year	6 months	MD, MN, MT
1 year	1 year	CO
2 years	Resident	FL, SD
2 years	1 year	AR, GA, IN, LA, NJ, NC, VT
3 years	Resident	HI
3 years	6 months	UT
3 years	1 year	AL, AK, AZ, CA, DE, MO, TN
4 years	1 year	PA
4 years	2 years	MS
5 years	Resident	MA
5 years	1 year	NY, TX, WV
6 years	1 year	KY
7 years	Resident	NH

Source: Compiled by the authors from National Conference of State Legislatures, state legislatures and state elections websites and state constitutions.

Citizenship, age, residency and filing fee requirements structure the potential pool of candidates.[24] And it is worth noting that these requirements are enforced. In 2014, for example, a California state senator was convicted of perjury and voter fraud and sentenced to three months in jail for falsely claiming to live in the district he represented. (He resigned from office, spent an hour in jail and two and a half years on probation, and was eventually pardoned by the governor).[25] In 2018 California adopted a law loosening the interpretation of district residency to diminish the chances that any other state lawmaker would run afoul of the requirement.[26] Florida's legislature had to tighten the state's residency requirements in 2014 when doubts were raised as to whether a number of its members actually resided in their districts.[27] Still, in 2017 a lawmaker had to resign after she pleaded guilty to perjury in a criminal case about where she actually lived.[28] Others had to scurry to avoid trouble. One Florida senator listed four different temporary addresses over a six-year period after redistricting placed her home outside the boundaries of the district she represented.[29]

Primary Election Rules

In almost all states, primaries are used to determine the party nominee for each office in the general election. The rules for primary elections, however, differ from state to state. In most states, the winner of the primary election is determined by a plurality rule—the candidate with the most votes wins. Often in primary elections there is only one candidate and the decision rule is therefore moot. And, of course, if only two candidates get votes, then the winner necessarily earned a majority. But ten states, almost all of them in the South, require a runoff if no candidate wins a majority in the primary.[30] The top two vote getters face each other in a *runoff primary* that is held a few weeks after the original primary. Because only two candidates are involved in the runoff, the winner is assured of receiving a majority of the votes cast. From the candidates' point of view, a runoff primary means an extended campaign with additional costs incurred.

The top vote getter in the first primary usually wins the runoff, but not always—in fact, he or she loses about 30 percent of the time. Sometimes the runoff becomes an intense battle between party factions. Consider, for example, the 2014 Texas Senate District 2 Republican primary. The incumbent, family physician Bob Deuell, faced two challengers in the March primary. One challenger, Mark Thompson, was a local therapist, working with visually impaired clients. The other, Bob Hall, was a retired businessman and head of the local Tea Party organization. Deuell received 48.5 percent of the vote, Thompson managed 12.7 percent, and Hall garnered 38.8 percent. Under the rules used in most primaries Deuell would have been declared the winner because he obtained the plurality of votes—in this case he outpolled his nearest opponent by ten percentage points. But Deuell finished just shy of a majority, so under the rules in Texas a runoff against the second-place finisher, Tea Party activist Hall, was scheduled for June. The results for the two contests are presented in table 2.4.

TABLE 2.4 2014 Texas Senate Runoff

March primary	49,172 votes cast:	Deuell	23,847 (48.5%)
		Hall	19,085 (38.8%)
		Thompson	6,240 (12.7%)
June runoff	36,160 votes cast:	Hall	18,230 (50.4%)
		Deuell	17,930 (49.6%)

There are a several things to note about this case. First, the incumbent, Deuell, received almost four thousand more votes than either of his opponents in the March primary. But he lost in the June runoff by three hundred votes. Second, there were thirteen thousand fewer votes cast in the June runoff than had been cast in the March primary. Third, the fall-off in votes cast was almost entirely at the expense of Deuell. He received almost five thousand fewer votes in June while Hall's vote total only fell a few hundred votes. Clearly, Tea Party supporters were more motivated to turn out for the runoff than were Deuell's supporters. The incumbent had foreseen this scenario; as one reporter noted, "Deuell knew a low-turnout runoff would help Hall, boosted by tea-party fervor."[31]

Another important question about primaries involves voter eligibility. The basic issue is who can participate in a party's primary election. Slightly over half of the states use some version of a "closed" primary, meaning only registered party members are allowed to vote in the contest. Other states use a variant of "open" primaries, wherein party registration is not a requirement to cast a vote. In open primaries, it is possible for independents or even supporters of the opposing party to cast a ballot. Thus the composition of primary electorates varies across the states.

There are many states where one party dominates in the general election. In other words, there is not much competition between the major parties. Elsewhere we note that nationwide about 40 percent of state legislative races are uncontested by one of the two major parties. In some states the proportion of uncontested races is much higher. In these situations, the primary election may be the only way for voters to enforce some accountability on their elected official. It does not happen often, but if legislators stray too far from the policy expectations of the electorate, the primary can even become the instrument of retribution. This is what happened in Oklahoma in 2018 when a host of challengers ran against incumbent Republicans who were viewed as unsupportive of teachers and the public education system. Republicans enjoyed a large majority (over 70 percent of the seats) in the state House. There were 74 incumbent GOP representatives. Of those, seven could not run again because of term limits and seventeen others retired or ran for another office. Thus, fifty Republican incumbents were left to seek reelection to the House. Through a concerted effort by the Oklahoma Education Association and other public school advocates, many of those fifty were challenged in their primary and eleven of them were defeated. In other words, 22 percent of the GOP incumbents who ran for reelection lost in their primary. One Oklahoma newspaper called it "the most extraordinary primary season in state history" leading to "unprecedented turnover."[32] And it was in the primary where accountability was enforced because all thirty-nine GOP incumbents who survived their primary won in the general election.

Timing of Primary Elections

In 2018 slightly more than half the states held primary elections in May or June, but two states (Illinois and Texas) held them in March, while five eastern states waited until September. While no state held its primary in July—Alabama and Georgia scheduled runoff elections for that month—about a dozen did so in August. For potential candidates, earlier primaries mean they must decide at an earlier date if they are going to run. An earlier primary also means they must develop a campaign organization and begin fund-raising sooner than some might prefer. For voters, an early primary translates into a longer campaign season. For the political parties, early primaries push forward the candidate recruitment process. In contrast, late primaries, particularly those held in September, mean the parties must be well organized because the schedule leaves only about eight weeks between the primary and the general election. As soon as the primary is over, the party must be prepared to offer assistance to the nominees, who in turn must be ready to hit the ground running.

Redistricting Practices

Every ten years, after a new federal census is taken, states must redraw their legislative district lines to realign electoral boundaries with shifting populations. They must do this because of the "one person, one vote" principle. In this country, "one person, one vote" has been interpreted by the courts to mean that legislative districts must have equal populations. While most people understand this, there are three things about the process that many do not realize: the state government is responsible for drawing the congressional district lines within that state in addition to drawing state legislative lines, the process for drawing these lines is not the same in all states, and the criteria for drawing the lines are different for congressional and state legislative districts (although the state is responsible for drawing both).

Each state determines the process for drawing legislative and congressional district lines within that state. For most, the procedure is to have the legislature create the districts through statutory law, which means the plan must be approved by a majority in each chamber and by the governor. If one party controls both chambers and the governor's office, or what we call unified government, then the district lines are likely to be drawn to enhance that party's electoral fortunes. In other words, a partisan gerrymander is probable under unified government.[33] In the 2011–2012 redistricting cycle there were several examples of partisan gerrymanders. Perhaps the most far-reaching was Wisconsin's, which became the subject of a lawsuit, *Gill v. Whitford*. In 2016, a federal district court declared the state's gerrymander to be so substantial that it violated the U.S. Constitution, the first time in over thirty years that a federal court had struck down a redistricting case based on partisan gerrymandering.[34] The case was appealed to the U.S. Supreme Court, which remanded it back to the district court on procedural grounds. The district court was scheduled to rehear the case in April 2019. Concerns about Wisconsin's redistricting practices appear well grounded. A report following the 2018 election found that, while Democrats carried the governorship and four other statewide elections and received 54 percent of all the votes cast in State Assembly races, they only won 36 percent of the Assembly seats.[35]

If divided government exists—if one party controls the legislature and the other party controls the executive branch, or if one party controls the Senate but the other party holds a majority in the lower house—then each party can check the other. In this situation, the plan that passes is apt to protect the political status quo. According to one study, in the last redistricting cycle, eighteen states produced redistricting plans that protected incumbents, regardless of party affiliation.[36]

For this reason, the election prior to the initiation of the redistricting process is critical because it determines the partisan makeup of the legislature that will redraw the lines. In this regard, the Republican Party appreciated the importance of the 2010 elections for the upcoming redistricting process for state legislative districts. The Republicans also understood the importance of state legislative control for the congressional redistricting process. They made a concerted effort to win control of as many states as possible that year. Employing a strategy they called REDMAP (Redistricting Majority Project), the Republicans identified the legislative chambers most likely to flip, and they devoted more than $30 million to those races. Their strategy proved astute; the GOP won control of twenty-two additional state legislative chambers.[37] This greatly advantaged them during the 2011 to 2012 redistricting cycle because they controlled the process in a majority of states. Based on the Republicans' success in the 2011–2012 cycle, Democrats are now focusing on state legislative elections in the run-up to the next redistricting cycle. As one activist Democratic recently remarked, "Everything that makes our democracy fair or unfair all comes down to the state level."[38]

Nonetheless, it is important to note that the overall partisan effect of redistricting is often less than what the public (and media) imagines.[39] There are constraints on how much gerrymandering can occur; among these, for example, are rules requiring district compactness and geographical contiguity.[40] In the Wisconsin case, for example, even Democratic Party leaders recognized that the geographic population distribution works against them. The House Democratic Floor Leader admitted that even if legislative district lines had been drawn by an independent entity in 2018, his party probably still would not have won a majority of districts.[41] This is because Democratic voters tend to be heavily clustered in urban districts. Nonetheless, the vote-to-seat distribution would likely have been more equitable than is currently the case under Wisconsin's gerrymandered maps.

There is evidence suggesting that legal constraints (such as compactness) are more strictly adhered to by independent redistricting commissions.[42] As a legal scholar notes, "Nearly all legislatures refuse to relinquish redistricting power voluntarily. That is why we're seeing a number of voter initiatives attempting to create independent commissions that take this power out of the hands of self-interested political actors. . . . But that option is limited to states that have an initiative process."[43]

In 2018, voters in five states addressed the issue of redistricting and gerrymandering in one way or another, and all did so through the initiative process. In May, Ohio voters revamped that state's redistricting commission to reduce the influence of elected officials. In November, Missouri and Colorado voters did the same. And two states, Michigan and Utah, passed ballot measures to create redistricting commissions for the first time. At least sixteen states now place power over the drawing of legislative districts outside the immediate control of the legislature.[44]

Most of these use an independent redistricting commission to draw the district lines. This does not necessarily make the process less political. As a redistricting analyst notes, "Reformers often mistakenly assume that commissions will be less partisan than legislatures when conducting redistricting but that depends largely on the design of the board or commission."[45] Each of the commissions works in a somewhat different way, differing on how commissioners are selected and whether the legislature has the opportunity to veto or modify the commission plan. The use of redistricting commissions is especially popular in the west, where the initiative process is prevalent. Independent redistricting commissions now exist in nine western states: Alaska, Arizona, California, Colorado, Hawaii, Idaho, Montana, Utah, and Washington.

Unusual redistricting procedures are employed in Iowa and Missouri. In 2018 Missouri passed a state constitutional amendment creating the post of state demographer. Assuming the measure withstands likely legal challenges, in the next round of redistricting following the 2020 census the nonpartisan state demographer will be charged with drawing legislative district lines using a statistical test to ensure fairness. The maps based on this process will then be submitted to the state's two redistricting commissions (one for state House districts and one for state Senate districts). This process is somewhat similar to the one long used in Iowa.[46] There the drawing of district lines is done by nonpartisan legislative staff, and they must follow specific criteria, developing district maps "without any political or election data including the addresses of incumbents."[47] The Iowa legislature can pass or reject the first redistricting plan submitted by the nonpartisan staff, but it cannot amend it. If the first plan is rejected, the nonpartisan staff produces a second plan, which the legislature can again only vote up or down. If that plan is rejected, the nonpartisan staff produces a third set of districts. The legislature can amend that plan only after they first reject it. In the four rounds of redistricting since this process was instituted in 1981, the legislature has never gotten to the point where it has amended a plan. In some ways, this is surprising because the process often results in dramatic changes. After the 2001 redistricting, for example, 64 of the 150 Iowa legislators wound up in districts with at least one other incumbent, forcing many of them to retire from the legislature, move to an unoccupied district, or face a competitive election.[48]

Case Law and State Redistricting

The standards for drawing state legislative district lines are somewhat different from those used for congressional districts. The biggest contrast is in what passes for "one person, one vote." Recall that the courts interpret the phrase *one person, one vote* to mean that each district must have the same population as the next district—that is, districts within a state must be equipopulous.[49] But just how close to "equal population" must a plan be? For congressional districts within a state, the answer is extremely close. Thus, each congressional district within a state must have almost exactly the same number of people. In contrast, the courts have been more flexible when it comes to state legislative districts. The difference is that the interpretation of "equal representation" for congressional districts stems from Article I, Section 2 of the U.S. Constitution, but for state legislative districts, the relevant constitutional sources are the Fourteenth and Fifteenth amendments to the U.S. Constitution and appropriate sections of state constitutions.

The key state legislative redistricting case is *Reynolds v. Sims*, which was decided by the U.S. Supreme Court in 1964.[50] The 1960s were a time of major policy shifts by the Court in regard to redistricting and representation. And *Reynolds* was monumental for the states. The decision forced a number of them to abandon the practice of apportioning their senates by county while several New England states had to give up apportioning their lower houses by cities and towns. This was something of a radical departure from political traditions. The allocation of seats in the U.S. House is by state population, as directed by Article I, Section 2 of the U.S. Constitution. But the allocation of seats in the U.S. Senate is not by population but by political jurisdiction—that is, by state, and each state is allocated two senators (Article I, Section 3). Thus, Wyoming (with a population of about 575,000) has the same representation in the U.S. Senate as California (with a population of more than 39 million). There are both symbolic and political purposes to this equal allocation; it reflects the fact that all states are equal in the federal system of government. Many states, when devising allocation principles for their own legislatures, followed similar reasoning. They determined that districts be allocated by population for the lower chambers and by political subdivision for the upper chamber; in most states, this political subdivision was the county. There would be one senator from each county, regardless of population. In 1960 in Florida, for example, one Senate district (Dade County) had a population of 935,000, and another (Jefferson County) had a population of 9,543. Each county had the same representation in the state Senate, even though one county had ninety-eight times more people! The U.S. Supreme Court ended this practice (and the use of any analogies to the U.S. Senate) with its decision in *Reynolds*.

The court did recognize, however, that many state constitutions required counties or other jurisdictions such as towns to remain intact when drawing legislative district lines. To facilitate these state constitutional stipulations, the U.S. Supreme Court permits some latitude in population deviation in the drawing of state legislative lines, and this often permits states to draw lines that keep political subdivisions such as counties, townships, or municipalities intact rather than being split among several legislative districts.

There are several other important considerations in redistricting. One is the matter of racial gerrymandering. The way district lines get drawn did not became an important issue for the federal courts until the 1960s, and one of the main reasons the courts finally became involved was because of racial discrimination in the way some states drew the district lines for their state legislatures.

Many of the early Supreme Court cases centered on the fact that states were intentionally diluting the voting strength of minorities. One of the ways this was done was by creating MMDs in urban areas. A 1973 Texas case, *White v. Regester*, is typical.[51] In San Antonio (Bexar County), where a sizeable Hispanic population resided, and in Dallas (Dallas County), where a significant black population lived, the creation of SMDs would likely have resulted in the election of some Hispanic and black legislators. But by using county-wide MMDs in each county, the majority of white voters could control the election. In a series of such cases in the late 1960s and 1970s, the U.S. Supreme Court discouraged the use of MMDs (without declaring them unconstitutional per se).

Campaign Finance Laws

Campaign finance laws differ among the states in several ways, most importantly in regard to the requirements for reporting donations and spending (known as *disclosure requirements*) and in regard to limits on how much an individual or group can donate to a campaign. While these requirements still vary between the states, decisions by the U.S. Supreme Court have greatly reduced the effect of the state-by-state differences. Most important in this regard was the 2010 case *Citizens United v. Federal Election Commission.*[52] By allowing direct spending on political advertising by corporations and unions, the Court expanded the potential for money being spent in state legislative campaigns. Perhaps more importantly, it enlarged the role of campaign spending by forces outside the control of the candidates themselves. Increasingly, these independent expenditures (IEs) strengthen the role of interest groups, nonprofit organizations often aligned with one political party or the other, and wealthy individuals in the campaign process.[53] By 2014, over $3.5 million in independent expenditures were reported in just one California Assembly race, and more than $1 million in independent spending occurred in each of five other state legislative contests.[54]

Independent expenditures continue to grow as a percentage of total spending in state legislative races. Tracking independent expenditures in fifteen states over time, a study reported that by 2016, IEs accounted for almost 23 percent of total spending in state legislative campaigns.[55] In the 2017–2018 electoral cycle, many organizations or individuals making independent expenditures did so in favor of Democratic candidates, and especially women candidates. For example, in Colorado in 2018 the Republicans held the state Senate by a narrow majority, prompting the Democrats to target five of the seventeen seats up for election. Democratic candidates in those races each raised between $300,000 and $500,000. But independent groups "poured in money under much looser campaign finance limits; state records showed at least $15 million of independent expenditures on advertising and staffing across the five key races."[56] The Democrats won all five Senate seats.

Term Limits

A final law that varies by state and affects the nature of elections is the limit on how many terms a legislator can serve. For most states, there is no limit; as long as an individual can continue to win elections, he or she can serve indefinitely. But, as noted in chapter 1, fifteen states impose term limitations. From the standpoint of elections, term limits have several implications. The most obvious is that because incumbents are eventually forced out, there is higher turnover in legislatures with term limits. Legislative turnover in states with term limits tends to average about fifteen percentage points higher than in states without term limits, although the precise nature of the term-limit law in a given state will affect the average turnover rate.

Another implication is that as a consequence of the forced turnover, there will be more open-seat elections (those in which there is no incumbent). Such contests tend to be more competitive. At the same time, most incumbents in term-limited states do not face a serious electoral challenge in the last few electoral cycles before they are termed out. Rather than take on an incumbent, strategic politicians will simply wait until the incumbent is termed out and the seat becomes open.[57]

The Candidates

Some years ago, in a book about running for the state legislature, we wrote, "No greater commitment to participation in the political process can be made than to stand for election. Most Americans give little thought to what is involved in running for elective office. Unappreciated is the tremendous personal cost in money, time, and emotion involved in seeking public office."[58] That observation still rings true.

Running for the legislature is a more daunting task than most realize. Indeed, between 35 and 40 percent of all legislative seats nationwide are uncontested—that is, only one major party candidate runs, so that person is automatically elected.[59] In some states, the figure is considerably higher. In 2018, over half of the state legislative races in Wyoming were uncontested by one of the major parties. In the 2014 general election in Georgia, 73 percent of Senate races were uncontested, as were an astounding 83 percent of House seats.

And it is not just that the general election may be uncontested; over 25 percent of incumbents did not have an opponent in either the primary or the general election.[60] This lack of competition has important consequences. Legislators who run unopposed appear to be more likely to "shirk"—that is, they are less likely to be actively engaged in the lawmaking and representational processes.[61]

Why is it so hard to get people to run for the legislature? Being a candidate for office demands a great deal of time and energy, often more than some aspiring politicians realize. A physician running for the Missouri Senate, for example, dropped out before the primary, explaining, "It was mostly the demands on my time. Trying to run two businesses—my work is somewhat unpredictable. All these things I could have known before hand, but I didn't realize how much work [running for office] was."[62] Psychologically, there is also the reality that all of the effort might be for naught; as one observer notes, "You have to be strong enough personally that you can risk being rejected."[63] A veteran lawmaker concurs, saying, "I don't like running for reelection every two years. It feels very much like a personal judgement. . . . I know it makes my stomach turn somersaults; I get anxious about it. Is this person going to vote for me? Did this person vote for me? Are you still going to vote for me?"[64] And there are potential financial costs associated with possibly winning office that might not pay very much. A physician running for the Minnesota House in 2018 worried about how she would be able meet her financial obligations if she won, fretting that "I can't pay back my student loans on a legislator's salary."[65] Thus, as an Iowa senator involved in recruiting others to run observed, "It's a huge commitment financially and on your family. So there's not a huge line of people—not even a small line of people who are interested in giving up four months of the year to serve."[66]

Candidate Type

When analyzing candidacies and campaigns, political scientists distinguish between three types of candidates: incumbents, challengers, and open-seat contestants. The incumbent is the current office holder. For the most part, incumbents enjoy substantial advantages in the American electoral system, and this is no less true of state legislative incumbents.[67] In a typical year, they win reelection more than 90 percent of the time.[68]

Challengers are candidates who run against incumbents. Because incumbents win so often, it is often difficult to find someone to compete against them. Almost all of the uncontested races mentioned earlier occurred in situations where no challenger could be convinced to run against an incumbent. There are, however, circumstances in which a candidate can pose a serious challenge to—and sometimes defeat—an incumbent. This is most likely to occur under one of the following scenarios:

1. *The race is in a marginal district.* A "marginal" district is one that is competitive, where the voters' preferences are split close to evenly between the two major parties or where there are a large number of independent voters. A "safe" district is one where members of one party almost always win. Thus, a Democratic challenger in a safe Republican district would face long odds. But in a marginal district, such a challenger might have a chance.

2. *Redistricting has occurred since the last election.* When the lines are redrawn, even longtime incumbents sometimes find they may lose. This is because the redrawing of the lines means there are some number of new voters in the district who might identify with the other political party or who may simply be unfamiliar with the incumbent.

3. *The incumbent has problems.* The problems could be policy based. The incumbent may have voted on an important issue in a way that has alienated a sufficient number of voters so that reelection is in doubt. For

example, any Montana lawmaker who votes for stricter gun control is likely to face stiff competition in the next election. Or, the incumbent may have become ideologically extreme beyond what the district's voters will tolerate.[69] But more often, problems in this context refer to personal failings such as ethical lapses or legal troubles. When personal difficulties become public, even an entrenched incumbent may lose. In 2018, a three-term New Mexico state representative known for her advocacy of tougher drunk-driving penalties was herself arrested for drunk driving.[70] She lost the general election. That same year a four-term state senator in New Hampshire lost his reelection bid after he was charged with domestic violence.[71]

4. *The U.S. president is unpopular and the incumbent legislator is of the president's party.* National trends can work against state legislative incumbents if they are of the same party as the president.[72] In 2006, for instance, several hundred Republican legislators were defeated by Democratic challengers in what was widely interpreted as a reaction against the administration of President George W. Bush. In 2010, the reverse occurred, as over seven hundred state legislative seats flipped from Democratic to Republican. This was viewed as a repudiation of President Obama. Incumbents of the president's party are more likely to be challenged, and more likely to lose, when the president is unpopular.[73] In 2018, Democrats won more than three hundred state legislative seats held by Republicans in an election that was framed as a referendum on President Trump.

The final type of candidate is an open-seat contestant. By definition, an open seat means there is no incumbent in the race. By eliminating any incumbency advantage, open-seat races are usually more competitive than races involving incumbents. In open-seat contests, both major parties typically run competent, qualified candidates. And because the race is anticipated to be competitive, it will likely will be more expensive.

Recruitment patterns are different for the three types of candidates. Incumbents do not have to be recruited; they have run successfully before and enjoy the advantages of name recognition, political contacts, and campaign contributors, as well as a track record of electoral success. Recruiting challengers is usually more difficult and may involve appealing to someone's sense of party loyalty to run even though the chances of winning are slight. It is usually easier for a party to find a good candidate to run in an open-seat contest because that contest appears more winnable.

Recruitment Agents

At one time, political parties controlled the recruitment of candidates. Party "bosses" determined who would run, when they would run, and for what office they would run. The party nomination was simply a matter of the party elite determining who would be the candidate. All of this began to change a century ago with the advent of the Progressive Era. Several reforms of the Progressive period were aimed at weakening the control of political parties, but in regard to recruitment, the most important of these was the creation of the primary election system (discussed earlier in this chapter). Primary elections weakened the ability of party bosses to control the nomination process by allowing voters to choose the nominees. This is not to say that parties are no longer important in recruiting candidates. Indeed, in recent years, the two major parties in various guises have become more active in encouraging people to run, especially in situations where control of the legislature may be at stake. But we are a long way from the pre-Progressive period when parties dictated the process. Beyond party leaders there are additional recruitment agents; in particular, interest groups may be active in seeking out potential candidates. Community groups and religious organizations sometimes play a role. A variety of interest groups, nonprofits, and "funding partners" often work with political parties to help recruit and support candidates. In this sense, the political party today is actually a broad network of allied or affiliated groups and individuals.[74]

A survey of nonincumbent candidates for state legislatures found that various party organizations were the most common recruitment agents but that numerous other agents were also involved.[75] According to the survey, the most active recruitment agent is the local party organization; 45 percent of the candidates said they had been approached and encouraged to run by a local party committee. This makes sense because it is ultimately the responsibility of the local party committee or chair to fill out the party's slate of candidates in an election in the area. Often, this means finding someone who is willing to be a "sacrificial lamb" when there is a seemingly invulnerable incumbent from the other party. State party officials and legislative leaders are more likely to become involved in recruitment when the parties are closely divided in the legislature. Under these circumstances, legislative leaders and state party officials identify which districts and races they think are winnable. These "targeted" races are the ones in which state party leaders and legislative leaders are the most likely to be involved, in terms of both recruiting "quality" candidates and promising campaign support to get them to enter the race.

Although interest groups and other associations (e.g., religious organizations) are not as prevalent as parties in the recruitment process, they are occasionally important. This is most likely to occur with groups that are closely allied with a particular party, such as labor unions with the Democratic Party or evangelical organizations with the Republican Party.

Self-Starters

Some candidates do not need to be recruited; they recruit themselves. In the survey mentioned above, nonincumbent candidates were asked to describe the circumstances surrounding their decision to run. When asked, "Whose idea was it to run for the legislature?" almost one-third of them said they were self-starters. About one-fifth had to be persuaded, and the rest (the largest group) were thinking about running when they received encouragement from others to do so. As we might expect, self-starters are more likely to run for open seats, while those who must be persuaded are often recruited to run against incumbents.

In the past few electoral cycles, there appear to have been more challenges to incumbents in the primaries—especially in Republican Party primaries in states where the Tea Party faction is particularly strong. As demonstrated by the Texas runoff example discussed earlier, some of these intraparty challenges have been successful, as a number of incumbent GOP legislators have been defeated in primaries in recent years. But, this is not just a Republican phenomenon. In 2018, the progressive wing of the Maryland Democratic Party challenged and defeated four veteran Democratic leaders, including two committee chairs and the Senate president pro tem, while, as will be discussed in chapter 4, six incumbent Democratic senators in New York lost their primaries to insurgent challengers.[76]

The Recruitment of Women and Minorities

As is true in most legislatures around the world, women and minorities in state legislatures are underrepresented relative to their proportions of the population. Although women comprise about 51 percent of the national population, only about 28 percent of all state legislators are women. The percentages for minorities are almost 10 percent African American (13 percent of the population nationwide), about 5 percent Hispanic (17 percent nationally), and about 1 percent Asian American (5 percent nationally). As one would expect, and as we will discuss in chapter 3, the percentage of legislators with a racial or ethnic minority heritage is highly variable by region and state, largely because the racial and ethnic mix varies by region and state. For example, more than 28 percent of Mississippi legislators are African American, about 40 percent of New Mexico legislators are Hispanic, and close to half of Hawaii legislators are Asian American or Pacific Islander, largely because each of these groups makes up a significant proportion of the population in these states.[77]

This sort of relationship does not, of course, explain the variation in female legislators across the states. Women are a majority of the population in every state except Alaska, but, prior to the 2018 election, the proportion of female state legislators ranged from 11 percent in Wyoming to 40 percent in Arizona.[78] The reasons for this disparity are many, including differences in political culture; partisan strength (female legislators are more likely to be Democrats); and the lingering reluctance, even today, of party elites in some states to actively recruit women as candidates.[79] The 2018 election resulted in impressive gains for women in many states. During the 2017–2018 electoral cycle, numerous organizations—some new, some established—were active in recruiting women to run for state legislative office and they met with a good deal of success. More women ran for state legislature than ever before and many won. Women took a majority of the seats in the Colorado House and the Nevada Assembly and achieved a near majority in the Oregon House. Many states, among them Virginia and Michigan, set new records for the number of women elected to the legislature.

There is, however, a pronounced gender gap between the parties in state legislatures.[80] A greater number of Democratic legislators are women and the gap between the parties continues to widen. In 1981, there were about five hundred Democratic and about four hundred Republican female legislators. But because Republicans at the time were a minority in most state legislatures, women actually constituted a slightly larger proportion of Republican legisla-tors. Over the next generation, more women from both parties were elected to the legislatures, but the increase was much greater among Democrats than Republicans. Prior to the 2018 election, there were 1,144 female Democratic legislators and 705 female Republican legislators. Because there were signifi-cantly more Republican legislators (4,121) than Democratic legislators (3,123) nationwide, this meant that Republican women made up a much smaller per-centage (17 percent) of their party in the legislatures than women constitute of Democrats in the legislatures (36 percent). This disparity increased as a result of the 2018 election, when Democratic women ran and won in record numbers while Republican women actually lost ground.[81]

Studies reveal that women, as a group, are less likely to self-start as candi-dates—that is, they are less likely to decide on their own to run for office and are more likely have to be recruited.[82] The first female speaker of the Ohio House noted of women, "They're harder to recruit. They're harder to convince to run."[83] Evidence of this difference is well established; in candidate surveys conducted in 1998 and 2002, 36 percent of male candidates were self-starters, while only 16 percent of female candidates fell into this category. Another sur-vey found that this "gender gap" continues to exist (38 percent of men and 22 percent of women were self-starters).[84]

It may also be that women are drawn to open-seat races. It was thought that, for this reason, states with legislative term limits might facilitate a higher rate of candidacy among women. Only recently, however, is there any evidence that this might indeed be the case.[85] Women candidates are also much more likely than men to say they were contacted and encouraged to run by state party officials or state legislative leaders. For this reason, efforts by the political par-ties to recruit women appear to be essential.[86]

One observer of women and politics argues that while women are often more reticent to run, they will do so when sufficiently upset or angry about current events, saying that "While men are often motivated to run by a desire to hold public office, women generally need to be triggered by an urge to 'do something.' Something got them angry enough or frustrated enough that they decided they needed to be the person at the table making that decision."[87] It appears that 2018 was such a time.

How Campaigns Are Run

There is a wide array of campaign practices found at the state legislative level. As noted at the beginning of this chapter, legislative campaigns in a few states are as professional, sophisticated, and expensive as congressional campaigns. Such races rely on paid consultants using the latest polling, advertising, social media outreach, and fund-raising techniques. These races, usually found in dis-tricts with large populations and known as *wholesale* campaigns, rely heavily on mass communication techniques to reach potential voters.

In contrast, legislative campaigns in states with small-population districts still rely on face-to-face, door-to-door *retail* campaigns that are designed to win over potential voters one at a time. Such campaigns are limited operations, involving the candidate and a handful of volunteers. Generally speaking, retail campaigns are more likely in races for lower chambers because, in most states, those districts have half or fewer people in them than do Senate districts (the median population of lower house districts is about 45,000; the median for Senate districts is roughly 125,000).

The most common campaign techniques found in state legislative races are direct mail and literature drops, billboards and yard signs, and "doorbelling."[88] These races are doorstep-to-doorstep and mailbox-by-mailbox efforts. They can be physically demanding and time-consuming, but for candidates without a lot of money, they allow them to make contact with potential voters. Time is valuable, and candidates who maximize their time campaigning are maximizing the impact of that resource. This is especially the case for a challenger, who typically does not enjoy name recognition and lots of campaign funds.[89] Chloe Maxmin is a good example of a candidate running a retail campaign. As a twenty-six-year old in 2018, she was the Democratic candidate for the Maine House in a rural district that had elected a Republican in each of the previous four elections. In a district of 35,000 people where the largest town is Waldoboro, population five thousand, she knocked on almost ten thousand doors over nine months. Her efforts paid off and she won the election.[90] Knocking on doors and engaging people directly can be an effective campaign tactic, but it is also fraught with perils, as Politics under the Domes 2.1 details.

Even relatively low-budget campaigns today make use of direct-mail advertising. Compared with the cost of television advertising, it is a relatively inexpensive way to reach potential voters, even if a candidate has to hire a mail consultant. A survey in three southern states found that more than 80 percent of state legislative candidates used direct mail and almost 30 percent of those candidates sent out at least seven different mailings.[91] As mentioned earlier, many candidates now make social media an integral part of their election strategy. It is also an important part of the fund-raising arsenal for legislative campaigns, allowing candidates to harvest valuable contact information from supporters and potential voters.[92]

The next few years are likely to bring substantial changes to legislative campaigns in many states. Campaign consultants and state parties continue to promote digital advertising as the ability to micro-target potential voters becomes ever sharper. Candidates can create and distribute their own campaign messages via social media platforms such as Facebook, Instagram, and YouTube. Micro-targeting techniques allow candidates to buy "pop-up" or banner ads on internet sites, steered to specific potential voters, at a fraction of the cost of advertising on more traditional media. During the 2018 legislative campaign, many candidates in Indiana employed such social media techniques.[93] In Senate District 29, the Democratic candidate used a Facebook ad to promote the roll-out of his first television ad. The Facebook ad cost less than $100 and reaped over five thousand impressions in three days. His Republican opponent started a Facebook ad almost two months before the election and garnered between ten thousand and fifty thousand impressions in a week. The ad cost him less than

$1,000. Such low-cost efforts are attractive in state legislative campaigns, where budgets are limited. As an Indianapolis political strategist argued, "You just get bigger bang for your buck through digital advertising. It is equally as powerful and more accessible than traditional advertising."[94]

Even traditional media are adapting to this new world; methods now exist to turn a traditional broadcast medium like television into an instrument for micro-targeting, as individual political data is merged with set-top box viewing information. Potentially, this will reduce the inefficiencies of delivering the political message outside the targeted constituency, which in turn may reduce the overall cost of television advertising for state legislative candidates.[95] But there are important issues involving protection of individual citizen data, message manipulations, and the potential lack of transparency in advertisements. These are issues that some state legislatures—Maryland's is a notable example—are addressing, as they seek to redefine the campaign playing field in a rapidly changing technological environment.[96]

In some states, legislative candidates do make use of television ads to reach voters. But for most candidates television is simply too costly and inefficient.[97] Take, for example, a candidate running for the Missouri House from a district in the Kansas City area. The television market for that area covers some two million people. Because the market is so large, buying commercial time is expensive. More important, because each House district in Missouri contains fewer than forty thousand people, almost all of the potential viewers in the media market will not reside in the candidate's district—indeed, a good portion of them will live across the border in Kansas. Thus, spending money on television ads would be remarkably wasteful.[98] Such inefficiencies potentially exist anywhere there is a large media market and small-population districts, such as lower house races in much of Connecticut, Georgia, Maryland, Minnesota, Tennessee, and Virginia.

POLITICS UNDER THE DOMES

The Art and Science of Doorbelling

Retail politics rule in most state legislative elections. Candidates typically find mass media to be too expensive and too inefficient to meet their campaigning needs. Instead, they literally introduce themselves to the electorate by knocking on doors.

Doorbelling is typically pursued by candidates in districts with smaller constituencies, where they have a reasonable chance to meet and greet a large percentage of potential voters. For example, in Maine, a state with small districts, "door-to-door campaigning is common, and most party organizers insist, essential. . . . They place a premium on face-to-face meetings." Ringing doorbells and talking with people can be an economical and effective way to campaign. But even in large districts, doorbelling can prove beneficial. A Texas Senate candidate commented, "I'm competing against TV, radio, and the demands of work life. The best way to get through to (voters) is by knocking on their doors." Validation for that proposition was provided by one of the Texans who answered his knock. The potential voter exclaimed, "There's nothing like the person-to-person contact. Coming out in [cold and rainy] weather likes this shows me he really cares." Indeed, such personal interactions promise long-term payoffs for a candidate. Several years after the fact, one Seattle-area voter happily recalled the time when his senator knocked on his door and "came in and we watched, like, half of a Mariners game together."

There are, however, potential pitfalls to doorbelling. One problem every candidate faces when knocking on doors is that nobody might answer. When this happened to a California Assembly candidate in 2018, she stuck a sticky note on the door with her phone number handwritten on it. The candidate reported that a few hundred people had called, remarking that "If you give your number out, you gotta return their calls." Her personal touch paid off, and she won her race.

Retail politics can have other drawbacks. One that many candidates admit is a simple fear of knocking on a stranger's door. A Vermont representative confessed that during her first run for the legislature, she was so scared of annoying people that she had to practice her spiel on a friend before screwing up the courage to take to the streets. Some downsides are physical, such as the plight of a California candidate who "knocked on 11,000 doors, met 7,000 voters and walked so many miles that he must now wear a knee brace," or an Indiana candidate who, in boasting about the large number of doors he had knocked on, declared, "I've got the blisters and the worn-out shoes to prove it." Dogs can pose a threat. A West Virginia candidate complained that her

reward for doorbelling was that "I got bit by a dog Friday and I got bit by a dog Saturday," while a Michigan candidate who deliberately tried to avoid homes with dogs was surprised when "we didn't see a dog, but about the same time I did see the dog, it saw me. . . . It came running out and jumped, and that was the first bite." And, of course, unstructured meetings can backfire, as they did for a young Iowa candidate: "I was out knocking on doors during the election, and I asked a woman—I thought I knew her, and I knew she was fixing to have a baby, so I asked her when the baby was due. It turns out she had it four months ago." The candidate ruefully observed, "You should never say things like that, especially if you're trying to get people to vote for you." Perhaps it is no surprise that in this case doorbelling did not work; the candidate lost the election.

Women candidates sometimes face additional obstacles. One young mother worried that, "I might have to take [my son] campaigning with me, too. Because I may not be able to leave him alone with [my husband]. So, I figure, "Well, I'll just take him with me." Put him in the car and go knocking on doors. But then I can see the GOP saying, 'Oh, she's dragging her son around for votes.' Because they've done that to me already!" Another candidate was pregnant with twins while she campaigned. She recalled proudly that "I knocked on thousands of doors. . . . But I did it with swollen ankles and two lives inside of me."

Minorities can suffer still other tribulations. One African American woman who was seeking reelection to the Oregon House in 2018 had a citizen call the police while she was knocking on doors in her district. According to the deputy who responded, the complainant had said that the representative appeared "to be casing the neighborhood while on her phone."

Another African American woman that same year, in this instance a twelve-year incumbent county supervisor running for a seat in the Wisconsin Assembly, was stopped by police while knocking on doors after they had received a call from a suspicious resident who thought the candidate and her seventy-one-year-old mother appeared to be "waiting for drugs at the local drug house."

Although doorbelling risks many hazards, both politicians and voters benefit from it in ways that neither of them may fully appreciate. For instance, the idea for a bill to relocate a county seat came to an Iowa lawmaker while he was knocking on doors during his reelection campaign, because "dang near every house that I went to, they were complaining [about it]." More generally, as a political science professor who lost a race for the Minnesota House reflected, "As a doorknocking candidate, you are forced every day to meet people whose political views differ from your own. At every door you may have to answer a critic or rethink your views. And the same goes for the voters themselves."

Sources: T. A. Badger, "Texas Candidates Go Door-to-Door," *Yahoo! News*, March 3, 2002; "Black Lawmaker Gets Police Called on Her While Canvassing in Neighborhood She Represents," *Governing*, July 5, 2018, http://www.governing .com/topics/politics/Oregon-Woman-Calls-Police-on-Black-Lawmaker-Canvassing-in-Her-District. html; Gus Burns, "Saginaw County Republican Politician Ann Doyle Endures Dog Attack in Bid for 94th District House Seat," *Saginaw News*, May 18, 2012; Andrew Garber, "1 State Senator, 2 Months, 99 Bills," *Seattle Times*, March 3, 2007; Charleston *Gazette*, "Legislative Hopefuls Struggle to Get Attention," November 6, 2000; John Fritze, "Voter Rolls Are Rising as Turnout Declines," *Indianapolis Star*, October 9, 2000; Morgan C. Matthews and Kathryn J. Lively, "Making Volunteer-Based Democracy 'Work': Gendered Coping Strategies in a Citizen Legislature," *Socius* 3 (2017): first published online, April 21, 2017, issue published January 1, 2017, https://doi.org/10.1177/237802 3117705535; Kyle Munson, "Munson: Is It Time to End Split in Lee County Seats?" *Des Moines Register*, May 6, 2014; Kathleen Murphy, "Vermont House Speaker: 'I'm Not Slick,'" Stateline.org, April 25, 2005; Jessie Opoien, "Constituent Called 911, Suspecting Drug Deal, on Dane County Supervisor Shelia Stubbs While She Canvassed for Assembly Seat, *Capitol Times*, September 19, 2018; Francis X. Quinn, "Democrats Foresee Big House Win," *Kennebec Journal*, September 30, 2002; Mattie Quinn, "Pregnant with Twins on the Campaign Trail," *Governing*, November 6, 2018, http://www.governing.com/23-percent-podcast/gov-jennifer-carroll-foy.html; James H. Read, "Doorknocking Is Democracy," *St. Cloud Times*, September 17, 2008; Nicole Riehl, "Aide to U.S. Senator Juggles Politics and College," *Gazette*, January 29, 2005; Otis R. Taylor Jr., "Buffy Wick's Experience Running Others' Campaigns Pays Off with Her Assembly Win," *San Francisco Chronicle*, November 12, 2018; Nancy Vogel, "Candidate's Millions Go toward Entry-Level Job," *Los Angeles Times*, October 26, 2004.

If the stakes are sufficiently high and the race is tight, however, candidates and political parties have little choice but to spend money, even if in inefficient ways. As we noted at the beginning of this chapter, candidates for several legislative districts in Virginia in 2017 spent millions of dollars. Much of that money was used to buy television airtime in the Washington, D.C., area—one of the most expensive television markets in the country. In Florida in 2018, one state Senate race cost an astounding $12 million—an amount one might more likely associate with some congressional districts or U.S. Senate races. Florida Senate districts contain about 500,000 people, so costs are high because there are many people to contact. This particular district was in Miami, which meant purchasing television ads was expensive.[99] And the race was forecasted to be close. All of these factors help drive up the cost of state legislative elections.

In some instances, cable television can be a reasonable alternative. Cable audiences are more narrowly segmented (e.g., *Bass Fishing for Beginners*); and as a consequence, advertising rates are lower than for network television. Moreover, precisely because audiences are segmented, a legislative candidate can target specific types of people, similar to direct mail. Even with cable, however, it is usually the case that much of the audience lives outside the district or—even worse—lives in the district but does not vote. The advantage of direct mail is that candidates (or their mail specialists) can use lists of registered voters to communicate with the individuals who are likely to participate. Radio also enjoys the advantage of being inexpensive, with segmented listening audiences, but—similar to cable—there is no guarantee that listeners live in the candidate's district or will turn out to vote.

Consequently, in many state legislative districts traditional campaign techniques continue to reign. These include building name recognition through yard signs, billboards, newspaper ads, campaign brochures, and the face-to-face contact achieved through going door-to-door and attending local events. One candidate, a twenty-four-year-old running (successfully, as it turned out) in the Atlanta, Georgia, area, summed up his strategy in this way:

> This campaign was all about name recognition. . . . There are just too many races in this area to get any real ink. . . . Every candidate had some form of equity to run on—money, connections, experience. My equity was time. . . . Being twenty-four helped a lot. At nine p.m. I can still be running from house to house; these other guys just can't do this, not in a hot Georgia summer.[100]

This candidate also made heavy use of phone banks, saying, "[We] sent up a phone bank of volunteers . . . working to call people and talk about the campaign. . . . We must have made two thousand calls."[101] "Retail politics" remains the apt description for most state legislative contests.

Turnover, Party Competition, and Elections

One of the more dramatic changes that occurred in state legislatures over the past century is a decline in membership turnover. *Turnover* refers to the percentage of new members coming into a legislative chamber. A high turnover rate means there are many inexperienced lawmakers, increasing the likelihood that the legislature is not an independent force in the policymaking arena. A low turnover rate means there is almost no "new blood" infused into the institution. Both situations are unattractive from an organizational point of view. The preferred case is one in which there is enough turnover to ensure competition between parties and viewpoints and to facilitate new ideas being introduced, but not so much change in membership that the legislature has no "institutional memory" or ability to act as a coequal branch of government.

Historically, there has been a clear decline in the average turnover rate in state legislatures. In the 1930s, turnover averaged more than 50 percent in senates and almost 60 percent in lower houses. This represents high turnover; it means that on average, half of senators and three of every five House members had not served in the previous legislative session. But over the next five decades, there was a steady decrease in turnover. By the end of the 1980s, turnover averaged 22 percent in senates and 24 percent in lower houses. And remember, these are averages for all states; some experienced even lower turnover rates. For instance, the California Senate averaged 11 percent turnover and the Assembly averaged 16 percent—rates comparable to those found in Congress. Turnover in each chamber of the Arkansas, Delaware, Illinois, New York, and Pennsylvania legislatures averaged 15 percent or less for each electoral cycle in the 1980s.

The decline in turnover was brought about by several variables. First, and perhaps most importantly, many legislatures had become more professionalized in the 1960s and 1970s, which, as we will examine in greater depth in chapter 3, means they had longer legislative sessions, better member pay, and more staff and other resources. The job became more demanding, but it also became more attractive for many legislators, and the incentive to stay increased. Second, electoral competition declined in many states (or, to be more precise, in many districts in these states). More seats became "safe" for one or the other party, and fewer incumbents were defeated. One recent study found that the median reelection rate for incumbents in state legislatures has been over 90 percent since 1992, and in several electoral cycles, the median was over 95 percent.[102] These two variables—a greater incentive for incumbents to stay and a greater electoral advantage for incumbents when they sought reelection—largely explain the decline in turnover.

Term Limits and Turnover

As noted in chapter 1, in the 1990s a movement to limit the number of terms a lawmaker could serve swept across many states. Supporters of term limits attribute many positive consequences to them. Most of these consequences are reviewed in other chapters; here we focus on the effect of term limits on turnover. And there is no doubt that, as advertised, term limits have increased turnover.

Since 2000, turnover in term-limited legislatures has averaged about 14 percentage points higher than in states without term limits (36 percent compared to 22 percent; these figures are the same for upper and lower chambers), although the gap has been as high as 18 percent in some years. It is clearly a substantial difference and one that is directly tied to term limits.[103] Variables such as redistricting or an unusual "wave" election can further magnify the effects of term limits; term-limited legislatures in the 2010 wave election averaged 42 percent turnover!

Competitive versus Noncompetitive States

Prior to the November 2018 election, Republicans held many more state legislative seats across the country than did Democrats (Republican held 56 percent of the seats, Democrats 43 percent, and 1 percent were nonpartisan or held by a minor party). This advantage was largely the result of two wave elections when

Republicans picked up over seven hundred legislative seats from the Democrats in 2010 and over three hundred seats in 2014. Partisan swings of this magnitude are historically rare, but appear to be becoming more common. In 2018 Democrats returned the favor by picking up more than three hundred seats; after the election the overall distribution of Republicans and Democrats in state legislatures had narrowed to 52 percent to 48 percent in favor of the Republicans.

But the relative closeness of the overall distribution of seats between the parties masks sizeable differences in specific states. In some states, one party dominates most elections, which usually translates into a lopsided legislative majority for that party. These are typically referred to as *one-party states*. In others, the contest for control of the legislature is much closer, with each party having a reasonable chance for majority status. But even in these states, not all legislative districts are competitive. It may be, for example, that 40 percent of the seats are "safe Democratic," 40 percent are "safe Republican," and only the remaining 20 percent are truly competitive. But the competitive 20 percent of the seats determine which party will control the legislature. Consequently, both parties (and other interests) invest a lot of money in the campaigns for these "targeted" seats.

Recently, the number of legislatures controlled by each party has swung back and forth in rather dramatic fashion. Before the 2006 election, Republicans controlled twenty state legislatures, Democrats controlled nineteen, and ten were split (Republicans held a majority in one chamber, and Democrats held a majority in the other chamber).[104] But the 2006 and 2008 elections produced a swing in favor of Democrats. The 2010 Republican tsunami washed away the Democratic gains of the previous two electoral cycles, and Republicans have controlled more legislatures than have Democrats through the rest of the decade.

But for our purposes, the issue is not simply which party controls the legislative chamber; it is also about the degree of control. In some states, one party is firmly in control because it holds a large majority of seats; for example the Republicans hold more than 70 percent of all seats in the South Dakota, Tennessee, and Wyoming legislatures while the Democrats hold more than 70 percent of all seats in the Hawaii, Massachusetts, and Vermont legislatures.[105] But in other states, the difference between majority and minority status is razor thin. After the 2018 election, Republicans held a one-seat advantage in the Minnesota Senate. There were at least a dozen chambers in which a shift of just three seats from one party to the other would change party control of the chamber. These chambers are "marginal" in that either party has a chance to win control in any given election. Colorado is an example of a state where legislative control is usually marginal, and as a consequence campaigns are competitive (and potentially expensive) in most electoral cycles.

A related issue is that of *divided* versus *unified* government. When one party controls both chambers of the legislature and the governor's office, they are able to largely dictate policymaking in the state. But when the parties have split control, policymaking authority is divided and policy either is a product of compromise or becomes stalemated—*gridlock* is the term typically applied.

While gridlock has been a dominant feature of the national government for the past decade, most states are currently in a position of unified governance (now also referred to as "trifecta government"). By the summer of 2014, unified government existed in thirty-eight states, leaving only eleven states experiencing divided government. This was the highest number of states with unified government in over half a century. The number of states with unified government has remained high throughout this decade; in 2018 at least thirty-six states experienced unified government (twenty-two Republican and fourteen Democrat). The upshot is that many people now look to the states rather than the federal government for policy leadership because decision-making in the states is less apt to be gridlocked.[106]

The Effect of Region

The electoral fortunes of the two parties are not the same everywhere. Some states are traditionally—meaning over the last several decades—Democratic strongholds (e.g., Massachusetts), some are traditionally Republican havens (e.g., Kansas), and some change over time. In the past two generations, the biggest shift of partisan strength was in the southern states. For decades, the Democrats controlled southern state legislatures consistently and with overwhelming majorities. Indeed, one analyst reported that "many state manuals from this period did not bother to record the party of state legislators because the idea that legislators might not be Democrats simply did not occur to the authors in this era."[107] Democratic Party dominance was so great in some southern states that in some years, there were literally no Republicans in the legislature. In 1961, for example, there were no Republicans in the Alabama House or Senate, the Arkansas Senate, the Louisiana House or Senate, the Mississippi House or Senate, the South Carolina House or Senate, or the Texas Senate.[108]

Today, of course, the situation is quite different. In 2018, the Republican Party was the majority party in both chambers of every legislature in the South. And in many instances, these majorities were substantial—for instance, the GOP held at least two-thirds of the seats in both chambers in Alabama, Arkansas, and Tennessee. Indeed, competition is so limited that many districts in the South go uncontested by one major party or the other.[109]

The rise of the Republican Party in the South was such a dramatic event that it obscured the fact that other regions also experienced significant partisan shifts.[110] The Mountain West went from being largely Democratic to solidly Republican over this same time period.[111] The Pacific coast states and many of the northeastern states shifted in the opposite direction—from being Republican states to being Democratic states.[112]

In other words, the relative strength of the two major parties shifts over time in different regions of the country. By focusing on the national scene only, these state legislative shifts—like geologic plate tectonics—often go unnoticed. But these regional and temporal shifts have important implications. The most obvious is policy change. But a second one is that recruitment patterns shift as well. As a party gains in strength, it is better able to attract quality candidates to run because such candidates realize they have a chance of winning. And ultimately, these regional shifts begin to surface in the congressional parties.

Conclusion

In some ways, electoral trends in the state legislatures reflect congressional trends. When incumbents run, they usually win more than 90 percent of the time and usually by substantial vote margins. And overall, competition between the parties is vigorous; over the past two decades, neither party has held more than 57 percent of the state legislative seats nationwide.

But a closer look reveals that many differences exist at the state level. First, although there is relative parity between the parties nationwide, there are a number of states in which one party dominates elections. Second, term limits alter the electoral dynamic in fifteen states by putting a time limit on incumbency. Third, the recruitment of women and minorities varies greatly in different states and in different regions of the country. Finally, the nature of campaigning is highly variable. In some states where districts are large and electoral stakes are high, campaigns may look a lot like congressional campaigns. But in other states—indeed, in most states—legislative campaigns are still relatively inexpensive, involving voluntary organizations and retail politics.

One way in which state legislatures do not reflect congressional trends is in the area of policymaking. While gridlock is the congressional norm these days, many state legislatures have moved with great determination in the policymaking arena. This is largely due to the partisan realignments that have left more and more states with unified government.

Chapter 3

The Changing Job of State Legislator

Safiya Wazir campaigning door-to-door in New Hampshire. A former refugee from Afghanistan, Wazir won her race for a seat in the state House of Representatives in 2018. AP Photo/Holly Ramer.

In 2018, a Republican, Brian Boner of Douglas, represented Wyoming Senate District 2. A Democrat, Mike McGuire of Healdsburg, represented California Senate District 2. Although both Boner and McGuire were state senators and tasked with many of the same responsibilities, the conditions of their legislative service differed dramatically.

Senator Boner served in an organization in which members see themselves as citizen-legislators. The Wyoming legislature meets for only sixty days over a two-year period—typically forty days in odd-numbered years and twenty days in even-numbered years, with the latter meeting limited to budget matters. For his legislative service, Senator Boner received a per diem—a daily payment—of $150 for each day the legislature was in session, and $150 a day for two days each month the legislature was not in session. Assuming the legislature met for the full sixty days it was allowed to meet over two years combined with the monthly stipend, Boner and his colleagues got paid $15,000 biennially, or $7,500 a year. This modest sum was supplemented by an additional $109 a day per diem to cover living expenses during the session and for travel days for lawmakers living outside of the capital, Cheyenne. The low pay and limited time demands mean that no member of the Wyoming legislature considers himself or herself a full-time legislator, one who financially supports himself or herself solely through the legislative wage. Senator Boner, for example, listed his occupation as farmer/rancher.[1]

Little in the way of staff assistance or facilities was provided to Senator Boner. Wyoming lawmakers do not have offices in the capitol, only a desk on their chamber floor. They are not provided personal staff. Contact information provided to the public for most members is simply their cell phone number.

Senator McGuire's working conditions were remarkably different. Service in the California legislature is considered a full-time position, much like service in the U.S. Congress. Over a two-year period, the legislature is in session about 240 days. Senator McGuire and his colleagues were paid $107,242 a year (raised to $110,459 starting December 3, 2018).[2] In addition, California legislators were entitled to a $192 per diem for each day the legislature was in session.

Senator McGuire also enjoyed impressive staff assistance and facilities. He had a personal office in the capitol and five district offices: Crescent City, Eureka, San Rafael, Santa Rosa, and Ukiah. Across his various offices he had thirteen staff members working for him: a chief of staff, a legislative director, three legislative aides, a district coordinator, two executive assistants, three office assistants, a district representative, and an administrative assistant/scheduler. Staff members not only helped the senator with his legislative responsibilities but they also managed his media and constituent relations.[3]

As the comparison of conditions in the California and Wyoming legislatures suggests, legislative service differs across the states. In this chapter, we will investigate what the job of state legislator is like in different settings. The concept of "legislative professionalization" will be examined, allowing us to explore differences across the fifty state legislatures in member pay, the time demands of service, and staff and facilities. We will also look at who serves in the legislature, how long they serve, and what their service entails. We will conclude with an examination of the different legislative career opportunity structures found in the states.

Legislative Professionalization

"Legislative professionalization" is a concept that assesses the capacity of both legislators and legislatures to generate and digest information in the policymaking process. Professional legislatures, such as the U.S. Congress, are those with unlimited legislative sessions, superior staff resources, and salaries sufficient to allow the members to pursue service as their full-time occupation. Thus, more professional legislators and legislatures are better equipped to play an active role in policymaking than are their less well-equipped counterparts. A number of different measures of legislative professionalization have been devised over time, but they all revolve around member salary, time devoted to legislative activities, and staff support.[4]

The theoretical implications of professionalization for legislators and legislatures are listed in table 3.1. As we might expect, as legislative salaries increase, lawmakers have greater incentive to continue service in the legislature. But increasing pay has an additional, less appreciated, impact on legislators: it also allows them to focus their energies on their legislative responsibilities rather than having to juggle them with the demands of other occupations.

The implications of legislative time demands condition the impact of pay on member behavior. On the one hand, when limited demands are made by legislative service, as in Wyoming, legislators do not need much salary to compensate for their service. Indeed, when legislatures meet for only a month or so, members may not have to sacrifice much time (and income) from their regular jobs to serve. On the other hand, when a legislature meets year-round, as in California,

TABLE 3.1 Implications of Professionalization for Legislators and Legislatures

Professionalization Component	Implications for Legislators	Implications for Legislature
Salary and benefits	• Increase incentive to serve, leading to longer tenure • Increase ability to focus efforts on legislative activities	• Lead to members with longer tenures, creating a more experienced body • Attract better-qualified members
Time demands of service	• Reduce opportunities to pursue other employment and increased need for higher salary to compensate for lost income • Increase opportunity to master legislative skills	• Make more time for policy development • Make more time for policy deliberation
Staff and resources	• Increase ability to influence policymaking process • Increase job satisfaction • Enhance reelection Prospects	• Make legislature a more serious policymaking competitor with the executive

Source: Adapted from Peverill Squire, "Measuring Legislative Professionalism: The Squire Index Revisited," *State Politics & Policy Quarterly* 7 (2007): 213.

lawmakers must be paid enough to support themselves and their families to compensate them for forgoing income from outside occupations. Thus, at the extremes of time demands, the implications of its relationship with salary are straightforward. But in the midrange of time demands, where legislatures meet for several months each year, calculations get more complicated. In these states, the point at which financial incentives are sufficient to compensate for lost income is not clear.

Legislative time demands have a second implication for legislators. The more days that a legislature meets each year, the better lawmakers come to grasp the complexities of the legislative process. Thus, longer sessions give members a better chance to master arcane rules, procedures, and norms.

The level of staff resources in a legislature has several clear-cut implications for legislators. First, more staff leads to better-informed legislators, which allows members to exert greater influence in the policymaking process. Second, as lawmakers enjoy having greater impact on policymaking, their job satisfaction likely increases.[5] Finally, more staff improves member reelection prospects by enhancing their ability to provide constituent services.

The institutional implications of legislative professionalization are straightforward. First, higher salaries allow lawmakers to devote more time and energy to legislating without the distraction of a competing occupation and thus can lead to longer serving and therefore more informed and effective members.[6] Second, higher salaries are likely to attract better-qualified legislators in terms of academic credentials, occupational status, and the like. Third, meeting for more days each year gives lawmakers more time to develop legislative proposals and more time to deliberate on them, thereby improving the quality of public policy.[7] Fourth, increased staff resources make the legislature a more equal partner with the executive branch in policymaking.[8]

Thus, the components of legislative professionalization have slightly different implications for legislators than for the institutions in which they serve. It is also clear that the combination of these components constitute something that is not captured by each of them individually. Professional legislators are not just longer serving but also better equipped as policymakers for reasons beyond their longevity. And professional legislatures are stronger competitors in the policymaking process for more reasons than just their being composed of veteran members.

What Difference Does Professionalization Make?

Legislative professionalization influences legislator behavior and legislative output in important ways. As we would expect, membership turnover declines as professionalism levels increase and members engage in more campaign-related activities and enjoy greater electoral security.[9] Lawmakers in more professional legislatures are more likely to adopt and use Twitter, have more contact with their constituents, are more attentive to constituent concerns, and are more representative of voters' views than are their counterparts in less professional legislatures.[10] Member voting behavior is affected, with lawmakers in more professionalized legislatures asserting greater independence from their parties and missing fewer roll-call votes.[11] Professionalization alters collaboration patterns among legislators, particularly in term-limited states.[12] Legislative efficiency—the percentage of bills passed and the number of bills enacted per legislative day—goes up with professionalization level, as do the prospects for producing accepted conference committee reports.[13] Lawmakers invest their leaders with less power as professionalization increases.[14] Members in more professionalized legislatures spend more time on legislative activities and make greater use of information from outside groups in developing policy.[15] Bureaucrats are more effectively constrained and have less influence on legislative outcomes, and government programs are more likely to be terminated in more professionalized legislatures.[16] And, because they have more information at their disposal, more professionalized legislatures are better able to counter gubernatorial influence in the budget process, to better resist a governor's policy agenda, to assert their own agendas, and to better calculate the prospects for veto overrides.[17]

Perhaps the most visible impact of professionalization is on the policy decisions legislatures make. The inclination to reform government practices and to adopt more complex regulatory policies increases with professionalization.[18] More professional legislatures adopt more complex tax policies, and at the same time they are also better able to make the changes necessary to keep those policies competitive.[19] Higher levels of professionalization are associated with the adoption of more innovative approaches to new technologies, stronger environmental and renewable energy programs, and more progressive state immigration policies.[20] More legislative attention is devoted to intersectional issues impacting women and minorities as professionalization levels increase.[21] Increased professionalization produces greater investments in higher education, boosts the likelihood of the adoption of performance-based funding, and leads to better-funded state pension systems.[22] More generally, professionalized legislatures are better able to mediate policy disputes, reducing the motivation for interest groups to turn to citizen initiatives in the states that allow them.[23] And they are better able to learn from the policy successes of other states, to devise innovative policies of their own, and to experience smoother rates of policy change.[24] In turn, less professionalized legislatures are more likely to simply copy legislation produced by other bodies.[25] Thus, the increased analytical capacity produced by professionalization translates into different policy choices.

There are potential downsides to professionalization. Because of their greater policymaking capacity, more professionalized legislatures change policies more rapidly. This induces greater uncertainty in financial bond markets and causes states with more professionalized bodies to suffer lower credit ratings.[26] And as a result of their greater innovativeness, more professionalized legislatures are also more apt to have their legislation invalidated by the U.S. Supreme Court than are their less professionalized counterparts.[27]

Despite legislative professionalization's net advantages, a negative relationship between it and public ratings of legislatures has been documented.[28] Examining this relationship more closely, it appears that people who identify themselves as conservatives are generally more disenchanted with professional legislatures while liberals express greater contentment.[29]

Professionalization Levels in Current State Legislatures

The legislative professionalization movement began in earnest in the 1960s, largely because of the efforts of California Assembly speaker Jesse Unruh, who pushed the California legislature to professionalize, and the Citizens Conference on State Legislatures, which joined with Unruh to take the reform movement nationwide.[30] During the next decade, many legislatures improved member pay, extended the legislative session, and improved staff resources. But the drive to professionalize leveled off in the 1980s. Since then, a few legislatures have continued to professionalize, but most others only held their ground or even regressed a bit.[31] As shown in table 3.2, taking into account inflation, in the aggregate legislatures in 2018 paid their members several thousand dollars less than they did in 1979, while over that same time period the length of legislative sessions has increased by just a few days and the number of staff per lawmaker has edged up only marginally.

How do professionalization levels currently compare across the fifty state legislatures? The most widely used measure compares a state legislature with the U.S. Congress on the three dimensions of professionalization: member pay, legislative days in session, and staff resources.[32] A score of "1" indicates that a state legislature perfectly resembles Congress in terms of professionalization, and a score of "0" indicates a complete lack of resemblance. As the median (.203) and mean scores (.225) for the fifty state legislatures suggest, most are only faintly similar to Congress (see appendix, table A.3). There is, however, considerable variation in legislative professionalization across the states. A handful of

TABLE 3.2 Professionalization Components for State Legislatures, 1979 and 2018

Indicator	1979	2018	Change from 1979 to 2018
Mean Member Salary	$33,700[a]	$31,292	- $2,408
Median Member Salary	$27,850[a]	$24,108	- $3,742
Mean Days in Session	62.4	74.3[b]	+11.9
Median Days in Session	58.5	61.8[b]	+ 3.3
Mean Staff per Member	3.7	4.5[c]	+ 0.8
Median Staff per Member	2.7	3.3[c]	+ 0.6

[a]   1979 salary calculated in 2018 dollars
[b]   Data are for 2013–2014 sessions
[c]   Data are for 2015

Source: Calculated by authors from data in various editions of *Book of the States* and http://www.ncsl.org/research/about-state-legislatures/staff-change-chart-1979-1988-1996-2003-2009.aspx.

legislatures, most notably California, Massachusetts, and New York, might be considered professional along the lines of the U.S. Congress. In contrast, legislatures ranging from Montana at 0.116 to New Hampshire at 0.048, have almost nothing in common with Congress and are considered "citizen legislatures." Most state legislatures, however, share at least some characteristics with their more professionally oriented counterparts.

Examining the Components of Professionalization: Salary and Benefits

One reason professionalization levels vary across the states is the salaries they pay their legislators. Most states offer an annual salary, but seven states pay only a daily wage, Vermont pays a weekly wage, and New Mexico does not pay any wages at all. In 2018, the annual salary that state legislators got paid varied dramatically, from $107,242 (raised to $110,459 starting December 2018) a year in California to $100 in New Hampshire to, nothing in New Mexico (see appendix, table A.4). Note that in every legislature, except for Virginia, members of both houses earn the same sum. In Virginia, the difference between the two houses stems from a 1992 decision by the House of Delegates to reduce their salaries by 2 percent in sympathy for a 2 percent pay cut imposed on state employees. The Senate chose not to follow suit, and the salary between the two houses has differed ever since.[33]

Overall, state legislative salaries are not impressive, with a median of only $24,108. Lawmakers are paid more than the state's median household income in only six states. Indeed, in many states, the legislative salary is well below the average household income. Wages paid to legislators in a majority of states have actually lost ground to inflation over the past four decades.[34] Thus, service in most legislatures is not financially enticing. This is not true in other federal systems. American legislative salaries pale in comparison to those paid to state and provincial lawmakers in Australia, Canada, and Germany.[35] City council members in many of the largest cities in this country are also paid much higher salaries than are their state legislators.[36] As shown in table 3.3, in 2018 Los Angeles City Council members were paid a salary of $191,000, almost double what members of the California legislature—the country's best-paid state legislators—made. Perhaps it is no surprise, then, that almost half of the city council's members were former state lawmakers, including one who had served as Assembly speaker. Similarly, higher salaries have enticed Minnesota lawmakers to leave the legislature to run for county supervisor posts.[37] For much the same reason, an Arizona lawmaker has proposed tying state legislative pay to the salaries given county supervisors in his state's largest counties, saying "I don't want to disparage our county supervisors, but I think state legislators have a greater responsibility, and wouldn't it be nice if we had the same level of pay?"[38]

It is important to point out that in many states the official legislative salary can be somewhat misleading. Most states offer lawmakers additional payments to cover expenses, usually called a "per diem." Some of these expenses require the submission of vouchers documenting the incurred costs. North Dakota

TABLE 3.3 **Salary Comparison between the Best-Paid State Legislators and City Council Members in Their State's Largest City**

State	2018 State Legislator Salary	State's Largest City	2018 City Councilor Salary in Largest City
California	$107,241	Los Angeles	$191,000
Pennsylvania	$87,180	Philadelphia	$129,632
New York	$79,500	New York City	$148,500
Michigan	$71,685	Detroit	$80,730
Illinois	$67,836	Chicago	$117,833

Sources: City council salaries are from https://www.detroitnews.com/story/news/local/detroit-city/2018/01/16/detroit-leaders-accept-pay-hike/109512180/; http://www.latimes.com/local/lanow/la-me-school-board-raises-20170710-story.html; https://nypost.com/2018/03/22/city-council-is-pushing-through-a-whopping-increase-in-its-operating-budget/; https://opengovus.com/chicago-employee; http://www.philly.com/philly/news/politics/20160809_Despite_six-figure_salary__city_council_is_still_a_part-time_job_for_some.html.

legislators, for example, are given $1,682 a month to cover lodging in Bismarck. But they have to submit receipts documenting their expenses; thus, as one representative noted, "In no case can you put money in your pocket."[39] Most state legislative expense payments, however, are provided without the submission of any documentation. Indeed, California legislators can collect a per diem even when they are absent.[40] Still, some of the expenses per diems are intended to cover are real, even if legislators do not have to produce receipts to demonstrate them. As one Minnesota lawmaker observed, "There's a big difference between living expenses and salary."[41] But to the extent that the money does not cover incurred expenses, it can add to a legislator's income. Such lenient rules led one former Arizona lawmaker to confess, "In all the years I was there, I didn't have expenses but I got thousands of dollars. . . . This is loot."[42]

Taking all of this into account, it is not simple to calculate the actual amount of money lawmakers make. One estimate of state legislative salaries with unvouchered expenses included is presented in the appendix in table A.4. These estimates are conservative because they are calculated only for the regular legislative session. In many states, legislators are also entitled to collect per diems for other days when they are performing legislative business, such as serving on an interim committee, which would give them the opportunity to claim more expense money. Moreover, per diems paid to state lawmakers receive favorable income tax treatment, meaning members get to keep almost all of it.[43] In New York it is even legal for members to use their per diems to help purchase a house in Albany for their use during the legislative session. When the member sells the house, he or she gets to keep any capital gains they may have made. As one observer notes, "It effectively allows them to pocket the per diem."[44]

Benefits are often afforded legislators as well. Health and dental insurance are made available to most lawmakers, with the state often covering part or all of the cost.[45] Pension plans are offered to legislators in all but ten states and some of those plans help compensate for low salaries. New Mexico, for example, does not give its lawmakers a salary, but they are eligible to collect a state pension at any age once they have served for at least ten years. Pensions for Texas legislators are tied not to their $7,200 annual salaries, but to the much higher salaries paid to state judges.[46] After eight years in the legislature a member can begin drawing a pension at age sixty (or at age fifty after twelve years of service). A 2013 estimate of benefits found that three Texas legislators, all with forty or more years of service, were entitled to annual pensions of more than $120,000.[47] An analysis of the pension plan available to Kansas legislators revealed that, "All told, a salary shy of $15,000 makes a lawmaker eligible for a pension that any teacher, road worker, prison employee, or Kansas bureaucrat could qualify for only if their actual pay ran north of $90,000."[48] Lawmakers in states that pay more generously also benefit from lavish pension plans. In Illinois, "The average retired lawmaker who had 20 years or more of service receives an annual pension payout of nearly $96,000, and that lawmaker's estimated total payout over the course of retirement will total more than $2.1 million. However, those retirees on average each contributed just $127,000 toward their pensions, meaning they will earn back what they directly contributed after less than two years in retirement."[49]

Overall, estimates in Maine reveal that although state legislators were paid only $12,215 annually during the 2017–2018 biennium, with their various benefits counted it costs the state $28,988 a year for each of them.[50] At the higher end, Illinois lawmakers earn a base salary of $67,836, but it costs the state over $101,000 each year to have them on the payroll.[51] Given the array of benefits offered, it may be understandable why the *Des Moines Register* titled an article examining them, "Being a Lawmaker: It's the Best Part-Time Job in Iowa."[52] Stories on better-paid legislatures hit much the same note. One detailing the generous benefits granted Pennsylvania lawmakers began, "How would you like Cadillac health care benefits for you and your spouse in retirement for as little as $75 a month? Become a state legislator."[53]

Lawmakers may also enjoy perks beyond per diems and pensions, although many of the flashier ones were taken away when state budgets ran into trouble during the Great Recession. Legislators in California, for example, used to be able to select a vehicle to use while in office; the state purchased it and leased it to the lawmaker. Now lawmakers are only allowed to get reimbursed for mileage for their own vehicles, a change that saved the state money.[54] Other benefits some legislators enjoy are of lesser monetary value but are still prized. Missouri reimburses state lawmakers 100 percent of the cost of any college course they take if they earn an "A" grade, 75 percent if they earn a "B," or 50 percent for a "C" or passing grade.[55] Every Alabama legislator used to be given two tickets and a parking pass to the annual Iron Bowl football game between Auburn University and the University of Alabama. A reform bill passed in late 2010—just after the game that year—prohibited that practice. But lawmakers still get special access to face-value tickets unavailable to the general public.[56] Texas legislators can purchase upscale furniture made by inmates working for the Texas Correctional Industries for well below what comparable products would sell to the general public.[57] Finally, a few perks are more a matter of convenience than dollars. For instance, because parking spaces are limited, Virginia legislators are allowed to park illegally in Richmond during the legislative session.[58] An unlisted California Department of Motor Vehicles office located in the state legislative office building allows lawmakers to avoid the usual long lines to register their cars and renew their licenses. (The office also handles constituent problems legislators bring to them.)[59] And until one Arizona lawmaker got caught driving 97 miles per hour in a 55 miles-per-hour zone—and bragged to the officer who pulled him over that he occasionally drove as fast 140 miles per hour—he and his colleagues were exempt from being given speeding tickets. In response to the uproar that ensued after the body camera video from the traffic stop was made public, the state's governor issued an executive order authorizing police to ticket state legislators who speed.[60]

Still, even with per diems and other benefits included, legislative pay in most states is less than what the public probably thinks. The median salary is only $32,611, and the total pay in fourteen states is less than $20,000 a year. How low is the wage in some states? A Montana lawmaker recently protested that "It is beyond ironic that we make less than a teenager working in a McDonalds in Helena."[61] When state health insurance costs rose dramatically in the middle of the last decade, some Nebraska senators saw their entire paycheck consumed by the added expense. One legislator even ended up paying the state $40 above his salary to cover his health insurance payment. He sheepishly admitted, "When I took the job I knew how much it paid. But I did have to do a little explaining to my wife."[62] Given the time lawmakers devote to their job, the pay some get is miniscule. According to a North Carolina representative, "Everybody I know that's down here is being supported from either having been very successful in business, having an income that's not affected by their being here, or their spouse is working and helping them pay bills."[63] A Georgia representative made the same point to a reporter, saying "There are three kinds of people in the General Assembly: the independently wealthy, the retired and the broke."[64]

How are state legislative salaries determined? Constitutions set legislative salaries in five states: Alabama, New Hampshire, New Mexico, Rhode Island, and Texas. A 1947 constitutional amendment set Alabama's legislative pay at $10 per day.[65] In 2012 voters replaced it with another amendment tying salaries to the state's median household income.[66] The now absurdly low salary of $100 a year in New Hampshire was set by an 1889 amendment to the state constitution and has been left untouched ever since.[67] New Mexico's constitution allows members no compensation beyond a per diem and mileage.[68] Texas established its salary in 1975 when voters approved a constitutional amendment increasing legislative salaries to $7,200.[69] Voters in Rhode Island amended their constitution in the mid-1990s to set member pay at $10,000 annually but provided for an automatic yearly cost-of-living adjustment tied to federal government inflation figures.[70]

POLITICS UNDER THE DOMES

The Battle to Raise Legislative Pay in South Dakota

In 2018, South Dakota lawmakers were paid $6,000 for their service, a sum that had not changed since 1999. That made them among the lowest paid state legislators in the country. Still, the prospects for improving their situation were not particularly good, in part because the South Dakota state constitution (Article 21, section 2) requires a two-thirds vote in each house to "fix the salary of any or all constitutional officers including members of the Legislature." Getting that level of support for a legislative pay increase is a politically daunting task.

The House Majority Whip, Leslie Heinemann, a Republican from Flandreau who lists his occupation as Dentist/Farmer/Small Business Owner, accepted the challenge and introduced a measure to change the law to set legislative salaries at 20 percent of the state's median household income. He fretted, however, that "There isn't enough of us in the Legislature that have a backbone to be able to vote for an increase, and I don't see that changing."

Other legislative leaders backed a pay raise, but suggested that it be done through a constitutional amendment. The Speaker of the House told his members that by going the amendment route "You're not setting your pay if you choose to vote for this. You're asking the people to set your pay." Other lawmakers, however, were skeptical about any amendment's prospects. One worried that "This is going to become a referendum on politics in general. . . . It's going to get beaten badly at the ballot, and that will set the cause back to raise salaries immensely because no legislator in the next ten years after this fails is going to want to touch that thing because the people will have spoken." The House passed a resolution to send such a constitutional amendment to the voters, but the measure died in the Senate. A Senate bill for the creation of a compensation commission to set salaries also failed to gain traction.

Those decisions left South Dakota lawmakers debating whether to pass the pay-increase mechanism as introduced by Representative Heinemann. They knew that for it to pass they would have to get a two-thirds vote in each house. The arguments they made for and against the measure echoed those made by their counterparts across the country. Supporting the pay raise, a senator challenged his colleagues to "Look around the room. We're retired or self-employed. The average person cannot give up their time to come out here and serve." Another senator who had once proposed to cut legislative salaries in half, confessed that he had changed his mind on the issue, saying "I've done a little grandstanding in the past, I will admit." Referring to the proposed measure, he said "This is an ask that is honest. This is an ask that is still appropriate." On the House side, one representative argued "The question is how big of a financial sacrifice are we expected to make? . . . The salary has not been adjusted for inflation or cost of living in 20 years." In response, one of his colleagues observed, "Here we are complaining that we need more money to come into this beautiful building and do our civic duty . . . If the salary isn't good enough for you, then don't run."

In the end, the Senate passed the measure on a 28 to 6 vote and the House followed suit by 52 to 15; both tallies making it over the two-thirds hurdle. That means that, depending on the state's median household income, in 2019 their salary would increase to somewhere between $10,200 and $10,500 a year. While it represents a large percentage increase, it still left the legislature as one of the lowest paid in the nation.

Sources: Brookings Register, "Voters Could Decide on Raise," January 26, 2018; Dana Ferguson, "South Dakota Lawmakers One Step Closer to Raising Their Salaries," *Argus Leader,* March 5, 2018; Bob Mercer, "SD Senate Votes for $4,500 Pay Raise," *Rapid City Journal,* March 6, 2018; South Dakota Legislature, Legislative Research Council, "House Bill 1311," https://sdlegislature.gov/Legislative_Session/Bills/Bill.aspx?Bill=1311&Session=2018; "South Dakota Legislator Salaries," sdlegislature.gov/docs/interim/2017/documents/DEXE11132017-N.pdf.

Compensation commissions currently exist in nineteen states.[71] Lawmakers are comfortable delegating power over their salaries to them because, as a Minnesota politician noted, "To make it less of a political football is a good idea."[72] Only in California, Oklahoma, and Washington, however, do commissions set legislative salaries without requiring the legislature to render some judgment on the decision.[73] Thus, lawmakers in those three states can get raises while still being able to publicly protest them.[74] In other commission states, the legislature plays a part in setting their pay. The particular role, however, varies in subtle but significant ways. In West Virginia, the state legislature must take positive action to put the commission's pay proposal into effect. The legislature may reduce the proposed salary but not increase it. Thus, legislators have to vote in favor of any pay raise, putting them in the much same political hot seat they would have occupied in the absence of a compensation commission. In contrast, in Michigan and Utah, the compensation commission's proposal goes into effect unless the legislature votes it down. Consequently, by taking no action—and not requiring lawmakers to go on record in support—pay raises in those state can be achieved without much political pain. Missouri changed its commission procedures to make it easier for raises to be implemented, discarding a process whereby legislators had to both approve a commission-recommended pay raise and appropriate the money for it—putting them on record in favor of a raise twice—in favor of one in which the commission's recommendation automatically goes into effect unless it is rejected by a two-thirds majority in each house. But even when the rules are structured in a favorable way, it can still be difficult for lawmakers to push through a pay raise. In 2017, Missouri legislators voted down a proposal to increase their salaries after the governor berated them for contemplating it.[75]

Only in Arizona do compensation commission recommendations get put before the voters. This places a significant obstacle between lawmakers and any pay raise. In 2006, the commission's recommendation to increase legislative salaries to $36,000 from $24,000 was defeated at the polls. Two years later, the state's voters overwhelmingly rejected a more modest proposal to raise salaries to $30,000. And in 2014 voters again turned down a proposal to increase salaries, this time to $35,000. As a consequence, Arizona's lawmakers have not enjoyed a pay increase for two decades.

The process by which pay raises are achieved matters, because proposed legislative salary increases are almost always controversial. In states where members have control over setting their own salaries, their sense of political self-preservation inevitably conflicts with their financial self-interests. Publicly, lawmakers offer two main justifications for legislative pay raises. The first is that they put in a lot of time and effort and deserve higher salaries:

- The Georgia Speaker of the House, a Republican: "These are really full-time jobs. . . . When I walk into an Ingles supermarket in Blue Ridge in July and a guy comes up and wants to ask me a question about an issue or wants my help on something very legitimate, I can't tell him, 'We're out of session, I am off the clock.' It's a year-round job, and it's a very demanding job. A lot of good people are having to leave."[76]
- The Kentucky Speaker of the House, a Democrat: "People should be paid for their work. And I see a lot of people who do a helluva lot less work in Frankfort than every legislator I know and make three times the salary."[77]
- The Oklahoma Speaker of the House, a Republican: "The session may last four months, but a legislator's work goes well beyond session. Last week, for instance, legislators began the process of conducting interim studies in preparation for next session. Legislators are also busy in their districts developing policies, meeting with constituents and learning about local needs."[78]

The second justification offered by legislators is that higher salaries are needed to allow a broader array of people to serve:

- The New York Speaker of the Assembly, a Democrat: "[A] depressed salary will eventually discourage qualified people from pursuing office. This is particularly dangerous for an elected legislature that must represent all segments of the State's population. Low legislative salaries compared to . . . the private sector tend to discourage member of the middle and working classes, particularly people with families, from seeking public office. The people who can afford to pursue these positions will disproportionately become the retired, [and] the independently wealthy . . ."[79]
- A Louisiana representative, a Republican: "I have colleagues in the Legislature who are leaving simply because they can no longer afford to serve. Eventually, our Legislature will consist of only the very wealthy or retired people."[80]
- A North Carolina senator, a Democrat: "We want to make sure we get a great diversity of people who serve as legislators. . . . Increasingly, the only people able to serve are those that are retired, those that are wealthy or those who are self-employed."[81]

Lawmakers fear they will pay a price at the polls if they support a salary increase. Asked about the salary his state's legislators receive, one Oklahoman expressed disgust, "I think they're overpaid. . . . Makes me want to go into the legislature, so I can have a cushy job and easy money." More charitably, another added, "It's quite a bit of pay for what they do, really."[82] Given such attitudes, lawmakers typically temper their financial expectations. Almost two decades ago, for example, a proposal to increase their meager pay came before the Kansas House. Early in the vote, the chamber's electronic display showed the measure almost passing, fifty-seven votes in favor to sixty-three votes opposed. But after it became clear that the pay increase would not garner the necessary majority to pass, a number of lawmakers changed their votes from "yes" to "no," and the final tally showed that the bill lost, forty-six to seventy-five. A representative who supported the pay proposal remarked, "I think they chickened out. If you had a secret ballot, that bill would have passed 125 to nothing. The fact is the members are running scared."[83]

An Indiana lawmaker pushing a pay raise in that legislature offered a similarly scathing assessment of his colleagues, lamenting, "Legislators, when it comes to their own pay, are gutless, just gutless. They're just afraid they won't get reelected."[84] And there is good reason for them to be nervous because pay raises can easily become an issue used against them in their next campaign.[85] Consequently, legislators have every incentive to concoct schemes to allow them to get pay raises without having to take political responsibility for them. In 2007, Indiana passed legislation tying legislative salaries to those paid to the state judges. Members of the Indiana legislature are now paid 18 percent of the salary paid to a state judge. This convoluted plan works to their advantage because increases in judicial salaries are linked to salary increases for state employees. So, when Indiana lawmakers make the politically easy vote to give state employees a raise, judicial salaries automatically increase, and when judicial salaries go up, legislators also get paid more.[86] Such an indirect pay-raise mechanism is not unique. In Florida, state law provides that legislators get the same percentage salary increase as general state employees.[87] A little-noticed constitutional amendment passed by Massachusetts voters in 1998 increases (or decreases, as it did in 2013) legislative pay every two years by the percentage change in the state's median household income.[88] The process in Rhode Island provides lawmakers an automatic cost-of-living boost. Since 1995, legislative salaries in Pennsylvania have been linked to the Consumer Price Index for the Mid-Atlantic region, a figure that is usually a bit higher than its national counterpart.[89] Alabama legislative salaries are tied to the state's median household income, and, as examined in Politics under the Domes 3.1, in 2018 South Dakota lawmakers set their salaries at 20 percent of their state's median household income. Removing pay decisions from legislators' hands in some fashion usually works to their benefit; between 1992 and 2017, those in states where commissions set their pay received much higher average salary increases than did their colleagues in states where they control their own wages.[90]

The validity of that last observation is documented by a novel step taken in 2018 by New York state legislators. After having not gotten a pay increase in twenty years, they used the budget bill to create a special compensation commission charged with determining an appropriate raise for them. At the end of the year the commission proposed raising legislative salaries to $110,000 in 2019—which would place New York's lawmakers just slightly behind their California counterparts that year—$120,000 in 2020 and $130,000 in 2021. The special commission also proposed that these increases be coupled with a limit on how much outside income legislators could earn and the elimination of additional stipends given to committee chairs and most other legislative leaders.[91]

In the end, how much does pay matter to those contemplating legislative service? It is important because it influences who serves and how long they serve. The low wage in Kansas, for example, caused one representative to resign so he could take a more lucrative position. He explained, "It's a simple matter of two jobs I love, one that pays and one that doesn't. It hurts a lot of us financially. Some make a real sacrifice to serve. I have to do what is best for my family."[92] A veteran Washington representative who also works as a part-time nurse reflected that "If I had a couple of kids at home, and I was worried about how I was going to pay for their college, I don't think I would have stayed in the Legislature for 20 years."[93] Many legislators say that taking time away from their regular occupations is costly. An Oregon senator admitted, "I didn't realize what kind of hardship it was going to be on me financially" because the job "is 24/7 and we don't treat it that way salary-wise." He calculated that he was losing money by serving because he had to close his general contracting business.[94] A member of the Washington House gave up his business designing septic systems because "I was having customers calling while I was working on [legislative] stuff and couldn't do them both well. I had to make a choice."[95] A Vermont lawmaker arrived at the opposite decision, opting to leave the legislature because he could not balance its demands with running a media company: "I was reluctant to step away from it. . . . I didn't really want to. But I didn't really see how I could [continue to serve] while trying to have a viable small business on the side."[96]

Because of such pressures, a Florida representative expressed what may be a widely shared sentiment among his colleagues around the country: "I wouldn't advise the average person to think about [legislative service] because it can put you at real financial risk. . . . I've been blessed to have this opportunity. I wouldn't trade it for the world. But I'm not sure that I could do it again."[97]

Examining the Components of Professionalization: Time Demands

Similar to member pay, the time demands made by legislative service vary across the states. Unlike the U.S. Congress, which meets annually for as many days as it wishes, most state legislatures operate under two potential time limitations: how often they may meet and how long those meetings may last. Because the original state legislatures were viewed as vital checks on gubernatorial power and because it was thought that regular sessions enhanced representation, they were required to meet annually. But during the early decades of the nineteenth century, the public came to distrust state legislatures; consequently, annual sessions were replaced with biennial sessions because it was reasoned that meeting less often would give lawmakers less time to create mischief. By the beginning of the twentieth century, only six states still had annual sessions; the rest met biennially, except for Alabama, which met only once every four years.[98]

Over the course of the twentieth century, the trend was a return to annual sessions. By 1960, nineteen states had annual sessions. The number of legislatures meeting annually continued to escalate over the next four decades, in large part in response to the professionalization revolution of the 1960s and 1970s. In 2008, Arkansas voters decided to allow their legislature to meet every year; Oregon voters did likewise in 2010. Those decisions leave just four states with legislatures that only meet every other year—Montana, Nevada, North Dakota, and Texas.

It is important to add, however, that annual sessions are not always created equal. Among the legislatures that meet every year, seven—Arkansas, Connecticut, Louisiana, Maine, New Mexico, North Carolina, and Wyoming—have one year out of every two during which the session is limited, with varying degrees of strictness, to budget matters.[99] Such sessions can be brief. In Wyoming, the legislature usually meets for no more than twenty days during the budget sessions it holds in even-numbered years. This provides little time in which to consider state spending, which even in a small-population state like Wyoming is several billion dollars a year. In 2014, the legislature actually settled the budget in only nineteen days, leaving one lawmaker to muse, "I think we'd be much smarter going 21, 22 days."[100]

Although the trend toward annual meetings is widespread, it is not universal. Montana's 1972 constitution established annual sessions, but the state's voters passed a referendum two years later returning the legislature to biennial sessions. Voters reaffirmed that decision again in 1982 and 1988.[101] And in Texas—the only large state with a legislature that meets every other year—efforts to move to annual meetings have been rebuffed, with one senator commenting, "There's not a single Republican who would vote for that" because "I think one of the reasons that Texas does as well as it does is because the Legislature meets as infrequently as it does."[102]

Even as most states have moved to meeting annually, session lengths continue to be limited in a majority of legislatures. Currently, only eleven states do not place any limit on the length of the regular legislative session.[103] In twenty-eight states, constitutional provisions establish the limits. For instance, the Georgia Constitution restricts the legislature to meeting for no more than forty legislative days in one calendar year.[104] Session length limits in Alabama, Alaska, Indiana, Maine, and South Carolina are imposed by law. Legislative rules limit the number of days in session in Arizona, California, and Massachusetts. Finally, indirect limits on legislator compensation, such as cut-off dates for per diems or mileage reimbursements, are used in three states—Iowa, New Hampshire, and Tennessee. In Iowa, for example, legislators can no longer collect their per diem after 110 calendar days in session in odd-numbered years or 100 calendar days in even-numbered years. This gives them a financial incentive to limit their time in session.

Thus, the formal time demands made on legislators by legislative sessions vary by state. The Utah legislature, for instance, is considered part-time and meets for fewer days than most legislatures. The 2018 session started on January 22 and finished on March 9, covering forty-five calendar days, the constitutional limit. Floor sessions were actually held on thirty-three days. They also met in special session for one day in July.[105] In contrast, the Michigan legislature is considered a full-time body. The eighty-two days the Michigan Senate and eighty-three days the Michigan House were scheduled to meet in floor sessions in 2018 might not seem imposing. But those meetings were distributed from January to December, with only July being session free, meaning that members were in a position where the legislature commanded much of their time during the course of the year.[106]

Moreover, as a Michigan Senate staffer pointed out, "To claim session days are the extent of a senator's work is false and disingenuous. Senators and staff work many hours outside of session helping constituents, holding committees, meeting in their districts and more."[107] Lawmakers do spend more time on matters related to their legislative service than the number of days spent in session suggests. A survey of members in all fifty states revealed the median legislator sees his or her position as being two-thirds of a full-time job.[108] Not surprisingly, lawmakers in more professional legislatures reported spending more time on the job than did their colleagues in less professional bodies. But even in South Dakota—the legislature where members reported spending the least amount of time on legislative matters—legislators still estimated that their efforts constituted more than one-third of a full-time position. This is in large part because, beyond their responsibilities associated with the legislative session, lawmakers report spending considerable amounts of time providing constituency services as well engaging in campaign-related activities.[109] Thus, as one South Dakota representative commented, "It's more like a second job, and it's a first job when you consider you're trying to do the people's business. I sure don't feel like it's a half-time job. It's a mammoth job."[110] A Vermont representative concurred, noting about her service that "I've never been so busy in my whole life, even though it's a part-time job."[111]

Examining the Components of Professionalization: Staff and Facilities

State legislatures started with almost nothing in the way of staff or facilities. Even by the middle of the twentieth century, most lawmakers were provided little assistance.[112] The professionalization revolution of the 1960s and 1970s produced impressive increases in staffing in most, but not all, state legislatures.[113] Today, almost every state legislative chamber provides professional and clerical staff to standing committees. Roughly half of the states provide members with year-round personal staff, but fewer than ten states provide district staff and offices.[114] Overall, a few states, such as California, Florida, New York, and Texas, operate with staff and facilities comparable to those of the U.S. Congress. Many other states provide much less in the way of assistance or facilities. Indeed, in a few places lawmakers have no personal offices, leaving them with only their desk, much like elementary school students.

Personal staff and district offices make the biggest difference in how legislators fulfill the tasks assigned them. Personal staff expands the reach of lawmakers, allowing them to acquire and digest greater amounts of information. District offices let them maintain a physical presence in their districts, thereby making it easier for them to stay in contact with their constituents. In New Jersey, for example, "These offices have staffs of as many as four or five people who are responsible for legislation, constituent services, administrative support, community outreach, and the myriad of functions that respond to the needs of the residents in each district."[115] An Illinois lawmaker noted that his constituents often "don't know where to turn," and that his district staff "send them in the right direction."[116] Along the same lines, a Pennsylvania representative commented, "The district office . . . provides taxpayers and residents a one-stop shop for state government services."[117] District staff also allows members to keep tabs on what their voters are thinking. An Illinois representative observed that in his district office, "We get a lot of responses to what is in the newspaper. . . . Generally, they are calling to vent, but they also want to make sure what they are saying is heard."[118] Lawmakers in more professionalized legislatures are particularly attuned to the importance of providing assistance to their constituents. A New York Assembly member comments that "Serving constituents is an integral part of the job. I know that on some other levels of government phones ring and ring and nobody answer them . . . (but) that doesn't happen here. . . . Constituents are full-time and legislation is also full-time."[119] Personal staff and district offices generate electoral benefits for lawmakers.

Legislative staff also assist members in coping with the multitude of policy demands being made of them. A Louisiana lobbyist acknowledged that legislators need such help because "When you think about 2,000 bills that may be introduced and start talking about different [policy] areas . . . lawmakers [themselves] don't have the expertise to really do it all and switch that quickly."[120] Information is central to legislative decision-making, and the staff helps generate and make sense of it. Assistance can also help keep lawmakers from making mistakes. When the Missouri General Assembly passed a special corporate income tax cut in 2015, it was estimated that it would reduce state revenues by $15 million annually. But in the first year it actually reduced revenues by $155 million. The chair of the House Budget Committee admitted, "We had bad information when we passed that bill. I think if we'd have had the correct information, we wouldn't have passed it."[121] Sometimes legislative errors are more embarrassing than costly. In 2017, the staffing-limited New Hampshire General Court passed what was supposed to be a fetal homicide bill. But, as one lawmaker observed, "The bill as drafted allows for physician-assisted suicide and allows a pregnant woman to commit homicide without consequences." The legislature had to scramble to fix the errors.[122]

Who Serves?

The stereotypical state legislator is a middle-aged white male lawyer. In reality, this stereotype fits less well today than in the past. Lawmakers today are drawn from a wide range of the general population. Their ranks have become increasingly diverse, better mirroring the people they represent.

Age

The notion that the archetypal state legislator is middle-aged is largely accurate. In 2015, the average lower house member was fifty-five years of age while the average state senator was slightly older at fifty-seven years. Overall, the youngest legislatures were Florida and Michigan at an average of fifty-one years of age, while the oldest was New Hampshire at sixty-four years of age. Lawmakers in term-limited states were on average three years younger than their counterparts in states without term limits. Women lawmakers were on average two years older than their male colleagues as we would anticipate because many of them delayed running for office while their families were young.[123]

Few young people are elected to state legislatures. Less than 5 percent of state lawmakers are thirty years of age or younger. Only occasionally does a very young person get elected. In 2018, Kalan Heywood, a nineteen-year-old second-year student at Cardinal Stritch University in Milwaukee, won a seat in the Wisconsin Assembly.[124] But he was not the youngest state legislator elected in recent years. In 2014, Saira Blair made national news when she was sent to the West Virginia House of Delegates at the age of eighteen. Blair served for two terms while also attending West Virginia University. But her final year in office was tarnished by the sort of mistake social media makes possible: a Snapchat video showed her singing along to the racially charged lyrics of a Lil' Wayne song. The irony was that this behavior allowed a twenty-five-year-old running for her seat to say in regard to Blair's actions that "It shows a massive lack of maturity."[125]

Women

The first women were elected to a state legislature in 1894, when three won seats in the Colorado House. By the time the first woman was elected to Congress in 1916, women had already served in the Arizona, Colorado, Idaho, Oregon, Utah, Washington, and Wyoming legislatures.[126] The number of female lawmakers grew over the course of the twentieth century, reaching more than one thousand by the mid-1980s. In 2019, a record 2,088 women were state legislators, a figure representing 28.3 percent of all legislative seats.[127] Women held more than 40 percent of the seats in Colorado, Nevada, and Oregon. Although they are still far from holding legislative seats in proportion to their share of the population, those serving now hold many of the most powerful positions. In 2018, for example, women served as Speaker of the House in Colorado, Iowa, Maine, Oregon, Tennessee, and Vermont. And they hold committee chairs in rough proportion to their numbers in state legislatures.[128]

African Americans

The first African American state legislator was elected in Vermont before the Civil War. Reconstruction saw the election of many African American lawmakers in southern states, but no African Americans were elected there again for decades after it ended. Indeed, the number of African Americans serving in state legislatures grew at a glacial pace through the first half of the twentieth century. Since then, their numbers have increased more rapidly.[129] By 2018, 673 African Americans held state legislative seats, constituting 9.1 percent of all state legislators. They were, however, concentrated in a relatively small number of states. Thus, in seven mostly southern states (Alabama, Georgia, Louisiana, Maryland, Mississippi, North Carolina, and South Carolina), African Americans held more than 20 percent of seats, while three state legislatures (Montana, North Dakota, and South Dakota) had no black members.[130]

Hispanic Americans

As with African Americans, the number of Hispanic legislators has only become noticeable in recent decades. In 2018, just over 330 Hispanic Americans held state legislative seats. Again, they were concentrated in a relatively small number of states. Indeed, no Hispanic Americans served in eight state legislatures. The state with the largest percentage was not Arizona, California, or Texas—although they all have sizable contingents—but New Mexico. This is not surprising, because Hispanic Americans have long been integrated into New Mexico's political culture. Even as far back as 1912, when the state was admitted to the union, more than 40 percent of the lower house and 20 percent of the Senate was Hispanic American.[131] The prominence of Hispanic Americans in the California and Texas legislatures is of much more recent vintage. In each, almost no Hispanics were elected before the 1960s, and caucuses composed of Hispanic members were only first created in the 1970s.[132]

American Indians

As of 2018, the National Caucus of Native American State Legislators, an organization that "provides a forum for discussion among Native American legislators," reported eighty-one members from twenty-two states.[133] In recent decades, the largest number of American Indian state lawmakers has been in Oklahoma. Among them was T. W. Shannon, a member of the Chickasaw Nation, who in 2013 became the first American Indian to be elected Speaker of the House in the state's history. Maine is the only state that has seats reserved specifically for representatives from Indian tribes—one each in its lower house for the Passamaquoddy, the Penobscot, and the Houlton Band of the Maliseet. The status of these members is similar to that of territorial representatives in the U.S. House in that they have seating and speaking privileges and draw salaries like other members, but they cannot participate in floor votes. In recent years tensions between several of the tribes and the Maine state government have caused them to withdraw their representatives from the legislature.[134] South Dakota subdivides two of its multimember House districts into four single-member districts in an effort to increase the prospects for American Indians to win seats in its legislature. As a minority within the minority Democratic Party, American Indians serving as lawmakers in that state have expressed frustrations with getting their policy preferences enacted. But they argue their absence from the legislature would leave the members of their community without any voice in the policymaking process and so they continue to serve.[135]

Explaining the Number of Women and Minority Legislators

What accounts for the differences in the diversity of state legislative membership? In the past, legislative professionalization has demonstrated differing relationships with the percentage of women and African American state legislators. A quarter century ago, women were found to be less likely to serve as legislative professionalization scores increased, but African Americans were more likely to serve.[136] Today, the evidence on these relationships is mixed. Some studies still find a negative relationship between professionalization and the number of women serving in a state legislature; others report no relationship.[137] African Americans, however, continue to be more likely to get elected to professional legislatures.[138] Latino legislators, however, are more likely to be elected to less professional bodies.[139]

But there are other variables beyond professionalization that matter. Most important for minorities, their share of legislative seats increases with their share of state population.[140] Women are more likely to get elected to legislatures using multimember districts; minorities are less likely.[141] State political culture also matters, with more women getting elected in New England and in the Rocky Mountain states and fewer women gaining seats in southern states. Partisan differences also emerge with different variables explaining where Democratic and Republican women get elected to state legislative seats.[142] It also appears that minority women enjoy an electoral advantage relative to minority men, in part because they experience less hostility from white voters and also because they tend to have better educational credentials and more political experience.[143]

The Impact of Women, Minorities, and Intersectional Interests in the Legislative Process

Having more women and minorities elected impacts the legislative process. Regardless of their backgrounds or leadership positions in a legislature, women lawmakers evidence a special concern for representing women.[144] But partisanship influences the way women legislators pursue such representation. Republican and Democratic women often offer different policy solutions to problems.[145] On contraceptive coverage legislation, however, moderate Republican women have successfully acted as "partisan bridges" to their Democratic women colleagues.[146] Generally, women's issues are pursued more vigorously in chambers controlled by Democrats.[147] But the ability of women lawmakers to influence legislative outcomes is mixed, with impacts being felt on some issues associated with women but not on other issues.[148]

Over time, as their numbers have increased, African American lawmakers have moved into leadership positions, particularly in those chambers where the black caucus is an important part of a Democratic majority.[149] Consequently, African American legislators have gained greater influence in the policymaking process.[150] This matters, because it appears that African American lawmakers are inherently more motivated to pursue and protect the political interests of blacks than are other legislators.[151] Indeed, where black legislators constitute a larger percentage of the members of a legislature, they have enjoyed a greater ability to shift budget priorities to match their constituents' preferences.[152] But there is also evidence that on issues such as immigration and same-sex marriage, black lawmakers have adopted more progressive positions than their constituents hold.[153]

The legislative success of Hispanic lawmakers varies considerably across the state legislatures.[154] Similar to the situation with blacks, where Hispanics constitute a larger block of members, Hispanic lawmakers influence policy-making.[155] And, as African American legislators are sensitive to the concerns of black constituents, Hispanic lawmakers are more attentive to the interests of Hispanic constituents than are other legislators.[156] Thus, it appears that having a minority member serving as one's state legislator has substantive policy implications for minority voters.

But not every relationship we might anticipate operates in quite the same fashion. For example, the amount of American Indian legislation introduced and passed in a state is unrelated to the number of American Indian members in the legislature. Instead, it is driven by the size of the American Indian population in the state and the existence of legislative committees focused exclusively on American Indians.[157] And who fits in what group is not always clear. There is evidence that multiracial legislators occasionally face resistance in their efforts to join minority caucuses.[158]

It is important to note that the overlap of characteristics, such as being an African American woman or a Hispanic male—what are termed intersectional interests—has also been found to have profound impacts on the legislative process.[159] Lawmakers who are women of color, for example, exert greater influence on state welfare reform policies than do their colleagues who are white women or men of color.[160] Interviews of African American women legislators reveal that while they see themselves as representing women's issues broadly, they often emphasize a different set of specific policies than do other women lawmakers.[161] Indeed, African American women sponsor a distinctive selection of legislative bills.[162] But even among black women legislators there are generational differences in how they approach women's issues.[163] And while black women and men lawmakers often vote similarly, the content of their legislative agendas differs.[164] All of this confirms the value of acknowledging the existence of intersectional interests.

Finally, although women and minorities are now getting elected to state legislatures in increasing numbers, it is crucial to recognize that their experiences in office can still be unpleasant. A thirty-two-year old black woman serving her second term in the Ohio House reported that she had been stopped by security when entering the statehouse and told that because she did not "look like a legislator" that she had to submit to extra screening. Officials later claimed that she looked "too young" to be a legislator.[165] The only African American woman lawmaker in Vermont resigned in 2018 because of the "threats and online race-related harassment" she had received.[166] That same year a group of armed anti-immigration protestors outside the Arizona capitol confronted a state representative who is a Navajo and demanded to know if he was in the country legally.[167] And the only Latina Republican in the Wisconsin Assembly was humiliated when during a social gathering one of her party's leaders said he was buying drinks for everyone "except Jessie because she's Hispanic." He then proceeded to buy beverages for the others and not her, and later made unwanted sexual comments to two other female lawmakers.[168] Clearly, even as more of them serve in office, women and minority lawmakers continue to endure indignities that their white male colleagues do not suffer.

Diversity by Other Measures

In recent years, state legislatures have become increasingly diverse in ways beyond age, gender, race, and ethnicity. The number of openly lesbian, gay, bisexual, transgender, and queer (LGBTQ) state legislators, for example, has grown significantly over the last two decades. In the 2018 election, 119 openly LGBTQ lawmakers won seats, taking them in thirty-seven of the forty-six states that held elections, including the first to ever get elected in Indiana, Kansas, and Nebraska.[169] Members of this group now constitute just under 2 percent of all lawmakers nationally.[170] As might be anticipated, larger contingents of LGBTQ legislators are found in more liberal states, such as California, Maryland, Massachusetts, and Washington. But they have been elected to office in conservative states as well. Indeed, several served in the Utah legislature before any were elected in Florida.[171] And in 2018 five LGTBQ candidates won seats in the Texas House and the first openly gay man was elected to the Alabama House.[172] The first transgender state legislator in the country's history was elected in Virginia in 2017. Three more were victorious in 2018, one in Colorado and two in New Hampshire.[173]

Openly LGBTQ lawmakers now find greater acceptance among their colleagues and have served as speaker of the house in California, Colorado, Oregon, and Rhode Island.[174] As more LGBTQ people are elected to a legislature, more pro-LGBTQ-rights legislation gets introduced and adopted. But at the same time, their service appears to generate a backlash; more anti-LGBTQ-rights legislation also gets introduced and passed. On balance, however, electing more LGBTQ legislators produces more pro-LGBTQ-rights laws.[175] As one close observer notes, "It's one thing for a state legislator to propose an anti-trans bathroom bill in their state legislature when there is no trans person in the room. . . . It is much harder for legislators to put forward hateful legislation when they know they are affecting the lives of one of their colleagues."[176]

Another example of the increasing diversity of state legislatures is the number of foreign-born lawmakers. A count a decade ago revealed seventy-nine state legislators who hailed from thirty-six different foreign countries.[177] According to 2014 data, 21 percent of the 105 Asian Pacific Americans serving in state legislatures that year had been born outside the United States.[178] Foreign-born legislators currently serve in many states. Among those holding office in 2018 were Romy Cachola, a Hawaii representative born in the Philippines, Evandro Carvalho, a Massachusetts representative born in Cape Verde; Ed Chau, a California Assembly member born in Hong Kong; Anne Dauphinais, a Connecticut representative born in Bermuda, Hoon-Yung Hopgood, a Michigan senator born in South Korea; Jean Jeudy, a New Hampshire representative born in Haiti; Hy Kloc, an Idaho representative born in Germany; Sabi "Doc" Kumar, a Tennessee representative, born in India; Fue Lee, a Minnesota representative born in Thailand; Teresa Alonso León, an Oregon representative born in Mexico; Yuh-Line Niou, a New York Assembly member born in Taiwan; Rady Mom, a Massachusetts representative born in Cambodia; Llhon Omar, a Minnesota representative born in Somalia; Juan Pichardo, a Rhode Island senator born in the Dominican Republic; Victor Ramirez, a Maryland senator born in El Salvador; and Hubert Vo, a Texas representative born in Vietnam. Most foreign-born legislators arrived in the United States as children or young adults, became established in their communities, and then committed themselves to public service. Many have taken a special interest in working to help assimilate immigrant communities in their districts and states.[179] In 2018 a number of foreign refugees decided to run for the legislature in response to what they perceived to be a rise in anti-immigrant sentiment in parts of the country.[180] One from Afghanistan, Safiya Wazir, won a seat in the New Hampshire House.[181]

Education Levels

State lawmakers are, on average, better educated than the people they represent. According to analyses conducted in 2011 and 2015, roughly 75 percent of legislators have an undergraduate degree and 40 percent hold an advanced degree of some sort. Both percentages rank far ahead of the general population. There is, however, considerable, and perhaps predictable, variation across the states. The best-paid legislature, California, also had the highest percentage of members who are college graduates, at 90 percent. The state that pays its members only $100 a year—New Hampshire—had the lowest percentage, at 53 percent.[182]

Most legislators attended public colleges, and a majority attended one in the state where they now hold office. Some state universities enjoy large numbers of alumni in the statehouse. For instance, in recent sessions just under a third of lawmakers in Indiana and Louisiana attended Indiana University–Bloomington and Louisiana State University, respectively. But there is no guarantee that having alumni in the legislature produces budgetary bonanzas for state universities. In 2011, about a third of the South Carolina General Assembly had attended the University of South Carolina. But that relationship did nothing to protect the university from suffering substantial budget cuts.[183] Overall, however, it appears that legislatures with a higher percentage of members who attended state colleges support greater funding for public higher education, and this relationship has become even stronger since the end of the Great Recession.[184]

Occupations

In the nineteenth century, agriculture was the predominant occupation of state legislators. But by the early twentieth century, lawyers started outnumbering farmers.[185] Comparing occupational data across the last century reveals that the percentage of lawmakers who were lawyers actually declined during this period, although not dramatically.[186] In 1909, 20 percent of legislators were attorneys; by 2015, that figure had slipped to 14 percent. The percentage of farmers holding legislative office declined much more precipitously, to 5 percent in 2015 from 25 percent one hundred years earlier, roughly parallel with the decrease in farmers as a percentage of the nation's population. A Washington senator recently observed that when he first started in the legislature in 1992, "There were people who had tree fruits, blueberry farms, hops, grapes. . . . Now I think I can say I'm the only one in the Senate whose primary living is farming."[187]

Lawmakers today are drawn from a variety of occupations. A plurality actually comes not from law or agriculture but from business.[188] Some own small businesses while others hold management positions in larger companies. Real estate agents, insurance agents, and funeral directors have traditionally served in state legislatures as a way of both performing public service and generating clients, and members of those occupations are still found in most legislatures.[189] But, many lawmakers in 2018 were employed in careers not usually associated with politics: an aquatic biologist in the Idaho House, a CrossFit trainer in the Nevada Assembly, a cybersecurity specialist in the Minnesota House, an airline pilot in the Georgia House, an environmental toxicologist in the Delaware House, a freelance court reporter in the Massachusetts House, a hospice chaplain in the Arkansas House, a landscaper in the Connecticut House, a locomotive engineer in the Arizona House, a longshoreman in the Pennsylvania House, a motivational speaker in the Tennessee House, a pipeline safety inspector in the New Mexico House, a theater education director in the Maine House, a marriage counselor in the Colorado House, a tree nurseryman in the South Dakota House, a UPS delivery driver in the West Virginia House, and a welder in the Kansas House. Under occupation one Alaska senator listed doctor, pilot, reindeer herder, and businessman, while a Massachusetts representative recorded small business owner, yoga instructor, and film editor. Lawmakers' earlier work experiences are also varied. Before the minority leader in the Connecticut House became a lawyer, she had been a model, a competitive body-builder, and a WWE "ring girl," while the House Speaker had been a union official and a combat medic in the Army Reserve, and he continued to be a high school football coach while in office. Such diversity infuses the lawmaking process with a breadth of experiences and expertise.

The number of lawmakers claiming full-time legislator as their occupation has increased over time. Only three legislative chambers had any members who claimed full-time status in 1909. As shown in table 3.4, today some have at least a few full-time legislators; several have significant proportions. Members saying they are full-time lawmakers are much more likely to be found in more professionalized legislatures than in less professionalized bodies. In the Pennsylvania House, for example, 59 percent of members identify their occupation

TABLE 3.4 Legislative Salary and Self-Identified Occupations of Members in Selected Lower Houses, 2018

		Percent of Members Who Self-Identify Occupation as:				
State	Annual Base Salary	Full-Time Legislator	Attorney	Insurance, Real Estate, Funeral Director	Farming, Ranching, Fishing	Retired
Pennsylvania	$87,180	59	10	1	0	>1
Massachusetts	$62,548	31	15	3	0	1
Wisconsin	$50,950	30	6	6	5	0
New Jersey	$49,000	18	20	3	0	0
Delaware	$45,291	22	5	5	2	7
Minnesota	$45,000	9	7	3	4	10
Arkansas	$40,188	0	11	5	9	14
Colorado	$30,000	32	14	2	2	5
Connecticut	$28,000	10	14	7	0	7
Iowa	$25,000	1	8	3	14	21
Mississippi	$23,500	1	28	11	5	5
Tennessee	$22,667	0	9	13	3	18
West Virginia	$20,000	0	17	5	1	21
Virginia	$17,820[a]	0	25	4	3	12
Idaho	$17,358	0	9	4	16	20
Georgia	$17,342	0	13	7	3	11
Maine	$12,215	>1	3	4	3	20
Nebraska	$12,000	0	8	10	16	10
Nevada	$9,043	0	19	2	0	10
Utah	$9,009	0	16	4	5	8
Kansas	$7,093	0	8	3	11	18
North Dakota	$7,080	0	4	5	18	16
South Dakota	$6,000	0	7	9	23	13
Montana	$4,079	0	5	4	18	18
New Mexico	$0	0	19	3	3	16

[a] Salary is the mean of the Senate and House of Delegates salaries.
Source: Data gathered by authors from state legislative websites.

as legislator. Pennsylvania's figure is unusually high, however; observers believe many lawmakers in other professionalized legislatures are also really full-time legislators, but they fear admitting it publicly because of the possible negative electoral repercussions of being labeled a career politician.[190] Outside of the more professional legislatures, few, if any, members say they make their living from public office. For instance, only 1 percent of Iowa or Mississippi House members claim to be full-time lawmakers, and none claim such status in more than half of the lower state houses listed in table 3.4.

Lawyers still play a prominent role in legislatures, in large part because they develop skills that lend themselves to success in the legislative process.[191] But while they constitute roughly a quarter of the membership in some legislatures, remarkably few serve in others. In 2017 the Kansas Senate had no licensed lawyers among its members. Their absence created some special problems because state statutes required senators to be active attorneys in order to serve on certain state commissions. More problematically, as one veteran member noted, "Whenever you have a legislative body whose job is to write laws without any lawyer whatsoever, that's some valuable insight you're going to lose."[192]

The percentage of legislators who are in farming or ranching today is strongly related to agriculture's role in a state's economy. Thus, 23 percent of North Dakota House members and 18 percent of Montana and South Dakota members identify themselves as farmers or ranchers. In contrast, no members of the Connecticut, Massachusetts, Nevada, New Jersey, or Pennsylvania House do. Every legislature listed in table 3.4 had at least some real estate agents, insurance agents, and funeral directors serving; a few had more than 10 percent of their members from those occupations.

Finally, much larger percentages of those who are retired are found in lower-salary state legislatures—for example, more than 20 percent of the members in Idaho, Iowa, Maine, and West Virginia legislatures. In contrast, only 1 percent of Massachusetts and Pennsylvania House members are retired. It is not surprising that service in less professional legislatures is attractive to retired people because they usually enjoy other sources of income and flexible schedules.

Although state legislators are drawn from a wide range of different occupations, working-class Americans are underrepresented in their ranks. This discrepancy becomes more pronounced as legislative professionalization increases.[193] The concern is that there are too few lawmakers to speak on the working class's behalf. As a Vermont legislator and dairy farmer who "wakes up at 4:30 a.m. during the session to milk his herd before he heads off to Montpelier" observes, "Most people that are in the Statehouse, serving, they're either retired, so they're collecting Social Security, or they're self-employed, so that you can arrange to have time off. . . . What you're missing in the middle is the average working person that doesn't have a business, is not self-employed . . . in order to survive they've got to work five days a week for 40 hours." He worries that the "average working person" gets ignored by the legislature: "They're the ones we're supposed to be helping out the most, so that they can support their families . . . And they're the voices that we don't hear down there [at the capitol]."[194]

The Job of State Legislator

Most lawmakers do not serve in legislatures that meet year-round. Yet, as noted by the time study discussed above, although they are thought to be performing a part-time job, their legislative tasks can be all-consuming. This forces them to juggle their legislative responsibilities with demands from their regular occupations and families.

Thus, during the legislative session, life for a legislator can be hectic, as the blog of Alabama representative (now state senator) Cam Ward reveals:

Monday: Usually up early to get into work at my real job. . . . Pack clothes for the week in Montgomery. Lay in bed and read legislation before going to sleep sometime after midnight.

Tuesday: Get up around 6:30 am to help get my daughter off to school. Go to office and get some work done on economic development job first. Then leave for Montgomery. . . . First meeting is at 11:00 am with House GOP Steering Committee. . . . Meeting ends a little after noon. Since I have about 15 minutes before next meeting I usually eat a Power Bar for lunch before going to my Rules Committee meeting at 12:30. Session begins at 1:00 pm. While listening to debates I usually read bills coming up the next to be voted on while returning e-mails from the House floor. In the course of the day I get an average [of] maybe 10–15 calls to return. . . . In between all of this I get prepared for my own bill to come up for a vote by lobbying other members in the chamber. . . . Session usually ends around 5:30 pm . . . then I typically have a couple of receptions to go to before we finally get to dinner around 7:00 pm. After dinner, around 9:30 pm I go back to the hotel to check in for the night and then read bills and return e-mails for a couple of hours before going to bed.

Wednesday: This is the day we spend in our committees. I try to get to the State House by 8:00 am so I can have my bills in order for the day. . . . First committee of the day for me is the Judiciary Committee. . . . We usually meet for about 3 hours. I usually have some of my bills in other committees at this same time so I rush up from the basement where Judiciary meets to the 6th floor and present my bills in front of other committees. . . . As soon as I am done I go back to the basement and finish up the Judiciary Committee meeting. At noon I go to the House GOP Caucus meeting where we usually talk about what will be going on in the House for the rest of the week. . . . At 1:30 pm I go to Education Policy Committee and get out by 2:30 pm. I then go back to my office where I return calls, speak with student groups visiting the capitol and handle constituent issues. I go back to the hotel around 5:00 pm and make phone calls and work for my economic development job until 6:30 pm and then go to dinner. . . . I get back to my room at about 9:30 pm where I respond to e-mails and read the news clips for the day.

Thursday: After breakfast I go to the State House where I return phone calls to constituents for about an hour and a half to two hours. Then at 9:30 am I [have] the Rules Committee meeting where the agenda for the House debate that day is set. At 10:00 am I rush to get down on to the House floor for the beginning of the session. . . . Once on the House floor we debate bills until around noon when we adjourn for lunch. We go back into session at 1:15 pm and usually go until about 3:30 pm before adjourning. . . . On the drive home I return calls the entire way back to Alabaster.

Friday: I spend as much time as possible working on my economic development work.

Saturday: Usually 3 out of every 4 Saturdays each month I have an event on this day. I try to get up early and respond to mail that I have received throughout the week. Sometimes that can be an hour and a half long chore there. Then we all have breakfast before I head off to my [district] event.

Sunday: After church we come back home where I will work in the yard for a couple of hours, then go back to my office in the house to work for a couple of hours preparing for the week. I read legislative bills until about 4:00 pm.[195]

A Massachusetts representative characterizes his work life this way: "Most of our job is meeting-based. . . . It's based on going from meeting to meeting to meeting."[196] Even when the legislature is not in session, a lawmaker's time can be devoured by legislative commitments. Constituents make demands on legislators, who devote a great deal of time and effort to responding to them. A Michigan senator estimated that she spent thirty hours a week communicating with people in her district.[197] Staff, of course, can help with the workload. A Hawaii senator confessed, "One day I tried to do all the responding [to constituents] myself. I started at 8 in the morning. I did not go to meetings, and I didn't go answer phone calls or respond to faxes. It took me until 8 in the evening almost to complete it all."[198] And requests for assistance come year-round, not just when the legislature is in session. A Nevada senator and pastor noted of his congregation members, "They'll come out after services and say, 'Great sermon—and, by the way, my son's in jail and I'm wondering what you can do to help.'"[199]

Lawmakers are expected to play an active role in the communities they represent and to be seen by their constituents. A Louisiana representative advises, "You need to be visible, available, and accessible."[200] According to a New York senator, "When I get off that train and I'm back in my district, I'm not going home, I'm going to a block association meeting and a community board meeting."[201] A story about one of California Senator Jerry Hill's "Java with Jerry" town hall meetings at a senior center reported that "He took questions for nearly two hours. Will the Legislature increase funding for health care for the disabled? The political will isn't there. What's the deal with red light cameras? It's a law enforcement money-making tactic with too many high fines. Single-payer health insurance? He supports it but doesn't see it going anywhere this year."[202] Given constituents' expectations, it is not surprising that a Wisconsin representative admitted, "If there are two people [at an event in the district], I try to be there." As a result, one day he attended an arts and craft show in Melrose and a spaghetti dinner in Sparta. The next day, he went to a lumberjack breakfast in Sparta, a smelt fry in Millston, and another spaghetti dinner in Sparta. He joked, "In this job, you'd better like fish, pancakes, and chicken."[203]

Lawmakers in less professional legislatures are not exempt from such time pressures. South Dakota lawmakers devote several weekends during the legislative session to "cracker barrels," meetings during which the members in a district solicit public input about the issues facing their constituents. Because many legislators have to drive long distances to get back home for their cracker barrels, these events represent a considerable time commitment. One South Dakota senator observed, "We have no time for ourselves, but we really should get to the people."[204]

Serving in the legislature can take a toll on family life because most lawmakers do not bring their families with them to the capital. Thus, many legislators spend several months apart from loved ones. For those with children, this can cause particular unhappiness. During a floor debate on whether to call a special session of the legislature, a Utah representative argued against it by reading a letter written to him by his seven-year-old daughter: "Dear Dad, I miss you so much. I wish you got voted off, because I want you to stay home."[205] When another Utah lawmaker opted to retire, he explained, "Last week, I missed a talent show. Last Wednesday, we're here until 11 p.m. and when I got home, the kids were already asleep. . . . The next morning, I left at 6:45 a.m. and kissed my kids, who were still sleeping."[206] A North Carolina representative who also chose to leave struck the same theme, saying "the titles of husband and father are much greater and I must devote the time to my young family while I still have that opportunity."[207]

The burden on female legislators may be particularly heavy. An Iowa representative noted with some irony that, given her various responsibilities, "One minute I'm making laws, and the next minute I'm cleaning toilets."[208] Similarly, a Wyoming representative reflected that after a session ended one day she "had to go buy a washing machine. . . . Merging daily life with legislative life was interesting."[209] Women with young children often feel especially stressed. One lawmaker and mother recalls wondering during a legislative session, "What are the kids doing? Do they miss me? Are they having fun? What's going on at home? I hope they went outside and didn't sit in front of the TV and watch *Caillou*!" Another admitted "My children ate a lot more fast food. Truly. I gave up laundry. My husband took over the laundry."[210] An Iowa legislator who gave birth in early 2018 brought her infant with her to work. According to a news report, she toted "the newborn to and from meetings at the Capitol, gently rocking her in a bassinet on the House floor and balancing bottles, blankets and bill numbers as she runs up and down stairs." She said she was driven to this predicament because her husband is a farmer "so it's not like he can strap a Babybjorn to his chest and be hopping in and out of payloaders and tractors and chasing after cows." At the same time she knew her constituents deserved representation: "They elected me to do a job, and I needed to be here."[211]

Older lawmakers can also feel torn by home pressures. A longtime Indiana representative lamented that although serving was "an honor and a privilege," at the same time, "being a legislator is also a very selfish endeavor that forces a person's family to take a back seat sometimes." He resigned to spend more time with his grandsons.[212]

All legislators can find the juggling act required of them to be frustrating. Toward the end of one legislative session, an Iowa senator admitted, "I'm a perfectionist. I haven't done anything well for the past few months. I haven't spent enough time with my family or my law practice or on my legislative work."[213] And the job can be overwhelming. A Wyoming representative confessed,

"I woke up in the middle of the night three times after dreaming about working on the Medicaid reform bill. . . . I was not expecting the Legislature to take over my dreams."[214] Consequently, public service can exact a personal toll. A Washington senator, angry about having constituents impugn his efforts, took to the floor to rail about it. In an emotional outburst, he challenged his critics, saying, "I've had enough. If you don't like the way we do this job, you need to come down here and do it yourself."[215] At times, his colleagues across the country are apt to share the sentiment.

Ethics

Most Americans do not think that state legislators rank particularly high in the country's political hierarchy. Yet they make decisions that impact almost every aspect of daily life. Much rides on lawmakers' votes; accordingly, they receive considerable attention from people and organizations with interests at stake before the legislature. Because of this, a California senator admitted, "It's a very seductive business. People want to be your friend. They shower you with gifts and meals and, while blowing smoke on your head, make you feel like you're the most wonderful person that ever stepped in the halls of Sacramento."[216] A Florida lawmaker offered a similar assessment: "There's this atmosphere of availability and perks. Freebie liquor. Freebie parties. Freebie food. It's almost like a temptation. You have to be strong-willed to be true."[217] Because of their power and the attention it attracts, legislators constantly confront ethical dilemmas.

Most of the ethical concerns raised about lawmakers involve the appropriate use of their office. Part of the concern is triggered by the reality that legislators often have other occupations, which potentially poses a conflict of interest in terms of the legislative agendas they pursue. There is evidence validating such apprehensions.[218] A study of the Michigan legislature, for example, found that "the owner of a septic system installation business . . . sponsored legislation to waive seasonal vehicle weight limits for those doing emergency septic work. A real estate management company president sponsored a bill that would make it harder to sue landlords about bed bug infestations. And [a] co-owner of a [car dealership] introduced a bill . . . that would require the state to pay for some auto dealer training programs."[219] Such potential conflicts abound in every legislature. One Missouri senator sponsored a bill to make it more difficult to sue businesses for racial discrimination at the same time his rent-to-own stores were being sued on such grounds, while another senator who was also a veterinarian pushed a measure to limit malpractice suits against veterinarians.[220] A Maryland delegate was investigated for "his involvement with a medical marijuana company while pushing for regulations and legislation affecting the burgeoning industry."[221] In Illinois, two Chicago police officers elected to the House of Representatives co-sponsored legislation to allow any police officer serving in the legislature to count his or her legislative service time toward their police pension (and double count that time for their legislative pension too).[222]

How do lawmakers defend such behavior? In 2014, the Indiana Senate Committee on Financial Institutions was chaired by a former bank CEO who ran a consulting firm that worked with financial companies. When asked about potential conflicts, the senator pointed to an institutional conundrum: "If no lawmaker could participate in any legislation regarding their fields of expertise, the legislature would be paralyzed. We depend on those with unique knowledge to offer their input, leadership and expertise in those fields."[223] An Iowa senator defended his sponsorship of a narrowly targeted tax cut that would benefit his machine shop by saying it was good public policy and that the perspective he brought to the legislature was important because "We have way too many people who have been in government their whole lives and don't know how to make sure that a payroll is met."[224] More often, legislators usually see themselves as rising above any possible conflicts. Another Indiana lawmaker, in this case a school district superintendent, expressed no qualms about voting on education issues, claiming, "When I'm here, I'm a lawmaker representing all of my constituents."[225]

Despite such assurances, questions still surface. When in 2011 the Texas House considered a measure to regulate the payday loan industry, the opposition to it was led by a member who owned twelve payday loan offices, leaving one of his fellow Republicans to ask during the debate, "Mr. Elkins, do you know the meaning of the term conflict of interest?"[226] South Carolina legislators who are practicing lawyers bill clients for millions of dollars to appear on their behalf before state boards and commissions, entities whose budgets and missions are overseen by the legislature. Good-government groups, such as Common Cause, raise questions about potential conflicts, but lawmakers respond that tough discloser requirements prevent any malfeasance.[227] Some legislators worry that stringent financial disclosure requirements may discourage people from running for office. In response to an attempt to force Oregon lawmakers to reveal their outside income sources, a senator commented, "We can make this as difficult as possible for someone to serve in the legislature. If we say we're not going to trust anybody, we're not going to trust anybody."[228] Apprehensions about disclosure requirements do appear to inhibit some potential candidates.[229]

Ethical concerns are also raised about the efforts of lobbyists to curry favor with legislators through free meals, trips, and gifts. State laws vary in how such lobbying efforts are treated. But even where rules are strict, they can be skirted. In Iowa, for example, ethics rules prevent legislators from accepting any gift of more than $3 in value. But those rules are waived for receptions where all 150 lawmakers are invited. Consequently, in 2017, lobbyists spent $326,976 on such events, many with open bars and lavish spreads of food.[230] (Such temptations have another price. One Florida representative complained, "You've heard of the 'Freshman 15' you pick up at college? It's the same here [in the legislature]."[231] For that reason, a Nevada Assembly leader advised his new colleagues to exercise "portion control" because "There are lots of cheese plates and crackers at get-togethers. . . . Pace yourself."[232] The recommendation in Texas is "don't try to go to all the events, and when you do go, don't eat the desserts."[233] To make legislative life even more challenging, a first-term Rhode Island lawmaker identified a related problem involving alcohol: "We have fundraisers every single night. . . . I didn't graduate from college that long ago, but I don't know how anyone's liver can handle four nights a week of fundraisers. My liver can't."[234] A report on the California legislature painted a similar picture: "Fundraisers are a daily occurrence at the downtown bars and restaurants around the Capitol; there were 19 evening functions over the course of three days last week . . . including a "margarita mixer" and a "tequila tasting."[235])

Ethics regulations in some states are loose and allow for all kinds of gifts. According to an analysis of contribution records compiled by one Missouri representative, his colleagues "accepted more than $40,000 worth of Cardinals and Royals tickets in 2013, including tickets to the Cardinals' playoffs and World Series games. . . . They also accepted more than $15,000 in Rams, Chiefs and [University of Missouri] Tigers football tickets, $8,200 in Tigers basketball tickets and $2,300 in Blues hockey tickets."[236] Voters tend to look askance at such largesse. After it was revealed that eleven Nevada legislators had accepted free tickets to a Rolling Stones concert, a public opinion survey found that 58 percent of Nevadans supported a ban on lobbyists' gifts.[237] It is important to appreciate that lobbyists engage in these activities to create goodwill with lawmakers and gain access to them. Votes are almost never explicitly traded for tickets or the like.

Outright corruption, however, does occur. Some cases are blatant and involve considerable sums of money. In 2018, a former Speaker of the New York Assembly was convicted of receiving almost $4 million in illegal compensation for actions he took in office to help, among others, several real estate developers.[238] A few years earlier, the Speaker of the Massachusetts House was convicted for taking $65,000 in bribes while an Alabama speaker was found guilty of using "his office to steer more the $2 million in contracts to his businesses."[239] Rank-and-file members also succumb to temptation. A long time South Carolina senator resigned after he pleaded guilty to diverting $160,000 in campaign contributions to his personal use.[240] Among those caught in a scandal enveloping the Arkansas General Assembly in 2018 was a former lawmaker who pleaded guilty "to conspiring to accept over $80,000 in bribes in exchange for influencing Arkansas state legislation and transactions, including steering approximately $245,000 in Arkansas General Improvement funds to his co-conspirators." He "also pleaded guilty to devising a scheme to conceal the bribe payments as donations" to the church where he served as a pastor.[241] Another Arkansas lawmaker pleaded guilty to taking $38,000 in bribes to direct $600,000 in government funds to two nonprofit organizations, one of them a bible college.[242]

In other cases, smaller sums are involved. In 2018, a Pennsylvania lawmaker was convicted of accepting $4,000 in bribes. A few years earlier several of her colleagues had pleaded guilty to receiving between $1,500 and $8,000 in illegal payments.[243] Among three Alaska legislators convicted a decade ago was a Speaker of the House, who had been secretly recorded telling an oil company executive that he "had to cheat, steal, beg, borrow and lie" to help defeat a tax provision opposed by the oil industry.[244] In return for his efforts, the lawmaker had received $1,000 in cash, a check for $7,993, a public opinion survey conducted for his reelection campaign, and the promise of a high-paying job with the company. Another convicted legislator received between $2,100 and $2,600 in cash and a $3,000 summer job for his nephew.[245] The unimpressive amounts of money passing hands prompted an Alaskan humorist to sneer, "The fact of the matter is, we all want to bribe a politician. We all thought it'd take a Mercedes or a Porsche. Nobody knew you could buy a politician for the cost of a used riding lawn mower."[246]

Some corruption is more subtle, such as the case of a Colorado senator who wrote to her state's Association of Realtors' political action committee, an organization that had opposed her election, requesting a payment of $1,400 in "reparations." She went on to threaten, "There are going to be some very important issues ahead of us. You have a choice. So do I."[247] Although the senator was forced to resign, a grand jury later declined to indict her. An Oklahoma representative was not as fortunate. After he was convicted of trying to bribe another lawmaker to drop out of an election for the state Senate by offering her an $80,000-a-year job in the state medical examiner's office, he was fined and sentenced to a year in jail.[248]

Although the preceding cases were isolated acts by individual lawmakers, other incidents have evinced more systemic and widespread corruption. In recent decades, a number of major scandals have enveloped state legislatures. Often known by colorful labels or FBI code names such as AzScam (Arizona), Boptrot (Kentucky), Shrimpscam (California), Operation Lost Trust (South Carolina), and Tennessee Waltz, these investigations resulted in a number of members and others involved in the legislative process being convicted and sent to jail.[249] Widespread problems of this sort are more likely to surface in some places more than in others. A 2017 survey of knowledgeable observers in every state found that corruption in the state legislature was thought to be extremely common or very common in six states: Alabama, Arkansas, Kentucky, Louisiana, Oklahoma, and Pennsylvania. Corruption was believed to be uncommon in the Idaho, Iowa, Kansas, Maine, Minnesota, and Montana legislatures.[250]

Over time, scandals large and small have prompted legislatures to adopt progressively tighter ethics laws. Consequently, state lawmakers operate under much more stringent regulations today than their predecessors a generation or two ago.[251] Indeed, lawmakers in forty-seven states face more rigorous ethics rules than do members of Congress.[252] There is a pronounced relationship between legislative professionalization and ethics laws. The stringency of lobbying regulations and the vigor with which they are enforced increases with professionalization.[253] More professional legislatures are also more likely to adopt stricter campaign finance laws.[254]

Even with considerable regulation, state legislatures have still had to contend with a number of episodes involving a variety of misbehaviors on the part of their members and staff. In 2018, for example, Arkansas legislators issued futile calls for the resignation of a state representative who was charged with having failed to file any state income taxes between 2003 and 2017.[255] Illinois lawmakers were more successful in pushing out a colleague who was alleged to have sent nude photos of an ex-girlfriend to other men in what was characterized as an online "catfishing" escapade.[256] Given that there are 7,383 state legislators across the country, it is not surprising that some of them engage in unethical or illegal behavior, but the expectation is that such incidents are isolated events.

More troubling is evidence of legislative cultures that tolerate misconduct. In late 2017 and early 2018, a number of state legislatures got swept up in the "#MeToo" movement.[257] By mid-2018, at least thirty lawmakers across the country had resigned and another forty were punished because of alleged sexual misconduct.[258] The misbehavior involved was often egregious. A Florida newspaper editorial said of the investigative report about one state senator's actions that it "reads like a 1960s bodice-ripper without the romance."[259] A California senator resigned before his colleagues expelled him for an assortment of alleged offenses, among them that he "made unwanted advances on a twenty-three-year-old Sacramento State [legislative] fellow working in his office and twice invited her to his home to go over her résumé for a full-time position. . . . The Senate investigation found that he likely had no intention of offering her the job."[260]

Such episodes indicate that state legislatures have allowed unacceptable behavior to fester. When the California Legislative Women's Caucus surveyed female staff members in late 2017, most of them concurred with a characterization of the capitol as a "boy's club." They also expressed skepticism about how any complaints they made might be treated. More than three hundred women signed on to a "We Said Enough" campaign, objecting specifically to the "groping, lewd comments, and suggestions of trading sexual favors for legislation while doing business in Sacramento."[261] A survey of Minnesota House members and staff revealed that 20 percent of them had experienced or witnessed sexual harassment in their workplace.[262]

Not all of the indignities inflicted on women working in state capitols were predatory in nature, but they were still demeaning.[263] An Arizona lobbyist for conservative causes went public with her complaint that a representative had "told me I shouldn't be in his office because he was told I had 6 month [old] twins at home and [he] didn't know how I was feeding them when [I was] at work. He [then] proceeded to tell me that I must be working because my husband doesn't make enough . . . [and that] I must not be pro[-]family because I'm a working mom." The lobbyist wrote that "Honestly, we talk about sexual harassment, but I've never felt more harassed or condemned by anyone in my life."[264] Other censured behaviors were either creepy—one California state senator was reproached "for giving unwanted hugs"—or juvenile—another senator was scolded for "giving an unsolicited noogie."[265]

Many state legislatures discovered that they were ill prepared to respond to the demands placed on them by the #MeToo movement. One analysis reported that "the majority of state legislative chambers across the country have no publicly available records of any sexual misconduct claims over the past 10 years."[266] Legislators scrambled to devise policies to address the problems uncovered. Roughly a dozen legislative chambers updated their rules governing harassment claims and about half of them inaugurated or revised harassment training programs.[267] The Indiana General Assembly, for example, passed legislation that for the first time instituted a sexual harassment policy and required training on it.[268] Some lawmakers rebelled at being forced to undergo sexual harassment training. A Republican representative in South Dakota protested that her "constituents didn't send me here to spend two hours trying to solve a problem that doesn't exist." But a male GOP colleague countered that "Anybody who's been around in the last year who says it wasn't worthwhile needs to do a serious check as to what their attitude is. . . . I think it's important that we take things seriously and not pooh-pooh things and not see things as a waste of time because it very well could have a profound effect on how we conduct ourselves, how we conduct our business and how we deal with each other."[269]

In the end, it is not clear how much these reform efforts will change statehouse cultures. Doubts were raised, for example, about attempts to address sexual harassment issues in Indiana, New York, and Oregon.[270] When asked to assess the impact of the #MeToo movement on a Colorado legislature that had been shaken by harassment allegations during its 2018 session, two women members arrived at different conclusions. One said "It was miserable—I felt like this place was haunted by complaints and no one was listening. . . . When I look back at it, I feel unsupported. . . . I feel a lack of protection and a lack of understanding."[271] In contrast, the lawmaker whose accusations initiated the investigation said, "I have fantastic male colleagues who stood by me and defended me. We've created a culture where our male colleagues are more engaged and having those conversations. We have signs all over the Capitol it is changing, but it will take time."[272] The California lobbyist who instigated that state legislature's investigations observed that "This is an issue that we are all still evolving on. Things that were acceptable 12 years, 12 months, 12 weeks ago—we are realizing as we continue to have these conversations that they're not acceptable. . . . This isn't something you get to take a class or a training, and then check the box and you're good."[273]

Whether voters would hold accused legislators to account also was not clear. Some lawmakers alleged to have misbehaved ran again and some won both their primary and the general election.[274] Others did not fare well. One Arizona state representative who had been expelled for sexual harassment ran for a state Senate seat believing that the charges against him would actually work in his favor. Republican voters disagreed and he finished last in his primary. And the Arizona representative who had insulted the conservative lobbyist (and the same lawmaker in the speeding incident) was also rejected by Republican primary voters.[275]

Legislative Careers and Legislature Career Opportunity Types

As demonstrated in this chapter, state legislators operate in diverse settings. This reality impacts their working experience. Given the different contexts in which lawmakers operate, state legislatures offer members one of three possible legislative career opportunities. The particular career opportunity a legislature offers is dictated in part by its level of pay. Some pay well enough that members can contemplate service as their primary vocation. Most, however, do not offer sufficient compensation for members to forgo their regular occupation. So, based simply on the level of pay offered, we would anticipate that some legislatures entice members to consider legislative service as their career while others do not.

Given the place of state legislatures in the American political hierarchy, however, there is a third potential career option. Some legislatures may be particularly well suited to serve their members as a springboard to higher political offices. That is, the current position is just a way station on the road to a more coveted elective post.

Thus, legislatures offer their members one of three possible career opportunities. One is a *springboard legislature*, a body that gives members substantial electoral advancement opportunities. Among legislatures that do not offer members good prospects for moving up, some may be considered *career legislatures* because they offer members sufficient financial compensation such that they can support themselves and their families from their legislative service. The other category is *dead-end legislatures*, bodies in which members cannot use their service to advance politically and which pay so poorly that they cannot realistically be a member's primary source of income.[276]

The existence of term limits in fifteen states influences their career opportunity classification. By definition, term limits remove the possibility of service in the legislative house becoming a career. (An argument could be made that the more generous limits in Louisiana and Nevada leave open the possibility of effectively becoming career bodies if either state were to significantly increase its level of pay.) But term limits appear to have increased the number of states that fall into the springboard category. In states that have them, term limits have created something of a conveyor belt from the lower house to the Senate, with large numbers of former lower house members moving to the upper house as they get forced out of their current post (and as Senate incumbents are forced out, creating open seats). Across the fourteen term-limited states with bicameral legislatures in 2009, a mean of 69 percent of Senate seats were held by former lower house members; the mean for the states without term limits was only 41 percent.[277] Term limits have not, however, altered the career opportunity structure in every state in which they have been introduced. California, for example, was considered a springboard body even before voters forced members of the Assembly to eventually leave.[278]

Conclusion

State legislators operate in a wide range of institutions. Some legislatures are professionalized along the lines of Congress. Members in these bodies are able to devote themselves to legislative service and have staff to assist them in their efforts. Other lawmakers serve in much less professionalized legislatures. They must juggle public service with the demands of their other occupations.

Moreover, they have little in the way of staff to help them with their legislative work. Different kinds of people are attracted to service in different kinds of legislatures. Legislatures offer different career opportunities to their members based on the salaries and political advancement opportunities they provide.

In the next chapter, we shift our focus to questions of legislative organization and structure, specifically the roles played by legislative parties, leadership, and standing committees. Each will be assessed in the light of contrasting levels of legislative professionalization. We will also more fully investigate questions about the impact of career opportunity structures on legislative organization. Being a springboard body, for example, has important consequences for legislative organization and member behavior. Legislators in springboard bodies tend to be more responsive to constituents on policy preferences than are their counterparts in other sorts of legislatures.[279] Organizationally, members of springboard legislatures make different sorts of demands of their leaders than do members of career or dead-end legislatures.[280]

Chapter 4

Legislative Organization across the States

New York Assembly Speaker Carl Heastie on the Assembly floor in 2019. AP Photo/Hans Pennink.

I n 2018, Philip Gunn served as speaker of the Mississippi House and Joe Aresimowicz served as speaker of the Connecticut House. Both leaders were granted comparable formal powers. Both, for example, exercised the authority to appoint members and chairs for almost all of the committees in their chambers.[1] But the similarities in their situations were superficial because the organizations they oversaw are remarkably different.

Speaker Gunn enjoyed an unusual position compared with his counterparts in other states. Except for a speaker pro tempore, there are no other party leaders in the Mississippi House—even the minority leader is only an informal post. Indeed, the speaker is chosen by the entire House membership, not by a party caucus, as is usually the case.[2] The lack of party organization is a remnant of the time when, as noted in chapter 2, only Democrats held seats in Mississippi. In the absence of a two-party system, there was no need for the development of complicated party leadership structures.[3] In contrast, in Connecticut, where Republicans and Democrats have long competed on even terms, the House is organized around party. It has an elaborate leadership structure. Speaker Aresimowicz was joined in the majority party leadership by a majority leader, one deputy speaker pro-tempore, eight deputy speakers, three assistant deputy speakers, seven deputy majority leaders, a party caucus chair, a chief majority whip, a majority whip-at-large, a deputy majority whip-at-large, six assistant majority whips, and eleven assistant majority leaders. Another twenty-eight representatives held positions in the minority party leadership structure.[4]

Committees were also organized differently in the two houses. In Mississippi, the legislative workload in the House was divided among forty-seven standing committees. The Connecticut House has evolved an unusual committee system. In 2018, it employed twenty-six standing committees, all of which were joint committees, meaning that members of the House and the Senate served together on them.

It is worth pointing out that neither the Connecticut House nor the Mississippi House was organized in the same fashion as the U.S. House. Indeed, examination of the organizational features of the ninety-nine state legislative chambers reveals that none of them exactly mirrors its federal counterpart. Moreover, although legislative houses share some notable organizational similarities, they each have distinctive features. Thus, state legislatures are not smaller or simpler versions of Congress or copies of each other. They have evolved a wide range of organizational structures, all of which influence the processes by which they make decisions and the policies they produce.

In this chapter, we examine the roles legislative parties, leadership, and standing committees play in state legislatures. Each constitutes an important and distinct part of the legislative system; yet they are intertwined. Each merits examination.

Where Are Decisions Made in State Legislatures?

Parties are the main organizational vehicles for state legislatures. Committees do much of the legislative work in them. Leadership makes the various parts of the legislative process function together. Collectively, parties, leaders, and committees structure how state legislatures make decisions. But there is often tension between party leadership and the committee structure: "There is an inherent contradiction between party and committee leadership. Party leadership is centralized; committee leadership is decentralized. Where committees are strong and independent, party leadership is weak. Where party leadership is strong, the committees are either weak or simply agents of the party leaders."[5]

There is considerable variation in the relative strength of committees and leaders across state legislatures. Overall, committees gained a good deal of information-processing ability and policy independence during the legislative professionalization push of the 1960s and 1970s. In many states, the committee system remains strong and provides a critical stage in the screening and shaping of substantive legislation.[6] But some see that independence waning in recent years, especially as the parties have become more polarized. One keen observer noted, "With increasing partisanship and the expansion of partisan staffing in many Senates and Houses, partisan considerations have grown in importance while substantive considerations have declined. Standing committees have ceded some of their authority to majority party caucuses and top legislative leaders."[7]

Ultimately, who are the most powerful decision-makers in a state legislative house—standing committees, party caucuses, or legislative leaders? In 1981, lawmakers were surveyed and asked to identify the most important decision-making entities in their chambers. Committees were thought to be an important decision-making center in eighty-one of the ninety-nine houses. In only three states were committees deemed to be unimportant in both chambers. Committees shared power with the leadership, the party caucus, or both in almost two-thirds of the houses. Committees, however, held dominant power in only about 15 percent of legislative chambers. A more recent study found that the locus of power within a legislature occasionally changes, suggesting that the 1981 findings likely need to be modified.[8] Certainly, this is apt to be the case for the role of committees in legislatures that have adopted term limits.[9]

Legislative Parties

In one way or another, political parties organize every state legislature, except for Nebraska, which is nonpartisan. As a classic text observed, "In most two party legislatures, the presiding officer is selected by the majority party caucus, the members of which will normally unite behind that choice in balloting on the floor of the house or senate."[10] Leaders are chosen in an organizational session usually held in December, after the election but before the convening of the legislature in regular session. If there are several people in the majority party caucus seeking a post such as the Speaker of the House, there will be a vote in the caucus to choose the party's nominee. The nominee must then be approved by the entire membership of the house. Obviously, the normal process is for all the members of the majority party to vote for the majority party nominee and that person becomes speaker. Although that is what happens most of the time, the past thirty years have witnessed the occasional formation of bipartisan coalitions to elect legislative leaders, something that does not happen in Congress. Chambers in Alaska, California, Connecticut, Illinois, Louisiana, Massachusetts, Montana, New Hampshire, New Mexico, New York, North Carolina, Pennsylvania, Tennessee, Texas, Vermont, and Washington have experienced one or more such coalitions.[11] In a closely divided Tennessee Senate, for example, Democratic Speaker John Wilder was reelected in 2005 only when two Republicans defected from their party's candidate and voted for him.

Wilder lost the position in 2007 when a Democrat jumped ship to vote for the Republican candidate.[12] In 2009, the forty-nine Tennessee House Democrats joined with Kent Williams, a renegade second-term Republican representative, to make him speaker on a 50–49 vote, frustrating the desires of the rest of the Republicans who thought they held the majority. Williams's victory was accompanied by "loud booing" and shouts of "traitor," "sell-out," and "Judas" from the public gallery.[13]

Why would some members of the majority party vote against their own party's nominee, throwing in with the minority party nominee? This is a risky maneuver because if it is unsuccessful, these "turncoats" are likely to be punished. They will be given less desirable committee assignments and any bills they introduce are apt to be buried by the leadership. They may even be kicked out of their party caucus, as Tennessee Speaker Williams was by the Republicans after he was elected with Democratic votes. (Williams took to officially labeling himself a "Carter County Republican" in honor of his home county.) Leadership might encourage a challenger to run against them in the next primary election.

Such "revolts" by some members of the majority may be the result of ideological factions with strong issue differences. In Alaska, the three Republicans representatives who joined with the Democrats to take control of the House in 2017 did so because of a shared vision about how to fix the state's fiscal problems.[14] But the more typical situation is one in which deep dissatisfaction with the actions and conduct of an incumbent leader leads disaffected party members to seek an accommodation with the opposition party. In the Missouri House in 2008, for example, although they were members of the majority, a group of unhappy Republicans approached the Democratic minority leader to investigate the chances they might combine forces to overthrow the speaker. The minority leader observed that the majority had "some serious problems of sticking together, and their major priorities aren't going to pass. . . . There's some discontent within the [GOP] caucus."[15]

Some bipartisan coalitions last over a full session or two; others are, in the words of a Connecticut representative, only "one-day dates."[16] And some of the coalitions make for very odd bedfellows. In 1981, Republican votes elevated Willie Brown, a liberal African American Democrat from San Francisco, to the speakership of the California Assembly. Brown went on to become the bane of California Republicans; indeed, the term-limits movement in California was partly pursued by the GOP as a means of dislodging him from the speakership that their votes had originally made possible.[17]

Although party is the main organizing device in state legislatures, party competition is not a given; at different points in time, many states have been dominated by a single party. As noted in chapter 2, as recently as the early 1960s, there were no Republican legislators in Alabama, Arkansas, Georgia, Louisiana, Mississippi, South Carolina, and Texas, and there were only a handful in Florida, Maryland, New Mexico, North Carolina, Oklahoma, Tennessee, and Virginia. Over the course of the next forty years, the situation changed, in some states dramatically.[18] By the beginning of the 2000s, both parties were represented in every legislature, although each party had a few chambers in which it enjoyed very large majorities. The process of moving from a one-party house to a two-party house has important consequences for legislative organization, with partisan structures such as caucuses developing only after the minority party's size reaches roughly one-third of the seats in a chamber. At that point, voting also becomes organized by partisanship rather than by factional allegiances.[19]

Parties in state legislative chambers differ from those in Congress and among each other in several additional ways. They vary in the power exercised by party caucuses. In some legislative chambers, party caucuses are powerful, even to the point of making votes binding on certain important issues, as in the New Mexico and Oklahoma legislatures.[20] But in other legislative chambers, caucuses are weak or even essentially nonexistent. The importance of party caucuses also varies over time. As many as one-quarter of the strong-party caucuses in the 1950s were not considered powerful by the 1980s.[21] In Colorado, caucus decisions used to be binding on member floor votes. But in 1988, Colorado voters passed the GAVEL (Give a Vote to Every Legislator) amendment outlawing the practice.[22] The importance of party caucuses appears to be a function of the size and the degree of party competition in the chamber. The more evenly matched the parties and the smaller the chamber, the greater the importance of caucuses.[23]

Parties also vary in the power and influence exercised by legislative campaign committees.[24] In some states, party campaign committees controlled by the legislative leadership are responsible for raising the bulk of the money members spend on their reelection efforts. In New York, for example, legislative candidates get almost no money from their state party organizations. Instead, legislative campaign committees raise substantial sums for their election efforts. These committees also help recruit candidates to run for the legislature.[25] In other states, responsibility for raising campaign funds falls almost entirely on the members themselves. Overall, the power and influence parties have to affect the ability of their members to achieve their policy or career goals vary substantially across states and over time.

There are, however, some state legislative chambers that have come to operate similarly to Congress. When the majority party is split into ideological factions, some state legislative leaders have resorted to enforcing their version of a "Hastert Rule." Named for a former Speaker of the U.S. House of Representatives, the "Hastert Rule" is actually an unofficial norm imposed by Republican leaders in Congress since the late 1990s. It holds that the GOP leadership will not bring a bill to the floor for vote unless a majority of the party caucus supports it. Sometimes called the "majority of the majority" rule, it has been in effect in some state legislatures as well, with Idaho and Virginia being examples. If the majority party leader decides to operate by a "Hastert Rule," bipartisan voting coalitions become less likely—especially on important legislation. The role of the minority party, even if it is relatively large minority, becomes diminished. Where a Hastert Rule is not used, the likelihood of bipartisan coalitions increases.

Legislative Leadership

Legislatures are created as egalitarian institutions, with each legislator exercising a single, equally weighted vote. State constitutions provide for minimal leadership, typically a speaker in the lower house and a president in the upper house. Over time, however, most legislatures have evolved much more elaborate leadership structures, with floor leaders and a host of whips, deputies, and assistants. Such leadership structures arise because of the need to try to organize the preferences of legislators and to coordinate their efforts to reach decisions. But because of the reality that legislators are created equal, being a leader is challenging. A former speaker of the North Carolina House likens trying to lead lawmakers to "pushing a wheelbarrow full of frogs."[26]

Unlike legislators, leaders are not created the same. Some enjoy far more power than others. One reason they differ is the leadership structure in which they operate. Where there are fewer leadership positions, more power can be concentrated in the top leader's hands. As suggested by the comparison between the Connecticut and Mississippi houses that opened this chapter, leadership structures vary across state legislatures.[27] Among the lower houses, Louisiana and Mississippi have just two leaders: a speaker and a speaker pro tempore. The other extreme is anchored by the Connecticut House, which in 2018 has seventy leadership posts. Regardless of the number of leadership posts, as table 4.1 shows, the top leader in every lower house is called the "speaker."

Senate leadership structures also vary in size and, at the top, they are more complicated and confusing than those found in lower houses. Formally, the

TABLE 4.1 The Top Leader in State Legislative Houses, 2018

Legislative Leader Title	Upper House[a]	Lower House
Lieutenant governor/president	AL, GA, MS, TX, *WV*	
President	AK, AZ, CO, FL, HI, IL, IA, KS, KY, LA, ME, MD, MA, MN, MT, NH, NJ, OH, OR, RI, UT, WI, WY	
President pro tempore	AR, CA, CT, DE, ID, IN, MI, MO, NV, NM, NC, ND, OK, PA, SC, SD, VT, VA, WA	
President/majority leader	NY	
Speaker/lieutenant governor	*TN*	
Speaker	NE Unicameral	All 49 lower houses

[a] States in italics allow members of the senate to elect a senator to be president or speaker and to serve as lieutenant governor.
Source: National Conference of State Legislatures, "2018 State Legislative Leaders," August 9, 2018, http://www.ncsl.org/legislators-staff/legislators/legislative-leaders/2017-state-legislative-leaders.aspx.

lieutenant governor is the president of the Senate in twenty-four states, holding a position that in most of them is similar to that of the vice president in the U.S. Senate. In the other twenty-six Senates, the president is elected by the membership. To confuse matters further, in both Tennessee and West Virginia, the Senate elects one of its own members to serve simultaneously as the leader of the chamber—called the "speaker" in Tennessee and the "president" in West Virginia—and as lieutenant governor. Moreover, although the members of the Nebraska Unicameral are referred to as "senator," they are, like in Tennessee, presided over by a speaker. A novel twist in New York is the norm that the Senate president also holds the title of majority leader.[28]

Looking across the state Senates, however, real leadership power is vested in the president or president pro tem in the vast majority of them. Thus, as table 4.1 implies, although many lieutenant governors serve as Senate president, they essentially perform a ceremonial role. Only a few, notably the lieutenant governors in Georgia and Texas, exercise significant power within their Senates.[29] But it is important to understand that leadership powers are not chiseled in stone; they can be and occasionally are altered. The lieutenant governor in Alabama used to enjoy great power in the Senate, but the position lost much of its authority as the result of a partisan conflict in 1999.[30] In the years since that blowup the office has regained only some of what it lost.

As in the lower houses, the size of Senate leadership structures varies substantially. In Louisiana, Mississippi, and Texas, only a president pro tem supplements the president. In Nebraska, the speaker serves with an Executive Board chair. Other Senates operate with far more leaders. The Connecticut Senate had thirty-six leadership positions in 2018. What makes this structure particularly noteworthy is that the thirty-six positions were spread across a thirty-six-member body, meaning every Connecticut senator held some leadership title!

Legislative leadership positions also vary in tenure. Longer leadership tenures are considered important because they are thought to increase the power wielded by leaders, especially relative to the executive.[31] Speaker careers in the lower houses have generally gotten gradually longer since 1901.[32] But several different patterns emerge across the states. In Pennsylvania and Wisconsin (both among the more professional legislatures in the country), the increase in leadership tenure has been slight because even during the earliest periods, leaders in these two states served at least two terms or occasionally even three terms. In Georgia, Mississippi, and South Carolina (one-party states for much of the past century), longer speakership tenures emerged very early on and quickly became the norm. Because of this, each of these lower houses has had considerably fewer speakers over the past century than almost any other lower house. The predominant pattern in the majority of states, however, is a decided increase in speakership tenure only in the past three to four decades, coinciding with professionalization efforts in most of them.

The imposition of term limits truncated the trend toward longer leadership service in the legislatures that have them. In California, for example, no speaker served in successive sessions until C. C. Young did so between 1913 and 1919.[33]

Longer tenures became the norm from that point on, with Willie Brown establishing the record, serving as speaker from 1981 to 1995. With the introduction of term limits, a California Assembly career could only be six years at most (until 2018 for the reasons discussed in chapter 1), and consequently recent speakers have held the post for only two to four years. As speaker-elect Karen Bass noted the day before she took over in the Assembly in 2008, "My speakership will be like all the other ones post–Willie Brown: short."[34] Indeed, in the twenty-three years following Brown's long tenure, the Assembly had twelve different speakers. But term limits do not necessarily change things in every legislature. In South Dakota, speakers rarely served for even four years even before term limits; thus, the adoption of term limits has not altered speakership careers there at all.

POLITICS UNDER THE DOMES

Who Controls the New York Senate?

Given the American two-party system it is reasonable to assume that the majority party in every legislative chamber will control it, save for the nonpartisan Nebraska Unicameral. But, while that assumption holds in the U.S. Congress, it is occasionally violated at the state legislative level.

Take, for example, the New York Senate. In 2009, Democrats held a majority of thirty-two to thirty and appeared to be in control of the chamber for the first time since 1965. But that June, in a surprise move, two Democrats voted with all of the Republicans to name a new Senate president, effectively putting the GOP in charge. A few days later, however, one of the renegade Democrats returned to the party, producing a 31 to 31 split between the two parties. Under normal circumstances the state's lieutenant governor would have broken the tie, but because the Democratic governor had resigned, the elected lieutenant governor had moved into that office, leaving the lieutenant governorship vacant. Consequently, the New York Senate was paralyzed for weeks. But when the second Democratic Senate defector returned to the party in July, control of the chamber reverted to the Democrats. That same day they passed 135 bills that had been stymied by the political impasse.

Democrats retained control through the 2010 legislative session. But the elections that year put the GOP back in the Senate majority. When the Senate organized, a faction of four disgruntled Democrats opted to separate from the rest of their party and form their own caucus, called the Independent Democratic Conference (IDC). The IDC members claimed that they were motivated by a desire to "push for commonsense solutions to problems facing this state, [to] break the hyper-partisan gridlock that has gripped this chamber, and [to] work to restore the public's trust in its public officials." As punishment for their defection, the leader of the Senate Democrats assigned his rebellious colleagues to minor committees. Unhappy with this turn of events, the IDC senators approached Republican leaders about working with them. Calculating that adding four votes to their bare majority would give them more room to operate, Republicans not only gave the IDC members better committee assignments, they also named them committee chairs. Consequently, not only did the IDC members get to enjoy the opportunity to exercise power as committee chairs, they also got to enjoy the additional pay stipend that comes with those posts in New York.

When Democrats regained the majority following the 2012 elections, the assumption was that the IDC senators would rejoin their Democratic colleagues. But, again to everyone's surprise, the IDC's leader declared that the "time has come for coalition government," and the group again threw its support behind the GOP, making their combination the effective majority. And to further complicate Senate affairs, another Democrat, Simcha Felder who represented a Brooklyn district, decided to caucus not with the Democrats or with the IDC, but with the Republicans.

Although its membership fluctuated, up until 2018 the IDC continued to be allied with the Republicans, leading one reporter to comment, "To the uninitiated, the State Senate looks more like a multi-party coalition in a European parliament than a product of the American two-party system." There were incentives for the IDC to maintain the coalition. Members of the IDC were rewarded with committee chair positions and their caucus was given its own funding, just like the two major party caucuses. Their members were given some say on setting the legislative agenda. And it was reported that the IDC's leader "managed to get $100 million for the New York City Housing Authority in the budget and more capital funding than any other senator."

The coalition finally fell apart in April, 2018. New York Governor Andrew Cuomo, a Democrat, announced that he had

brokered a deal between his party's two Senate factions. The IDC members would return to the Democratic Party fold and the IDC leader would be named the Deputy Democratic Conference Leader. The Republicans, however, still maintained their majority because the other Democratic defector, Senator Felder, opted to continue to caucus with them. And the GOP took immediate revenge on their former coalition partners. The four IDC senators who chaired committees lost those positions and thirty-nine IDC staffers were fired.

Why were IDC members willing to give up what they had? The answer is likely a sense of political self-preservation. Given the rise of the progressive wing of the Democratic Party in 2018, IDC members had reason to fear that they would be punished in their primaries. As the leader of one liberal Democratic Party club said, "We're going to remember those who were in bed with the Republicans—the party of Trump." The IDC members hoped that rejoining the Senate Democratic caucus would appease vengeful Democratic voters. But they were wrong. In the September primary, six of the eight IDC members were defeated, including their former leader, even though they had heavily outspent their insurgent challengers. And in the general election the Democrats won more than enough state Senate seats to take full control of the chamber without having to ask for Senator Felder's support.

Sources: Elizabeth Benjamin, "The Daily Politics," New York Daily News, July 10, 2009; Fredric U. Dicker, "State Senate's Gone Coup-Koo," New York Post, June 9, 2009; Thomas Kaplan, "Top Breakaway Democrat Favors G.O.P. Coalition in State Senate," New York Times, November 28, 2012; David Lombardo and Rachel Silberstein, "39 Ex-IDC Staffers Purged after Unity Deal," Times Union, May 19, 2018; David Lombardo and Rachel Silberstein, "Ex-IDC Senators Stripped of Committee Posts," Times Union, April 6, 2018; Kevin Lovett, "Independent Democrats Not Ready to Abandon NYS Senate GOP," *New York Daily News*, November 23, 2015; Jesse McKinley, "New York's Democrats Ended a 7-Year Civil War: Now Comes the Hard Part," *New York Times*, April 5, 2018; Jesse McKinley, "What Is a Majority Vote in the State Senate? The Answer Goes beyond Simple Math," *New York Times*, February 25, 2014; Casey Seiler, "Avella's Defection Strengthens Senate Coalition," *Times Union*, February 26, 2014; Casey Seiler, "IDC Will Once Again Partner with Senate GOP," *Times Union*, January 2, 2017; Vivian Wang, "Democratic Insurgents Topple 6 New York Senate Incumbents," *New York Times*, September 14, 2018; Adam Wisnieski, "Klein and Co. Upset Democrats Some More," *Riverdale Press*, February 2, 2011.

Why have speakers in most legislatures served for longer in recent decades? It is, of course, likely that professionalization, which encourages members to serve longer, has done the same for their leaders. But it is also the case that speakers have come to serve for more years because of reforms elsewhere in the political system that had implications for legislative leaders' political career ambitions. Most notably, laws allowing governors to serve longer in office impeded political advancement opportunities for legislative leaders by forcing them to wait longer for the opportunity to move up the electoral ladder.[35] In North Carolina, voter approval in 1977 of a constitutional amendment removing the one-term limit on governors convinced members of the lower house to allow their speaker to serve for more than two years.[36] A third variable explaining longer leadership service is the appearance in the legislatures of a politician with unusual political skills, allowing him or her to permanently shatter any one- or two-term tradition.

What do legislative leaders actually do? The top jobs are multidimensional. According to a speaker of the Kentucky House, "I deal with 100 people on a daily basis on a variety of things from committee meetings, to office space, to personnel problems, to constituent requests, to what we are going to do in the next session." Comparing it to his previous position, he claimed, "It's a more time-consuming job than when I was [Kentucky] attorney general."[37] Not only do leaders have to manage the legislative process, but they must also manage facilities and, most challenging of all, people.

How much power do legislative leaders really wield? Typically, leaders of the majority have a number of formal powers at their disposal.[38] As will be discussed below, top legislative leaders make the vast majority of committee assignments and usually name committee chairs. In a handful of statehouses, the top leader even selects his or her floor leader. And as will be examined in chapter 5, many leaders enjoy power over the referral of legislation to committees and over the flow of legislation to the floor. Both powers give a leader the chance to determine a bill's fate.[39] Finally, the authority to recognize speakers and make parliamentary rulings give a leader considerable opportunity to fashion debates and votes to his or her liking.

Legislative leaders use their powers in a "carrot and stick" fashion. The carrot is that leaders can greatly assist members by helping them get favorable committee assignments, progress up the legislative leadership ladder, and pass legislation. The stick is that members who fail to do the leadership's bidding can be punished in ways large and small. One Rhode Island representative who got on the wrong side of his leaders complained, "If a bill has my name on it, it won't go anywhere," and that his lone assignment was to "the committee that never meets."[40] An even higher cost was paid by a Republican Indiana senator who posted a critical tweet of the president pro tem, a party colleague. The penalized senator lost his assistant majority floor leader post, his designation as the ranking member of the Judiciary Committee, and his press secretary. Perhaps even more humbling, his seat in the chamber was moved from the front row with other GOP leaders to the back row among rank-and-file Democrats.[41]

Angry leaders can engage in remarkably petty behavior. When a Republican member of the California Assembly continually irritated the Democratic majority, the speaker took action against him, ordering the member moved out of his capitol office to another room known as "the doghouse" that was only half the size. The next year, a Democrat who failed to provide the speaker a critical budget vote found herself booted out of the capitol altogether to an office building across the street where no other lawmaker was housed. Such antics are not confined to California. A Florida House speaker banished a member of a failed rebellion against him to a purgatory "in the Capitol basement, shoehorned into an office so small his secretary set up her office in the hallway."[42] The depths of spiteful punishment, however, may have been plumbed by a California Senate majority leader. When three of his caucus members attended the fund-raising dinner of a political group the leader did not support, he authorized that the locks on their capitol offices be changed. Each of the locked-out senators had to first meet with the majority leader and make amends before getting a new key.[43]

Such powers give leaders leverage they can use to get their members to do their bidding without any explicit quid pro quo. Along these lines a former California Assembly member recalled an incident that "involved a bill dealing with Continental Airlines taking over Western Airlines. I was opposed to the bill and was giving an impassioned speech . . . against the bill when [Speaker] Willie [Brown] walked by my desk and said, 'Don't get too wound up, you're voting for this bill.' I paused, looked at Willie and concluded, 'Now that I have given you all the opponents' arguments, I am voting for this bill.' I sat down and the bill passed."[44] Lawmakers quickly come to understand that it is in their long-term interests to vote the way leaders want. While informal, persuasive leadership styles tend to be successful in Congress, more formal and hierarchical leadership authority is effective at the state legislative level.[45]

But, as always, the authority accorded to leaders across legislatures varies. Recent attempts to gauge the power of lower house speakers examined several different formal aspects of leadership authority, among them the ability to appoint other legislative leaders, committee chairs, and committee members, as well as the office's tenure potential and control over various resources and parliamentary procedures. By these calculations, speakers in West Virginia, New Hampshire, and Arizona generally enjoy the greatest power, and those in Alaska, Hawaii, and Wyoming have the least ability to influence legislative action. But, importantly, it appears that the powers exercised by speakers in most states ebb and flow over time.[46]

It is also the case that the power accorded to leaders varies by career opportunity type. In general, legislators in springboard legislatures invest less power in their leaders, preferring instead to have the ability to promote their own ambitions and agendas. Legislators in career bodies grant their leaders greater power.[47] Paradoxically, however, the process of professionalization may actually work to reduce leadership power from what it had been in the past as lawmakers with greater informational resources at their disposal opt to assert greater individual influence in the legislative process.[48] Perhaps not surprisingly, compared with their counterparts in other legislatures, "term limited legislative leaders have less control over legislative members, the rules, and the agenda," only overcoming their lack of apprenticeship and the experience it produces if they possess strong leadership skills.[49]

In every legislature, however, the power leaders enjoy ultimately depends on the power a majority of members is willing to delegate to them. Thus, leaders often find that they must defer their own policy preferences to those of the members who put them in power. In 2005, for example, the Connecticut House speaker strongly opposed civil unions for same-sex couples. But when he learned that a majority of the House favored such a bill, he allowed the measure to come to a vote despite his personal opposition.[50] Similarly, although Willie Brown was hailed as the "Ayatollah of the Assembly" during his long tenure as speaker in California, he stayed in the top post in large measure because he sublimated his policy preferences to those pursued by the members of his party caucus.[51] Leaders have to pick and choose when to exercise their power. The longest-serving speaker in the history of the Idaho House, Bruce Newcomb, observed, "You only have so much political capital. One of the most important things to learn as a leader is to not waste your political capital on small matters or on fights you cannot win."[52] Thus, under most circumstances, leaders seek to facilitate the policy preferences of their members, or at least their supporters, rather than promoting their own preferences. As a former speaker of the Vermont House confessed, "I was captive to my caucus, and that, I believe, is a major reason I managed to serve five terms."[53]

To this point, our discussion of leadership has focused on the roles and powers of majority party leaders. This emphasis is appropriate because state legislatures almost always make decisions by majority rule. (There are situations in which some state legislatures employ supermajority rules, but they tend to be rare.)[54] Thus, the goal of majority party leaders is straightforward. Assuming that they can get their majority to act cohesively, they win. But what of minority leaders? The ability of the minority party to exert influence in the legislative process varies by state and chamber.[55] But, under most circumstances, even if the minority party leadership can keep its members together, they cannot win unless they are joined by some number of majority party members. In the sixty-seven-member Minnesota Senate, for example, the minority leader has acknowledged that the majority "can pass anything they want to pass as long as they have 34 [votes]. It doesn't matter if I have 33 [votes]. I can't prevail."[56]

Given this reality, what then is the goal of minority leaders? Generally, it is to put their members on record pursuing policies that might in the future win them the majority. The Democratic minority leader in the Idaho House—a high-altitude adventure guide outside the legislature—described his role this way: "I run a more vocal opposition. . . . Don't go along to get along. . . . If I hide and go back to my happy outdoor place, I've failed in my responsibility to the minority." Given that his party is overwhelmingly outnumbered and always loses, being its leader can be "wearying and depressing," but he notes, "This is nothing. . . . I was trapped by a storm once in a tent at 17,000 feet with someone who spent five days throwing up. If there's one thing a high-altitude guide is really good at, it's suffering." Most minority party leaders in state legislatures can commiserate.[57]

Committees

Every state legislature operates with standing committees, bodies that exist from session to session and that have the power to recommend legislative proposals to the full chamber. Standing committees are devices that allow legislatures to handle bills and other legislative matters efficiently by dividing the workload among lawmakers. Committees can be power centers in American legislatures because of the position they occupy in the legislative process. Legislation that is introduced is usually referred to a standing committee, and the decision that committee makes on whether to recommend a bill or an amended version of it to the full chamber may dictate the measure's ultimate fate. This is known as the "gatekeeping power."

It might be assumed that the power of standing committees is universally great because of the influence such bodies exercise in the U.S. House and Senate. In reality, the power of standing committees varies, both across state legislative houses and over time within a house.[58] During the 1960s, for example, committees in the Illinois House favorably reported 81 percent of the bills referred to them, and committees in the Illinois Senate favorably reported 83 percent of the bills referred to them, evidence of limited gatekeeping power. By the early 1980s committees in both houses were exercising considerably more gatekeeping authority, with House committees recommending only 46 percent of bills and Senate committees recommending 65 percent of bills.[59] In California, committees in the Assembly and Senate recommended 76 percent of bills referred to them in the era just before the adoption of term limits and 83 percent after limits took effect, suggesting that committees lost gatekeeping power with the advent of term limits.[60] It is worth pointing out that, although their behavior shifted over time, committees in neither Illinois nor California could be said to exercise significant gatekeeping powers. Instead, the real gatekeepers in both legislatures were party leaders.

There also are notable differences in standing committee structures across state legislatures. One important difference is revealed in table 4.2. Although the ninety-nine state legislative houses handle roughly the same set of policy decisions, they can divide up the workload in divergent ways. The Maryland House, for example, has 141 members but uses only seven standing committees. (An eighth standing committee, Consent Calendars, comprises only the speaker

TABLE 4.2 Standing Committees in the Maryland House of Delegates and the Mississippi House of Representatives, 2017–2018

Maryland House of Delegates (141 Members; 7 Standing Committees)

Appropriations

Economic Matters

Environmental and Transportation

Health and Government Operations

Judiciary

Rules and Executive Nominations

Ways and Means

Mississippi House of Representatives (122 Members; 47 Standing Committees)

Accountability, Efficiency, Transparency	Judiciary En Banc
Agriculture	Legislative Budget
Apportionment and Elections	Local and Private Legislation
Appropriations	Management
Banking and Financial Services	Marine Resources
Compilation, Revision, and Publication	Medicaid
Conservation and Water Resources	Military Affairs
Constitution	Municipalities
Corrections	Performance-Based Budgeting
County Affairs	Ports, Harbors, and Airports
Drug Policy	Public Health and Human Services
Education	Public Property
Energy	Public Utilities
Enrolled Bills	Revenue and Expenditure General Bills
Ethics	Rules
Executive Contingent Fund	State Library
Forestry	Technology
Gaming	Transportation
Insurance	Universities and Colleges
Interstate Cooperation	Ways and Means
Investigate State Offices	Wildlife, Fisheries, and Parks
Judiciary A	Workforce Development
Judiciary B	Youth and Family Affairs

Sources: State legislative websites. Maryland's Consent Calendars Committee was not counted.

and the majority and minority leaders.) All but one of the standing committees has subcommittees. Delegates typically have only one standing committee assignment and serve on a single subcommittee. In contrast, the Mississippi House, with 122 members, divides up its work very differently. It has forty-seven standing committees, none with subcommittees. Representatives usually serve on five to seven standing committees.

An altogether different standing committee system from that found in most state legislatures and Congress evolved in Connecticut, Maine, and Massachusetts. Legislatures in those states rely almost exclusively on joint standing committees. Members from each house serve on the same committee, with a cochair from each house. In practice, joint committees greatly reduce the need for conference committees to reconcile legislative differences between the two chambers, thus arguably making the legislative process more efficient.[61] With joint committees, however, the distinction between separate houses is blurred, raising questions about the rationale for their independent existence. Vermont abandoned joint committees in 1917 because they were thought to invalidate bicameral principles.[62] Having separate committee systems in each house increases the number of obstacles that interests must overcome to get legislation passed and therefore arguably increases the power and informational resources each house enjoys.[63]

Another difference between standing committee systems in state legislatures and in Congress is their stability. The standing committee system in Congress does not change often. In contrast, standing committees come and go more regularly in state legislatures. When party control changes in a state legislative chamber, the tendency is for the newly elected majority party to create committees focused on its policy priorities and to abolish committees emphasizing the other party's interests.[64] After the Democrats took charge of the Minnesota House following the 2018 elections, they created several new committees and subcommittees "focusing on climate change, clean water, early childhood education, labor and corrections." The incoming speaker said that her party was "creating committees to give attention to issues that affect Minnesotans' lives but which have not received enough consideration previously." In turn, the outgoing GOP speaker charged that the new majority was "growing the committee structure by 30 percent, primarily by adding committees that cater to their activist base and special interests."[65]

But even absent a change in party control, state legislative committee systems typically reconfigure themselves from session to session. Although it was under GOP control the entire time, between the 2013–2014 and 2017–2018 legislative sessions the Mississippi House dropped the Legislative Reapportionment and Tourism standing committees and a select committee on Railway Development and replaced them with new standing committees on Drug Policy and Revenue and General Expenditure Bills. Additionally, the standing committee on Performance Evaluation and Expenditure Review (PEER) morphed into the standing committee on Performance-Based Budgeting. Whatever its source, instability in standing committee systems is associated with a decline in legislative efficiency because of a loss of member expertise.[66]

There are two questions about how standing committees are composed in state legislatures that merit special attention. First, does the majority party stack committees with a greater percentage of its members than their representation in the chamber would warrant, as happens in the U.S. House with the powerful Rules and Ways and Means committees? In general, state legislatures usually follow proportional representation rules. One examination of legislative rules in the late 1990s revealed that in twenty-five of ninety-one Houses, an explicit rule mandated proportional representation, and in another forty-five Houses, the practice was usually followed even though it was not formally required.[67] In Alaska, for example, Uniform Rule 1(e) states, "On each standing committee the minority is entitled to the number of seats that is proportional to the number of minority members compared to the total house membership or to one seat, whichever is greater."[68]

Committee stacking, however, does occur, and it is more likely to happen when rules allow it and the majority party controls a chamber by only a slim margin.[69] Typically, the committees that get stacked are those the majority wants to ensure it controls, such as rules committees that manage the legislative process and budget committees that determine how the government raises and spends money. When in 2012 the Virginia Senate was evenly split between the Republicans and the Democrats (with twenty seats for each party), the GOP seized on the tie-breaking vote granted to the Republican lieutenant governor to take control of the chamber. Not only did they name Republicans to chair every standing committee, but they also stacked several important committees in their favor. The Rules Committee, for example, comprised twelve Republicans and four Democrats.[70]

From the majority leadership's perspective, stacking powerful committees so as to be able to dictate outcomes is a reasonable strategy. When the Republicans took control of the Georgia House in 2005—the first time they had organized the chamber since 1870—they went well beyond simply stacking committees in their favor to produce the outcomes they wanted. They adopted a creative scheme to allow the majority party leadership to directly shape committee decisions. The rules were rewritten to give the speaker the right to appoint an unspecified number of "hawks," majority party members empowered to swoop in and participate as full voting members on any standing committee at any point in time.[71] Thus, by calling in the hawks (three of whom were eventually appointed), the GOP leadership would be able to force a committee to make the decision it wanted even if several committee Republicans preferred to side with the Democrats on a bill or an amendment. Democrats were predictably outraged by the creation of the hawks, with their leader griping that, "There's some political whoring going on."[72] In fact, a somewhat similar position had previously been used in the North Carolina House, where the majority party leaders and a designated legislator were considered "floater voters" and were allowed to participate and vote on all committees.[73] And in the Illinois House the speaker is authorized to appoint temporary replacements for committee members who are "unavailable," a system that allows lawmakers who do not want to cast an unpopular vote to be replaced by another member who is comfortable doing the speaker's bidding. In 2016, more than six hundred temporary committee appointments were made.[74] Such blatant efforts to stack the deck in the majority's favor are, however, rare.[75] And in the Georgia House, Republicans opted to abolish hawks in 2010.[76]

After party ratios are set, the question becomes who gets to serve on each committee. Committee assignments are handled in different ways in different legislative houses, as documented in table 4.3. The vast majority of assignments are made by the top leader in a chamber—the speaker in the lower house and the president, president pro tem, or majority leader in the Senate. There are, however, some notable deviations. In six lower houses and eleven Senates, a "committee on committees" gives out committee positions, although in several chambers, the top leader chairs the committee and greatly influences the assignments it makes. The committee on rules acts as a committee on committees in three Senates. Party caucuses make committee assignments in the Hawaii House.[77] Up until 2017 caucuses organized around congressional districts did so in the Arkansas House; now the speaker selects committee members, drawing equal numbers for each committee from each of the four congressional district caucuses.[78]

Rules allow the minority party a role in assigning its members to committees in roughly 40 percent of state legislative houses.[79] Some rules give complete power to the minority party. In Illinois, for example, "The Minority Leader shall appoint to all committees the members from the minority caucus and shall designate a Minority Spokesperson for each committee."[80] Rules in some other Houses only require that the minority leader be consulted. For instance, in the North Carolina House, "Before appointing members of committees, the Speaker shall consult with the Minority Leader."[81] Even where the appointing power is not bound to do so by the rules, they often follow the minority party leadership's assignment preferences for minority party members.[82] But if they are not compelled to follow them, appointing powers can choose to ignore minority party wishes when it suits their needs.

No limitations are placed on the appointing power's ability to make assignments in a majority of Houses. For instance, the rule in the Michigan House states, "The Speaker shall appoint all committees, except where the House shall otherwise order."[83] In these chambers, the appointing authority is constrained only by his or her political calculations, and leaders can use committee appointments with an eye toward encouraging member loyalty to party positions.[84]

Some chambers, however, do limit the appointing power's freedom to make committee appointments by requiring other considerations to be taken into account. One such constraint is a reliance on member seniority, where members who have served for longer have the opportunity to select the committees on which they serve. Assignment rules in most states do not mention seniority, but a few do.[85]

Seniority as an absolute rule is used only in the Arkansas and South Carolina Senates, although each employs it in a slightly different way. The Arkansas Senate divides its committees into three different groups. Senators are then assigned committees using something like a professional sports draft: "The most

TABLE 4.3 Standing Committee and Chair Appointment Powers in State Legislatures, 2017

Appointing Authority	Senate		Lower House	
	Committee Members[a]	Committee Chair	Committee Members	Committee Chair
Speaker	TN	TN	AL, AR, *AZ*, CA, *CO*, DE, FL, GA, ID, *IL*, IN, IA, KS, KY, LA, ME, MD, MA, MI, MN, MS, MO, MT, NV, *NH*, NM, NY, *OH*, OK, OR, RI, SC, SD, TN, TX (half), UT, VT, VA, WA, WV, WI, WY	AL, AZ, AR, CA, CO, DE, FL, GA, ID, IL, IN, IA, KS, KY, LA, ME, MD, MA, MI, MN, MS, MO, MT, NV, *NH*, NM, NY, *OH*, OK, OR, PA, RI, SD, TN, TX, UT, VT, VA, WA, WV, WI, WY
President	AZ, FL, HI, *IL*, KY, LA, ME, MD, MA, MS, *NH*, *OH*, OR, RI, TX, UT, WA, WV, WY	AZ, FL, HI, IL, KY, LA, ME, MD, MA, MS, *NH*, *OH*, OR, RI, TX, UT, WV, WY		
President pro tempore	DDE, ID, IN, *MO*, NY, *OK*, PA, SD	DDE, ID, IN, MO, NY, OK, PA, SD		
Majority leader	CO, *IA*, MI, *NV*, WI	CO, IA, MI, MN, NV, ND, WI		ND
Committee on committees	AAL, AK, CT, GA, MT, NE, NJ, NM, NC, ND, VT	AAL, AK, CT, GA, MT, NJ, NM, NC, VT, WA	AK, CT, NJ, NC, ND, PA	AK, CT, NJ, NC
Committee on rules	CA, KS, MN	CA, KS		
Chamber election	VA	NE		
Committee election				SC
Use of a seniority rule	AR, SC	AR, SC, VA	TX (half) MS (in part)	
Party caucuses			HI	HI

[a] States in italics allow significant minority party input into committee assignment decisions.
Sources: State legislative web pages and Council on State Governments, *The Book of the States, 2017 Edition* (Lexington, KY: Council on State Governments, 2017).

senior member of the Senate shall select first and shall choose either a Class "A", Class "B" or Class "C" Committee. The next senior member shall then choose a position on either a Class "A", Class "B" or Class "C" Committee. The seniority rotation procedure shall continue, without regard to party affiliation, until the member with the least seniority makes his or her selection. After the member with the least seniority makes his or her selection, the most senior member shall select his or her second Class "A", Class "B" or Class "C" Committee. The seniority rotation procedure shall continue until the member with the least seniority selects his or her second Class "A", Class "B" or Class "C" Committee."[86] In the South Carolina Senate, after it is determined how many positions are available for each party on each committee, the clerk calls members in order of their seniority and

> Each member, upon his or her name being called during the first call of the roll, shall select four (4) unfilled Standing Committees on which he or she wishes to serve (and shall also select at this same time a seat on any or all of the Ethics, Invitations and Interstate Cooperation Committees so long as a vacancy exists). Each member must select either the Finance or Judiciary Committee during the first call of the roll. When the prescribed number of seats provided for a particular party within a Standing Committee has been filled, the President shall announce that the seats available for either the Majority or Minority party are filled. When the roll is called for the second time, it shall be called in reverse order of continuous service and each member upon his or her name being called, may select one additional unfilled Standing Committee on which he or she wishes to serve.[87]

Seniority is applied in more limited ways in the Texas and Mississippi Houses.[88]

What is noteworthy about the rare uses of seniority at the state legislative level is that they differ almost completely with the use of seniority in the U.S. Congress. As will be noted below, to the extent that a seniority rule is followed in both the U.S. House and Senate, it pertains to who becomes a committee chair. Seniority is only one of many pieces of information that are used in making committee assignments in Congress.[89] In contrast, in a few state legislative chambers seniority dictates committee assignments.

Constraints other than seniority exist in the assignment process in some other chambers. The Alabama speaker makes all appointments, but, according to the rules, he or she "shall proportion, as reasonably as possible, committee appointments in a manner which is inclusive and reflects the racial diversity, gender, and political party affiliation of the members of the body. Political party affiliation and racial diversity should be considered in instances where at least ten members of the body are affiliated with a political party or are members of the same race."[90] In Minnesota, "A committee of the House must not have exclusive membership from one profession, occupation or vocation," so the agriculture committee cannot be composed entirely of farmers, the judiciary committee entirely of lawyers, or the education committee entirely of teachers.[91] (Typically, agriculture and judiciary committees are loaded with farmers and lawyers, respectively, in large part because of the expertise such members can impart to the institution.)[92] In several houses, the appointing authority is specifically directed to take into account member desires, as in the California Assembly, where, "In appointing Members to serve on committees, the Speaker shall consider the preferences of the Members."[93] Indeed, across state legislatures, member preferences are typically honored by those who make committee assignments.[94] This is to be expected because, as already noted, leaders retain their office only with the consent of those they lead. Irritating too many members with unwanted committee assignments might put a leader's job at risk. Even with the best of intentions, however, there are a limited number of preferred committee slots, creating more demand than can be satisfied. A former Vermont speaker who "enjoyed" absolute assignment power admitted, "I really disliked making committee assignments. It seemed no matter what I did, I couldn't avoid having thirty or more members furious at me because they had been 'dumped' into committees on which they didn't want to serve."[95]

Given the latitude that leaders typically enjoy in the committee appointment process, it would be easy to envision the creation of committees that are politically or ideologically unrepresentative of the larger House membership. In fact, most committees in state legislatures are representative of their parent house.[96] This suggests that committees are intended to provide the chamber with information and issue expertise rather than being designed to skew policies away from what the chamber's median legislator would accept. The few legislative committees that do not reflect the preferences of the larger chamber are likely to emerge in houses where committee assignment rules give considerable weight to member choices, member seniority is taken into account, or member committee property rights are observed. Representative committees are encouraged by rules that require parties to be proportionally represented and that give the minority party greater say on their members' committee assignments.[97]

Compared with the committee appointment process, fewer rules control the designation of committee chairs, as also shown in table 4.3. Committee chairs are commonly determined by the top leader. In most legislative chambers, as in both houses of Congress, committee chairs are reserved for majority party members. Obviously, when a bipartisan coalition takes control of a house, members from each party are typically named to top committee posts. But in a handful of legislative chambers, minority party members are traditionally designated to lead a few committees even in the absence of a bipartisan coalition. In the Texas House, for example, about a third of committee chairs were given to minority party Democrats in 2013.[98] And once in a while, the partisan monopoly is broken even in bodies without any history of such bipartisanship. In the Missouri House in 2011, three Democrats were given committee chairs by a staunchly Republican speaker.[99] Giving the minority party some committee chairs can, of course, buy the appointing power more friends and their goodwill, but it risks alienating majority party members who were denied the positions.

Unlike in Congress, where both houses still largely observe an unwritten seniority rule that the majority party member with the longest consecutive service on a committee automatically becomes its chair, seniority dictates who takes control of committees in only a few state legislative chambers. Explicit seniority rules are used in the Arkansas, South Carolina, and Virginia Senates.

But only the South Carolina Senate operates with a rule that is similar to those found in the two houses of Congress: "In the selection of the Chairman of the Standing Committees, the senior member of the Committee from the majority party, in terms of seniority within the Committee, shall be the Chairman of the Standing Committee." To keep too much power from being concentrated in the hands of the most senior members, senators are limited to chairing a single standing committee.[100] In the Arkansas and Virginia Senates, the most senior member of the majority party on a committee becomes its chair, but seniority is measured by service in the full body, not on the committee, so a senator could chair a committee without ever having served on it before.[101]

Where discretion is allowed, leaders can use the power to name chairs as a way to reward friends and punish enemies. As a New Jersey senator explained, "It's pretty simple. . . . In a battle for leadership, the winners usually give the key assignments to their supporters, and the people who were the strongest against them under most circumstances suffer the consequences." A senator on the losing side agreed, stating simply, "It's about payback."[102] Even the most unsophisticated lawmakers understand this reality.

Career Opportunity Types and Committee Membership and Leadership

As discussed in chapter 3, a legislative house can offer its members one of three different career opportunities. These different career types link up with the way legislative chambers are organized. Career legislatures, where members anticipate serving for many years, are bodies where seniority is apt to be more highly valued. Consequently, committee leaders and members of the most powerful committees are senior lawmakers. In contrast, springboard legislatures, where members look to use their current position as a quick route to higher office, prize seniority much less. Thus, legislators with little seniority gain access to positions of power much more quickly than they would in career bodies. Dead-end legislatures fall between the extremes of career legislatures and springboard legislatures. Because dead-end legislatures offer little incentive to stay or little opportunity to move up, lawmakers may not serve in the body for very long. But members of dead-end houses find it rational to invest power in more senior members who understand the legislative process and who are able to help less senior members achieve their legislative goals.[103]

The Value of Legislative Experience

Experience matters because the legislative process is, as will be documented in chapter 5, complicated. Lawmakers face a steep learning curve in educating themselves about byzantine rules and procedures.[104] In addition, the issues involved in public policymaking are complex. A beleaguered new member of the Texas House recounted, "It's kind of like being back in college, and every day you have a series of mini-seminars on various topics. . . . You'll have meetings with funeral directors and people about water and then the motorcycle people were in yesterday, and colleges and high schools and middle school, electricity, oil and gas. It's all over the map."[105] At the end of his first term as member of the Louisiana House one representative said in amazement about serving on the tax committee, "It was like drinking water from a fire hose. . . . Everything was coming at us."[106] A Vermont legislative leader revealed that at the conclusion of the legislative session he "went to a number of new members . . . and I said 'I want you to know that it's OK that you come to the conclusion that this is way harder than you thought it would be.' And every single one of them said, "It is way harder than I thought it would be.'"[107] After the conclusion of her first term in office, a young Hawaii representative had to be hospitalized for two weeks for "burnout and exhaustion from trying to 'do it all.'"[108]

Accordingly, a first-term member of the Florida House observed, "This is billed as a part-time job, but it's a full-time job getting adjusted to it."[109] And the adjustment period can be overwhelming. A Washington representative admitted, "My first term I spent looking at the ceiling, admiring the architecture."[110] Many new legislators must come to grips with the realities of how the system really works. A first-year member of the Iowa House confessed, "Initially, I was disappointed when I learned that floor debate is not where the decisions are made."[111] A colleague concurred, observing, "It's not like your high school textbook on how a bill gets passed. You might as well toss that out the window. I had this idea about these big, grand debates. . . . But already I'm learning that a lot of it goes on outside the chamber, out of the public eye. Some issues are decided before they come to the floor."[112]

New lawmakers have much to learn, and part of their socialization process occurs through hazing. Much of this behavior seems silly, such as the note purportedly from the governor handed to a new member of the Mississippi Senate. The message claimed that the governor had a close friend who was interested in the lawmaker's first bill and asked him "to call a Mr. L. E. Fant" to sidestep problems that might lead to a veto. The phone number was, of course, for the Jackson city zoo, and veteran legislators had a good laugh at their new colleague's expense.[113] A more common form of this rite of passage is to give a new member a difficult time on the initial bill he or she brings to the floor.[114] The first time a Texas senator spoke in support of a bill she authored, her colleagues inundated her with questions, most of them picayune. After she withstood the onslaught, the measure passed unanimously.[115]

Such hazing actually serves a purpose by reminding new members that they are just single members of a larger body that requires agreement among a majority or more to accomplish anything. In recent years, legislatures have become much more aware of the need to socialize and educate their new members; consequently, more than half of them have instituted formal orientation and training sessions.[116] During these meetings, veteran lawmakers share their experiences as a way to help bring their new colleagues up to speed.[117] A California Assembly speaker, for example, advised his recently elected colleagues, "Keep your mouths shut. Don't get out there and offer your opinion on every issue. Listen. Do your homework and do it again."[118] A Rhode Island Senate majority leader warned them to be humble in their efforts, because "you are going to be amazed to find that not everyone agrees with you."[119] Along these same lines, a

Nevada majority leader dampened his new colleagues' expectations, disclosing that "you won't change the world in one day, or one session."[120] The reason for such guidance is simple. As a veteran senator in New Jersey observed with only slight hyperbole, becoming a good legislator takes time: "You don't do it in your first four or five years. In your first three years, you're lucky to know where the bathroom is."[121]

Conclusion

Parties, leaders, and committees are central to the functioning of every state legislature, as they are in the U.S. Congress. But the particular configuration of each and the relationships among them differ across legislative chambers. In some houses, leaders dominate; in others, committees make the important decisions; and in still others, power is vested in party caucuses. Moreover, party, leadership, and committee structures and the powers they exercise can and do change over time. Understanding how parties, leaders, and committees are constituted and how they interact is critical to understanding how a legislative house as an organization operates. It is the context in which legislative decision-making occurs, and (as we will point out in subsequent chapters) the context is critical. Comprehending how the mix works in one legislative chamber, however, may provide only limited insight into the operations of other legislatures. For one thing, the division of seats between the parties may make a difference; in chambers where only one or two seats separate the majority from the minority party, leadership is likely to exert more control. The key thing to understand is that the relative power of leaders and committees is just that—relative. Circumstances change, lawmakers and leaders come and go, and norms such as seniority may erode or strengthen over time.

In the next chapter, we will see how the relationships among leaders, committees, and the rank-and-file members of the parties help define the legislative process. Again, just as there are substantial differences across legislatures in the roles played by parties, leaders, and committees, the rules under which legislation is considered also vary significantly. The complexity of the legislative process emphasizes the importance of the structures and players discussed in this chapter, each of which is invested with power as a means to help the legislature make decisions.

Chapter 5

The Legislative Process in the States

Sen. Carolyn McGinn, R-Sedgwick, left, chair of the Senate Ways and Means committee, along with Sen. Laura Kelly, D-Topeka, and Sen. Jim Denning, R-Overland Park, right, listened Tuesday, January 30, 2018, as proponents and opponents of a bill that would halt KanCare 2.0. gave testimony before the committee. Thad Allton/*The Topeka Capital-Journal* via AP.

Diagrams showing "how a bill gets passed" are commonplace. Such schematics outline various formal steps in getting a bill passed into law. Unfortunately, these presentations only take us so far in gaining a real understanding of the legislative process. At the outset, we need to recognize that these sorts of diagrams do not give the full picture. Indeed, they are usually presented in such a way that readers are left to infer that the process is straightforward and rational, almost sterile. In fact, it is an accurate description of the process that only some bills follow. Typically, these are minor bills making technical adjustments to existing laws or bills on which there is overwhelming agreement. In most legislatures, these measures account for half—perhaps three-fourths—of all enactments. But for bills involving conflict and disagreement—that is, almost any legislation of political significance—the process involves many more twists and turns than textbook diagrams suggest.

To put it another way, there is the *textbook* version of the process, and then there is the *contextual* version of the process. Both are necessary to gain a full understanding of how a legislature operates. The textbook version (which we explain in this chapter) details the formal steps in the process. These formal steps are part of the "rules of the game" that must be understood and mastered if we are to understand how bills are passed. But the rules do not operate in a vacuum.

The legislative game involves many players—legislators, staffers, the governor, political parties, bureaucrats, lobbyists, and many others. The relationships among the multitude of players largely define the context in which lawmaking occurs. And this is just as important to understand as the rules. Do the leaders of the House and Senate get along? Is one political party dominant in the state, or is there a competitive party system in which both parties have a chance to hold legislative control? How popular is the governor? Is Senator A still angry with Senator B? Is someone going to challenge Representative X in the next primary election? Which lawmakers are retiring, and which are running for another office? These and other issues provide the context in which the process plays out. We will discuss contextual factors in chapter 6.

In this chapter, we begin by examining the broad differences in rules and legislative procedures across the states. Second, we review the different types of bills—and different procedural tracks—that are found in legislatures. Third, we present the basic "textbook" version of the steps in the legislative process (recognizing that the contextual version is also important). Fourth, we discuss the dimension of time as it applies to legislatures. Fifth, we explore the appropriations process as a special subset of legislative bill making. We conclude this chapter with an initial look at some of the contextual factors that affect legislative decision-making as a prelude to a more detailed discussion in chapter 6.

Variation across the States

The process by which a bill gets passed is not quite the same across the fifty state legislatures or even between chambers in the same legislature. Although the basic procedure and purpose of the process is roughly comparable in all states, each legislature has some quirks or oddities that have developed over time and make its process at least a little distinctive. For example, in the South Dakota legislature, a move to "defer the bill to the 41st Legislative Day" is a common motion. Because there are only forty days in a legislative session in South Dakota, this motion effectively kills the bill. It is a prevalent motion in standing committees; probably 30 to 40 percent of all bills sent to committees are deferred to the forty-first legislative day, and thus no further action is taken on them.

It is important to appreciate that legislative "rules and resources do matter in systematic ways" and that the variations in these rules affect how power is distributed in a legislative chamber.[1] These differences can be important for at least two reasons: first, they can mean the difference between a bill passing and not passing, and second, they can determine where the "tipping point" for passage is located. For example, in Illinois, until the end of May, bills require the usual simple majority for passage. After May 31, bills require a three-fifths (60 percent) majority in order to pass. Thus, late in the session the person who provides the tipping point (what political scientists call the "pivot point") is no longer the "median vote" (the fifty-first legislator in a one-hundred-member House), but is someone a bit further away from the median (the sixtieth legislator in a one-hundred-member House) voting in support. Depending on the partisan distribution in the chamber, this means the pivot point may shift to someone in the minority party. To put this another way, votes late in the session may require a bipartisan coalition in order to pass. It should be evident that this rule may affect the flow of legislation in the session. While this rule applies to virtually all bills in Illinois, some states employ a similar rule but only for budget bills.

Table 5.1 shows the number of bills introduced and the percentage passed in a recent two-year period. We include the bills in both regular sessions of the biennium. We can make several observations about these data. First, there is a wide range in the number of bill introductions across the states, from 572 in Wyoming to more than 31,000 in New York. New York, however, is an extreme case, with nearly twice as many bill introductions as the next-most-prolific state (New Jersey, with almost 16,000 introductions). But four other states (Illinois, Minnesota, Massachusetts, and Texas) have at least 6,000 introductions each. The median is about 2,600 bill introductions; the two states closest to the median are Iowa and Tennessee.

Given the thousands of bills introduced, for the most part, state legislatures pass relatively few of them. Only eleven states passed more than one thousand bills each. But a more appropriate measure is the *proportion* of bills passed, and, as figure 5.1 indicates, most legislatures are not easy marks in this regard. In about half of the states, less than 25 percent of the bills that are introduced become law. Clearly, most bills die along the way.

This is not, however, the case everywhere. In a few states, most legislation that is introduced is passed; in 2015–2016, these states were Arkansas, Colorado, Delaware, Idaho, Nevada, North Dakota, South Dakota, Utah, and Wyoming.[2] These are all states with small-sized or medium-sized populations and short sessions. And except for Arkansas and Delaware, they are all Northern Plains or Rocky Mountain states. But rather than geography, the passage of a high proportion of bills in these states is more likely the result of specific rules and operating procedures. Colorado, for example, limits each legislator to five bill introductions per session—a rule that encourages lawmakers to be selective about what they introduce, focusing on only proposals they think have a decent chance to pass. The Wyoming Senate limits each senator to seven bill introductions; the Florida House has a limit of six bills for a regular session.[3]

TABLE 5.1 **Bill Introductions and Enactments, 2015–2016 Biennium**

State	Total Bills Introduced in 2015–2016	Total Bills Enacted into Law, 2015–2016	Bills Vetoed	Percent Total Bills Enacted into Law 2015–2016)
Alabama	2215	634	3	28
Alaska	615	110	6	18
Arizona	2410	698	14	29
Arkansas	2371	1589	0	67
California	5140	1615	266	31
Colorado	1368	751	5	55
Connecticut	4318	500	10	11
Delaware	1075	628	1	58
Florida	3195	499	10	15
Georgia	2237	635	317	28
Hawaii	5281	497	16	9
Idaho	1080	724	6	67
Illinois	10364	3506	44	34
Indiana	3068	474	2	15
Iowa	2447	287	2	12
Kansas	1260	217	4	17
Kentucky	1384	267	7	19
Louisiana	3057	1015	23	33
Maine	1880	622	238	33
Maryland	5051	1329	195	26
Massachusetts	14015	1395	5	10
Michigan	3365	832	9	25
Minnesota	7673	187	6	5
Mississippi	5274	739	5	14
Missouri	3932	269	42	7
Montana	1187	457	52	38
Nebraska	1155	505	10	44
Nevada	1013	556	7	55
New Hampshire	1946	608	23	31
New Jersey	15923	498	114	3
New Mexico	1915	166	42	9
New York	31514	1108	222	3
North Carolina	1985	426	3	21
North Dakota	854	484	1	56
Ohio	1004	180	3	18
Oklahoma	3852	760	22	20
Oregon	2895	972	0	33
Pennsylvania	3860	214	16	5

State	Total Bills Introduced in 2015–2016	Total Bills Enacted into Law, 2015–2016	Bills Vetoed	Percent Total Bills Enacted into Law 2015–2016)
Rhode Island	4871	1444	7	29
South Carolina	1765	308	3	17
South Dakota	845	494	10	58
Tennessee	2837	1026	1	36
Texas	6276	1323	42	21
Utah	1936	886	7	41
Vermont	1153	186	2	16
Virginia	5783	1536	27	26
Washington	3616	563	14	15
West Virginia	3503	538	46	15
Wisconsin	3660	748	7	20
Wyoming	572	324	3	56
Total	**199,995**	**36,329**	**1,918**	**18%**

Note: Figures are for bills only and do not include resolutions and are for regular sessions in two consecutive years, not including any special sessions.

Source: Council of State Governments, Lexington, Kentucky, *The Book of the States*, 2016 and 2017 editions, table 3.19. Figures for Idaho and Alaska are corrected from those that appear in *The Book of the States*. Figures for Delaware, Illinois, Iowa, Massachusetts, and South Carolina are from 2013–2014 due to missing data for 2015 and 2016. Figures for states with odd-year elections (Louisiana, Mississippi, New Jersey, Virginia) are from 2014–2015. Tennessee figures are for 2016 only due to missing data in 2015.

Such limits are typically dictated by chamber rules, and the limits may change from one year to the next.

In Idaho, bills are not automatically introduced; rather, a standing committee must approve them for printing. This process means that each year, three hundred to four hundred proposed bills are never printed and therefore never formally introduced. Some of these bills are simply held by the sponsor, but many are not introduced because the committee refuses to print the proposal. Thus, although table 5.1 indicates that Idaho passed 67 percent of the *bills that were introduced*, the legislature actually passed a considerably lower percentage of the *total proposals that were drafted*. In other words, about 25 percent to 30 percent of the proposals were eliminated before they were formally introduced. Obviously, this gatekeeping function grants standing committees in Idaho extraordinary power.

State constitutions in North Dakota and South Dakota place strict limits on the number of days the legislature can meet (sixty days total over a two-year period in North Dakota; seventy-five days total in South Dakota). Wyoming also has constitutional limits (sixty days in a two-year session). Consequently, the high proportion of bills passed in these legislatures does not reflect a permissive environment in which lawmakers are oblivious; it is more likely the case

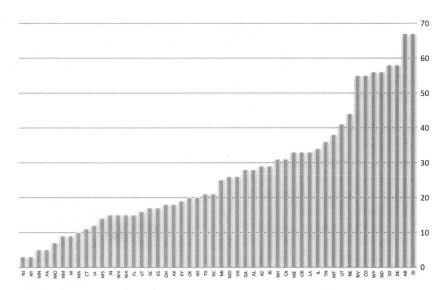

FIGURE 5.1 Percent of Bill Introductions That Are Enacted, 2015–2016

that the rules and procedures keep legislators focused on bills with legitimate prospects for passage.

This is not the case everywhere. In New York, many bills that have no chance of passing are introduced. As one analysis of New York politics observes, "Many bills are introduced with no real legislative intent. . . . A bill that does not pass in one session must be reintroduced in the next or it will be dropped. A large proportion of those that fail will show up again. . . . One of the first functions of a legislator's staff at the beginning of the session is to dust off last year's bills for introduction."[4] Lawmakers in New Jersey behave similarly. One report notes that the state legislature is "notorious, much like New York, for re-filing legislation. It is a common practice for legislators to reintroduce all their bills from the previous session. . . . This results in a decent amount of legislative clutter."[5]

In Massachusetts, citizens have a right to write their own bills and to petition their legislators to introduce them on their behalf.[6] This procedure inflates the number of bill introductions, the vast majority of which have almost no shot at passing. Indeed, Massachusetts lawmakers can signal that they do not actually support a bill they are introducing on behalf of a constituent by indicating they are bringing it "by request."[7]

At the extremes of table 5.1 (either very high or very low levels of bill introductions), an inverse relationship generally exists between the number of bills introduced and the proportion passed. That is, all the states where large numbers of bills are introduced show low bill passage percentages. Thus, the states with the highest number of introductions—New York (thirty-one thousand bills), New Jersey (almost sixteen thousand) and Massachusetts (thirteen to fourteen thousand)—have enactment rates of 3 percent, 3 percent, and 10 percent, respectively. In contrast, states with few bill introductions tend to have much higher enactment rates.

But this inverse relationship between introductions and enactments appears to hold only at the extremes. For the rest of the states, other variables take primacy. These variables include the number of local bills (proposals that apply only to a specific locality and not statewide) introduced, the number of appropriation (budget) bills, unified or divided party control of the legislature, and whether carry-over provisions exist. Each of these variables will be discussed in turn.

In a few states, especially those with a "local act" system of local government chartering, a good deal of municipal, county, and other local jurisdiction business is conducted through the legislature. In Alabama, for example, the House has nine standing committees that are each dedicated to local legislation for a specific county, for example the "Baldwin County Legislation Committee."[8] Much of this local legislation is noncontroversial, and as long as local lawmakers are supportive, the bill will pass without much dissent. In some states, local legislation comprises a hefty slice of the workload—perhaps several hundred bills. In some years, more than half the bills introduced in Alabama involve local government issues.[9] One recent study reported that about 60 percent of the bills introduced in the lower houses in Georgia and Louisiana were local bills, as were more than 30 percent in North Carolina and Ohio.[10]

The ways in which appropriation bills are handled vary by state. In some, such as California, Massachusetts, and Wisconsin, the entire state budget is typically handled in a single omnibus measure, while in Minnesota all the state agency budgets are rolled into about a half-dozen large appropriation bills. In other states, each individual department or office has a separate budget bill, so there may be dozens of different budget bills. Some have even more. Arkansas averages several hundred appropriations bills, and Idaho usually has about one hundred budget bills each session. In most cases, the appropriations have been worked out in committee and between leadership in the two chambers before the measures are sent to the floor, so budget bills have a high degree of success on the floor. Thus, a legislature in which the appropriations process is divided into dozens or hundreds of bills is apt to have a higher overall "batting average" when it comes to determining the overall passage rate of legislation. In a few states, omnibus bills extend beyond budget items to include substantive policies. Minnesota and Connecticut are well known for rolling dozens of policy bills into omnibus legislation. Toward the end of the 2018 legislative session in Minnesota, the governor vetoed a 989-page bill (SF 3656) that, according to one lawmaker, would take about thirty hours for an average reader to plow through.[11] This omnibus bill contained both budget funding and policy items for a range of issues from insurance coverage to transporting sugar beets to guidelines for public funding of art projects to cosmetology licensing requirements. (All of this was in the measure despite the fact that the Minnesota constitution mandates that bills have a single subject.) Thus, in Minnesota it is not unusual to have dozens, or even hundreds of small bills rolled into a few omnibus bills at the end of the session to be negotiated among the governor, the House, and the Senate. Such measures, known around the state capitol as "garbage bills," are now so common that the term *garbage bill* is referenced in the frequently asked question (FAQ) section on the Minnesota Legislature's website.[12]

There are other legislatures that operate in a similar fashion. Recently, the New York legislature, often in concert with the governor, has produced a "Big Ugly," a single bill that incorporates a number of disparate policies.[13] Obviously, if twenty or thirty small bills that were introduced separately are eventually rolled together into a single omnibus bill and passed, the statistics on bill passage rates can distort the actual number of bills passed in the session.

Party control of the legislature matters as well. If the Republicans control one house and the Democrats the other, bills introduced in one house are more likely to die when they reach the other house. A good example is New York, where historically the Democrats have controlled the Assembly and routinely pass some bills knowing they will be killed in the Senate, where the Republicans usually hold the majority. The same procedure works in reverse—the Senate passes some bills knowing they have no chance of getting through the Assembly. But members from both parties can claim credit and score points with their partisan backers even though they realize the bills one chamber passes have little chance of actually becoming law.

About half of state legislatures make use of a "carry-over provision" between the first and second years of a biennial legislative session. A carry-over provision stipulates that a bill that was not passed in the first year of a session stays alive in the second year of that same session. Thus, if a bill passed the Senate, was sent to the House, and was awaiting a committee hearing when the legislature adjourned, it could be picked up in the process and considered when the legislature reconvened the following year. In other words, the bill would not have to be reintroduced in the first chamber and forced to start all over again. The specifics of how these provisions work varies by state.[14] States with carry-over provisions may have a higher passage rate because the same bill does not have to be reintroduced.[15] Of course, all bills must start anew following a general election because the new legislature is not the same one that previously considered them.

Other procedural rules can make a difference as well. Some states, for example, impose strict deadlines on when bills may be introduced during a session. Such rules tend to limit the number of bills introduced, again impacting the percentage that get passed.[16]

Finally, it is worth noting that analyzing passage rates is just one aspect of an overall assessment of the legislative process. It is probably true that bills today are longer and more complicated than they used to be, a phenomenon also associated with congressional legislation. Moreover, we know that some bills are much more important than others. And this leads us to the recognition that there are actually different tracks that legislation may follow.

The Three Tracks of the Legislative Process: Bills That Die, Bills That Fly, and Bills That Crawl

Many observers have sought to explain the legislative process by analogy. Making laws has been compared to sausage making, the "torturous upriver runs of spawning fish," a casino with multiple games of chance, and the work of an improvisational jazz band, to name just a few.[17]

Perhaps the legislative process is best described as having at least three different processes, or tracks. These tracks correspond to different types of legislation. As indicated in table 5.1, most bills do not make it through the process to become law. They die, and they usually do so in committee. These bills are like boxcars that are pulled off onto rail spurs, where they sit for the remainder of the session.[18]

In contrast, of the bills that do pass, most encounter little or no opposition and pass easily. As Frank Smallwood, a political scientist and former state legislator, noted years ago, "It is important to realize that very few of these bills dealt with the creation of new statutory law from scratch. Instead, the overwhelming majority involved incremental amendments to existing state laws."[19] They are often referred to as "technical" or "housekeeping" measures, meaning that they make only small changes in the current body of law. Take, for example, House Bill 476, "an Act empowering each county to create regulations for the maintenance of for-profit cemeteries," and the route it followed through the Delaware General Assembly. HB 476 was introduced in the Delaware House on June 20, 2018, was reported favorably by the Administration Committee on June 27, passed the House on a floor vote of 40 to 0, and passed on the Senate floor 20 to1 on July 1. It took a mere twelve days to pass both chambers. Only one lawmaker voted against it.[20] Such noncontroversial bills fly along the legislative tracks like express trains. They are not unusual. In 2018, 59 percent of the bills that passed the Virginia General Assembly did so unanimously—not a single "nay" vote was cast in either chamber.[21]

A much smaller but generally more significant group of bills are those on which legislators (and no doubt others) have differing opinions. These bills often involve contentious issues and represent a significant shift in thinking about policy options. In other words, they involve changing the status quo in some meaningful way. And that is precisely the problem for such a bill's supporters. Changing the status quo means changing the relative costs and benefits for some number of people and groups. There is a sort of inherent inertia in the legislative process that must be overcome. Even what seems like a relatively simple matter can meet resistance. Take, for example, mandatory seat belt laws. Today, for most people, the need for such laws seems obvious. But when seat belt bills were first proposed, they encountered resistance from many quarters. Some citizens saw them as a government invasion of privacy. Police recognized that enforcement would be difficult and time-consuming. Other people were concerned about the nature of punishment for noncompliance: Would it mean a fine? A suspension of the driver's license? A night in jail?[22]

Many bills involve issues more controversial than seat belts. On such matters, there is enough opposition to change that it makes the crafting of significant public policy a difficult and artful endeavor. Here, there is no fast track, but rather a slow, winding route that seems always to be uphill, working against the inertia of the status quo. And often, even if the legislative train makes it to the final station, it will not be composed of quite the same set of cars that began the journey. Such bills often require the sponsors to compromise with opponents in order to assemble a winning coalition. Amendments are added and provisions deleted like boxcars being switched in and out in an effort to find the right combination to pull the bill through. Sometimes it takes several years to find the right combination for passage. Taking such a "long view" does not come easily in legislatures operating under two-year or four-year electoral cycles.

A special case of a bill that almost always crawls is the budget. The precise way the budget is crafted differs from state to state, as shown in table 5.2. Twenty states pass a biennial (two-year) budget; the rest pass annual budgets.[23] In most states, such as Tennessee and Maryland, the governor plays the key role because the legislature is largely reacting to the parameters established in the executive budget. In other states, such as Idaho and Colorado, the legislature plays a significant independent role, often ignoring the governor's budget proposal. As noted earlier, some states produce a single, massive appropriation bill—usually known as the "omnibus budget bill"—but in others, the budget is set through dozens of smaller appropriation bills (often a separate budget for each state agency).

But regardless of the differences that may exist, the budget process is the same in all states in one aspect: it is the one piece of legislation that must be passed. The phrase, *must be passed*, requires some explanation. In truth, states can usually continue to operate with maintenance-level spending even if the legislature and governor have not approved a budget for the new fiscal year. After all, Illinois went more than two years (2015–2017) without an approved budget

TABLE 5.2 State Budget Cycles

Budget Type	States
Annual Budget (30 States)	AL, AK, AZ, CA, CO, DE, FL, GA, ID, IL, IA, KS, LA, MD, MA, MI, MS, MO, NJ, NM, NY, OK, PA, RI, SC, SD, TN, UT, VT, WV
Annual Session, Biennial Budget (16 States)	AR, CT, HI, IN, KY, ME, MN, NE, NH, NC, OH, OR, VA, WA, WI, WY
Biennial Session, Biennial Budget (4 States)	MT, NV, ND, TX

Source: National Association of State Budget Officers, *Budget Processes in the States* (Washington DC, 2015), 8–15.

and Pennsylvania's 2016 budget impasse lasted almost a year. Both states continued to operate, but only under serious fiscal stress, as many vendors were not paid and some state universities and local governments went without their share of state revenues. Thus, we can say that the budget bill must pass because the state government (and often local governments such as school districts) cannot fully function without the funds appropriated through it. Appropriations is such a central function of the legislative process that, in many states, the legislature is likely to adjourn within days of the budget bill's passage. We will have more to say about the budget process later in this chapter.

Most of the following discussion will concentrate on the third track—the legislative process as it applies to the bills on which there is substantial disagreement. This may be a small subset of all bills, but these are almost always the ones that generate media interest, that affect some significant component of the population, and that have real consequences beyond "technical" or "housekeeping" matters. In terms of political significance, these are the bills that carry the freight.

Steps in the Legislative Process

Some years ago, the National Conference of State Legislatures published a report on "How the Legislative Process Works." It concluded that "There is only one generalization about the legislative process in the 50 states that requires no disclaimer—every state does things differently than every other state. The lawmaking procedure is never precisely the same in all 50 states, or for that matter, in the legislative chambers of the same state."[24] That characterization is accurate. But it is also true that, despite quirks and oddities, there are some general principles that apply everywhere.

For instance, the American legislative process is designed to be deliberative and slow. Several organizational and procedural features are specifically intended to promote this, including three-readings rules, standing committee systems, reconsideration rules, and (except for in Nebraska) bicameralism. The process described here is a generic model—a few of the stages may vary in detail from one legislature to the next.[25] This is true, for example, of "three-readings rules"—they do not necessarily appear in all legislatures. A few states actually require only two readings.[26]

Introduction and First Reading

As discussed in Politics under the Domes 5.1, the ideas for bills come from many sources. The governor typically outlines a few in a state-of-the-state address at the outset of the legislative session. Some are requested by administrative agencies. Many bill ideas come from interest groups. Others are suggested by constituents and a few are devised by the lawmakers themselves. Regardless of who develops the idea, a bill is eventually written. In some cases, an interest group may draw up an initial draft, or the legislator or his or her personal staff might develop a proposal, but most of the time staff attorneys who work for the legislature draft bills. In some states, the process differs. In Connecticut, a legislator proposes a bill by writing a brief summary of its intent. Bills are only written in full statutory language at the request of legislative committees.[27] Regardless of who draws up the original version, a bill must be sponsored and introduced by a legislator. (But as is often the case with the states, this generalization has some exceptions: Under certain conditions, the governor in Alaska and the governor or Supreme Court chief justice in Oregon can introduce legislation without a legislative sponsor.)

Drafts become bills when they are "dropped" or "placed in the hopper"—that is, given to the clerk of the chamber, who assigns an identification number (e.g., H1000 for a House bill, S1000 for a Senate bill). The bill is then introduced and "read" for the first time. In reality, the bill is normally not read in its entirety. More likely, the bill number, sponsor, and bill title are read. The bill title is actually a synopsis of the measure and its intent and identifies the relevant section or sections of the state code of laws.

Referral to Standing Committee

For several reasons, the committee stage is typically a critical phase in the legislative process. Because so many bills are introduced, legislatures divide up the workload for reviewing them by creating a standing committee system. As discussed in chapter 4, the organization of these committees is not the same from one state to another. But typically, each chamber will have somewhere between ten and thirty standing committees, most of which deal with a specific subject area (e.g., Business and Commerce Committee, Education Committee, Transportation Committee). In most chambers, each legislator is assigned to about three committees and each committee has perhaps ten to fifteen members. But there are divergences in how this works across the states.

Because a different array of legislators sits on each committee, the ideological position and policy preferences of one committee may differ from those of other committees. They may also be different from the overall array of preferences of the chamber. Thus, it can make a difference which committee receives a particular bill. Although one committee might be predisposed to hold and kill a particular bill, another committee might choose to act favorably on it. And although different committees have jurisdiction over different topics, it is not always obvious to which committee a specific bill should be referred.

POLITICS UNDER THE DOMES

"There Ought to Be a Law," or Why Legislators Introduce Bills

State legislators introduce some two hundred thousand bills every two years. Where are the ideas for all those measures generated? And given the slim odds that any one of them will get enacted into law, why are so many of them introduced?

First, it is important to understand that lawmakers conceive few of the proposals contained in the legislation they author. Rather than acting as policy innovators, legislators act as policy entrepreneurs. They scan the political horizon looking for ideas that interest them. As an Iowa senator recently confessed about a measure determining how long rural students could be permitted to ride school buses each day, "This bill was not the bright idea of any of the legislators in this room. This bill was brought to us."

Second, lawmakers have many different motivations for introducing legislation; consequently, there are many kinds of bills. Obviously, some measures, such as those involving appropriations, are routine matters the legislature must address every year or two. Other pieces of legislation are developed by the executive branch to deal with administrative matters or local governments to address issues pertinent to them. Still others are drafted by lobbyists or organizations such as the American Legislative Exchange Council (ALEC) to promote the interests of those they represent.

There are, however, many additional motivations for lawmakers to introduce bills:

There ought to be a law: State legislators, like most Americans, get exasperated by things. Unlike the rest of us, they are in a position where they can directly do something about it. As a California legislator acknowledged in regard to his authorship of bills, "You get mad and you want to make change. . . . I found that's what motivates me." Accordingly, an aggrieved Washington senator filed a bill to require employers to pay to fly an employee business class for long-distance business trips, explaining, "I got to thinking about the fact that my employer has to supply me with an ergonomically sound chair. But if they ask me to go to Washington, DC, they can stuff me in the back of the airplane." A Florida senator, stuck in a traffic jam and irritated by drivers cutting in front of him, literally thought to himself, "There ought to be a law," and proceeded to write a bill to require police to issue tickets to "me-first" drivers who cut off other motorists.

That's a good idea: Lawmakers occasionally stumble across ideas that strike them as worth pursuing. When an Oregon senator met with a community college political science class, the students suggested a special tax break for working students. As one of them recalled, the senator "liked the idea, got out his cell phone and called into legal counsel to have it drafted for us."

To take a political stand: Most minority party members realize that the bills they introduce face long odds. Still, they propose measures as a means of putting their policy preferences on record. As a minority party member in Georgia noted, "It's important for us to introduce and work on passing legislation we think would benefit the state to at least demonstrate to those we represent what exactly it is that we are fighting for."

Constituent requests: Legislators often introduce bills that have been proposed by their constituents. Indeed, a Wyoming representative admits, "Almost all of my legislation comes from constituent requests." A Utah senator observed that "Each legislator has to decide how responsive he or she will be to the people who elected them. . . . I choose to open bill files when people bring me an issue that they are deeply concerned about." In many cases, introducing a bill to make the constituent happy is all that matters to the lawmaker; getting the measure passed is somewhat beside the point.

Personal policy expertise and interests: As shown in chapter 3, legislators come from a variety of occupational backgrounds and they often draw on their personal experiences for policy proposals. An Alabama representative, for example, acknowledged, "I am one of these horrible lowlifes in our society commonly referred to as an attorney, so I often bring a number of these bills that I think will improve the criminal justice process."

Personal convictions: Some bills are introduced not because their authors think that they are politically popular, but because they believe the policies they contain are morally correct. In 2018, Idaho representative Melissa Wintrow introduced legislation that would have "prohibited anyone convicted of misdemeanor domestic assault from owning, possessing or purchasing firearms for a period of two years." The idea had been brought to her by two young women who had lost their mother to domestic violence. In introducing the bill to her colleagues on the House floor, Wintrow said "We need to stand for families and for the women and children who are being murdered. . . . I've never believed more strongly in anything, and I've never been more nervous in presenting a bill—because there's a lot at stake." After the measure failed to advance she admitted to being "devastated," but vowed to introduce it again in the next legislative session.

Policy incubation: Legislators occasionally introduce a measure on an issue knowing that it is unlikely to resonate with their colleagues. Facing certain defeat, they still put the bill before the legislature simply to initiate a conversation. Taking such a long-term perspective is known as "policy incubation." As an Iowa senator acknowledged after proposing a bill allowing for doctor-assisted suicide, "My purpose is to start the dialogue. I have no illusions about its prospects for passage this year." A Georgia representative known for tackling controversial issues explained his perspective on policy incubation this way: "In molding opinion, it takes time, a lot of patience and the willingness to [introduce] a lot of bills. . . . It might not be until the third or fourth year that something germinates."

Policy fads: In September 2013 a Maryland second-grader was suspended from school for having gnawed a pastry into the shape of a gun and then pointing it at his classmates. This incident got a great deal of media attention, and a number of lawmakers seized the opportunity to exploit it for their political benefit. Consequently, in 2014 legislators in Florida, Missouri, and Oklahoma were given the opportunity to pass "Pop-Tart" bills that would allow schoolchildren to play with pretend guns without facing punishment.

Media attention: Sometimes, just threatening to introduce a bill can get a lawmaker media attention, something many of them crave. Following the 2016 presidential election an Iowa representative announced he would introduce a "suck it up buttercup" bill that would target any state university that spent "taxpayer dollars on grief counseling for students upset" by Donald Trump's victory. Within days he had given sixty-five interviews on the proposed legislation with news outlets in nineteen states. He admitted that he was "absolutely flabbergasted at how much attention it's gotten." When the lawmaker later learned that no state university was using state tax dollars for additional counseling services, he decided against actually introducing the measure.

Cheap political points: Bills are occasionally written to score cheap and easy political points with supporters. When a lawsuit threatened the tradition of a Christian prayer at the beginning of Rowan County, North Carolina, commission meetings, two representatives from that county introduced a bill stating, "The North Carolina General Assembly does not recognize federal court rulings which prohibit and otherwise regulate the State of North Carolina, its public schools, or any political subdivisions of the State from making laws respecting an establishment of religion." The measure had glaring constitutional flaws, but the lawmakers who authored it knew many of their voters likely approved.

Political satire: In 2017, Texas Representative Jessica Farrar introduced House Bill 4260, a measure designed to "encourage men to remain 'fully abstinent' and only allow the 'occasional masturbatory emissions inside health care and medical facilities' because these were the 'best way to ensure men's health.'" She was motivated to author the legislation because she was "fed up with the various legislative bills introduced by men addressing women's healthcare."

Tit-for-tat: When a Maryland delegate from the Washington, D.C., suburbs introduced a bill to ban black bear hunting, her colleagues in the far western reaches of the state were furious. To them, black bears were nuisances and they did not appreciate a metropolitan-area delegate who did not have her garbage cans regularly violated telling them how the animals should be treated. As a response, one western delegate proposed a bill to trap bears and release them around the rest of the state. The delegate knew his measure had no chance to pass, but he fumed, "I'm trying to make the point that the people who put bills in for someone else's area, they don't live with bears, they don't understand the situation. They think they are cuddly and cute with names like Fuzzy and Boo Boo."

A fourth-grade class requests it: Fourth-grade classes often study state government, and this leads many of their teachers to suggest proposing a bill as a class project. In 2014, for example, fourth-grade classes prevailed on New York lawmakers to introduce legislation to name the wood frog the state amphibian and yogurt the state snack; Michigan lawmakers had to choose between competing measures developed by different fourth-grade classes to name a state amphibian—one class pushed for the spring peeper frog, the other Blanchard's cricket frog; Utah legislators were lobbied by a fourth-grade class to name the quaking aspen the state tree, and Missouri fourth-graders pushed their legislature to name jumping jacks the state exercise.

Self-interest: In 2018 a California senator introduced a measure to "allow sitting legislators and congressmen who hold inactive licenses as certified public accountants to continue using the title." At the time the measure would only apply to the senator and to the U.S. representative who had asked him to introduce it. The lawmaker said he didn't know if he would use the CPA designation again if the bill became law. It passed in the Senate, but it did not come up for a vote in the Assembly.

Legislators see lawmaking as their primary function. Still, at times people may wonder about some of the legislation they propose. A Montana governor complained, "Some of these legislators, they draft bills just to get an effect from the people. . . . And unfortunately, it kind of makes some of them look bat-crap crazy." But as a Washington senator noted for introducing many measures rationalized, "You get elected to legislate and introduce bills. What are you here for, to sit?"

Sources: Jill Carroll Andrade, "Keeping in Touch," *State Legislatures* (February 2006): 29–31; *Athens Banner-Herald*, "Lawmakers Differ on Lawmaking: Active or Passive," February 17, 2002; Joanne Beck, "Byron-Bergan Fourth-Graders Tout Yogurt in Albany," *New York Daily News*, June 13, 2014; Steve Bousquet, "Gov. Rick Scott Signs Bills on Vouchers, Guns and Sports Stadiums," *Miami Herald*, June 20, 2014; Michelle Breidenbach, "NYS Senate Approves Skaneateles Fourth-Graders' Request to Make Wood Frog State Amphibian," Syracuse.com, June 10, 2014, http://www.syracuse.com/news/index.ssf/2014/06/nys_senate_approves_skaneateles_fourth_graders_request_to_make_wood_frog_state_a.html; Madeleine Brown, "Quaking Aspen a Step Closer to Becoming Utah's State Tree," *Deseret News*, February 10, 2014; Kelly David Burke, "Montana Governor: State Bills Makes GOP Look 'Bat-Crap Crazy,'" http://www.foxnews.com/politics/2011/03/23/montana-governor-state-bills-makes-gop-look-bat-crap-crazy/; Jeff Charis-Carlson, "Kaufmann Won't Introduce 'Suck It Up Buttercup' Bill," *Iowa City Press-Citizen*, January 6, 2017; Mary C. Curtis, "A State Religion? What's Next, North Carolina, Secession?" *Washington Post*, April 4, 2013; Tim Engle, "Jump to It: Missouri Now Has an Official State Exercise," *Kansas City Star*, July 10, 2014; Tim Fitzsimons, "The 0.1 Percent: State Lawmaker Sam Park Looks to Build a Diverse Coalition in Georgia," NBCnews.com, October 12, 2018, https://www.nbcnews.com/feature/nbc-out/0-1-percent-state-lawmaker-sam-park-looks-build-diverse-n919521; Andrew Garber, "1 State Senator, 2 Months, 99 Bills," *Seattle Times*, March 3, 2007; Madalyn Gunnell, "Utah Lawmakers Filed a Record 1,359 Bills This Year—One of Them to Shame Lawmakers Who Create Too Many," *Salt Lake Tribune*, March 5, 2018; Alexander Hertel-Fernandez, "ALEC has Tremendous Influence in State Legislatures. Here's Why," *Washington Post*, December 9, 2013; Debbie Howlett, "Legislators Target Road Rudeness," *USA Today*, May 4, 2004; *Iowa City Press-Citizen*, "Iowa Bill Would Legalize Doctor-Assisted Suicides," January 30, 1992; Molly Jackman, "ALEC's Influence over Lawmaking in State Legislatures," Brookings Institution, December 6, 2013; Alexei Koseff, "This Law Would Affect Just Two People in California, Including Its Author," *Sacramento Bee*, May 9, 2018; Mike Lear, "House Approves 'Pop Tart' Bill to Protect Kids Pretending to Have Weapons in School," Missourinet, April 11, 2014, http://www.missourinet.com/2014/04/11/house-approves-pop-tart-bill-to-protect-kids-pretending-to-have-weapons-in-school/; Brooke A. Lewis, "New Bill Takes Aim at Men's Masturbation Habits," *Houston Chronicle*, March 12, 2017; Taryn Luna, "When Jerry Hill Gets Ticked Off, You Might Get a New Law," *Sacramento Bee*, May 16, 2017; Tara McClain, "Students Press State for Tax Break," *Statesman Journal*, March 10, 2005; Kim Norvell, "'Suck it Up Buttercup' Lawmaker Hangs Up on Canadian Journalist," *Des Moines Register*, November 18, 2016; William Petroski, "Rural Students Could Ride Buses Over 2.5 Hours Daily under Bill Passed by Iowa Senate," *Des Moines Register*, February 20, 2018; Representative Cam Ward, "Post from the Legislature," March 27, 2007, http://www.politicalparlor.net/wp/2007/03/27/bills-for-the-week/; Jill Rosen, "Peeved Politicians Offer Up Payback," *Baltimore Sun*, March 27, 2006; Brian Smith, "A State Amphibian? Lawmakers Introduce Dueling Bills over Michigan's Official Frog," MLive.com, May 16, 2014, http://www.mlive.com/lansing-news/index.ssf/2014/05/a_state_amphibian_lawmakers_in.html; *Tulsa World*, "Bill Would Allow Chewing Pop-Tarts into Gun Shapes in Oklahoma Schools," January 8, 2014; William L. Spence, "Session Takes a Toll on Idaho Legislators: Lawmakers' 'Passion Projects' Bring Heartache and Sleepless Nights," *Spokesman-Review*, March 29, 2018.

In lower houses, the referral decision typically rests with the speaker. But, again, variations are seen across the states. In some Houses, a committee (a committee on committees or a rules committee) makes the referral. In the

Virginia House, the clerk makes the decision with direction from the speaker. In the Maine House, the full membership votes on the initial referral.[28] The referral can be a critical decision that, literally, determines the fate of a bill. In 2014, for example, the Indiana House speaker took away a proposed constitutional amendment banning same-sex marriage, a measure he supported, from the Judiciary Committee to which it had been referred initially and gave it instead to the Elections and Apportionment Committee, where he correctly assumed it would receive a favorable recommendation.[29] Referrals can also be used to kill bills. A former Vermont speaker confessed that through the strategic use of his referral power, "I sent my share of bills off to death row during my tenure."[30]

Committee Hearings

The most extensive review of a bill almost always occurs in committee. It is important to note that this is the only stage in the entire legislative process during which the public can speak before the legislature on proposed legislation.[31] Only lawmakers may introduce bills and only they may speak on the chamber floor during debate. Thus, the committee stage is important because points of view from a wide array of individuals and groups can be entertained. On rare occasions public voices can dominate a hearing, especially on topics that generate strong ideological or emotional reactions, such as abortion or guns. In 2017 a Texas Senate hearing on illegal immigration and sanctuary status resulted in 450 people signing up to testify over a sixteen-hour hearing in the Senate State Affairs Committee.[32] When in 2013 the Hawaii legislature considered legislation to allow same-sex marriage, more than one thousand people signed up to testify. The hearing consumed fifty-seven hours over five days and was characterized as "a citizens' filibuster."[33]

Although private citizens or government officials may give some of the testimony, the reality is that interest group lobbyists usually provide much of it. Lobbyists are an integral part of the legislative process and this is particularly evident at the committee stage. Committee hearings are about providing information to lawmakers, and lobbyists are key purveyors of it.

The committee chair is the pivotal person at this point in the legislative process. In most legislatures, control over the hearing process is in the hands of the chair. The chair usually decides when (or even if) a bill will be heard. As one committee chair stated, "[P]art of the power and part of the responsibility and part of the privilege of being a committee chairman is to set the agenda."[34] Control over the agenda confers considerable power on chairs.

There are a few state legislatures in which every bill must receive a hearing in committee. For the most part, such a rule means the committee chairs are not as powerful since they do not hold absolute veto power over a bill by refusing to schedule it. There are seven state legislatures in which both chambers have a requirement that all bills be heard in committee (all are either New England or Rocky Mountain/Plains states). There are four states where all bills in the House must receive a committee hearing and another four states where only Senate bills must be heard in committee.[35]

Committee Action and Second Reading

Assuming a bill receives a hearing, the committee may report it to the entire chamber ("to the floor") with one of several recommendations. What the committee chooses to do at this stage is usually critical to the success or failure of a measure. The most common committee actions at this stage are to table the bill (hold it in committee) or to issue a report to the floor recommending that the bill "do pass" (a favorable recommendation), "do not pass" (unfavorable recommendation), or be amended (change some aspect of the bill). There are other potential recommendations, but they are less common (e.g., return the bill to the sponsoring legislator, send it to the floor without a recommendation, refer the bill to another committee, or replace a bill with an entirely new one).

In most states, an unfavorable recommendation ("do not pass") is a rarity; if the committee does not like the bill, they will simply hold it in committee. But there are a handful of states, such as Colorado, South Dakota, and New Hampshire, in which all bills are required to be reported to the floor.[36] In these states, a "do not pass" recommendation is a common report because the committee does not have the option of holding the measure.

For the most part, legislators on the floor follow the recommendation of the committee report; because most of them did not hear the testimony and discussion in committee they use the committee recommendation as an informed "cue" for voting. In essence, it is a system based on trust and deference: the lawmaker trusts the members of the committees on which he or she does not sit to make the right decisions based on the information provided in the committee hearing, and therefore defers to his or her colleagues' recommendation.

There are, however, times when the system does not work in quite this way. On issues that attract a lot of attention and emotion, such as abortion, guns, or taxes, legislators are as likely to put faith in their own ideological orientation or political "gut reaction" as they are to trust the committee report. It is also the case that on some issues, the party has come to a position in caucus and members are expected to adhere to that position. Sometimes this means that the party leadership or caucus has taken a stance while the committee had the bill under consideration. Under these circumstances, the committee decision may be a foregone conclusion, and much of the testimony is more for show than anything else. This may be especially true on salient issues that currently divide the parties, given the increased polarization evident in many legislatures.

In the end, however, the committee recommendation is usually the determining factor. On average, perhaps 90 percent of the bills that receive a favorable recommendation from a committee will pass on the floor. But deference to committee recommendations varies across chambers. One study found that more than 95 percent of committee bills cleared the floor in the Arkansas, Pennsylvania, and Vermont Houses but less than 80 percent passed in Delaware, Georgia, Ohio, and Wisconsin.[37]

On some occasions, a majority of house members wish to pursue a bill, but the committee to which it was referred prefers to kill it. In a number of chambers, a discharge procedure exists to pull such a bill out of the committee's grasp, allowing it to come to the floor. The rules governing discharge procedures vary. In some chambers, the discharge motion requires only a simple majority; in other houses, an extraordinary majority is needed.[38] In the Illinois House all bills that are introduced are first assigned to the Rules Committee to then be reassigned to other committees. The Rules Committee, however, is controlled by the speaker and measures he opposes are kept in that committee to kill them. They can be discharged, but only by the unanimous consent of the House![39] But even when only a majority is required discharge petitions are rarely deployed, in large part because the majority party controls the committees and therefore has an incentive to resist them, as do committee chairs.[40]

In many states, the committee report is made when the bill is on the calendar for the second reading. Again, in most cases, the bill is actually only read by title. A day or two after this second reading and issuance of the committee report, the bill moves to the third reading calendar.

Third Reading, Debate, and Floor Vote

Once more, the bill is read (again, typically by title only), and at that point lawmakers debate its merits on the floor before taking a roll-call vote. Although floor debate occasionally makes for high drama, the reality is that by this point, leadership, most legislators, many lobbyists, and other close observers already know the outcome. Leaders poll members of their party, often in a caucus meeting, to find out how individual lawmakers intend to vote. Thus, there is little mystery about the likely outcome. In the New York Senate, for example, 7,109 bills were brought to the floor for a vote between 1997 and 2001. Not a single one was defeated.[41] Because leaders typically control which bills get brought up for a vote on the floor, they can choose to only call up measures that are going to pass. A study of the Illinois House noted that the speaker's almost complete agenda control "allows him to make sure his supporters are in the chamber before calling a bill, or to call a vote after opponent lawmakers have left the chamber."[42] Thus, a leader's calculations are simple; as a speaker of the Missouri House—another body where almost everything brought to a vote passes—noted, "There were several controversial issues where the votes just weren't there. They weren't even close. There's no use wasting the House's time if you don't have 82 (votes out of 163 members)."[43]

In most states, passage of a bill requires a simple majority of those present and voting. Thus, if the chamber has one hundred members and five are not present or abstain from voting, the bill requires forty-eight votes for passage (50 percent plus one of ninety-five present and voting equals forty-eight). However, some chambers require a true majority (also known as a "constitutional majority") of the entire membership, even if some are absent or not voting. The Indiana House is one such body. In order to pass the chamber, a bill must receive 51 "aye" votes.[44] The practical implications of voting standards are twofold. First, it is harder to pass legislation in a state using a "real majority" rule. Second, in a state with this rule, a lawmaker can help defeat a bill by simply "taking a walk," because being absent has the same effect as voting no but avoids placing the member in the position of actually going on record as voting against the measure. Consequently, what appears to be a minor difference in rules—present and voting majority versus real majority—can lead to large differences in outcomes and in legislators' behavior. And where it is not clear which voting standard is to be used, as has been the case in the New York Senate, legislative chambers can tie themselves in parliamentary knots.[45]

Given that in many chambers the majority party leadership only brings bills to the floor for a vote if they are confident that the measures will pass, the minority party often feels impotent. One tactic the minority party might, under certain circumstances, be able to pursue to gain some leverage is to deny the majority the required quorum to conduct official business. This is usually only an option where a supermajority quorum requirement exists, most notably the two-thirds standard currently found in Indiana, Oregon, Tennessee, and Texas. Where a supermajority is required to conduct business, the minority party—assuming it is of sufficient size—can use the rule to its advantage. When broken quorums happen, as they have in Oregon, Texas and Wisconsin in recent years, they get considerable media attention. But they are rare events, and they usually only slow down, not prevent, the majority party from working its will.[46]

Another possible strategy is to deploy a filibuster in those chambers with rules that allow for one. A filibuster is an effort to slow down the legislative process to the point at which all floor business comes to a standstill. It is a tactic used by an individual or minority group of legislators when they object to a measure but do not have enough votes to otherwise prevent its passage. Although filibusters are usually only associated with the U.S. Senate, unlimited debate is allowed in roughly one-third of state legislative houses.[47] In some chambers that allow for unlimited debate, the rules make it easy to bring a filibuster to a stop; in others, it is more difficult to do.[48]

Typically, legislators engage in filibusters as a last resort. In 2007, for example, having failed to stop the bill or amend it to their satisfaction, Democrats, who were in the minority in the Missouri Senate, filibustered a GOP measure dealing with a novel mechanism to fund construction at the state's public universities. Operating as a tag team, the Democrats held the bill hostage to a filibuster during a fifteen-hour debate, starting at 8 p.m. on a Monday evening and ending at 11 a.m. the next morning. Although the filibuster successfully blocked the bill from coming to a vote in the short term, the Republican majority ultimately prevailed. They did so by employing a seldom-used parliamentary procedure, one that had been invoked only nine times during the previous four decades. After the GOP broke the filibuster, they passed the bill—minus funding for two major projects scheduled to be built at the University of Missouri campus in Columbia, the district of the Democratic leader of the filibuster.[49]

Occasionally, filibusters do stop a bill. In 2018, Democrats in the South Carolina Senate talked for three straight days in opposition to an abortion ban bill they opposed, eventually forcing the majority Republicans to withdraw the measure because the session was scheduled to end soon and other legislation needed to be debated.[50] Filibusters can also force concessions. Again in 2018, a daylong filibuster in the Missouri Senate resulted in supporters of a utility rate structure bill amending it to address the opponent's major reservations.[51]

While the classic filibuster involves one or more legislators commanding the floor by continuing to speak without limit, there are other delaying tactics that may be employed. Using a coordinated series of ten-minute speeches to stretch out deliberations and thereby kill bills as a legislative deadline looms is referred to (for no known reason) in the Texas House as "chubbing."[52] In 2017, a band of twelve angry conservative Republicans, upset that several of their bills had been thwarted by the GOP leadership, used the technique to derail more than one hundred noncontroversial bills in retribution. Given the time of year when it occurred, it was called the "Mother's Day Massacre."[53]

Another dilatory ploy is to make a motion that a bill be read in its entirety, rather than just by title. This tactic is especially effective in part-time legislatures with strict limits on session length. In 2016, minority party Republicans in the Oregon House, feeling that their concerns were being ignored by the Democratic leadership, requested a full reading of House Bill 4014, a fifty-one-page measure implementing rules and regulations for commercial marijuana production. The reading of the bill, "which began in the morning and extended well into the afternoon," was just one of a series of procedural moves deployed by the unhappy minority party members. The bill eventually passed, but the Republicans' concerns were noted, as the delaying tactics caused several committee hearings to be postponed.[54]

Another obstructionist tactic is to propose dozens of amendments to a bill on the floor. This maneuver is favored by Senator Ernie Chambers in the Nebraska Unicameral. Chambers is known for introducing a myriad of amendments to bills he does not like. In 2005, he introduced thirty-one floor amendments to a resolution to establish a state constitutional guarantee of the right to hunt and fish. With tongue in cheek, Senator Chambers introduced amendments that included the right to "hunt for the Holy Grail," to "hunt moonbeams and daydreams," to "hunt for who let the dogs out," to "hunt for the Fountain of Youth," and about two dozen more nonsense provisions. His efforts along these lines are occasionally successful, especially when they are used near the end of a session when time becomes precious. But because of them he often incurs his colleagues' enmity. As one noted, "In Washington they call it a filibuster. In Lincoln, they call it Ernie."[55]

Even when a bill does pass on the floor, that action may not settle the matter because the vote can be reconsidered within a specified time frame (usually twenty-four to forty-eight hours), if someone who voted for it proposes to do so. Reconsideration is the legislative equivalent of "buyer's remorse"—the term for a buyer making a purchase and almost immediately regretting it. Consumer protection laws often allow for buyer's remorse and give the buyer a limited number of days to back out of a deal. Reconsideration works the same way. If a bill is passed and then at least one lawmaker who voted for its passage has second thoughts, he or she may call for reconsideration of the measure. Although rare, it occasionally happens that a bill will pass, be reconsidered, and then fail.

Of course, the process can work the other way as well—a bill may fail, be reconsidered, and pass. In fact, the latter case is actually the more likely scenario, especially in a body with part-time legislators who are pressed for time toward the end of the session. It occasionally occurs that the leadership has not clearly communicated that they favored a particular bill. If the rank-and-file members are uncertain about a measure, they are likely to vote against it. If that happens, the majority party leadership may call for a brief recess, assemble the members of the party in caucus, and explain that the legislation in question is a "good" bill and should pass. When the legislators reconvene on the floor, there will be a call for reconsideration, and the vote will be retaken. In 2018, the Mississippi House initially voted down a measure to create a state lottery. The bill was a priority for the governor and he successfully pressured enough lawmakers that the following day the House reconsidered the bill and passed it.[56]

Same Steps in Second Chamber

There may be differences in the specifics of the legislative process between the two houses in a state, but for the most part, the basic outlines are the same. This means a bill again has to undergo three separate readings, committee hearings and action, and, if the bill gets that far, a floor vote. Again, the committee stage is usually critical. It is often the case that a bill will pass the first chamber but not the second. It may be that the committee that receives the bill in the second chamber has different policy preferences compared with the original committee. Perhaps only the committee chair in the second chamber is strongly opposed to the bill, but that alone may be enough to keep it in committee if the chair refuses to hold a hearing. It may be that the Republicans are the majority party in one chamber, but the Democrats are the majority in the other chamber. There are numerous ways in which the political context in one chamber may be differ from the context in the other chamber. And this, of course, makes it harder to build the sort of coalition necessary to pass the bill in both chambers.

There may also be scheduling obstacles. About twenty states impose deadlines by which bills from one chamber must clear a standing committee and pass the floor and be sent to the other chamber. In most states this is known as the "crossover date." As one might expect, almost all the state legislatures with crossover deadlines are part-time; examples include Kansas, Mississippi and West Virginia. Of the full-time legislatures, only California and Illinois employ crossover deadlines.[57]

Potential Conference Committee

Even if a bill passes in each chamber, it is possible that it does not pass with the same wording. To become law, it must pass both chambers in precisely the same form. Suppose, for example, the House passes a bill that lowers the drinking age for all alcoholic beverages from twenty-one to eighteen years of age. But when the bill goes to the Senate, it is amended, and the new version stipulates that the drinking age law will be lowered from twenty-one to nineteen years of age, and only for beer and wine (one would still have to be twenty-one years old to purchase "hard" liquor). Clearly, this is not the same bill that was passed by the House. So now what happens?

The typical procedure is that the original chamber votes on whether to accede to the changes made by the second chamber. If they accept the changes, the bill is then sent to the governor. If the original chamber does not accept the changes, a conference committee may ensue. A conference committee is an ad hoc body (in other words, one is created anew for each such instance). The rules governing conference committees vary from one state and chamber to the next, but generally these committees consist of about six to ten legislators (usually three to five from each chamber) appointed by the presiding officer or party leaders in each chamber.[58] The task of the conference committee is to craft a compromise—a bill that both chambers will accept. If the chambers passed substantially different bills, then the conference committee has a great deal of policymaking discretion. The conference report must be accepted by a floor vote in each chamber; otherwise, the bill is dead. Likewise, if the conference committee cannot agree on a report, the bill is dead. In most states floor amendments are not permitted on conference committee bill reports; thus the chambers must accept either the conference version or no bill at all. The "take-it-or-leave-it" nature of the conference bill means that conference committees have substantial power over the issue under consideration.[59] As one expert explains, "Conference committees . . . are the least visible phase of the lawmaking process. And, although they may have a low profile, it is in conference committees that some of the most important action in the legislative game takes place."[60]

While conference committees can be an important part of the process they are not used in every state. Some legislatures, most notably New York, make little use of them.[61] Differences between the houses in New York are typically resolved through negotiations between their leaders.[62] But in many legislatures, "going to conference" is a common procedure, so much so that conference committees are sometimes referred to as the "third chamber." And in some states, they play a central role in the budget process.

The Governor's Desk

When a bill is passed by both chambers (in the same exact form), it is sent to the governor. The governor may sign the measure into law or veto it. (On occasion, a governor will allow a measure to become law without his or her signature, as Ohio's governor did with a 2018 bill extending concealed weapon rights to military veterans. In this case, the governor did so not because he opposed the measure but as a way to protest the legislature's failure to pass other gun legislation he favored.)[63] Vetoes are most likely to occur when the governor is affiliated with one party but the legislative majority is from the other party—again, a condition known as *divided government*. There are exceptions, of course. In 2018, California governor Jerry Brown vetoed 201 of the 1,217 bills passed by the legislature, or 16.5 percent, even though both chambers were controlled by his own party, the Democrats.[64] Some governors are far more likely to veto legislation than are others, regardless of party control in the legislature. Over the course of his rocky relationship with the Maine legislature from 2011 to 2019, Governor Paul LePage vetoed 642 bills, "more than all other Maine governors combined going back to 1917 and 80 times as many as his predecessor."[65] If the governor does veto a bill, the legislature still has the opportunity to pass it into law through an override. Overriding a veto is not easy; in most states, it can only be done if an extraordinary majority (typically two-thirds or three-fifths, see table 6.2) of the legislators in each chamber votes to do so. Few vetoes are overridden; in 2016 the figure was just under 3 percent.[66] But when a governor aggravates the legislature, lawmakers can turn on him or her with a vengeance. Although it requires a two-thirds vote in both chambers to override a gubernatorial veto in Maine, in 2018 the legislature did just that on twenty of the forty-three bills Governor LePage vetoed, even though the governor's party controlled one of the two chambers.[67]

The role of the governor in the legislative process, however, is often far greater than wielding a veto threat. Most significant legislation involves detailed negotiation between the governor and the legislative leadership. Some of this legislation is set forth as the part of the governor's legislative agenda—problems the governor addresses in the state-of-the-state address given at the beginning of the legislative session. We will discuss the governor's role in the legislative process in greater detail in chapter 6.

Legislative Time

As we discussed in chapter 3, most state legislatures only meet for a few months each year. In 2018, for example, the overwhelming majority were in session for four months or less.[68] The most immediate implication of this reality is that part-time legislatures operate under severe time pressures. Lawmakers must deal with many issues, some complex and difficult, some minor and easy, all in a limited time frame. It is human nature to defer the complex and difficult issues. Part of this may be procrastination. But another part of it is that complex, difficult issues require more study, more negotiation, and more time to develop the compromises and coalitions that are necessary for passage. Therefore, most of the critical issues facing a legislature do not get resolved until the end of the session, if they get resolved at all. This creates a legislative logjam as the end of the session draws near.[69] To help combat this problem, many state legislatures establish deadlines for bill introductions, committee reports (called "funnel days" in Iowa), and (as mentioned earlier) the transmitting of bills from one chamber to the other. Although bill deadlines help, there are always exceptions to them. Rules can be waived, and in many states, a few "privileged" committees—typically budget, state affairs, rules, or leadership committees—do not have to abide by the deadlines.

Because of all of this, one astute observer notes that "political time differs from ordinary approaches to time in that it is not linear."[70] Legislative actions have a different pace, and time has a different (ever-increasing) value as the legislative session moves from beginning to end. Generally, at the start of the session, the legislative pace is leisurely. Many events on the social calendar are scheduled for early in a session. These gatherings are hosted by a variety of associations and interest groups, each trying to get a little "face time" with legislators.

During the legislative day, bills are being sent to committees and committee chairs schedule hearings. Little action occurs on the chamber floor at this time—largely because there are few bills to discuss or on which to vote because most of them are still at the committee stage. As the session progresses and bills begin to move from committee to the floor for debate, possible amendment, and floor vote, legislators find their time increasingly divided between committee hearings, floor sessions, and caucus meetings as the leaders and the rank-and-file members discuss priorities and strategies. As committee deadlines pass and most of the standing committees suspend operations for the year, the floor action comes to dominate, punctuated by occasional caucus meetings. Meanwhile, one or more conference committees are likely negotiating, behind closed doors, the bills that passed in both chambers but in different versions. Finally, in the waning days of the session, action shifts again, at least in many legislatures, to the behind-the-scenes negotiations between party leaders in each chamber and, often, the governor or his or her key staffers.

The end of the session is almost always hectic, with bills moving rapidly from one chamber to the other, some of them being strategically held back by the leadership as bargaining chips, the fate of individual legislators' pet bills hanging in the balance, negotiations on critical bills breaking down and resuming again, nerves fraying, and tempers flaring. Tensions can run high. Toward the end of Missouri's 2017 session, a Republican senator and a Democratic senator joined together on the chamber floor to sing the spiritual, "Kumbaya," but to no avail; "no other senators audibly joined in and no progress on any bills happened the rest of the day."[71] Typically, however, most of the activity centers on those in leadership positions. Rank-and-file members are left out of the action until they are needed to vote. As the final days approached during a session of the Maine House, the speaker warned his members, "Bring plenty of reading material. Bring musical instruments if you want. We will be doing a lot of waiting around."[72] His prediction proved accurate. A reporter observed that bored lawmakers "snapped rubber bands across the room during a break while leadership huddled to work out last-minute details."[73] Such behavior is not confined to Maine. During the final late-night hours of one Missouri session a Wiffle ball game was played in a capitol corridor while the chamber's leaders hashed out needed compromises; in North Carolina an "impromptu dance party" broke out in a hallway.[74] Such antics are an accepted part of the process. During the final hours California Assembly members are known to play "legislative bingo" in which they are secretly assigned odd words and phrases—the names of the seven dwarfs, "bromance," and the like—that they have to discreetly work into floor debates.[75] Some members look askance at such pranks. In the Iowa Senate, a first-term member took to the floor during the last day of a session to complain, "Here we are supposed to be representing the people, and we're down here playing Solitaire while we're supposedly passing these significant pieces of legislation." The Senate leader, who was busy with negotiations, sloughed off the complaint, noting, "Freshmen [legislators] are always shocked by what goes on. Next year he won't even mention it. He'll probably be playing games."[76]

Unorthodox legislative maneuvers are occasionally employed in the last few days to try to salvage dying proposals. In California, the scheme used is called "gut and amend." A low-profile and noncontroversial measure is amended to incorporate a more controversial proposal in a last-ditch effort to pass it.[77] In Idaho, a similar maneuver is referred to as "radiator capping," where one bill is substituted for another and the only thing in common between the two is the bill number; it is analogous to taking the radiator cap off one automobile and placing it on a different car. This mostly happens at the end of the session, when one chamber "radiator caps" a bill from the other chamber. Comparable techniques are found in a number of states. As in California, the process in North Carolina is called "gut and amend," while in Oregon it is known as "gut and stuff," in Kansas as "gut and go," and in both Hawaii and Pennsylvania it is "gut and replace." In North Dakota and South Dakota the action is referred to as a "Hoghouse Amendment" (named for an incident that occurred in the South Dakota legislature in 1920, when a bill was gutted and replaced by another to fund a hog barn at South Dakota State University). Utah lawmakers actually plan ahead for such last minute moves by introducing "boxcar bills" at the beginning of the legislative session. Boxcar bills are placeholders; empty shells that are only filled with substantive legislative language if needed near the end of a session.[78] Such last-minute ploys are under attack in some states because critics argue that they do not allow adequate time for public input on the "new" bill.[79] In September of 2018, the League of Women Voters and Common Cause sued the state of Hawaii over such practices, claiming that "Gut and replace and other deceptive practices have been used for years to cut the public out of the conversation. Enough is enough."[80]

Perhaps not surprisingly, errors are made in the hectic rush of the last few days of a legislative session. A Florida senator admits, "There's no way, when you are passing 50 bills a day, that you can look at every word. There's just no way."[81] Arguably, the most egregious mistake made in the waning hours of a recent session occurred in Arizona. The House speaker brought up a bill to create a tax refund program intended to encourage the state's citizens to purchase cleaner-burning-fuel vehicles. Although lawmakers had not seen the bill before, because it was the speaker's measure, they assumed it was error-free. But as one representative later confessed, "The bottom line is that we are asking questions as we are thumbing through bills we've never seen before."[82] Had lawmakers greater opportunity to review the measure closely, they might have caught the mistake that extended the program to 1 percent of all vehicles in the state rather than 1 percent of all newly registered vehicles as the speaker had intended. The error was expensive; projected to cost the state only $3 million to $10 million, the program actually cost almost $450 million before the mistake was fixed.[83]

Ultimately, during the final days or even hours, consensus begins to build among legislators and media alike that some particularly dicey legislation is the *going home bill*—meaning it is the key issue that needs to be resolved before the legislature can adjourn for the year (*sine die*, literally translated as "without day," and meaning in this instance "with no appointed day" or "indefinitely") and everyone can go home. It may be a transportation issue, a social issue, or a tax reform question. More often than not, however, it is the budget bill. But whatever the going home bill turns out to be that year, after it is resolved, the legislature will adjourn soon thereafter. No matter that there are still bills left on the calendar; no matter that there are still important issues to address. They will have to wait until next year; it is time to go home. After all, in forty or so of the states, the legislatures are part-time organizations with part-time pay, and the members need to get back to their families and jobs.

The Budget Process

Although most other bills can wait until the following year, the one bill that the legislature must pass is the appropriations (budget) bill. Technically, of course, some states do wait "until next year" to pass a budget because twenty states have a biennial budget cycle, meaning they pass a budget for a two-year period. The remaining thirty states have an annual budget cycle, so they must pass the appropriations bill(s) every year. But even in the biennial states, budget adjustments must usually be made in the "off year" because the economy may have slowed or because unforeseen expenditures such as natural disasters may have occurred.

Budget bills have to pass because almost every other bill the legislature passes has a price tag associated with it—it creates a program or law that must be administered by state agencies, or it authorizes the construction of roads, bridges, public university buildings, or other aspects of the physical infrastructure. All of these things cost money. And most of that money is appropriated through the state budget process.

What makes the budget task especially challenging is that almost all states require that expenditures be balanced by revenues. States can borrow money (bonding) for large-scale projects like highways or university buildings, but they cannot do so in the same manner that the federal government does. Therefore, state legislatures are far more constrained by economic realities than is the federal government. And this means that governors and legislatures must make hard choices about what to fund and what to forgo. When the economy takes a downturn, these choices are especially painful. During the Great Recession of 2007–2009, almost all states experienced substantial budget shortfalls, forcing the legislature to make significant spending cuts, to raise taxes, or to have to do both. A consequence of tight budgets is that other issues, particularly new initiatives that require spending, get squeezed off the legislative agenda. Fiscal difficulties in 2009, for instance, meant, as a Maryland senator put it, "The budget is going to suck 99 percent of the oxygen out of the State House."[84]

Since the 1950s, as many legislatures became more professionalized, as discussed in chapter 3, executive dominance of the budget process has lessened, and legislatures have become more equal partners in setting priorities.[85] Indeed, longer legislative sessions give more professionalized legislatures the time they need to battle the executive over the budget.[86] Lawmakers also have increased institutional information resources devoted to the state budget. The fiscal policy expertise of California's Legislative Analyst's Office, for example, is held in high regard by legislators of both parties and is used to inform their decisions on the budget.[87]

The rules under which budgets are adopted are similar in most of the states. In forty-two states, a simple majority is all that is required to pass the budget.

Another six states use majority rules under most circumstances. In Illinois, a majority vote is all that is needed up until June 1, after which date a three-fifths vote is required. This supermajority vote penalty gives the majority party incentive to get the budget passed on time. But even that incentive is not always enough to produce an on-time budget—especially when one party controls the executive branch and the other party controls the legislature, as was the case in Illinois during the budget stalemates of 2016 and 2017.

One important consideration that does vary is the nature of the penalty if the budget deadline is missed. In some states, missing the budget deadline simply means the state continues to operate under a "maintenance budget" based on the previous year's funding. In others, most state services must be curtailed or shut down entirely. For legislators, the political costs of an actual budget shutdown can be substantial.[88] And there may be a personal cost as well. In 2018, Alaska lawmakers passed legislation that cuts off their per diem if they have not passed a budget by the 121st calendar day of their legislative session.[89]

Pork barrel spending—the appropriation of government money to fund local projects without much scrutiny—occurs in almost every legislature.[90] In New York, the euphemism used is "member items," and they constituted more than $475 million doled out through the State and Municipal Facilities Program (SMFP) in the 2019 budget.[91] A veteran Republican senator acknowledged that her "member items" included, "$371,000 for a University at Buffalo rural dentistry program that services 3,500 people, including a new expansion of free dental benefits to veterans and low-income seniors in her district; $500,000 for various law enforcement capital needs in her district; $150,000 to help the Chautauqua Lake Association remove invasive species and $95,000 to remove weeds at the lake; $200,000 for the Cattaraugus Youth Bureau, which will partly go to provide services to homeless and runaway youths; $200,000 from a multiregional breast cancer education and support group; money for health food programs in Cattaraugus County; and two symposiums in her region for lupus patients and their families."[92] One critic of "member items" complained that "It's just pork. There is nobody even pretending that there is statewide importance to any of these. . . . There is no process. No airing. There's complete discretion."[93] Such money is given out to help members get reelected and to assist party leaders in securing needed support from their members. A California Assembly member admitted, "Pork is never allocated on the basis of need. It is always allocated on the basis of politics, and usually to buy votes."[94] To get a gas tax increase measure through the legislature in 2017, California legislative leaders "earmarked nearly $1 billion worth of special items, from $100 million for a University of California, Merced parkway project (to corral Democratic Assemblyman Adam Gray), to a $400 million extension of the Altamont Corridor Express commuter rail line (to win the support of Republican state Sen. Anthony Cannella)."[95] Consistent with such claims, an analysis of "member initiative spending" in the Illinois legislature revealed that monies were directed toward electorally competitive districts, districts represented by legislative leaders, and districts represented by moderate members who were being wooed by legislative leaders.[96]

Influences on Legislative Decision-Making

Ultimately, each legislator must decide how to vote on each bill. As a Vermont legislator noted: "No matter how complex the issue, no matter how much you know, or often don't know, the ultimate choice always boils down to a simple affirmation or rejection of the issue at hand. A roll-call can be very rough. It's the moment of truth. There is no place to hide, no luxury of equivocation or vacillation. Every perplexity, ambiguity, and uncertainty must be frozen into one of two words: Yes, or No."[97]

It is true that the roll-call vote on final passage of a bill is a visible decision because most votes are recorded and published in the legislature's official journal. A recorded vote is, therefore, evidence that may be used for or against the legislator in the next election campaign. Lawmakers are sensitive to this reality and occasionally take votes in such a manner as to protect themselves from possible attack by a future political opponent. For instance, when the Missouri Senate voted on a controversial measure to allow legislators and other elected officials to invest in ethanol plants that receive state financial incentives, they did so by taking a head count vote—one that recorded only the final tally, not how each individual senator voted on the measure.[98] Democrats in the California Assembly took such subterfuge one step further. When a bill to reduce the penalties for possessing crack cocaine failed to pass, the Democratic majority successfully moved to have the vote, on which many of them had voted in the affirmative, expunged from the official record. That action left no trace of a vote that might have haunted lawmakers in the next election.[99]

But it is important to understand that many decisions on how to vote on an issue are often made earlier in the process—sometimes in committee, frequently on floor amendments or procedural motions, and occasionally in party caucus.[100] And there are other decisions to be made that do not require a vote at all—whether to introduce a proposal, for example. These decisions are generally not recorded but may be just as important—indeed, often more important—than the final roll-call vote. Thus, as Politics under the Domes 5.2 demonstrates, the final vote may not be an accurate reflection of where a lawmaker actually stands on an issue.

The story of "how a bill gets passed" is the culmination of many different decisions. Among the most important influences are partisanship, party leadership, committee actions, legislative staff, constituency considerations, and lobbyists. The relative importance of these variables varies by legislature and chamber and over time; they shift with the political context at any given moment. Parties often frame issues and structure legislative action so that partisanship becomes an immediate frame of reference for decision-making.[101] Party leaders tend to be strongest in larger legislatures and when the two parties are electorally competitive and turnover is high.[102]

Leadership also may be stronger when the parties are *polarized*—that is, when the ideological gap between the two parties is great. When polarization occurs, the role of political parties (and especially party leadership) in determining the outcome of legislation is substantial.[103] On important bills with ideological or partisan significance, the majority party will tightly control the agenda, will likely instruct committee chairs on which bills to prioritize, and will make every effort to ensure that all their members vote the party line. Lawmakers, especially those in the majority party, will go along because leadership can help maximize the party's electoral chances and thus maintain the party's majority status.[104] The ability of the majority party to control the flow of legislation, while generally greater in states than in the Congress, is nonetheless not uniform across all states. To put it simply, institutional and procedural rules vary, and this fact has important consequences for the flow of legislation.[105]

It is clear that polarization has increased in state legislatures, just as it has in Congress. But the degree of polarization varies from legislature to legislature. Over the past several years a handful of states, notably Colorado, California, and Wisconsin, have been more polarized than Congress. That means that in these legislatures the ideological gap between most Democrats and most Republicans was even greater than it was in Washington, D.C. But that was not true of all legislatures. Scoring much lower in polarization were Rhode Island, because its Republican lawmakers tended to be moderates, and Louisiana, because its Democrats tilted conservative.[106]

POLITICS UNDER THE DOMES

"I Voted for That Bill Before I Voted Against It": Why Floor Votes Don't Necessarily Tell the Whole Story

In many cases, the only formal vote of record is the final floor vote on a bill, the vote that occurs after the third reading, in response to the question, "Shall the bill pass?" And if any vote gets reported in the media, it is almost always this one. But votes that occur before the final floor vote may be just as important. These votes occur in committee, on floor amendments, and on procedural motions. Consider the following hypothetical example involving House Bill 1 (HB1): "An Act to Create the Center for the Study of Legislatures at State University and to Fund the Center at $200,000 in an Annual Appropriation."

Representatives Smith and Jones are both from districts in Polsbytown, where State University is located. Representative Smith is a State University graduate and a strong advocate for the university. Representative Jones is a graduate of a rival school, Tech College, and privately is not very supportive of State University.

Both representatives Smith and Jones serve on the House Appropriations Committee, the powerful budget-writing committee. When the appropriation request for the Center for the Study of Legislatures (known hereafter as "the Center") is before the committee, Representative Smith makes a motion to increase funding for the Center to $500,000. The motion is defeated seven to thirteen (seven ayes and thirteen nays) in committee, with Smith voting for the increase and Jones voting against it (see table at end of box).

Another committee member makes a motion to fund the Center at $100,000. The motion carries with eleven ayes and nine nays, with both Smith voting against it (because it does not fund the Center at a high enough level) and Jones voting against it (because it provides too much funding). The bill is sent to the floor with a "do pass" recommendation.

On the House floor, a representative from Jewell City (where A&M Institute is located) moves to amend the bill to fund the Center at $100. The motion carries, with Representative Smith voting against it and Representative Jones voting for it on a voice vote. The bill is amended, sent to engrossment, and reaches the third reading. On the roll-call vote on final passage on the floor, Smith votes against the bill, arguing that a $100 appropriation is tantamount to killing the Center. Jones votes for the bill. It passes, and the Center for the Study of Legislatures is established at State University with funding of $100.

In the subsequent electoral campaign, Smith's opponent notes that Smith voted against the bill creating the Center. Meanwhile, Jones's campaign brochure states, "I voted to create the Center at State University."

But who really supported the Center at State University?

Tracking the Procedural Votes to Create the Center for the Study of Legislatures at State University

Procedure	State University's Position	Procedural Vote	Smith's Position	Jones's Position
Original bill introduced, funds the Center at $200,000	Favors	None	Supports the Center	Opposes the Center
Smith's motion in committee to increase funding of the Center to $500,000	Strongly favors	Fails 7–13	Yes	No
Motion in committee to reduce funding to $100,000	Opposes	Passes 11–9	No	No
Floor amendment to reduce funding to $100	Strongly opposes	Passes on voice vote	No	Yes
Final roll-call vote on HB1, as amended to fund the Center at $100	Strongly opposes	Passes 51–49	No	Yes

But party and ideology do not dictate every outcome. On highly salient issues, an important determinant of a vote is constituency. More than 85 percent of all state legislators represent single-member districts, which require them to be sensitive to local policy preferences. This, of course, is because district voters have the power to defeat a lawmaker in a subsequent election. As one legislative scholar put it, "The next election is what keeps representatives as constituency oriented as they are."[107] Thus, when a bill to get rid of a "big-government policy" mandating the use of renewable energy came before the GOP-dominated North Carolina House, it failed because many members understood that their constituents were attracted by the prospect of new jobs being created. The Republican author of the failed measure mused, "It's hard to be conservative when it affects your district."[108]

Constituency size is, however, highly variable between chambers and among states, as detailed in chapter 1, and that fact has implications for how members get pressured to vote. The smaller the district population, the more likely it is that the electorate is relatively homogeneous demographically, politically, and ideologically. The upshot of this fact for legislative decision-making is that constituency preferences are clearer, for the most part, in smaller districts. Again, the key phrase here is "on salient issues." Most bills involve minor changes to policy; consequently, they have little effect on the day-to-day lives of a lawmaker's constituents. In these instances constituents usually do not express any preferences. But on major issues—those few matters that voters might follow—legislators pay close attention to district opinion. After a West Virginia chemical storage tank leaked contaminants into a major river, tainting the drinking water for many of the state's residents, the legislature responded by passing stricter regulations on industry. The Republican Senate leader voted for the measure even though he did not think the new rules were needed, because "the public has pushed back."[109] Lawmakers are loath to resist the will of their voters when it is clearly expressed.

Although it is evident that the constituency can influence the way lawmakers vote on bills, it is important to be clear which constituency is pressuring a member. The usual assumption is that members are worried about how a vote might be used against them by the other party in the next general election. But sometimes, the constituency that matters is the "primary constituency," the voters a lawmaker counts on to ensure renomination if a threat emerges from within his or her own party.[110] The primary constituency can greatly constrain a lawmaker's voting behavior on issues that deeply divide the major parties. During the California legislature's epic partisan battle over the state's 2009 budget, the Assembly speaker observed, "One of the reasons why it's hard for my Republican colleagues to vote for revenue—more important than their tax pledge—is their next primary. If they vote for revenue, then they're going to be easily challenged in another primary. But the Democrats face the same thing: If we vote for deep, permanent cuts in health and human services, then we have to face our next primary, too."[111]

In this instance, California legislators appear to be more worried about upsetting voters in their next primary than upsetting voters in the next general election. To the extent that legislative districts are uncompetitive between the major parties—a problem noted in chapter 2—the primary constituency, not the district more generally, becomes central to lawmakers. This potentially pushes Democratic and Republican lawmakers further apart. It also means factional fissures within the party become paramount in the primary; one need only think of the "Main Street" versus "Tea Party" fight for control of the GOP in legislative elections in a number of states.

But most votes a legislator casts are not apt to become campaign fodder for a political opponent. The vast majority of them fly under his or her constituency's political radar. What influences a member's voting behavior when it appears that the public is not watching? Voting with the legislator's party is, of course, important. Indeed, in many cases, party even trumps personal views.[112] Sometimes a lawmaker's personal characteristics matter. On highly salient religious issues, for example, a legislator's religion is an important predictor of his or her vote, particularly among those with conservative Protestant affiliations.[113] Personal relationships can also matter; whether a legislator likes or identifies with another member may influence how he or she votes on a bill.[114] When asked why she voted against a bill to increase fines for talking on a cell phone while driving, a Georgia representatives admitted, "It's a protest because [party leaders] ignored my bill last year. . . . I'm just causing trouble. I'm not philosophically opposed—I'm just mad."[115] A lawmaker's votes can even be swayed by whom he or she sits next to on the chamber floor.[116]

Conclusion

In this chapter, we have focused on the more formal dynamics of the legislative process. Rules, procedures, and calendars all play critical roles in the legislative process. Recently, state legislative scholars have focused considerable attention on how differences in rules can make important differences in terms of control over the legislative process itself.[117] But other forces matter as well.[118] As we will discuss in chapter 6, the governor is usually an important actor; interest groups typically play a sizeable role in the legislative process; the bureaucracy is often involved; and in some states, even the voters can play lawmaker. These are some of the contextual factors that we mentioned at the outset of the chapter. As we shall see, the context differs across the states, and it differs by issue. The context can even shift within a state. Over time, the players change. New legislators are elected, as are new governors. Sometimes the goals of individual players change. New issues appear and some old issues fade away, creating new political cleavages while erasing others. Consequently, political circumstances change, and the relationships among players change. In other words, even when the rules—the textbook version of the process—stay the same, the context is always shifting.

Chapter 6

The Legislative Context

Supporters delivering signed petitions for a ballot initiative to the election division of the Oregon Secretary of State's office. AP Photo/*Statesman Journal*, Timothy J. Gonzalez, File.

In chapter 4, we discussed the structure and organization of the legislature, which represents the internal environment in which legislative decisions are made. In chapter 5, we examined how those internal processes work through the formal rules. But lawmakers do not make decisions in a vacuum. Other political forces are at play as well and must also be examined.

Outside pressures are pertinent for legislatures because they are supposed to be the "most representative" branch of government. Relevant external forces fall broadly into several types, including public opinion, organized interests, other state governmental institutions, the federal government, local governments, and fiscal constraints. All of these come into play, sometimes constraining what legislatures can do and sometimes effectively mandating what they must do.

Public Opinion, Constituency, and the Representational Role

Public opinion is an amorphous concept. For the individual legislator, it may refer to the array of policy preferences held by people within his or her district. Or it may refer to policy preferences on a specific issue at the district or state level. On one hand, these opinions may be largely unstructured, in which case the lawmaker may not be aware of the shape of public views unless they are documented in a survey, and even then they may be vague. On the other hand, opinions may be clearly articulated in a structured form through interest group communications or via the initiative or referendum.

Ample evidence shows that public opinion matters at the aggregate level in state legislatures.[1] In other words, states with more liberal residents (as measured by public opinion polls) embrace more liberal policies (as implemented through the legislature).[2] Indeed, public opinion on a specific policy issue is a strong predictor of policy adoption.[3] Generally, this relationship also is true at the micro level. When district opinion is clearly discernible, a lawmaker is likely to vote consistent with that opinion. But there are important qualifications to this statement. First, the linkage between district opinion and a legislator's vote is not the same in all states.[4] Second, constituent opinion may not be clearly discernible on many bills. Third, the perception of who the "constituency" is may not be consistent from lawmaker to lawmaker or even from issue to issue.

Representational Roles

There are a variety of activities that pertain to representation. Some are not directly related to policymaking but rather to communication with constituents and casework—efforts to facilitate an individual constituent's request for help with a problem.[5] We discuss the components of representation in chapter 7; here we focus on the question of policy representation.

Legislators are representatives of a larger body politic, and therefore public opinion is one of the dimensions considered in discussions of representation. This is usually framed in terms of representational roles—the way the individual lawmaker views his or her policy obligation to the constituency. The discussion is often couched in terms of the two opposing points of view described in chapter 1: the *delegate* and the *trustee* theories of representation.[6] The delegate theory contends that the proper role of the legislator is to take the same position on a vote as the majority of his or her constituents would take. In effect, the legislator is the agent operating on behalf of the policy preferences of the principals (constituents) he or she represents. Thus, when the elected representative holds one position on an issue but the constituency holds a different view, the agent's responsibility is to follow the preferences of the district, not the lawmaker's own inclination.

The trustee theory is that the legislator should vote his or her conscience, regardless of constituent opinion. The view here is that the legislator is elected to consider each issue and vote on the basis of his or her own best judgment. This trustee role is often called the "Burkean model" because of a trenchant description of it provided by Edmund Burke, an eighteenth-century English political philosopher and member of Parliament. The trustee role asserts that constituent opinion should be consulted and considered, but the legislator must make the decision he or she thinks is right regardless of its popularity.

A cogent example of this representational dilemma occurred several years ago in Idaho. In 2002, the U.S. Supreme Court voided the death penalty in Idaho and eight other states because their laws unconstitutionally stipulated that judges rather than juries should decide the sentences in capital punishment cases.[7] In response, the Idaho legislature rewrote the state law to require that juries determine the sentence in capital punishment cases, thus rectifying the constitutional flaw. The bill to do this, S1001, was the first measure to reach the Idaho Senate floor for a vote in 2003. Consequently, it was the first bill on which senators had to make a decision. For one rookie senator, Elliot Werk (D-Boise), it was an excruciating experience. Werk personally opposed capital punishment but was convinced that most of his constituents wanted it reinstated, saying, "My district has told me loud and clear that they are in favor of the death penalty."[8] The new lawmaker agonized over what he should do, spending a near-sleepless night grappling with his decision. The next morning, he went to the capitol and cast a vote to reinstate the death penalty, stating, "I'm not representing Elliot Werk in the Senate. I'm representing the people of District 17." The novice senator was clearly uncomfortable with the vote, but he felt strongly that the delegate role was the proper one to follow. In this case, constituent public opinion was the guiding force in his decision.

Sitting next to Werk was Marti Calabretta, a veteran Democratic legislator from northern Idaho. She voted against reinstatement of the death penalty, although she knew her constituents supported it. Senator Calabretta commented, "In this case, we have to lead our public. . . . I'll probably end up walking in every bar in the district and letting them yell at me."[9] Calabretta demonstrated the trustee role of representation. Although she knew her constituents would not agree with her, she believed her conscience on this issue outweighed the district's preference: "Bottom line, it's your vote."[10] The trustee-delegate conundrum is as old as representative democracy.[11] The dilemma is especially problematic in legislatures where single-member districts are the rule because it focuses the representational relationship on a specific geographic constituency and an individual lawmaker. Reflecting on the quandary, one senator admitted, "It's one of the great questions of political thought: 'Do you vote your conscience or do you vote your district?' By the way, it's unanswerable."[12]

Although the representational role dilemma is a classic problem for political philosophers to mull, for legislators, it rarely presents itself with such clarity as in the death penalty case. This is true for at least three reasons. First, most bills simply do not create a predicament for the legislator because the general public does not care enough about the issue to develop a strong preference. Recall from chapter 5 that most measures involve relatively minor, often technical, issues. These are bills about which the general public knows little and about which it has no opinion. There may be a specific interest group or two that cares about the legislation, but the larger public does not. One study found that most lawmakers estimated that their constituents had an opinion on no more than 10 percent of the bills before the legislature.[13] In other words, legislators believed there was no discernable constituent opinion on 90 percent of the measures before them. Obviously, this belief gives each lawmaker a good deal of room to reach his or her own decisions.

Second, even if an issue is salient and people in the district have strong opinions about it, there is no guarantee that everyone will share the same view. Constituent opinion is infrequently unequivocally and overwhelmingly on one side of an issue. One study found that most legislators claimed that their constituency held a clear position on no more than ten bills each year—not 10 percent of all bills, but ten bills in total![14] That constitutes less than 1 percent of the measures introduced in most legislatures. It is also possible that the legislator misperceives constituent opinion on a given issue. Not all voices in the district are heard equally, almost no scientific polling is done on issue positions within legislative districts, and therefore often the lawmaker has only a vague or general sense of what his or her constituents think about an issue. Consequently, he or she may overestimate or underestimate district opinion on any issue. A recent study documents that legislators "can systematically misperceive what their constituents want."[15]

Third, if constituent opinion is strongly and clearly on one side of an issue, it is likely that the legislator shares the same view as the constituency. After all, the lawmaker is "of the district" and probably shares many of the same demographic, political, and ideological characteristics as the majority of the community from which he or she was elected. Voters tend not to elect someone who is consistently out of step with them—at least they do not elect them more than once. Thus, for the most part, legislators think like the majority of people in their district.

Different Views of Constituency

One of the considerations complicating the relationship between the representative and the constituency is that "constituency" can be a vague term. One might think it is obvious who the constituency is: the people who live within the district that elected a particular legislator. And indeed, every lawmaker can tell you precisely the physical, geographic, and demographic parameters of his or her district. It is, "the entity to which, from which, and within which the member travels."[16]

But lawmakers often have some subset of people in the district in mind when they refer to their "constituency."[17] Thus, when legislators refer to their "constituency," they may in fact be referring to the entire geographic district, but sometimes they may mean "the people who voted for me in the general election," while at other times they might mean "the partisan core that votes for me in the primary election and actively supports me during the campaign." Indeed, in today's world of polarized politics, the "constituency" is often that faction of the party that dominates the primary election. Since so many legislative districts are safe for one party, the voters in the primary election become the key constituency. Thus, sometimes "constituency" seems to mean "people who are ideologically similar to me."

Sometimes, lawmakers are thinking of specific economic or organizational interests when they refer to "constituency." For example, labor unions are a core constituency for many Democrats—even if many of the union members do not actually live in the legislators' district. For some Republicans, ideological constituencies like the American Legislative Exchange Council (ALEC), a national organization that promotes conservative policies, have become a key reference group. Finally, legislators sometimes mean their "personal support group" of family, friends, and closest political allies.

In other words, "constituency" seems to be measured on a sliding scale. It is unlikely that legislators even recognize that they use the term in different ways in different contexts—it seems to be a subconscious shifting of the definition of the word, expanding and contracting depending on the issue at hand and perhaps depending on perceived electoral consequences. Often, therefore, it is not always clear to whom the lawmaker refers when he or she says, "My constituency is in favor of this bill." For the most part, then, constituent opinion is in the eye of the beholder. Or, to put it another way, constituent opinion depends on which constituency the eye is beholding.

It is also the case that the public does not pay attention to most votes in the state legislature. Media coverage of the state legislature is thin in many states, and if people are paying attention to any legislative news, it is likely to be news about the U.S. Congress. Moreover, we know that many state legislative elections are uncontested or not competitive. Holding legislators accountable for their policy positions is difficult under such circumstances. A study of roll-call voting in eleven states found that legislators rarely were punished, electorally, by voting contrary to district opinion.[18]

We do not, however, wish to discount the importance of constituent opinion under certain circumstances. In the rare instances in which the district expresses a clear and strong preference for a specific policy position, the legislator ignores it at his or her peril. It does not happen often, but lawmakers have been recalled from office or defeated in the next regularly scheduled election on the basis of a specific vote. In 2013, for example, two Colorado senators were recalled because of their vote on a gun control bill and in 2018, a California senator was recalled for supporting a gasoline tax increase. For the most part, politicians are risk averse, and they understand the implications of going against the majority of their district on an important issue.

Public Opinion, Organized Interests, and Lobbying

Although it may be true that the general public has little knowledge of or interest in most of the issues that come before the legislature, that does not mean that no one is paying attention. There are hundreds—if not thousands—of interest groups in a state, each of which may care deeply about what is going on in a particular policy area. Each of these groups seeks to communicate its position and influence decisions. They do this in a variety of ways, but most important from the legislator's perspective are lobbying and election-related activities. Interest group efforts are particularly influential on issues that fail to get much attention from the general public.[19]

The Lobbyists

Lobbyists today usually do not call themselves "lobbyists." In part, this is because the term has a pejorative air about it. But it is also because a lot of people who are registered as lobbyists spend only a small fraction of their time actually trying to persuade legislators to do their bidding. Such efforts are just one of the activities they perform as part of a larger job description, and they do not think of themselves primarily as lobbyists. For instance, the executive director of the state Blueberry Growers' Association spends much less time with the legislature than with the state Department of Agriculture, the state Commerce Department, and marketing groups. Only occasionally will a bill have a potential impact on blueberry farmers (perhaps a pesticide bill or tonnage limits for trucks on secondary roads), and at that point, the director will act as a lobbyist.

People in the lobbying business prefer to be called "public affairs specialist," "government relations director," "policy advocate," "legislative liaison," "legislative agent," or something similar. There are actually several varieties of lobbyists. Examine almost any secretary of state or state ethics commission website and you can find a list of registered lobbyists, usually in alphabetical order, and the clients each represents. For example, under "E" in the 2018 list of lobbyists on the Texas Ethics Commission website, one finds the following individuals:

- David Emerick, vice president and executive director of State and Local Government Relations, JPMorgan Chase & Company, one of the largest banking and financial services companies in the world. Emerick and his staff represent the interests of JPMorgan Chase in several states, among them Texas and Oklahoma. This is a typical pattern for corporate lobbyists; they often work a regional circuit, following events in several state legislatures.

- Jennifer Brown Emerson, listed as an "attorney/lobbyist." Among her clients in 2018 were Altria (a tobacco company), CenterPoint Energy (a utility company), Mallinckrodt Pharmaceuticals, the Port of Houston, the San Antonio Water System, the Texas Package Store Association (liquor stores), and the Texas Rural Water Association.
- Paul Emerson, a state financial analyst for the Texas Association of Counties. Emerson is a former legislative staffer and budget analyst for the Texas Legislature, where he worked for about a decade before moving to the county association. Although lobbying is not his primary responsibility, he is a registered lobbyist for the counties' association because of his state budgeting expertise. It makes sense that many former legislative staffers wind up working as lobbyists; they have experience, they have a deep understanding of the issues, and they have contacts in the legislature and understand how it works.
- Tommy Engelke, Executive Vice President of the Texas Agricultural Cooperative Council, a statewide industry association. The Council represents agricultural cooperatives from around the state. As executive vice president of the Council, Engelke's job is multifaceted, and lobbying the Texas Legislature is just one of his work responsibilities.[20]

These four individuals, from Emerick to Engelke, are all registered lobbyists in Texas, but the nature of what they do, and for whom they do it, differs. Most are "in-house" lobbyists employed by one organization to do their lobbying. David Emerick lobbies for a single company—albeit a large firm (JPMorgan Chase). Tommy Engelke is the vice president of an association of agricultural cooperatives in Texas. Paul Emerson represents a single organization, the Texas Association of Counties (TAC). As an organization of local government officials, TAC must follow many bills before the Texas legislature. This is true of all sorts of local governments, and in any state capitol one will find a large contingent of lobbyists representing counties, cities, school districts, public utility districts, and numerous other local government entities. Estimates are that about 30 percent of all lobbyists are government lobbyists.[21] In-house lobbyists are usually knowledgeable about the issues that are of primary importance to the organization they represent. Their organizational value is their subject-matter expertise.

In contrast, Jennifer Brown Emerson represents many different organizations, associations, and corporations. She is a "contract" lobbyist, or a "multi-client" lobbyist. Sometimes such lobbyists are referred to as "hired guns." Contract lobbyists may represent just a couple of interests, or they may represent a large number. Generally, they are not hired for their expertise in a specific issue area but for their knowledge of the legislative process and their contacts with legislators and legislative staff.[22] They are especially prominent in states such as Texas with large and diverse constituencies, or in states like California and New York with more professional legislatures.[23] Most lobbyists at the state level are in-house lobbyists, and the number of lobbyists with more than one client varies by state. Recent estimates are that only 17 percent of lobbyists in

Hawaii and 21 percent in Oregon are multi-client lobbyists, while 32 percent in Florida and Pennsylvania fit that category.[24]

Although they differ in focus, these are all conventional types of lobbyists in the sense that most fall into one of the categories discussed above (i.e., in-house corporate, single-issue, local government, contract). But, as shown in Politics under the Domes 6.1, lobbyists do not always fit a stereotype.

Interest groups and lobbyists are integral parts of the legislative scene. There are more than fifteen hundred registered lobbyists in large-population states such as Illinois, Ohio, or Texas. In smaller states, the number of registered lobbyists is much lower. Montana and West Virginia, for example, each list about four hundred registered lobbyists.[25]

What Lobbyists Do

For the most part, interest groups and their representatives (lobbyists) have a symbiotic relationship with legislators; lobbyists seek to be heard on behalf of their clients, and lawmakers seek information on the likely political and policy consequences of proposed laws. This information exchange goes on constantly in and around the capitol—it happens informally in legislators' offices and the capitol halls, and it happens more formally in committee hearings.[26] It occurs over dinner in the restaurants around the capital city, and it takes place over appetizers on paper plates at the numerous "Legislative Appreciation" gatherings, where each organization holds an open house to which all the legislators are invited. An analysis by the Ohio General Assembly Joint Legislative Ethics Committee reveals that in 2017 lobbyists in that state reported spending $702,000 during the legislative session. Over 75 percent ($536,000) of the reported expenditures went to "all-invited social events"—the term for the large social events to which all the legislators are invited.[27]

POLITICS UNDER THE DOMES

Lobbying outside the Box

The stereotypical lobbyist is a middle-aged white male lawyer who represents wealthy and powerful interests. There is, of course, a kernel of truth to this stereotype, and many successful lobbyists fit that profile. But not all influential lobbyists do. Take, for example, Marion Hammer.

Standing just short of five feet tall, Hammer was, in 2018, a seventy-nine-year old Florida grandmother. For the last four decades she has been the National Rifle Association's state lobbyist. A visitor to her Tallahassee office suite noted that "There's no fancy reception area, leather-covered chairs, or brandy decanters. . . . Just two or three rooms filled with paper, files, magazines, and a couple of older ladies clipping newspaper stories." But appearances can deceive. One former state senator recalls that "One night we were late here after a vote, and I offered to walk Miss Hammer to her car. She said, 'Oh, don't you worry about me. I'm safe enough.' She opened her bag and there was her .38

Special!" Hammer has been so successful in pushing the NRA's agenda that she is largely credited for Florida's reputation as the "Gunshine State."

It was Hammer who, in 1987, successfully lobbied the state legislature to adopt "shall issue" language for concealed weapons permits, denying law enforcement officials any discretion in issuing them. In 2005, Hammer was the force behind Florida's adoption of "stand your ground" legislation, which removed any legal duty to retreat and allowed for the use of deadly force in self-defense if a person reasonably thought he or she was at risk of death or great bodily harm. Other states followed in Florida's wake on both policies.

Hammer's success is not the simple result of being part of an organization that gives generous campaign contributions. She is powerful for two more subtle reasons. First, she spends an enormous amount of time working on the nuts and bolts of legislation, leaving others to take political credit. One reporter found that on a 2013 bill to prohibit schools from punishing students for playing with pretend guns (a Pop-Tart bill referenced in Politics under the Domes 5.1) Hammer worked "on the legislation's language with a staff lawyer for the Florida House of Representatives. Notably, no lawmakers [were] ever copied on the [email] correspondence, nor [was] there any indication in the documents that any elected officials [were] involved in the drafting process—the legislation did not yet have a formal sponsor." The state representative who introduced the resulting bill several months later confessed that on the gun legislation he sponsored, "[Hammer] works on it with the analyst. Then I look it over and file it. I'm not picky on the details."

Second, as the NRA's lobbyist, Hammer has access to a large number of gun-rights supporters and she can mobilize them. One former state lawmaker estimated that Hammer's emails reach hundreds of thousands of Floridians. Moreover, a political strategist noted with awe that "The number of fanatical supporters who will take her word for anything and can be deployed almost at will is unique." And Hammer demands complete loyalty from state legislators. One prominent state politician cautioned that "If you're with Marion [only] 95 percent of the time, you're a damn traitor."

Thus, although she does not fit anyone's stereotype of the successful lobbyist, Marion Hammer has an enviable record of getting the Florida legislature to do her bidding. She does not get what she wants through campaign contributions, although they do not hurt her cause, but because she does all of the heavy legislative lifting that sets the stage for getting a bill through the legislature, and then she can rally large numbers of Floridians to pressure their representatives to pass it.

But even with all of Hammer's skill and political pull, there are rare occasions when lawmakers go against her and the NRA. Following the horrific 2018 Marjory Stoneman Douglas High School shootings in Parkland, Florida, public pressure to take some action to stem the violence caused state lawmakers to pass legislation to ban bump stocks that increase the rate at which a rifle can be fired, to impose a three-day waiting period and raise the minimum age to buy assault rifles, and to allow schools to arm staff members. Hammer opposed all but the last provision. In this instance, however, lawmakers could safely ignore her and the gun rights supporters she represents because the other side of the debate mobilized a larger number of concerned voters.

Sources: David Cole, *Engines of Liberty: The Power of Citizen Activists to Make Constitutional Law* (New York: Basic Books, 2016), 105–8; Amanda Robb, "Inside the NRA's Florida Strategy,"

Rolling Stone, March 9, 2018, https://www.rol lingstone.com/politics/politics-news/inside-the-nr as-florida-strategy-128869/; Mike Spies, "The Unchecked Influence of NRA Lobbyist Marion Hammer," *The Trace*, February 23, 2018, https ://www.thetrace.org/features/nra-influence

-florida-marion-hammer-gun-laws/; Mike Spies, "I Spent a Year Reporting on NRA Lobbyist Marion Hammer, Read Her Emails with Florida Officials," *The Trace*, March 9, 2018, https://www.the trace.org/2018/03/marion-hammer-nra-florida -document-dump/.

Good lobbyists know as much—and often more—about what goes on in the legislature as do many of the lawmakers. As a study on lobbying notes, "Lobbyists have to know the legislative process in a particular state inside and out."[28] And this means both the formal process and the political context within that state. Lobbyists spend extraordinary amounts of time reading bills, attending committee hearings, meeting with legislative staff, talking to legislators, and consulting one another. They keep in touch with their clients. They often draft proposed legislation, and they research arguments in support of their own bills and to defeat the bills they oppose. They share these arguments with the legislators they view as their allies. They form coalitions with other groups when they think it is in their interest to do so. In states where legislative staffing is limited (which, as chapter 3 documents, is most states), when committees meet to discuss the relative merits of a piece of legislation, most of the testimony, pro and con, is provided by lobbyists. In short, next to the legislators, their staff, and perhaps a few members of the executive branch and the statehouse press corps, lobbyists (as a group) know more about the lawmakers and the legislative process than anyone else in the state.

Virtually all lobbyists engage in personal, face-to-face meetings with legislators and staff. One survey of lobbying techniques finds that 98 percent of registered lobbyists say they meet personally with legislators; 97 percent say they meet personally with legislative staff.[29] The latter interaction is especially common in the more professionalized legislatures.

The most effective lobbyists spend long hours at the legislature, staying in contact, touching base, and being seen, even if they do not have much on the agenda that particular day or week. As one observer notes, "Lobbyists who simply show up in the Capitol on decision day, introduce themselves to harried lawmakers, and ask for consideration of their clients' positions don't accomplish much. Indeed, no smart lobbyist would even think of operating that way."[30]

A great deal of the "social lobby" that envelops the legislative session is designed to give interest groups and their agents some "face time" in an informal setting. As a Missouri legislator noted, "dinners have historically served as a means of 'purchasing time' with legislators whose schedules are packed when they're in Jefferson City for the legislative session."[31] Such personal interactions provide lobbyists an opportunity to make lawmakers aware of their clients' legislative preferences.

The word often used in this regard is *access*. Lobbyists insist that the campaign contributions they make and the meals and drinks they buy for legislators do not buy votes, but they help guarantee access to the lawmaker when the lobbyist needs to discuss a bill. As one observer points out, "access" in this sense really means "access before others are given access"—a sort of preferential treatment.[32] Discussing the impact of campaign contributions, a Florida lawmaker admitted, "It does buy access. If somebody gives me a campaign contribution I'm going to remember it, and I'm going to remember who they are and when they come calling, I'm going to listen to them. It doesn't mean they've bought me. But they have bought access."[33] Legislators' time is limited, especially toward the end of the session. With multiple demands made on them, lawmakers must decide who to see first, whose e-mail or text message to respond to now, whose phone calls to return. A lobbyist who is personally known to the legislator is likely to be higher on that list. Lawmakers, however, come to understand the nature of their relationship with interest group representatives. Discussing lobbyists, a veteran Vermont senator warned his younger colleagues, "They play a role here. They are good people. They tend to be fun, they tend to be bright, but their loyalty is not to you. It's to the people who pay them."[34]

Testifying at committee hearings is also a frequent activity; a study of California, South Carolina, and Wisconsin lobbyists found that 98 percent of them reported testifying at legislative hearings.[35] Some of this testimony may be persuasive, involving information new to the committee members. But the reality is that the more effective lobbyists have already had one-on-one conversations with the chair and other committee members as well as with committee staff (in states where such staff exists). In these instances, their testimony serves to reiterate and emphasize specific points and to provide a public record of the interest group's position.

Meeting with legislators and staff and testifying before committees are direct lobbying techniques. But lobbyists also engage in indirect techniques, which are designed to mobilize citizens and interest group members in the process. Organizing public rallies, letter-writing and e-mail campaigns, and telephone banks and issuing press releases are examples. Increasingly, lobbyists send a "legislative alert" to the interest group's members, urging them to contact their legislator and providing e-mail addresses to do so. Even lobbyists representing state and local governments engage in such efforts.[36] But, as generating such grassroots pressure has become cheaper and easier because of technological innovations, there is evidence that lawmakers may no longer interpret the volume of such messages as an important signal about constituent preferences.[37]

Interest Groups and Campaign Financing

Another type of interest group activity is related to elections. Some interest groups publicly endorse candidates. Generally, these are single-issue groups or ones that are closely allied with a specific party (e.g., some environmental groups and the Democratic Party; some antiabortion groups and the Republican Party). Other groups (especially corporations) tend not to formally endorse candidates. Meanwhile, organizations of local government officials such as the Texas Association of Counties are prohibited by law from active electioneering.

Many groups that do not publicly endorse candidates nonetheless signal their preferences by contributing money to specific candidates. In most states, interest groups do this through their political action committees (PACs), which are the legal entity through which campaign funds are collected and disbursed. As discussed in chapter 2, however, different states have different campaign finance laws.

When it comes to giving campaign contributions, most interest groups and their PACS are risk averse. As with social lobbying, what interest groups generally want from their campaign donations is access. Again, as chapter 2 noted, incumbents are highly likely to get reelected; consequently, most PAC money flows to incumbents. It is uncommon for PAC money to actually buy a legislator's vote on a particular bill, especially at the floor vote stage. But campaign contributions may have an effect in less visible ways—such as whether a particular bill gets introduced or receives a hearing in committee. Some interest groups are strategic in targeting campaign contributions to legislators who are likely to be their policy allies on specific committees, and to people in positions of leadership who can influence committee assignments.[38] Although the impact of campaign contributions on policymaking is greater in some states than in others, almost everywhere they are likely to at least buy access.[39] As one scholar observed, "Legislators tend to be inclined to listen a little more attentively to a group's substantive arguments if that group has contributed to their campaign."[40]

When there is no incumbent—an open-seat contest—it is not unusual for a PAC to give money to both candidates in the general election. Such behavior is a form of bet-hedging. This is not true, however, of all interest groups and PACs. Single-issue groups, groups with a strong ideological bent, and groups that are generally allied with one political party are not bet-hedgers. They tend to be "all in" for the candidates who share their ideology or who support their issue. For these groups, the job is more about getting the "right people" elected than about lobbying in the traditional sense. For such groups, the outcome of the election largely determines their success in the upcoming legislature. Simply put, when the election results in a Democratic majority, the lobbyist for the state educational association is likely to have a more successful legislative session. When the Republicans win a majority, the lobbyist for the state business association is apt to do well.

A recent phenomenon in state legislative elections is the increasing involvement of some interest groups in what are known as "independent expenditures." Rather than contributing directly to a candidate's campaign, some organizations are more likely to run their own advertisements on behalf of or in opposition to a specific candidate. Groups that are most likely to engage in such activities are either single-issue groups or organizations traditionally allied with one political party.

This trend was evident even before the U.S. Supreme Court's *Citizens United* decision in 2010, but reports indicate it has accelerated since then.[41] In Maine, for example, independent spending in legislative races increased by 600 percent between 2008 and 2012 and was four times higher in September 2018 than it was at the same time in 2016.[42] In a 2016 election to fill a vacancy in the California Senate, $12.1 million was spent during the campaign—an extraordinary amount even by California standards. Over 75 percent ($9.6 million) of those funds were independent expenditures, outside the control of the candidates.[43] A similar situation obtained in a closely contested 2018 Florida Senate race; the candidates spent a combined $1.5 million while the parties and outside interest groups injected more than $10 million into the contest.[44] And such distorted ratios are not confined to large states. A 2018 special election that determined control of the Minnesota Senate saw the two major party candidates combine to spend roughly $150,000 while independent groups poured more than $1 million into the race.[45]

Finally, some groups and their lobbyists have the luxury of "going public" and trying to create public policy through instruments of direct democracy. Not all groups—in fact, probably not many groups—have the organizational or financial resources to undertake this sort of effort. But some do, and they use this tactic when it serves their purpose.

Term Limits and Lobbyists

As a general rule, term limits have given lobbyists an opportunity to exercise greater influence in the legislature, particularly in lower houses where there are usually fewer experienced lawmakers.[46] Term limits "reduce the incentive and capacity of state legislatures to gather information available from . . . other states," and increase the likelihood that legislators will look to adopt model legislation offered by interest groups.[47] The tobacco industry, for instance, appears to hold greater sway over unseasoned legislators in term-limited legislatures.[48] Lawmakers often have to turn to lobbyists for information, and the introduction of term limits has altered the relationship between the two in fundamental ways.[49] A longtime Missouri lobbyist for trial lawyers characterizes the changes in this way:

> You can use shorthand with people who have been there for over 20 years, because issues don't really change. . . . I could go to Harold Caskey (D-Butler, retired), who had been in the Senate for 25 years when I started lobbying, and just say "This is a peer-review bill." He would know exactly what it meant, exactly what it said, and exactly why we had problems with it. There was no need for education. In fact, during my first year of lobbying, a bill came up that we weren't expecting on the Senate floor. We literally sent in a business card with the bill number, a frowny face, and a two-word topic. It wasn't that the person just trusted everything we said; it was that he knew what the information on the card meant.

In contrast, when recently arming a much less experienced legislator to oppose a particular bill to which her organization objected, the lobbyist admitted, "So we had two of our members spend four hours with [the lawmaker] in her district on a Saturday, basically teaching her discrimination law."[50] With greater turnover produced by term limits, lobbyists have to continually educate new members to bring them up to speed on important issues. As a longtime

Louisiana lobbyist reflected, "I am now part educator, almost like a college professor. . . . When I first started, I was just a salesman."[51]

Public Opinion and Direct Democracy

One of the biggest differences between the federal government and state governments is that some of the latter operate with one or more forms of "direct democracy." The three instruments of direct democracy are the recall, the referendum, and the initiative. They are used in some of the states but not at all at the federal level.[52] One or more of these instruments is available in thirty-five states, and eleven states have all three.[53] And each of these mechanisms has the potential to affect the way the legislature conducts its business.

The Recall

At the state level, the recall is the least common form of direct democracy. Nineteen states allow for it, but the requirements for getting a recall election to the ballot differ among them. But nowhere is it an easy procedure to invoke. Nonetheless, as will be documented in chapter 7, in recent years recall elections have become more common. In 2011, one legislator from Michigan and another from Arizona were successfully recalled. In 2011 and 2012, more than a dozen Wisconsin legislators were subjected to recall elections over a controversial collective bargaining measure. Three were recalled and another resigned her seat once the petition signatures were submitted to the secretary of state's office. In 2013, two Colorado senators, including the Senate president, were recalled after voting in favor of a gun control measure. Within three years, seven state legislators had been successfully recalled and another resigned prior to the recall elections. That burst of activity, however, was unusual; over the next four years recall petitions were circulated against a total of twenty-two legislators in about a half-dozen states, but none of them even qualified for the ballot. Not until 2018 was another state legislator successfully recalled, when a California senator was removed from office over his vote to support a gasoline tax increase.[54]

Although only a small number of lawmakers have actually been recalled in recent years, the potential risk of recall is taken seriously by many legislators. In July 2007, the Michigan Taxpayers Alliance began holding seminars across the state to train its members about using the recall process, just in case the legislature voted for a tax increase. As one veteran observer of Michigan politics noted, "Make no doubt about it, threat of recall has a tremendous impact on the state Legislature, in both parties."[55] For example, recall petitions were filed in June 2008 against Louisiana House Speaker Jim Tucker and three other representatives after lawmakers voted for a bill that would increase legislative salaries. In response, two of the legislators threatened with recall recanted; one asked the governor to veto the measure, and the other published a letter of apology to his constituents in a local newspaper.[56] The governor vetoed the bill, likely saving these lawmakers from facing recalls.[57]

The Popular Referendum

There are two types of referenda. The more common is the "legislative referendum," an instrument allowing (or requiring) the legislature to put a proposal before the public for a vote. In all states but Delaware, this method is used to amend the state constitution; it requires (in most states) a two-thirds approval in each legislative chamber, after which the proposed amendment is referred to the public for a vote in the next regularly scheduled election.[58] By amending the state constitution, this type of referendum can have a major impact on the policy options legislators have available to them. The legislature has a direct role in this process because such amendments require legislative approval before they are submitted to the public.

This is not the case with the second type of referendum, usually called the "popular referendum." The popular referendum is a mechanism whereby voters can override legislative actions.[59] It exists in almost half of the states. When the legislature passes a law in these states, it is possible for the general public to, in essence, "veto" the legislative action. Indeed, in Maine it is formally called the "People's Veto." Popular referenda require the circulation of petitions to gather signatures of registered voters. If enough valid signatures are gathered, implementation of the law at issue is suspended, and it is placed on the ballot in the next election for the voters to accept or reject. Clearly, then, legislatures in states with the popular referendum are subject to an additional level of scrutiny. In 2016, Nebraska voters repealed a law passed by the Nebraska Unicameral that would have banned capital punishment as a sentencing option in murder convictions. In 2018, two laws passed by state legislatures were overturned by popular vote—one in Maine (reinstating ranked-choice voting) and another in Missouri (voiding a "right-to-work" measure). Overturning legislative action through the popular referendum can have an even broader effect than just a simple "public veto" of a single bill by causing legislators to subsequently recalibrate other policy positions they hold in light of the voters' decision.[60]

The Initiative

The most common instrument of direct democracy, in terms of its effect on state legislatures, is the initiative. The initiative exists in twenty-four states, about half of which are in the West. There are several varieties of initiative. The most important distinction among them is whether the initiative can be used to both amend the constitution and make statutory law (found in eighteen states) or only to make statutory law (found in six states). Essentially, the direct initiative process allows the public to bypass the legislature. By collecting the requisite number of signatures on a petition, the public can get a proposal— either a law or a constitutional amendment—placed on the ballot for a vote. If the required number of voters approve (usually a majority), the proposal becomes law (or becomes part of the state constitution, depending on the type of initiative). Clearly, both initiative types have the potential to weaken the policymaking independence of the legislature, but an initiative that amends the state constitution has a greater impact because it precludes further legislative action on the issue.[61] In contrast, a statutory initiative can be changed by the legislature by simply writing a new law. Although this is legally permissible, it may be politically difficult. After all, a majority of voters approved the plebiscite in the first place, and they are not likely to want the legislature to overturn their decision. But it does happen on occasion, as it did in Missouri when the legislature passed a bill gutting an initiative restricting "puppy mills" that the voters had adopted only a few months before.[62] And it is also the case that in writing laws and passing appropriations to implement voter initiatives, legislators can cleverly blunt their impact.[63]

There also is a subtle influence the existence of the initiative can have on the legislative process that merits mention. There are times when the mere threat of an initiative is sufficient to force the legislature to adopt policies it might otherwise reject. In 2014, for example, the Republican-controlled Michigan legislature passed a bill to increase the state's minimum wage, a move that was an anathema to conservatives. The reason they took that action was to head off a proposed ballot proposal that would have raised the minimum wage to an even higher figure. As one Republican representative admitted, "When offered death or injury, we took injury. . . . We didn't want to raise the minimum wage as much as we did."[64] In the absence of the initiative process, the legislature would have opted to do nothing.

Other state legislatures have felt pressured by threatened ballot measures. After the Alaska legislature passed a significant ethics reform bill in 2018, one activist noted, "This only happened because more than 45,000 Alaskans signed petitions to put a similar proposal, the Alaska Government Accountability Act, on the ballot."[65] That same year, California lawmakers were prompted to pass a data privacy law and a statewide ban on soda taxes to head off likely ballot measures on those topics.[66] Even a ballot measure that fails at the polls can still impact legislative decision-making. After Ohio voters rejected a sentencing reform proposal a Republican backer of the measure remarked, "Now legislative leaders are getting together to say what can we do to address this issue. . . . It's interesting how often big public policy changes occur in Ohio because of the threat that something might go to the ballot."[67]

The menace posed by a proposed initiative varies by state. The key is how difficult or easy it is to qualify proposals for the ballot. Consequently, states where it is relatively easy to get measures on the ballot, such as California, Colorado, and Oregon, find many more issues being decided by public vote than states where the standards for qualifying measures for the ballot are more difficult, such as Mississippi and Wyoming. The average number of initiative measures on the ballot in each biennium between 2010 and 2018 is provided in table 6.1. We chose to use the biennium because most legislatures operate on two-year cycles. Over each two-year period, for example, California has witnessed an average of almost ten propositions being decided by the public. To be sure, not all these propositions pass; between 60 and 70 percent of the measures put before the voters fail. Nonetheless, it is clear that states where the initiative is a viable instrument of direct democracy operate in a different policy

TABLE 6.1 **Average Number of Initiative Measures on State Ballot per Biennium, 2010–2018**

State	Average Number of Qualified Ballot Initiatives per Biennium
California	9.6
Colorado	6.0
Washington	5.8
Oregon	4.6
Massachusetts, Missouri, North Dakota	3.0–3.8
Maine, Montana, South Dakota	2.0–2.8
Alaska, Arkansas, Arizona, Florida, Michigan, Nevada, Ohio, Oklahoma	1.0–1.8
Idaho, Mississippi, Nebraska, Utah	fewer than 1.0

Note: Figures do not include 2019 and may slightly underestimate average figures. Most states do not have ballot initiatives in odd years, but a few do—especially Colorado, Maine, and Washington.
Source: Calculated by the authors from the National Conference of State Legislature's Statewide Ballot Measures Database, http://www.ncsl.org/research/elections-and-campaigns/ballot-measures -database.aspx.

environment than the rest of the states. For one thing, many of these initiatives involve fiscal policy—either mandating spending on specific items (e.g., education) or placing limits on specific taxes. Such constraints may have long-term consequences for the ability of the legislature to manage the fiscal needs of the state. A number of other initiatives address social policy, such as same-sex marriage or abortion, and some evidence suggests that the policies in initiative states more closely represent the preferences of the general public.[68] Perhaps, then, it is not surprising that voters like the initiative. In California in 2013, for example, 72 percent of survey respondents agreed that allowing voters to make laws and change public policies at the ballot box was a good thing.[69] From the California legislature's perspective, then, the threat posed by a potential ballot measure is real.

The Governor and the Legislature

One of the most important contextual factors that affect the legislative session is the relationship between the governor and the legislature. The relationship depends on several variables, but key among them is party affiliation. When the governor and the legislative majority are of the same party, the legislature is more likely to follow the governor's lead on important policy matters and legislation moves more easily through the legislative process. An analysis in Wisconsin shows that deliberation time on bills that became law dropped from 164 days to 119 days once the Republicans gained unified party control of the government in 2011.[70] Currently there are more states with unified government than any time since the early 1960s.[71] When the governor is from one party and the legislative majority is from the other party, divided government exists. In this circumstance, the legislative majority is far less likely to bend to the will of the chief executive and instead is more likely to pursue its own policy preferences, setting the stage for legislative conflict and gridlock.

But even unified government does not guarantee smooth legislative sailing.[72] This is especially true if the legislature feels that the executive is overstepping the boundaries of institutional authority. In Utah, where both the governor and large legislative majorities were Republicans in 2018, the legislature overrode three bills vetoed by the governor in a single day, prompted by a power struggle with the executive over his refusal to call a special legislative session legislative leaders wanted the previous year. As the *Salt Lake City Tribune* noted that this reflected "a yearlong turf war where part-time lawmakers contend the full-time governor is seizing too much power."[73] And, of course, as discussed at the beginning of chapter 1, in 2018 Missouri's Republican governor was forced out of office by the Republican-controlled state legislature.

Governors enjoy inherent advantages in dealing with state legislatures.[74] One is the electoral connection; the governor is elected statewide and can claim a statewide mandate, something no state legislator can do. Another is the ability of the governor to command media interest—journalists find it easier to report on the actions of one person than those of a complicated institution like the legislature. Finally, as the leader of the executive branch, governors enjoy an information advantage over lawmakers, who, except in the most professionalized legislatures, do not have comparable policy experts at their disposal. As a study of gubernatorial power observed, "Because legislatures house every governor's primary bargaining partners, the institutional resources of the lawmakers are crucially relevant."[75] Without the time and staff to generate their own independent sources of information, legislators are at a disadvantage when negotiating with the governor.

Setting the Agenda

Governors also enjoy the power of "agenda setting." This is the process of defining the issues for public consideration—and especially for the legislature's deliberation. The primary tools are the "state-of-the state address" and the "budget address," both of which are presented by the governor to the legislature at the beginning of the legislative session and are usually accompanied by considerable pomp, fanfare, and media coverage. These addresses are really about the governor telling the public and the legislature what he or she identifies as the critical issues for consideration, floating potential solutions to these problems, and proposing budgets to pay for them and other state programs.[76] It is unlikely that any governor will get his or her way on all the matters he or she offers as worthy of consideration. But what is important is that the governor sets the parameters of the public agenda and the legislature winds up reacting to it. The governor does not set the entire agenda, of course—not by any means. Most of the bills the legislature will pass are minor or narrow in scope and have nothing to do with the governor's legislative program. But a legislature, even at its best, can only deal with a limited number of major issues in any given year. And the governor has a powerful role in defining which of those major issues should be considered. Right or wrong, the media's end-of-session assessment of how the legislature performed is often based on how much of the governor's agenda was passed.

The governor, therefore, is sometimes referred to as the "chief legislator" and has some specific tools to help persuade and cajole the legislature to do his or her bidding.[77] Some of these tools are constitutionally derived, and because constitutions differ from one another, the specifics differ from state to state. Others are a matter of personal style and political circumstances and differ from one governor to the next, even in the same state.

Budgets

We have already mentioned the *agenda setting* power afforded to the governor by the state-of-the-state address and the media limelight. The budget message is in the same vein but can be an even more powerful tool. Governors emphasize their policy priorities through the budget they submit to the legislature. State budgets are complex documents, and in most states, the governor has a much larger staff to sift through the budget items agency by agency and line by line than does the legislature. Legislatures always find items to change in the governor's budget plan—cutting a little here, adding some favored projects there—but for the most part, the legislature is only in a position to react to the governor's plan and change things on the margins. And on the back end of this process, the governor usually enjoys considerable veto power, which means he or she can cut favored legislative programs if lawmakers alter the budget plan too much. Institutional designs also tend to favor the governor. Part-time legislatures and those subject to term limits operate at a decided disadvantage in budget conflicts with the governor.[78]

There are a handful of states in which the legislature operates as a truly independent force in budgetary matters. Idaho is one such state; over the years, the legislature has developed its own Legislative Budget Office, which is well staffed and highly respected and allows the Joint Finance and Appropriations Committee (the budget committee) access to independent budget analyses. Another is Colorado, where the legislature has a long history of budgetary independence, to the point that some governors have publicly complained about their lack of power over spending.[79]

Veto Power

Given that both federal and state governments adhere to "separation of powers" among the executive, legislative, and judicial branches, perhaps the most obvious tool the governor has at his or her disposal is the veto. As a legislative leader in Vermont advised his new colleagues, "With one pen [the governor] has as much power as all the rest of us."[80] Every governor enjoys some form of veto, but the specifics of that power vary across the states, as shown in table 6.2. The particulars (how long does the governor have to veto a bill? how many votes are required to override the veto?) are important, as they help define the degree of the institutional advantage accorded to the governor.[81] The key point is that the veto is powerful because it is usually hard for the legislature to override it. In most states, a veto override requires an extraordinary majority (either a three-fifths or a two-thirds vote).[82] And this extraordinary majority must occur in both houses. It is no wonder that few gubernatorial vetoes are overturned. Indeed, in New York, the legislature failed to override a single veto of the thousands issued between 1873 and 1976![83] (New York legislators turned this institutional weakness to their electoral advantage. Lawmakers passed and took credit for measures that constituents and special interests had requested even though they knew they were poor public policy. Members could do this with clear consciences because they were confident that the governor would veto the measures and those vetoes would be sustained.)[84]

For the most part, vetoes are more likely when divided government exists—that is, when the governor is from one party and the other party has a majority in the legislature. In 2018, the governor of Maryland vetoed thirty-nine bills and the governor of Illinois vetoed eighty-eight. In both states the governor was a Republican and the Democrats held a majority in the legislature.

TABLE 6.2 Gubernatorial Veto Power

Veto Power (from strongest to weakest)	Legislative Vote Needed to Override Veto:			
	Three-fourths (1 State)	Two-thirds (37 States)	Three-fifths (5 States)	Majority (7 States)
Line-Item Veto of Appropriations Language (23 States)		CA, CO, ID, IA, LA, MA, MI, MN, MS, MO, MT, NJ, NM, NY, OH, PA, WA, WI, WY		AL, AR, KY, WV
Line-Item Veto (21 States)	AK[a]	AZ, CT, FL, GA, HI, KS, ND, OK, OR, SC, SD, TN, TX, UT, VA,	DE, IL, NE	ME, MD
Package Veto (6 states)		NV, NH, VT	NC, RI	IN

[a]   Article II, Section 16 of the Alaska constitution states "Bills to raise revenue and appropriation bills or items, although vetoed, become law by affirmative vote of three-fourths of the membership of the legislature." Other measures require only a two-thirds vote for an override. Alaska is also the only state where the legislature sits and votes together on veto overrides.

Source: Adapted by the authors from National Association of State Budget Officers, *Budget Processes in the States* (Washington, DC: National Association of State Budget Officers, 2015), 49–51.

In addition to a general (or package) veto, which is used to block an entire bill, forty-four states (counting Maryland, which has a notably weak version) permit their governors to exercise some variant of a line-item veto on budget bills. The line-item veto allows the governor to object to specific appropriations (or occasionally provisions) within a bill without vetoing the entire measure. Ostensibly, this power is granted as a way to ensure fiscal responsibility, and some governors use it extensively for that purpose; in 2014 Missouri governor Jay Nixon issued over two hundred line-item vetoes totaling more than $275 million.[85] But it also appears that governors use it to shape spending to their partisan preferences as much as they use it to lower the overall budget.[86] In 2018, Louisiana's governor, a Democrat, vetoed forty projects from his state's construction budget, saving the state $39 million. A news story on the vetoes noted that most of the dropped projects were "located in parishes represented by Republicans who often vote at odds with the Democratic governor."[87]

In some states, it is easier for the legislature to override a line-item veto than to override a general veto; in others, it still requires an extraordinary majority. But in either case, the governor, by blocking or reducing an appropriation measure, calls attention to it and makes it more difficult for the legislature to reinstate the full amount. Because vetoes (either line-item or general) are difficult to override, the mere threat of a veto is often sufficient incentive for legislative leaders to negotiate with the governor before the legislation is passed.

This is not to suggest that governors always get their way when they break out the veto stamp. Although governors usually enjoy the upper hand, relations between the two institutions occasionally degenerate to the point where legislators ignore party and unite against the executive. In 2004, for example, strong disagreement over spending priorities led the Republican-controlled South Carolina House to take only ninety-nine minutes to override 105 of 106 vetoes issued by the Republican governor. Instead of cutting $96 million from the budget, as the governor wanted, the legislature agreed to cut only $250,000. The governor retaliated by accusing lawmakers of pork barrel spending, dramatizing his point by carrying two live piglets into the House chamber.[88] The governor's antics did little to improve relations with the legislature. The next year, they overrode 153 of his 163 vetoes.[89] Touchiness between the institutions lingered even longer. When discussing a proposal to increase capitol security a few years later, the governor joked, "I have yet to read ever about any terrorism attack on a state capitol, I just don't think it's a high priority target, although sometimes I would like it to be." Legislators were not amused by the jab.[90]

Other Gubernatorial Weapons

Another tool at the disposal of some governors is the special session. Most legislatures meet for only part of the year. The legislature adjourns *sine die* (literally "without day" meaning with no appointed day or indefinitely) and is not scheduled to return until the next regular session the following year (or in the case of biennial legislatures, the next regular session two years hence). Occasionally, however, the legislature may be called back for a special session—usually to deal with an emergency or to address an important issue left unresolved at the adjournment of the regular session. In about half of the states, the governor has the power to call the legislature into special session (in the other half, only legislative leaders have such authority). Because most lawmakers are not full-time but instead have "real jobs" outside their legislative duties, being called to special session is disruptive. Although this is true of all legislators, it is especially problematic for those who live great distances from the capitol and for those with young children.[91] As in the case with the veto power, the simple threat of calling a special session may provide the governor enough leverage to get the legislature to comply with gubernatorial priorities.

Sometimes the special session and veto powers can be deployed together to great effect. In 2016 Washington governor Jay Inslee, a Democrat, battled with the legislature over two issues: developing a supplemental adjustment plan to the two-year budget and completion of a strategy for future K–12 education funding.[92] Legislative sessions in even-numbered years in the state of Washington are sixty days, and on the sixtieth day the legislature adjourned without a budget agreement or a firm plan on how to address future education spending. So, as the legislature adjourned on Thursday, March 10, and legislators were preparing to return to their home districts, the governor immediately called them back for a thirty-day special session, beginning that very evening.

That night, Inslee vetoed twenty-seven bills, including some bills sponsored by Republicans and others sponsored by Democrats. He announced "There is no break and no rest; legislators need to balance the books." Focusing on the need for a budget agreement, Inslee stated that lawmakers would have to "step up to the plate and make the hard compromises that are necessary to get a budget."

Negotiations continued for almost three weeks; on the twentieth day of the special session the governor and the legislators reached a compromise on the supplemental budget. The legislature then acted to override the governor's twenty-seven vetoes, and in a twenty-minute flurry of votes, they successfully overrode all of them. The governor said he was comfortable with that outcome because the vetoes had been designed to force the legislature to focus on reaching the necessary budget compromises.

Most observers would argue that the governor used his special session and veto tools to great effect in 2016. But it was a different story in 2017, when the governor and legislature fought through three special sessions and an impending state government shutdown before finally agreeing on a budget. It is important to recognize that each battle between a governor and the state legislature follows its own script.

To varying degrees, governors enjoy at least two more advantages: patronage and campaign assistance. Most governors have several hundred appointments to make to advisory or regulatory boards and commissions. Such patronage matters, because "although some of these are more ceremonial than substantive, legislators covet them to prove their ability to reward friends."[93] Governors can also use their appointment powers to directly entice legislators. In 2006, for example, the Indiana governor, a Republican, offered one Democratic representative a $60,000-a-year position on the state Worker's

Compensation Board and another a $55,000-a-year post on the Indiana Parole Board. (Although legislative Democrats expressed outrage, a Democratic governor had made similar offers to several GOP lawmakers a decade before.)[94] And the governor can offer (or withhold an offer) to go out of his way to help a legislator who is expecting a difficult reelection campaign. If the governor is popular, the offer to come to the district and give a speech on behalf of the lawmaker and to help raise campaign funds is hard to refuse.

The point of this discussion is that the governor has many tools—some provide positive incentives, some threaten negative consequences, and some define the playing field. The branches may be separate, but they are not necessarily equal, and in most states, the legislature finds that it is playing uphill against the governor. What all this translates to is that on major policy issues, the governor is usually a central legislative player. Much of this action occurs behind the scenes, with the governor (or key staff members from the governor's office) meeting with legislative leaders (and their key staffers) to hammer out legislation that is acceptable to both legislative chambers and the chief executive.

The Bureaucracy

A considerable amount of the legislature's time is taken up with issues involving state agencies—the bureaucracy. First, the legislature must appropriate money for governmental operations. The budget process involves agency heads coming before the legislative appropriations committees to make their case for funds. The budget is almost always the biggest issue facing the legislature. Even if the governor takes the budgetary lead, the appropriations or budget committees are intimately involved in the process.

Second, the agencies initiate some of the legislative proposals brought before the legislature each session. Some of these proposals are advanced because the agencies seek authority to do something differently than they have been doing or see the need for a new program. Other proposals are developed because the agencies find that federal grant requirements or federal or state court action obliges the agency to operate in a different manner, and therefore the agency seeks legislation to bring them into compliance. In a typical legislative session, perhaps 10 to 20 percent of the bills introduced are at the behest of state agencies.

Third, the legislature depends on the bureaucracy to carry out laws after they are enacted. Legislatures pass the laws, but they do not implement them. State (and local) agencies determine how the laws will be put into effect. In 2008, for example, the Mississippi Legislature passed HB 509, amending Section 47-1-19 of the Mississippi Code. This section authorized inmates in the state prisons or county jails to perform public service work for nonprofit charitable organizations under certain conditions. HB 509 added the following language to the code: "In addition, it is lawful for a state, county or municipality to provide prisoners for public service work for churches according to criteria approved by the Department of Corrections."[95] This was a popular measure; it was approved unanimously in the Senate, passed on a vote of 114 to 3 in the House, and was signed into law by the governor. Very simply, the legislature extended the set of "nonprofit charitable organizations" to include churches. But what, exactly, qualifies as a church? And what, specifically, are the sort of activities that qualify as "public service work"? The legislature did not specify. But the bill did say "according to criteria approved by the Department of Corrections."

In other words, the legislature set a basic policy and then left the precise manner in which the policy is to be carried out to the administering agency—in this case, the Mississippi Department of Corrections. The legislature delegated some of its authority to the agency by authorizing the department to determine what sort of activities constitute "public service work" and over what sort of religious organization qualifies a church. This is a common practice; a legislature does not have the time or expertise to write legislation so precise that it covers every possible contingency that might arise. Instead, a legislature authorizes state or local agencies to fill in many of the details. Usually, agencies are required to develop rules and standards for how they intend to implement the law, and these rules and standards are then subject to review by the legislature.

Thus, the relationship between the bureaucracy and the legislature is complicated. According to one former legislator, from a lawmaker's perspective, "administrators variously are enemies, allies, whipping boys or behind-the-scenes resources."[96] But legislators and bureaucrats each need the other to make policy work. Legislatures give agencies both money (through the budget process) and authority (to implement the policy). Legislatures then seek to oversee the way the agencies carry out the policy mandate. This oversight function is challenging to perform because most state legislatures are part time and proper oversight is a time-consuming and staff-intensive exercise. Given that legislators see lawmaking and casework as their primary functions, there is not much incentive to engage in serious oversight in most states. And it is a time-consuming undertaking that, absent a public scandal, offers little political reward for those who engage in it. Thus, oversight is an important institutional function that is typically pursued with little enthusiasm by lawmakers. Most legislatures have committees to review agency rules, and virtually all of them hire auditing staff to review agency expenditures.

The authority of the legislature to review and potentially overturn agency rules varies by state. In about fifteen states, the legislature has no agency review authority. In most states, the legislature shares this authority with the governor, but in a few the legislature (or a legislative committee) can, on its own, negate a proposed administrative rule. Thus, the rule-making calculus for state agencies may be somewhat different, depending on the rule review authority of the state legislature.[97] Nonetheless, except for a few states, legislative oversight of the bureaucracy is thin. Moreover, the ability of lawmakers to legislatively design bureaucracies in such a way as to produce the bureaucratic outcomes the legislature wants is limited.[98] Given the time and staff costs of conducting oversight, it is no surprise that part-time legislatures are less likely than more professional legislatures to devote much effort to this function.[99]

The fourth way that legislators and the bureaucracy interface is through casework. Casework, or constituent service, involves lawmakers and their staffs seeking to solve problems for individual constituents. Many times, these problems involve a state or local agency, and legislators act as intermediaries between their constituents and the bureaucrats. Constituent service is an important part of the representative function performed by legislators and is especially valued in some legislatures.[100] Because each has something of value to the other—the lawmaker can give the agency budgetary and programmatic support, and the agency can give the lawmaker assistance in solving constituent problems—they have every incentive to work together. But ultimately, the legislator holds the upper hand. As an Iowa lawmaker observed about her interactions with state bureaucrats, "You get more flies with sugar than vinegar. I usually start with kind[ness]. Death and mutilation come later."[101]

Lawmakers receive two distinct benefits from the provision of constituent services. One is a sense of satisfaction. As a legislator confessed, "I have a lot of personal reward from getting somebody's social security check or whatever. . . . I remember a grandmother calling me up once because her grandson needed drug rehabilitation—we got him into a clinic. So you get a lot of personal reward that way."[102] The second benefit is political. Constituents who see a legislator as trying to help them solve their problems are potential voters in the next election, and evidence suggests that lawmakers who emphasize casework are rewarded at the polls.[103] Not surprisingly, almost all lawmakers today view constituent service as an essential part of their job.[104] One study found that almost three-quarters of lawmakers reported they received at least five requests for help from constituents each week. Almost 20 percent said they received at least twenty-five requests a week.[105] As state populations grow, bureaucracies to serve their needs grow as well, and unfortunately, so too do problems for legislators to help solve. Consequently, casework puts lawmakers in contact with agencies on a daily basis.

The Courts

Given the American system of separation of powers, we might expect only limited interaction between state courts and state legislatures. For the most part, each branch operates in its own sphere of influence with little direct interference from the other. State courts, for instance, tend to shy away from involving themselves in internal legislative disputes.[106]

The formal relationship between courts and legislatures varies across the states, and in only a few of them does it mirror the relationship between Congress and the federal courts. In just eight states, for example, does the governor nominate state court of last resort (usually, but not always, called the state Supreme Court) judges and the state Senate confirm them in a process like the one used in the federal government. In Connecticut, Rhode Island, and Tennessee, the governor nominates and both houses of the legislature confirm them. In most other states, the governor nominates or the voters elect judges and the legislature plays no role. But in two states, South Carolina and Virginia, neither the governor nor the voters play a role; instead the appointment of judges is left entirely to the legislature.[107]

From a policy perspective, the state court of last resort can negate laws passed by the legislature if the court determines that such laws violate the state constitution. Just how often this occurs, however, varies widely across the states and across time periods within a state. In some states, legislative acts are rarely struck down, while in others 30 to 40 percent of the challenges may be successful.[108]

When courts overturn laws, or reach decisions lawmakers do not like, the legislature can respond. If they choose, legislators can rewrite laws to address the court's concerns, or they can pursue alternative policies. Indeed, state legislatures are more likely to respond to decisions to overturn laws by their state courts than they are to federal court decisions that overturn their laws.[109] And on rare occasions, legislatures can respond with remarkable speed. When in 2014 the Massachusetts Supreme Judicial Court handed down a decision holding that state law did not prohibit the perverse practice of taking "upskirt" photos, the following day outraged lawmakers drafted a bill outlawing it, passed it in both chambers, and sent it on to the governor.[110]

State Courts and Policy Mandates

Typically, the influence of state courts on legislation is subtle. Policies adopted by the legislature are often shaped by court decisions at the bill development stage, as lawmakers anticipate potential legal challenges to a proposed law.[111] There is, for example, evidence that legislatures take the ideological orientation of their state supreme court into account when developing abortion and death penalty legislation.[112] Still, direct clashes between the legislature and the state courts occasionally occur. In 2005, the Kansas Supreme Court found on state constitutional grounds that the legislature was illegally underfunding public education. As a remedy, the court ordered the legislature to increase spending on schools by at least $285 million annually. Education funding issues have arisen in most states, and in many of them, the state court has taken a position similar to that in Kansas, which mandates the legislature to fund public education at a higher level.

Kansas Republicans, who held the majority in both houses, were outraged and railed about the "non-elected judiciary's willingness to usurp the will of the people."[113] Some GOP legislators argued that they should ignore the court's decision. One proclaimed, "I believe the Legislature's duty is to disregard this unconstitutional and unpermissive order of the court."[114] Another Republican suggested that the process by which Supreme Court justices get put on the bench be changed so as to require Senate confirmation, arguing that doing so would make it more likely that the court and the legislature would move in sync.[115] A third Republican legislator raised the possibility of impeaching the members of the court.[116] Other lawmakers, however, counseled restraint, with one saying, "I tend to be upset with the court, too, and you want to say 'stick it.' But I don't know what the ramifications of [trying to punish the court] would be. We could be in an even stickier situation than we are now."[117]

As the battle between the institutions dragged on, Kansas legislators jumped on opportunities to take swipes at the Supreme Court. The House, for example, cut $3.7 million from the court's budget, which, of course, is under the legislature's control.[118] It took two years for the funding issue to be resolved to the court's satisfaction. But, grudgingly, the legislature increased spending for the public schools. And in the end, although many legislators railed about the court's actions, the judicial appointment process was not changed.[119]

But by 2014, the education funding was again before the Kansas Supreme Court. Despite admonishments not to do so from the governor and legislative leaders, the court ruled once more that the legislature had failed to meet the state constitutional mandate for adequate school funding. Inter-branch sniping resurfaced, with the House Education Committee chair saying this was a budget issue "and clearly that duty lies with the legislative branch. I don't believe that's the place of the court." The Supreme Court responded by noting that it has the duty to determine if legislative acts are in line with the state constitution, and "the judiciary is not at liberty to surrender, ignore or waive this duty."[120] In 2018, under court order, the Kansas legislature was set to increase spending on public education, but some lawmakers wanted to tie the spending increase to a ballot measure that would strip the Court's authority to rule on the issue of "adequacy funding."[121]

By June, the legislature had devised a plan to increase funding over the next five years, but the state Supreme Court determined that the new funding scheme was still inadequate because it had not taken into account inflation for future spending. The Senate president vented her frustration, saying, "The unelected bureaucrats of the Kansas Supreme Court chose to continue the endless cycle of litigation," and opining that "when Kansas is on par with Nancy Pelosi's California for sky-high property taxes and families are fleeing the state, we can thank the Kansas Supreme Court."[122] It is likely that some legislators will continue to press efforts to pass a state constitutional amendment to limit the jurisdiction of the state supreme court in the matter of school funding.[123]

Kansas is not alone in this game of tug-of-war over the legislature's and court's roles in education funding. Similar turf battles were recently played out in states as diverse as New Hampshire, New Jersey, Ohio, Vermont, and Washington. And the legislative response in some of those states has been similar to that in Kansas. After the Washington Supreme Court issued a ruling that the legislature was not responding quickly enough to its order to increase school funding, an unhappy senator introduced one bill mocking the court's decision and another measure to reduce the number of justices.[124]

Other issues have triggered similar legislative outbursts against state courts. In 2018, Iowa Republican lawmakers, unhappy with a number of court decisions, proposed legislation cutting the judicial branch's budget and docking the chief justice's pay.[125] After Pennsylvania's Supreme Court declared that the state's congressional redistricting plan passed by a Republican legislature violated provisions of the state constitution, a number of GOP lawmakers vowed to impeach the justices.[126] West Virginia's House of Delegates actually took things one step further, charging the four sitting justices on the state's Supreme

Court of Appeals with a series of offenses and voting to impeach all of them.[127] None of these efforts came to fruition—West Virginia's impeachment cases largely fell apart in a morass of procedural problems—but they all signaled continuing discord between the legislative and judicial branches in a number of states.

State Courts, Direct Democracy, and Policymaking

In states where "direct democracy" instruments are commonplace, the courts play an important role because they must often mediate between the legislature and the proponents of various initiatives. Some of these issues directly affect the legislature, term limits being the obvious example. Today fifteen states have legislative term limits, but as noted in chapter 1, at one time or another, twenty-one states passed term limits—nineteen of them through the initiative process. In four of those states—Massachusetts (1997), Washington (1998), Oregon (2002), and Wyoming (2004)—the state supreme court struck down term limits as a violation of some aspect of each state's constitution. And in 2014, Illinois courts blocked a term-limit initiative from appearing on the ballot in that state.[128] But the courts in each of the remaining term-limit states upheld them, determining that there was no violation of the particular state constitution. Tax and expenditure limits (TELs) are another example of an issue in which the interpretation of voter initiatives taken by the state courts can have an important effect on a legislature's independence, in this case in its ability to craft a state budget.

The Fiscal Factor

As we discussed briefly in chapter 5, state budgets are constrained in ways the federal budget is not. For example, all states but Vermont have a balanced-budget requirement, although just how stringent that constraint is varies from state to state.[129] About half of the states have laws (either statutory or constitutional) that place specific limits on revenue or spending (e.g., a law limiting the increase in spending per capita to the rate of inflation).[130] Furthermore, a dozen states (almost all of them states with the initiative process) require a supermajority vote to raise taxes. Some of these mandate a popular vote—not just a vote by the legislature—to increase taxes. More than three-fourths of the states have restrictions on the type and amount of bonded indebtedness the state can undertake. What all this means is that state legislatures are much more limited than the U.S. Congress in their options for setting fiscal policy and devising budgets. Unlike the federal government, the states, for the most part, must live within their financial means. This often requires making difficult policy choices, all with political implications. Consequently, setting a budget that is acceptable to a majority in each chamber and to the governor can be a challenge. And in years of economic downturn, it can be a painful process for legislators. States are responsible, in whole or in part, for public education, higher education, health care, roads and highways, prisons, and a host of other public services and regulations. That leaves state lawmakers pondering, "Do we cut programs? Do we raise taxes? Do we do both? Do we do neither?" Lawmakers know that some segment of the population will be unhappy with whatever answer they reach.

During the Great Recession, as state revenues dropped by more than 10 percent in many places, almost every legislature had to make tough decisions about increasing taxes or cutting programs. States depleted their budget reserves ("rainy day funds"). Almost every state cut spending and government programs. By 2012, over a half-million public sector jobs had been eliminated.[131] At least thirty-three states were forced to raise taxes.[132] The point is that state legislators arguably face a more daunting budget process than do members of Congress because they are forced to make agonizing choices.

Legislatures have devised procedures to cope with the complexities of setting budgets. Most have come to rely on one of two mechanisms for getting the budget done. One option is to defer most of the budget decisions to the relevant standing committees (usually called the appropriations, budget or finance committees). These committees do the lion's share of the work in putting together the budget and the floor largely goes along with their recommendations. The other option is to delegate most of the budget-setting power to the party leadership in the two chambers, along with the governor. In New York, for example, it is widely understood that the governor, the Senate majority leader, and the Assembly speaker negotiate the final budget.

Many legislatures also have specific deadlines for revenue projections, committee reports on the budget, and final passage. For most states, the fiscal year begins on July 1, so the budget must be approved before that date. But, of course, disagreements can keep budgets from getting passed on time. Of the forty-one budgets in California between 1977 and 1978 and between 2017 and 2018, for instance, only twenty were passed on time.[133]

The Federal Factor

Obviously, state legislatures are greatly affected by the federal relationship. On some occasions, legislatures are constrained by federal actions; on other occasions, they are forced to act. Federal court decisions, congressional statutes, executive orders issued by the president, and federal agency rulings can all influence state legislative policymaking.[134] The federal grant-in-aid program (fiscal federalism) is especially important in this regard because federal money to states is often tied to specific policy or program requirements. In 2016, for example, the Tennessee General Assembly passed a drunken-driving law that accidentally ran afoul of standards set by the federal government, putting $60 million in federal road funds at risk. Lawmakers had to fix their error so that they did not lose millions in federal money.[135]

In recent years, the most high-profile instance of federal action affecting states is the Patient Protection and Affordable Care Act of 2010 (known as the ACA, or "Obamacare"). Because states varied widely in their own health insurance mandates, the net impact of the ACA differs from one state to another. The fact that states may set up their own health insurance exchanges or choose to use the federal exchange complicates matters. Furthermore, some states have chosen to expand Medicaid coverage under the ACA while other states have not.

The situation in which the national government creates policies that must be carried out by state governments is referred to as "coercive federalism," and it is a trend that accelerated during the administrations of President George W. Bush and President Barack Obama.[136] In response to the feeling that both the Bush and the Obama administrations pushed national mandates onto the states, many legislators became more aggressive in fighting back against what they saw as national government intrusion into state policy domains. As legislatures have become more capable over time, they appear to be more assertive of their own prerogatives and less willing to quietly comply with federal mandates. Of course, this is also clearly tied to political polarization and the ideological distance between the parties.[137]

Increased polarization at the national level affects state legislative behavior in other ways. When issues before the state legislature are framed as issues with national implications, legislators are more likely to vote along party lines. When national political implications are less evident, bipartisan votes in the legislature are more common.[138]

It is not just congressional actions that affect state legislatures, of course. By far, most of the laws struck down by the U.S. Supreme Court are state laws, not congressional acts. Some—perhaps most—of the more momentous U.S. Supreme Court decisions have had sweeping effects on states and their legislatures. The reapportionment cases of the 1960s are an obvious example. With *Reynolds v. Sims* the U.S. Supreme Court forced the states to reapportion legislative seats to more closely approximate the "one person, one vote" principle. The long-term impact on state legislatures was substantial, including increased representation of urban and suburban constituencies, which resulted in greater responsiveness to those interests at the expense of rural concerns.

A good illustration of how federal court action influences state legislatures and policymaking is the response to the 2005 U.S. Supreme Court case of *Kelo v. New London*.[139] In *Kelo* the Court asserted that a city had the authority to exert "eminent domain" (the taking of private property, generally for public good) even for a private economic development. Here, the U.S. Supreme Court essentially upheld an interpretation of the Connecticut Supreme Court that Connecticut law allowed such taking. Within one year of the *Kelo* decision, thirty legislatures had passed new laws clarifying and limiting the use of eminent domain in their respective states.[140]

The Local Government Factor

Local governments are creatures of the state government. They are created by the state and derive their powers from it; they have no independent constitutional standing. Thus local governments in their various incarnations—counties, cities, special districts, school districts, and the like—are dependent on state governments for their policing, regulatory, and taxing authority.[141]

All of this means that local governments are not sovereign; they owe their claim to govern to a grant of authority, usually called a charter, from the state government. The charter sets what local governments can or cannot do, and what they are required to do. In some states, local governments are given a fair amount of freedom to operate as they see fit (typically referred to as "home rule"). In others, the state—especially through the legislature—places strict limits on the powers of local governments. Such constraints can bring local governments into conflict with the legislature.

In the last decade considerable regulatory tension has arisen between some states and their local governments. One authority on this relationship observes, "Because states have vast legal powers over local governments, a state may order its local units to do all sorts of things: regulate private activities, provide services, refrain from using some types of taxes, limit tax rates, utilize a particular personnel system—the possibilities are enormous."[142] The tension can be especially intense between a state legislature and the larger cities and more urban counties within that state. Currently, many state legislatures are controlled by Republicans and they usually have conservative policy preferences. But urban areas typically elect liberal Democrats to office who push progressive agendas.[143] Thus, the potential for conflict is obvious. Since 2012, for example, forty cities and counties across the country have passed legislation raising their minimum wage above the level established by the federal government.[144] But in a number of states, Republican lawmakers have overturned such efforts. When Birmingham, Alabama, raised its minimum wage, Republicans in the state legislature passed a bill eliminating the power for any local government in the state to raise its own minimum wage. A GOP representative conceded, "While we say we want local control of certain things, I don't believe the minimum wage is one of those."[145] State lawmakers in Florida, Iowa, Kentucky, and Missouri have taken similar steps.[146]

Such measures are referred to as "preemption laws" and they are increasing in frequency as Republican-controlled state legislatures opt to limit the ability of Democratic-controlled local governments to pursue liberal policies.[147] Some preemption laws enjoy broad appeal and are found in many states. Laws limiting what local governments can do in regard to firearms regulation are found in forty-three states.[148] Other preemption laws target seemingly smaller matters. In 2018, for example, the Tennessee legislature passed a measure requiring the Tennessee Historical Commission to issue a waiver before any local government can remove a statue, monument, or historical marker. This action was taken after the city of Memphis had managed to take down two statues of Confederate leaders.[149] And Arizona's governor signed a bill preventing any city or county in the state from adopting a tax on sugary drinks.[150]

Local government officials resent preemption laws. When Columbia, Missouri, explored the idea of banning plastic bags, the Republican-controlled legislature stepped in and passed a bill blocking any such prohibitions. A Columbia city council member who had been a Republican candidate for the state House, responded, "While I'm opposed to local governments, or anyone, banning useful products, I am even more opposed to our state representatives getting involved in our local issues."[151] But states have the legal authority to pass such bills. As a North Carolina lawmaker commented, "If you don't like it, run for state government and try and change it."[152]

Conclusion

In important ways, state lawmakers are more constrained in their legislative actions than are members of Congress. There are at least three reasons for this reality. First, national laws, executive orders, and federal court decisions may limit or require certain actions by the states—although it is true that nowadays state legislators are more willing to try to resist such actions when they are viewed as unwarranted intrusions into state policymaking. In recent years, this "pushback" by some legislatures has had a decidedly partisan tone to it; Republican-dominated legislatures resist the ACA just as Democratic-dominated legislatures resisted the No Child Left Behind Act during the George W. Bush years and now resist some of the Trump administration's immigration policies.

Second, state legislators are constrained by fiscal realities not found at the federal level. The most important of these, of course, is the state requirement for a balanced budget. Almost all state legislatures must operate under such fiscal restrictions; this is not the case for Congress. The implications of this are great; when it comes to budgeting, state legislatures are forced to be closely attuned to state economic trends.

Finally, many state legislatures must consider their actions in light of the existence of the instruments of direct democracy. In particular, the initiative, the referendum, and the recall mean that state legislators may be bound by constituent desires in ways that members of Congress need not be.

Chapter 7

Are State Legislatures Representative Institutions?

A rally in support of the recall of a Colorado state senator in 2013. The senator was recalled. AP Photo, *The Gazette*, Michael Ciaglo.

Over the preceding chapters, we documented that although state legislatures share some important characteristics with Congress and with each other, by and large they are a varied lot. Each legislature enjoys a unique history and a distinctive configuration of organizational structures. Electoral contexts also vary, as do the powers the governor enjoys, the roles interest groups play, and the ability of voters to enact legislation. But beyond appreciating their variety, can we offer any assessments of state legislatures as representative institutions? Do they perform the many tasks expected of them by the people they represent and serve?

Evaluating the performance of legislatures is a daunting endeavor, and we have no simple answers to offer. Instead, we will compile bits and pieces of evidence to try to reach a realistic appraisal of the job they do. We will begin looking at how the public rates their legislatures and the information people have at their disposal to make those judgments. We then note the quandaries lawmakers often face as they go about trying to represent their constituents. Ultimately, we conclude that state legislatures, even if flawed, are representative institutions.

What Do Election Results Tell Us about Evaluations of State Legislative Performance?

In a representative democracy, the ultimate assessment of legislative performance occurs at the ballot box. After all, that is where voters can reelect or replace their lawmakers. Consequently, we might assume that if most incumbents get reelected, then the voters must be pleased with their performance in office. If legislators lose their reelection bids, then we might conclude that voters were dissatisfied.

As we noted in chapter 2, most lawmakers are successful in their efforts to retain office. The incumbent reelection rate across the states for 2001–2016 approached 94 percent, meaning that ninety-four of every one hundred incumbents who sought reelection were successful.[1] This is, of course, an impressive figure and is comparable to that for members of Congress over the same period. Even in the great Republican electoral wave of 2010, 87 percent of incumbents seeking reelection were successful.[2] As we would expect, legislators in more professional legislatures are able to exploit the additional institutional resources they enjoy for their electoral benefit and get reelected at a slightly higher rate than their counterparts in less professional bodies.

If incumbent reelection rates reflect voter satisfaction, then it might be concluded that the public thinks its legislatures are doing a good job. That assessment, however, is too simplistic. A number of explanations beyond voter contentment might account for these impressive reelection rates. As noted in chapter 2, more than one-third of all state legislative elections are uncontested by one of the major parties. In those districts, voters are not provided an alternative through which to express their possible dissatisfaction with the incumbent. We also noted that population distribution patterns and redistricting practices often conspire to make legislative districts safe for one party, again dampening potential competition and limiting the utility of election results as a measure of voter contentment. Finally, the fact that incumbents have the ability to raise the financial resources they need to communicate with the voters while their challengers generally do not also makes any purported link between reelection rates and voter satisfaction suspect.

Ample evidence also suggests that support expressed for an individual legislator does not necessarily translate into support for the institution in which the member serves. A 2013 survey in New York, taken at a time when the state government was routinely being called dysfunctional, revealed that although only 34 percent of respondents approved of the job the legislature was doing, 48 percent approved of their Assembly member and 56 percent approved of their senator.[3] Perhaps even more telling are the results from a 2007 survey of Illinois voters. Respondents were asked, "Suppose you could vote to keep all of the state legislators in office or to kick them all out and start with an entirely new legislature. If the election were held today, how would you vote?" Only 19 percent would have opted to keep the current legislature; 55 percent preferred instead to elect a whole new batch of legislators.[4] This is a striking result and an indictment of an uncompetitive electoral process given the fact that roughly 95 percent of Illinois incumbents get reelected.

There is one other kind of election that casts light on public evaluations of lawmakers. As discussed in chapter 6, in nineteen states voters are authorized to pursue recall elections, allowing them to remove legislators from office before the scheduled end of their terms. Recall elections are rare events, but, as table 7.1 documents, they are occurring with greater frequency in recent years. During the first six decades in which recall elections were allowed, only five such contests were held. During the next four decades, an average of roughly four recall elections occurred every ten years. But between 2010 and 2018 seventeen recall elections were called, as many as in the previous forty years combined.

Do these data point to growing public dissatisfaction with legislators? Of the seventeen recalls since 2010, twelve occurred in Wisconsin. All were politically motivated, with Democrats enjoying modest success in removing several Republicans who voted in favor of stripping government workers of many collective-bargaining rights, while Republicans failed in their efforts to oust several Democrats who had fled the state to prevent a quorum. In the remaining five cases, a Republican Michigan representative was recalled over

TABLE 7.1   Recall Elections for State Legislators, 1910 to 2018

Years	Number of Recall Elections	Number of Legislators Recalled
1910–1969	5	3
1970–1979	2	2
1980–1989	5	4
1990–1999	6	3
2000–2009	3	1
2010–2018	17[a]	8

[a] In addition, two lawmakers resigned rather than face recall elections.
Sources: Data gathered by authors, primarily from National Conference of State Legislatures, http://www. ncsl.org/research/elections-and-campaigns/recall-of-state-officials.aspx, and Ballotpedia, https://ballotpedia.org/State_legislative_recalls#2018.

his vote in support of state education financing reform, a longtime Arizona Senate GOP leader tainted by scandal was removed, two Colorado Senate Democrats were defeated because of their pro-gun-control votes, and a California senator lost after voting for a gas tax increase. In a sense, the lawmakers who lost recalls were removed from office because voters—at least those who participated in their recall elections—were dissatisfied. But it is worth pointing out that the majority of legislators who face recall elections survive them. And those who lose are often already in a weak political position. The California senator who lost in 2018, for example, only faced a recall election because he represented a competitive district that he had won by just a few votes. The leader of the recall effort admitted, "Lions don't go after all the gazelles, they work together to take down the weakest, slowest one. Let's think like a lion and use the recall process to pick off one member, their weakest member."[5] Still, even though recall efforts are launched against only a sliver of lawmakers and most fail, the fact that some succeed likely chills the actions of many of their colleagues.

How Highly Do Citizens Rate Their State Legislatures?

It appears that people like their local lawmakers, yet dislike the body in which they serve. How do citizens rate the performance of their legislatures? In a 1999 national survey that asked how much trust or confidence respondents had in a number of governmental institutions, people expressed less confidence in their state legislatures than in their local police, governor, public schools, or local courts.[6] Although this ranking might appear not to reflect well on the legislature, it is important to note that more than two-thirds of respondents had a great deal of or some trust or confidence in it. Thus, on the whole, state legislatures fare reasonably well in terms of public trust or confidence.

As we might expect, however, ratings of state legislative performance varies across the states. Approval scores for selected state legislatures in 2018 are shown in table 7.2. A majority of people in seven states approved of the performance of their state legislature. In contrast, less than a third of the population gave them a favorable rating in five states. The scores were mixed in the rest.

Across all of these states no obvious explanations for the ratings leap out. Intriguingly, as was noted in chapter 3, a negative relationship between professionalization and public evaluation of legislatures has been documented at other times. That is, generally the more professional the legislature, the less people approve of it.[7] This finding is true even though, as pointed out in chapter 3, contact between representatives and the represented increases with professionalization, as does policy responsiveness.[8]

But we may want to avoid reading too much into this relationship. While some newspaper columnists rail about the shortcomings of full-time legislatures, recent efforts to switch the professional legislatures in California and Michigan to part-time bodies failed to get enough signatures to even make it

TABLE 7.2 Public Approval of State Legislatures, by Approval Percent, 2018

State (Month of Survey)	Percent Approve	Percent Disapprove	Percent Don't Know/ Undecided
Utah (February)	63	30	8
Tennessee (March)	58	37	5
Georgia (March)	57	38	5
Mississippi (March)	56	39	5
New Hampshire (February)	56	26	18
Alabama (March)	53	41	6
Idaho (March)	51	40	9
California (March)	46	38	16
New York (February)[b]	44	37	19
South Carolina (February)	44	38	18
Colorado (November)[a]	43	31	26
Virginia (September)[a]	43	43	13
Maryland (February)	42	34	24
New Jersey (March)	37	41	22
Florida (February)	34	50	16
North Carolina (April)	32	35	32
Oklahoma (January)	31	57	12
Iowa (January)	26	48	26
Kentucky (April)	25	58	17
Minnesota (November)[a]	24	37	39

[a] The Colorado, Minnesota and Virginia surveys were conducted in late 2017.

[b] Separate questions were asked for the Assembly and the Senate. The number reported here is the average of the two.

Sources: (AL) NBC News/SurveyMonkey Alabama State Poll, April 12, 2018; (CA) PPIC Statewide Survey, "Californians and Their Government," March 2018; (CO), Colorado Political Climate Survey, January, 2018; (FL) Quinnipiac University Poll, "Nelson on Plus Side of Close Florida Senate Race, Quinnipiac Poll Finds," February 27, 2018; (GA) NBC News/SurveyMonkey Georgia State Poll, April 12, 2018; (ID) Idaho Politics Weekly, "Idahoans Have Higher Opinion of State Legislature Than Congress," May 6, 2018; (IA) Public Policy Polling, "NEW POLL: Iowans Reject Republican Tax Cuts, Overwhelmingly Support Public Services," January 8, 2018; Big Red Poll, April 11–15, 2018; (MD) Goucher Poll, February 21, 2018; (MN) Survey USA, http://www.surveyusa.com/client/PollReport.aspx?g=9ed21a28-1db6-466c-9cf1-dd22afcd5f9f; (MS) NBC News/SurveyMonkey Mississippi State Poll, April 12, 2018; (NH) Granite State Poll, "Sununu Remains Popular, Holds Lead over Prospective Democratic Opponents," February 13, 2018; (NJ) Quinnipiac University Poll, "Menendez Has 17-Point Lead over GOP Challenger; Quinnipiac University Poll Finds," March 13, 2018; (NY) Siena College Research Institute, February 5–8, 2018; (NC) Survey USA, http://www.surveyusa.com/client/PollReport.aspx?g=c23131ad-7e15-4068-9655-df1486ef9b7c; (OK) Sooner Poll, "Could Fallin Be the Most Unpopular Oklahoma Governor in Modern Times?" January 20, 2018; (SC) Winthrop Poll, https://www.winthrop.edu/winthroppoll/default.aspx?id=9804; (TN) NBC News/SurveyMonkey Tennessee State Poll, April 12, 2018; (UT) utahpolicy.com, "Utahns Give Hebert, Utah Legislature High Approval Ratings in New Poll," March 1, 2018; (VA) Quinnipiac University Poll, "Dem Tops 50 Percent; Up 10 Pts in VA Governor's Race, Quinnipiac University Poll Finds," September 19, 2017.

on to the ballot.[9] Moreover, surveys probing voters' views on various aspects of legislative professionalization produce a mixed picture. A national survey conducted in 2018 found that "Most respondents didn't know if being a state legislator was a full-time job."[10] That same year a survey of Michigan residents found that 48 percent of them supported the idea of reverting to a part-time legislature, while 35 percent opposed it and 18 percent were undecided.[11] An overwhelming 70 percent of Pennsylvanians agreed with calls for reforms to alter "The structure and operations of the state legislature, including the size of the legislature and term limits for elected officials."[12] At the same time, 54 percent of New Mexico residents backed the idea of paying their state legislators an annual salary while only 33 percent opposed it. And 65 percent favored extending the length of the legislative session; only 27 percent were opposed.[13] In 2015, New Yorkers were offered a choice. By a 59 to 35 percent margin they supported the idea of a full-time legislature while requiring a ban on all outside employment. But by virtually the same margins they also backed a part-time legislature with full disclosure of members' outside income.[14] Taking all of this together, it does not appear that voters really know what kind of legislature they might want.

Several other plausible explanations for legislative ratings also fail to find much support. Whether a state has imposed term limits or allows ballot initiatives does not appear to be related to how the public evaluates the legislature.[15] Voters also are not particularly troubled by the behavior of more polarized bodies.[16]

Instead, partisanship currently appears to drive how people evaluate their legislature, as demonstrated by table 7.3, which gives approval scores by party identification and party control of government across twelve states in 2018. In the states where one party is in full control of the government, supporters of that party generally approve of the legislature's performance. Thus 66 percent of California Democrats approve of their state legislature while 81 percent of Utah Republicans approve of their state legislature. In contrast, adherents of the out party express disenchantment. Approval ratings for legislatures in states where control is split are almost always much lower, with partisans from both sides giving their legislature lackluster scores.

How does legislative approval fluctuate over time? It seems clear that when the economy performs well approval scores move higher. When the economy performs poorly, as it did during the Great Recession, approval scores trend downward. Accordingly, looking at approval scores for the California legislature—an institution for which we have a long time series of data—the body received its highest average ratings in 1988 and 2017 (57 percent), both years when the state economy was booming, and its lowest average mark in 2010 (14 percent), when the state was mired in the depths of economic contraction.[17] This relationship suggests that public evaluations of legislative performance are tied to things such as the performance of the economy over which state legislators have little, if any, real influence. And that might raise a question about the basis on which people render judgments on their legislatures.

TABLE 7.3 Public Approval of State Legislatures, by Political Party and Party Control of Government, 2018

State (Month of Survey)	Party Control of Legislature Party Control of Governorship	Percent Approve	Percent Democrats Approve	Percent Republicans Approve
California (March)	Democratic Democratic	46	66	17
New Jersey (March)	Democratic Democratic	37	50	22
Colorado (November)[a]	Divided Democratic	43	60	27
New York (February)[b]	Divided Democratic	44	54	36
North Carolina (April)	Republican Democratic	32	29	42
Minnesota (November)[a]	Republican Democratic	24	31	22
Virginia (September)[a]	Republican Democrat	43	44	41
New Hampshire (February)	Republican Republican	56	54	62
Florida (February)	Republican Republican	34	17	55
Idaho	Republican Republican	51	18	72
Kentucky (April)	Republican Republican	25	20	31
Utah (February)	Republican Republican	63	27	81

[a] The Colorado, Minnesota, and Virginia surveys were conducted in late 2017.
[b] Separate questions were asked for the Assembly and the Senate. The number reported here is the average of the two.
Sources: (CA) PPIC Statewide Survey, "Californians and Their Government," March 2018; (CO) Colorado Political Climate Survey, January, 2018; (FL) Quinnipiac University Poll, "Nelson on Plus Side of Close Florida Senate Race, Quinnipiac Poll Finds," February 27, 2018; (KY) Big Red Poll, April 11–15, 2018; (ID) Idaho Politics Weekly, "Idahoans Have Higher Opinion of State Legislature Than Congress," May 6, 2018; (MN) Survey USA, http://www.surveyusa.com/client/PollReport.aspx?g=9ed21a28-1db6-466c-9cf1-dd22afcd5f9f; (NH) Granite State Poll, "Sununu Remains Popular, Holds Lead over Prospective Democratic Opponents," February 13, 2018; (NJ) Quinipiac University Poll, "Menendez Has 17-Point Lead Over GOP Challenger; Quinnipiac University Poll Finds," March 13, 2018; (NY) Siena College Research Institute, February 5-8, 2018; (NC) Survey USA, http://www.surveyusa.com/client/PollReport.aspx?g=c23131ad-7e15-4068-9655-df1486ef9b7c; (UT) utahpolicy.com, "Utahns Give Hebert, Utah Legislature High Approval Ratings in New Poll," March 1, 2018; (VA) Quinnipiac University Poll, "Dem Tops 50 Percent; Up 10 Pts in Va Governor's Race, Quinnipiac University Poll Finds," September 19, 2017.

How Much Do People Know about Their State Legislatures and Legislators?

Considerable evidence suggests that most citizens know little about their state lawmakers or the institution in which they serve. In 2006, for example, Utahns were asked in a survey to name their state senator or representative. Only 17 percent could name both of their legislators, and another 17 percent could name one of them. The remaining 66 percent of respondents either were not certain of their lawmakers' names or admitted that they did not know them.[18] Comparable results were obtained in a 2018 North Carolina survey. Only 17 percent of North Carolinians could correctly identify their state senator while 22 percent could identify their state representative.[19] A national survey taken that year reported remarkably similar numbers.[20]

The most powerful state legislators are also little known by the public. When New Yorkers were asked their opinion of Assembly Speaker Sheldon Silver in 2013, one-third of them could not offer one, suggesting that they were unfamiliar with Silver's name even though he had held the top post for two decades and was currently embroiled in a major scandal.[21] Two years later Silver's successor as speaker, Carl Heastie, was unknown to 73 percent of respondents even though he was the first African American to hold that position.[22] In 2018, almost three-quarters of Oregonians were so unfamiliar with Tina Kotek that they were unable to express an opinion on her, even though she was in her fifth year as the speaker of the State House and was the first lesbian in American history to have held such a lofty post.[23] Such results are not surprising. A 1998 New Jersey survey asked if respondents could name the Assembly speaker or the Senate majority leader. Only 2 percent could name the speaker, which was better than the 1 percent who could name the Senate majority leader.[24] Similarly unimpressive results were obtained in a 2018 North Carolina poll: Only 11 percent could name the State Senate president pro tem and 8 percent the Speaker of the House. At the same time, 77 percent of North Carolinians could name Cam Newton as the quarterback of the NFL's Carolina Panthers.[25]

Even some of the most basic information about their legislature escapes many voters. For example, in a 2018 national survey "About half [of respondents] couldn't say if their state had a one or two-house legislature."[26] In a 2014 survey only 44 percent of Tennessee residents could correctly identify which party controlled their legislature even though the GOP held more than two-thirds of the seats in both houses.[27] Perhaps most shockingly, a survey conducted two weeks before the 2007 New Jersey legislative elections revealed that three-quarters of the state's registered voters were unaware of the impending contests.[28] Collectively, these data suggest that although many people may express an opinion about their legislature's job performance, there may not be much substance behind those evaluations. But it should be acknowledged that on rare occasion, voters do pay somewhat closer attention. In the 2018 North Carolina survey alluded to earlier, 86 percent of respondents correctly identified the GOP as the majority party in the state legislature.[29] At the time, the state legislature had been at the center of a number of controversial public policy debates. Thus, only under exceptional circumstances do most Americans focus enough on their state legislatures to have even the most cursory information about them at their disposal.

How Much Information about State Legislatures Is Available?

Americans appear to know little about their state legislatures or legislators. But how much information about the institutions and their members is readily available to them? As Politics under the Domes 7.1 documents, there is almost nothing in popular culture to help voters understand legislatures or lawmakers. Perhaps even more troubling, there are fewer and fewer stories from the state capitol printed in newspapers and broadcast on television and radio every year. For some time, observers have lamented decreases in the number of reporters assigned to cover state legislatures.[30] Recently, the decline has been precipitous. Between 2000 and 2009, for example, the number of full-time statehouse reporters in New Jersey dropped to fifteen from fifty, with the *New York Times* completely eliminating its Trenton bureau.[31] A Washington State reporter estimated that the 2014 press corps in Olympia was only one-third as large as it had been in 1991.[32] In 2017 it was thought that the full-time press corps covering the Illinois state legislature was only 25 percent of the size it had been at the beginning of the 1990s.[33] In Oregon, the number of statehouse reporters shrank from thirty-seven as recently as 2005, to just thirteen in 2018.[34] Also in 2018, "A veteran of the Arizona Legislature noted that the state Senate needed only six chairs to accommodate all the reporters covering the chamber."[35] And these examples are not aberrations. A survey of statehouse reporters nationally found that their overall number had plunged 35 percent just between 2003 and 2014.[36]

The decrease in the number of reporters focused on the capitol has important implications for the public. In the last decade a shocking number of lower house speakers have run into ethical and legal problems, forcing them out of office, leading observers to suggest that they may be prone to misbehavior because they dominate their houses without much scrutiny by the media.[37] But the worry is not only about the absence of media watchdogs focused on legislative leaders. A veteran statehouse reporter in Florida, concerned by the loss of colleagues in Tallahassee, observed, "Twenty years of reporting from here have taught me that lawmakers behave differently when they know a hometown reporter is watching."[38] Events in the Massachusetts House one ugly night in 2000 support this assertion. According to an analysis of the incident:

> Massachusetts legislators drank, caroused and slumbered through an all-night session while their leaders added nearly $200 million to the state budget, apparently illegally recording the votes of absent members while the rank and file chanted "Toga! Toga! Toga!" on the House floor. Lawmakers partied in a committee office, purportedly shaved a freshman colleague's leg as a prank while he was sleeping, then fell asleep themselves in a cloakroom, snoring so loudly they could be heard outside in the hall. "Will the House please come to order?" one member implored. "No!" his giddy, giggling colleagues shouted back. . . . But one thing was left out of the follow-up [news] coverage: There

had been no reporters in the chamber that night, out of a Statehouse press corps that numbers in the dozens. It took days before the legislators' most egregious personal conduct was reported.[39]

Reflecting on these events, the speaker admonished journalists about meeting their professional obligations, placing some of the blame for the unfortunate episode on them, saying, "You bring in the light, and in the light we have to make these decisions."[40] A Rhode Island legislative leader recently expressed the same expectations. After one representative complained publicly about the "insane amount of drinking" at the State House, the leader defended the legislature and its members by observing that "If there was anything wrong, I'm sure the [*Providence*] *Journal*, the radio people, and the TV people would have reported it."[41] Everyone in state capitols operates under an assumption that the press may make their behavior public. The question then becomes what happens when the media is missing?

POLITICS UNDER THE DOMES

State Legislators on Screen

Politics is a common topic in American popular culture, but state legislators rarely register as characters. And when they appear on screen, the depictions of them are almost never positive.

Lawmakers are usually portrayed as either corrupt or cartoonish. Legislators and legislatures rarely take center stage in popular culture. According to a survey, out of the many thousands of movies that have been produced, only six have focused on state legislatures, and one of those movies, the 2006 version of *All the King's Men*, was a remake of the 1949 original. These productions have occasionally captured important facets of legislative behavior and process, but events in them were usually overdramatized and the lawmakers cast in a negative light. The single broadcast television series to feature a state legislator, *Slattery's People*, which ran in the mid-1960s, did provide a positive portrayal of a lawmaker. But poor ratings caused the program to be canceled midway through its second season. As two television historians concluded about the program's demise, "People wanted entertainment rather than conscience."

In recent years, shady legislators have been easy to find on television. Look, for instance, at HBO shows. On *The Sopranos*, New Jersey Assembly member Ronald Zellman was on the mob family's payroll, assisting them in fixing problems large and small. One of the recurring characters on *The Wire* was Maryland senator R. Clayton "Clay" Davis, a notoriously corrupt politician who continually pocketed bribes. And after Bill Henrickson was elected a Utah senator in *Big Love*, the Senate pinned him on statutory rape charges related to his polygamist lifestyle. Later, the leader of a competing polygamist sect attempted to murder him in the capitol.

State legislators fared little better elsewhere. In the second season of the Netflix program *Ozark*, a casino bill battle in the Missouri Senate resulted in one senator committing suicide after being black-mailed over his mental health problems, another senator selling his vote for a large campaign contribution, and a third senator being extorted to force her support. A Showtime production, *Brotherhood*, centered on "an ambitious" member of the Rhode Island House of Representatives, who was "not above bending the rules." In an episode of CBS's *The Defenders*, two Las Vegas defense lawyers were "shocked when their client, a state senator, is charged with the kidnapping and burglary of his mistress in the midst of a divorce case."

On the rare occasion when lawmakers are not being depicted as crooked or troubled, they are being portrayed as buffoons. Take Robert Lipton, a state senator on *The Office*. Lipton married one of the office accountants, but he was cuckolded when she was found to be carrying another man's baby. But that mattered little because the senator turned out to be a closet homosexual. All of this was, of course, played for comedic effect.

Do such depictions really matter? They may. In 2018, for example, a Deadspin .com humorist commented, "There are a great many things about this country I prefer not to think about, and one of them is that, while Congress is the absolute fucking worst, state senators and assemblymen are somehow 500 times more insane." For most Americans, politics is background noise in their lives. Although, as we have argued throughout this book, the decisions lawmakers make influence daily life in important ways, most people rarely focus on them or the institutions in which they serve. Consequently, the way legislators are portrayed in movies and on television are often the main images people see, and the ones that they likely carry with them rather than those of the real-life versions. When fictional legislators are always depicted in an unfavorable light, it tends to feed Americans' worst fears about politics and politicians.

Sources: Mordecai Lee, "Pop Culture as Civics Lesson: Exploring the Dearth of State Legislatures in Hollywood's Public Sector," *Public Voices* 12 (2012): 49–67, Drew Magary, "Shake Shack Is Our Most Overrated Fast Food Restaurant," Deadspin.com, September 4, 2018, https://adequateman.deadspin .com/shake-shack-is-our-most-overrated-fast-foo d-restaurant-1828796718; Christopher H. Sterling and John Michael Kittross, *Stay Tuned*, 3rd ed. (Mahwah, NJ: Lawrence Erlbaum Associates, 2002), 440, and additional information gathered by the authors from IMDB.com and other sources.

But beyond influencing legislative behavior, the lack of media coverage also impacts voters. Without newspapers, television, and radio paying attention to the legislature, it becomes much more difficult for people to learn about their lawmakers and the decisions they make. One study revealed that people living in and around Richmond, Virginia, where (because it is the state capital) the local newspaper gives considerable coverage to governmental affairs, were much better informed about state politics than people in the rest of the state who read local papers that focused on other topics.[42] Thus, it appears that people are not averse to learning about their legislature, but they have to be immersed in information about it for it to penetrate their consciousness. Unfortunately, another study revealed that considerably more newspapers were cutting back on coverage of state government and politics than were increasing it.[43] Current trends indicate that people in the future will be exposed to less information about state government through the traditional media of newspapers, television, and radio.

Potentially filling this information vacuum, at least partially, is an increasing cadre of bloggers and other nontraditional reporters who cover their state legislature on a daily basis.[44] According to a 2014 study, almost 20 percent of all statehouse reporters now work for nontraditional outlets, such as digital-only sites and nonprofit organizations.[45] These new media reporters are of many different types, from professional journalists to volunteers or political junkies. In many cases, they provide more detailed information about day-to-day legislative events than the traditional media provide, although they occasionally run into difficulties gaining press credentials allowing capitol access.[46] A major concern, however, is that many of the new media reporters offer overt ideological perspectives, meaning that consumers of them need to be wary.[47] While the quality of their reports varies, there is little doubt that because of them the flow of information about state legislatures today is actually more voluminous and represents a broader range of perspectives than what was available through the mainstream media in the past. There is little evidence, however, that many citizens take advantage of these various nontraditional news outlets. In December 2018, for example, a Twitter public list of statehouse reporters had 331 members but only fifty-nine subscribers.[48]

Institutionally, state legislatures have responded to the decline in attention from the mainstream media by exploiting new technologies to create alternative avenues to reach citizens. Every legislature has developed a website to make information available. The quality of these websites varies; wealthier states with better-educated populations have pages that are much more accessible and interactive than those in poorer and less well-educated states.[49] By and large, legislative websites have tended to foster civic engagement rather than interaction between the representative and the represented. They do, however, appear to be reasonably well used.[50]

Email has also increased the ease with which constituents can contact their legislators. Lawmakers have found it to be useful in engaging with constituents, although this is more the case with members of less professional legislatures than with their counterparts in more professional bodies. Legislators, however, are less sanguine about their email interactions pushed by interest groups.[51] Indeed, they have reacted negatively to blanket emailing efforts intended to influence them. A North Carolina senator, for instance, took to the floor to vent about an email he had received opposing proposed cuts in spending on public schools. By mistake, instructions from a school principal to her staff detailing how the message could be sent on to legislators had been left on the email. The senator complained to his colleagues, "It looks like they're using e-mail not so much to inform and request assistance, but to harass us."[52] For similar reasons, an Idaho senator got his state's technical staff to change the Senate's system so that people could not send emails to every lawmaker simultaneously. A member of the Idaho House sympathized with the Senate's decision, noting, "E-mail in the beginning was a personal expression of opinion from somebody in my district. E-mail is starting to become like getting 500 postcards that all say the same thing."[53] Several New York lawmakers have said that phone calls to their offices have a greater impact on them than do emails.[54]

State legislatures have exploited other new technologies to connect with the public. By 2018, almost every state legislative party caucus had a Facebook page and an active Twitter account, and a number were on Instagram.[55] Many also posted videos on YouTube. Indeed, some caucuses were widely present across social media platforms. Arizona House Republicans, for example, had a blog and could be found on Flickr, Instagram, Facebook, Google+, Twitter, and YouTube. Some legislators use blogs as a way of keeping in touch with their districts; even more use Facebook for that purpose. Given that lawmakers are disproportionally drawn from the ranks of older generations, it took a while for these innovations to catch on. For instance, the first South Carolina legislator to post regularly on YouTube, a middle-aged lawyer, reflected, "Who would've thought it would've been me? I was dragged into the new age by my daughters."[56] But within a short period of time many of his colleagues across the country had figured out how to exploit social media.

But new technology has brought new problems. In 2018, several state lawmakers had to deal with legal and public relations difficulties involving their blocking of disgruntled constituents from posting on their social media accounts.[57] A Washington legislator got entangled in a dispute with the state Legislative Ethics Board because she embedded state-funded photos and videos on her campaign Facebook page. Had she simply provided links to this material rather than embedding it, she would not have run afoul of the state law governing the use of state materials.[58] Clearly, a raft of new skills are needed to operate successfully in the ever-changing world of technology, leading a Hawaii representative to marvel that even as a lawmaker "You almost have to be an expert in graphics and designing and mailing and newsletters and e-newsletters and social media, and . . . that you now have thousands of people that you now have to communicate with."[59]

More systematically, by 2016, at least one chamber in all fifty states offered live webcasts or television broadcasts of legislative proceedings; forty-two states also had webcasts of some or all committee hearings. Television broadcasts of legislative sessions—essentially state versions of C-SPAN—were available in thirty-four states.[60] How many people take advantage of these offerings, however, is questionable. A few years ago, the Minnesota House Public Information Services reported that its live and archive webcast streams had 11,652 distinct (meaning a unique Internet Protocol address) visitors—an unimpressive number in a state with a population of more than five million. Perhaps even more depressingly, the Virginia Senate estimated that it had only seventy to one hundred daily users of its streaming video.[61]

Twitter usage data for state legislative related accounts also are less than impressive. As of December 2018, not many legislative caucuses had as many as fifteen thousand followers, and several had far fewer—Massachusetts House Republicans, for example, had only 330 followers. By way of comparison, former president Barack Obama enjoyed over 104 million followers. Clearly, when it comes to covering events at the statehouse, these new media still do not yet enjoy the reach of the mainstream media.

Yet it is important to note that there are occasions when new media events attract considerable attention. When in 2013 Texas Senator Wendy Davis took to the floor in pink sneakers to filibuster an antiabortion bill, her effort and the accompanying uproar in the public gallery was live-streamed around the country. Clips were quickly uploaded to YouTube. Although Davis ultimately failed to stop the bill, she became an instant national celebrity, appearing on every network television Sunday talk show only days later.[62]

There is an additional source of information about state legislators that merits mention. Although the voting public may not pay close attention to their lawmakers, as noted in chapter 6, interest groups do. Various interest groups publish ratings based on how lawmakers vote on legislation of importance to the organizations. Most of these scores are given on a scale of 0–100, where a higher score indicates greater support for the rating group's policy positions. Occasionally, a group gives out letter grades. Some states have a number of different ratings generated. Following the 2015–2016 legislative session, for example, at least ten scorecards were available for Wisconsin voters; among those issuing them were the Metropolitan Milwaukee Association of Commerce, Wisconsin AFL-CIO, Wisconsin Professional Police Association, and Wisconsin Sierra Club. For voters who are sufficiently motivated to locate these ratings, they can provide insight into their legislators' policy preferences, at least in specific issue areas.

Do State Legislators Represent Their Constituents?

Given that people know very little about their state legislatures or legislators, we might surmise that lawmakers do not feel constrained by constituent opinion. After all, it often seems that nobody is watching them. A survey of legislators offers some support for this notion. Far more of them leaned toward a "trustee" orientation, meaning that they placed greater weight on pursuing policies that they considered to be right for their state than toward a "delegate" orientation, one in which they would strive to accurately represent the preferences of their constituents.[63] There also is evidence that lawmakers are more responsive to constituent service requests than they are to demands to take specific public policy positions.[64] These findings might indicate that most legislators feel comfortable substituting their own judgment on issues in place of those expressed by their voters.

Yet, as discussed in chapter 6, analyses of legislative roll-call voting suggest otherwise. Voters hold the same expectations for state legislators as they do for their members of Congress.[65] Consequently, state lawmakers' votes generally align with the preferences of the voters in their districts.[66] Indeed, legislators work hard to match their representational styles to the characteristics and needs of their constituents.[67] And in a survey, 88 percent of lawmakers assessed their performance in representing their constituents as either "excellent" or "good."

Indeed, they assigned themselves considerably lower scores on legislating than on representation.[68] Anecdotal evidence suggests that members take to heart what little they hear from their constituents. A Kansas lobbyist observed, "The home constituent who takes the time to contact their legislator can have a tremendous impact on the process. When a constituent wakes up and calls in on a property tax issue or a school finance issue, [lawmakers] pay attention."[69] Another lobbyist agreed, saying, "Legislators have been known, if they got four letters for it and two against it, to vote for it. They say, 'Well, I've got a mandate from the people.'"[70] Along these lines, a Missouri representative confessed that he switched his position on an important bill because "I got more calls telling me to vote for it than I did against it."[71] Ample evidence supports the assertion that rather than ignoring the folks back home, legislators are actually obsessed with voter opinion, and they do a good job of representing the policy views of their constituents, particularly when they actively monitor them and have specific information on their preferences.[72]

There are, however, caveats to this generally positive assessment. One recent study suggests that constituents do not do a particularly good job of holding state legislators electorally accountable for their legislative roll-call votes.[73] Indeed, in many cases voters appear to adopt positions communicated to them by their state legislators, even when those stances are inconsistent with the voters' previous positions. This suggests that they often defer to their elected representatives.[74] Legislators themselves also introduce bias into the relationship. Evidence shows that in 2012 and 2014 state legislators from both parties overestimated their constituents' support for conservative policies.[75] Another obstacle is that lawmakers may not know the problems their districts face as well as they believe.[76] And there are occasions when lawmakers get buffeted by conflicting demands from their constituents and their party leaders, leading them to engage in waffling on their support or opposition to specific bills.[77] Finally, what actually gets to the roll-call-vote stage in the legislative process has been shown to be more likely to reflect the issues deemed important by more affluent voters rather than those identified by low-income voters, again possibly distorting the representational process.[78]

The Dynamics of Representation at the State Level

Earlier, we pointed out that the public seems to hold individual legislators in higher regard than they hold the legislative institution. We are far from the first to note this; it is a phenomenon long recognized at the congressional level.[79] As others have documented, the public appears to judge the institution and the individual lawmaker on different criteria. More precisely, the judgment is made on different aspects of representation.

The Components of Representation

Representation is a complex concept; political theorists and political scientists recognize that it is a relationship in which designated agents (in this case elected officials) are responsive to the needs of the people they represent.[80] But there are numerous ways to be "responsive." "Policy responsiveness"—voting on legislation in a manner consistent with the district's wishes—is one obvious and important aspect discussed in chapter 6.

But there are other aspects of responsiveness. One is *service responsiveness*, what we call "casework" or "constituent service," and it is discussed in several places in this book. It entails helping individual constituents with problems. In its simplest form, it may involve nothing more than providing information, but it often involves "redressing grievances."[81] In these instances, the representative becomes an "ombudsman," acting as an intermediary and advocate for individual constituents in their dealings with state (or federal or local) bureaucracies. Many lawmakers take this part of the job seriously, as one northeastern legislator's comments exemplify: "I think that one of my personal priorities for any particular day is making sure my constituent stuff is done. I call people back. I let them know that I'm working on their problem immediately. . . . People ought to know that their representatives are responsive, and that they care and that they are going to try to help folks out."[82]

Another component is *allocational responsiveness*, which involves "securing government funds for the constituency."[83] This ranges from construction projects within the district to efforts to redefine funding formulas for state aid to local school districts.[84] A good example of allocational responsiveness is the reaction by Idaho senator Shawn Keough when the State Department of Transportation advisory board reordered the priority list of infrastructure projects in early 2009. The board, arguing that they needed to "spread the wealth" among all parts of the state, moved refurbishing of a much-traveled bridge in the senator's district from the top priority to number seven on the list of projects. The senator exclaimed, "I'm just astounded. . . . I think it's breathtaking that they would take the worst bridge in the state and . . . treat it in the manner they did. It's a pretty important issue for my district."[85]

By raising the issue publicly, Senator Keough put the transportation board on the defensive and forced the governor to take up the issue. As discussed in chapter 6, budgets in most states must be balanced, and this requirement means that it is more difficult for a state legislator to "deliver the pork" than it is for members of Congress. Nonetheless, there are almost always some building projects to be funded, and, as shown in chapter 5, lawmakers seek to exert control over those funds.

Several students of legislatures identify another aspect of representation as *communication between the constituency and the representative*. Earlier in this chapter we noted that legislators are exploiting newer technologies such as e-mail and Facebook to stay in touch with their constituents. But there are more traditional ways that legislators seek to do this as well. During the session, many legislators write and mail newsletters in an attempt to keep their constituents updated on legislative issues. Some write weekly columns for hometown newspapers. And when in their district, most lawmakers feel compelled to attend as many local events and meetings as possible. As one Massachusetts legislator put it, "There are always more events, meetings, and conferences to attend than one human can accomplish. . . . Legislators, as representatives, have to be constantly available to one and all."[86] Most lawmakers recognize the value of the service, allocation, and communication aspects of representation, and they work assiduously at them. It seems it is often on the basis of these activities that legislators are evaluated by their constituents. Indeed, given that representation is a complex concept, they pursue it in different ways depending on the contexts in which they serve.[87]

The Changing Dynamics of the Job

In chapter 3, we noted widespread variation among legislatures on a number of dimensions, including staff resources, compensation levels, and time demands. But, of course, the job entails more than just the time when the legislature meets. For one thing, casework does not end when the session concludes. And the obligation to attend meetings in the district does not disappear. It is almost certainly the case that the general public overestimates the amount of money legislators are paid and underestimates the amount of work involved in their job. Lawmakers themselves recognize early on that the job is far more than it seems on the surface. Many would agree with this statement by a Connecticut legislator: "I think in fairness, for somebody to do their job adequately, if you factor out the whole year, the extra hours to count when you're in session, campaigning, responding, you're really getting paid half-time for a full-time job. . . . To do the job adequately takes full time. I just don't think people recognize that."[88]

The job has changed in part because the number of constituents each lawmaker represents has increased. Since 1970, the population of the United States has grown by about 50 percent; because state legislatures do not add seats to accommodate population growth, the typical legislator today has 50 percent more constituents than his or her predecessors did a generation ago. A study conducted in the 1990s asked veteran lawmakers—those who had been in office for a minimum of fifteen years—about the changes that had occurred during their time in office. More than 91 percent said the pressures of the job had increased and more than 87 percent said the demand for constituent services had increased.[89]

Again, as noted in chapter 3, about three-quarters of legislators think that the job is at least the equivalent of a half-time position. Another study finds similar results; a typical state is Maryland, where 83 percent of the legislators claimed to work at least fifty hours per week during session and at least fifteen hours per week when not in session.[90] As populations grow, so, too, do the demands of the job.

The key thing here is that communication with constituents and casework are the activities that correlate highest with legislators' assessment of the amount of time they spend on the job.[91] And lawmakers believe it is an important part of what they do: Constituent service was rated as the "most important task" of the legislator in surveys of the Connecticut and New York legislatures.[92]

A Final Assessment

In 2005, a budget battle between the governor and the legislature forced the Minnesota government to shut down for several days. Lawmakers feared that constituents would vent their unhappiness over the legislature's role in the political mess when they saw them during public events, such as parades. One senator reported that the majority leader actively dodged any such abuse by marching with several neighborhood kids. "He spent the whole day with them. And he said it was great. Not one person yelled at him. He figured nobody would get mad at him if he had four little children walking around him."[93]

Fortunately, most state legislators do not need a pint-sized posse to protect them from the public. Generally, people like their lawmakers and are accepting of, if somewhat ambivalent about, the institutions in which they serve. Yet, except in rare circumstances, people actually know little about the legislature, its members, or the decisions they make. Unfortunately, little is likely to change about this reality. The mainstream media is becoming less and less useful as a source of information about the legislature, as news-gathering resources are drawn away from the capitol. Legislatures and legislators have seized on new technologies to try to reach their constituents, but it does not appear that people are all that interested in taking advantage of these opportunities. Elections could conceivably help alleviate the lack of information, but that can only happen when challengers have sufficient resources to make their case to the voters.[94] Sadly, most legislative elections are uncompetitive; indeed, in a shocking number of cases, seats go uncontested. That means much of the burden for overseeing the legislature falls onto interest groups. The good news is that the number of such groups is increasing in every capitol, meaning there are more and more eyes trained on the legislature. The bad news is that each interest group tends to see only its own policy trees and not the larger forest.

But people may be comfortable with this situation. Although state legislatures are flawed in some regard, with occasional scandals, policy mistakes, and an absence of political courage or policy boldness, voters still return incumbents to office in overwhelming numbers. And perhaps more tellingly, state legislatures do well in comparison with other legislative institutions. When a national sample was asked in 2007 which governmental body it trusted more when it came to matters of government spending and fiscal responsibility, 18 percent said Congress and 60 percent picked their state legislature.[95] Thus, when asked to evaluate the performance of state legislatures, a reasonable response might be "Compared with what?" Although state legislatures are far from perfect institutions and citizens may express some discontent with them, they appear to be preferred to many of the alternatives.

Appendix

TABLE A.1 The Fifty State Legislatures (in Alphabetical Order)

State	Legislature Name	Upper House Name	Upper House Size	Upper House Term	Lower House Name	Lower House Size	Lower House Term	Lower House Members Per Senator
Alabama	Legislature	Senate	35	4	House of Representatives	105	4	3.00
Alaska	Legislature	Senate	20	4	House of Representatives	40	2	2.00
Arizona	Legislature	Senate	30	2	House of Representatives	60	2	2.00
Arkansas	General Assembly	Senate	35	4	House of Representatives	100	2	2.86
California	Legislature	Senate	40	4	Assembly	80	2	2.00
Colorado	General Assembly	Senate	35	4	House of Representatives	65	2	1.86
Connecticut	General Assembly	Senate	36	2	House of Representatives	151	2	4.19
Delaware	General Assembly	Senate	21	4	House of Representatives	41	2	1.95
Florida	Legislature	Senate	40	4	House of Representatives	120	2	3.00
Georgia	General Assembly	Senate	56	2	House of Representatives	180	2	3.21
Hawaii	Legislature	Senate	25	4	House of Representatives	51	2	2.04
Idaho	Legislature	Senate	35	2	House of Representatives	70	2	2.00
Illinois	General Assembly	Senate	59	4[a]	House of Representatives	118	2	2.00
Indiana	General Assembly	Senate	50	4	House of Representatives	100	2	2.00
Iowa	General Assembly	Senate	50	4	House of Representatives	100	2	2.00
Kansas	Legislature	Senate	40	4	House of Representatives	125	2	3.13
Kentucky	General Assembly	Senate	38	4	House of Representatives	100	2	2.63
Louisiana	Legislature	Senate	39	4	House of Representatives	105	4	2.69
Maine	Legislature	Senate	35	2	House of Representatives	151	2	4.31
Maryland	General Assembly	Senate	47	4	House of Delegates	141	4	3.00

State	Legislature	Chamber	Size	Term	Chamber	Size	Term	Ratio
Massachusetts	General Court	Senate	40	2	House of Representatives	160	2	4.00
Michigan	Legislature	Senate	38	4	House of Representatives	110	2	2.89
Minnesota	Legislature	Senate	67	4	House of Representatives	134	2	2.00
Mississippi	Legislature	Senate	52	4	House of Representatives	122	4	2.35
Missouri	General Assembly	Senate	34	4	House of Representatives	163	2	4.79
Montana	Legislature	Senate	50	4	House of Representatives	100	2	2.00
Nebraska	Legislature (Unicameral)	N/A	N/A	4	N/A	N/A	N/A	N/A
Nevada	Legislature	Senate	21	4	Assembly	42	2	2.00
New Hampshire	General Court	Senate	24	2	House of Representatives	400	2	16.67
New Jersey	Legislature	Senate	40	4[b]	General Assembly	80	2	2.00
New Mexico	Legislature	Senate	42	4	House of Representatives	70	2	1.67
New York	Legislature	Senate	63	2	Assembly	150	2	2.38
North Carolina	General Assembly	Senate	50	2	House of Representatives	120	2	2.40
North Dakota	Legislative Assembly	Senate	47	4	House of Representatives	94	4	2.00
Ohio	General Assembly	Senate	33	4	House of Representatives	99	2	3.00
Oklahoma	Legislature	Senate	48	4	House of Representatives	101	2	2.10
Oregon	Legislative Assembly	Senate	30	4	House of Representatives	60	2	2.00
Pennsylvania	General Assembly	Senate	50	4	House of Representatives	203	2	4.06
Rhode Island	General Assembly	Senate	38	2	House of Representatives	75	2	1.97
South Carolina	General Assembly	Senate	46	4	House of Representatives	124	2	2.70
South Dakota	Legislature	Senate	35	2	House of Representatives	70	2	2.00
Tennessee	General Assembly	Senate	33	4	House of Representatives	99	2	3.00
Texas	Legislature	Senate	31	4	House of Representatives	150	2	4.84
Utah	Legislature	Senate	29	4	House of Representatives	75	2	2.58

(Continued)

TABLE A.1 (Continued)

State	Legislature Name	Upper House Name	Upper House Size	Upper House Term	Lower House Name	Lower House Size	Lower House Term	Lower House Members Per Senator
Vermont	General Assembly	Senate	30	2	House of Representatives	150	2	5.00
Virginia	General Assembly	Senate	40	4	House of Delegates	100	2	2.50
Washington	Legislature	Senate	49	4	House of Representatives	98	2	2.00
West Virginia	Legislature	Senate	34	4	House of Delegates	100	2	2.94
Wisconsin	Legislature	Senate	33	4	Assembly	99	2	3.00
Wyoming	Legislature	Senate	30	4	House of Representatives	60	2	2.00

[a] Illinois Senate seats are divided into three electoral classes. In each ten-year period, a senate seat has two four-year terms and one two-year term.
[b] New Jersey Senate terms are two years in the first election after redistricting each decade and are then followed by two four-year terms.

TABLE A.2 Constituency Size by State and House Chamber, 2013 (from Smallest to Largest)

State	Lower House Seats	District Population[a]	State	Upper House Seats	District Population
New Hampshire	400	3,309	North Dakota	47	15,391
Vermont	150	4,178	Wyoming	30	19,422
Maine	151	8,797	Montana	50	20,303
Wyoming	60	9,711	Vermont	30	20,888
Montana	100	10,152	South Dakota	35	24,139
Rhode Island	75	14,020	Rhode Island	38	27,671
North Dakota	94	15,391	Alaska	20	36,757
Alaska	40	18,378	Maine	35	37,951
West Virginia	100	18,543	Nebraska	49	38,133
Delaware	41	22,579	Delaware	21	44,083
Kansas	125	23,512	Idaho	35	46,061
Connecticut	151	23,815	New Mexico	42	49,650
South Dakota	70	24,139	West Virginia	34	54,538
Mississippi	122	24,518	New Hampshire	24	55,144
Hawaii	51	27,530	Hawaii	25	56,162
Arkansas	100	29,594	Mississippi	52	57,523
New Mexico	70	29,790	Iowa	50	61,808
Iowa	100	30,904	Kansas	40	72,349
Utah	75	34,001	Oklahoma	48	80,220
Missouri	163	37,081	Minnesota	67	80,901
Oklahoma	101	38,124	Arkansas	35	84,554
South Carolina	124	38,507	Connecticut	36	99,891
Minnesota	134	40,451	Utah	29	100,030
Massachusetts	160	41,830	South Carolina	46	103,801
Maryland	141	42,048	Kentucky	38	115,666
Kentucky	100	43,953	Louisiana	39	118,602
Louisiana	105	44,052	Maryland	47	126,145
Alabama	105	46,035	Oregon	30	131,002
Idaho	70	46,061	Indiana	50	131,418
Georgia	180	55,512	Nevada	21	132,864
Wisconsin	99	58,007	Alabama	35	138,106
Pennsylvania	203	62,925	Washington	49	142,274
Oregon	60	65,501	Colorado	35	150,525
Tennessee	99	65,616	Massachusetts	40	167,321
Indiana	100	65,709	Wisconsin	33	174,022
Nevada	42	66,432	Missouri	34	177,770

(Continued)

State	Lower House Seats	District Population[a]	State	Upper House Seats	District Population
Colorado	65	81,052	Georgia	56	178,432
North Carolina	120	82,067	Tennessee	33	196,848
Virginia	100	82,604	North Carolina	50	196,961
Michigan	110	89,960	Virginia	40	206,510
Illinois	118	109,171	Illinois	59	218,341
Ohio	99	116,877	Arizona	30	220,887
New York	150	131,008	New Jersey	40	222,483
Washington	98	142,274	Pennsylvania	50	255,476
Florida	120	162,941	Michigan	38	260,411
Texas	150	176,321	New York	63	311,923
Arizona	60	220,887	Ohio	33	350,631
New Jersey	80	222,483	Florida	40	488,822
California	80	479,157	Texas	31	853,168
			California	40	958,313
Mean		67,908	Mean		158,256
Median		42,048	Median		117,134

[a] Arizona, Idaho, New Jersey, North Dakota, and Washington elect two lower house members in each upper house district; thus, each lower house member represents as many constituents as the corresponding upper house member, and that is the number reported here. Maryland, New Hampshire, South Dakota, Vermont, and West Virginia have "mixed" electoral systems with some single-member districts (SMDs) and some multimember districts. For this table, the district population figure is calculated for the SMDs in those states, except for South Dakota. Nebraska's unicameral legislature is considered as an upper house and not included in this table.
Source: Calculated by the authors using U.S. Census Bureau data for 2013.

TABLE A.3 State Legislative Professionalization, 2015

State	2015 Rank	2015 Score[a]
Alabama	34	.175
Alaska	8	.296
Arizona	14	.264
Arkansas	24	.207
California	1	.629
Colorado	12	.268
Connecticut	13	.267
Delaware	27	.203
Florida	15	.245
Georgia	42	.149
Hawaii	7	.321
Idaho	35	.169
Illinois	9	.294
Indiana	40	.156
Iowa	17	.241
Kansas	31	.181
Kentucky	36	.162
Louisiana	29	.187
Maine	41	.154
Maryland	10	.278
Massachusetts	2	.431
Michigan	5	.401
Minnesota	25	.204
Mississippi	37	.161
Missouri	16	.243
Montana	45	.116
Nebraska	21	.230
Nevada	30	.182
New Hampshire	50	.048
New Jersey	20	.233
New Mexico	43	.140
New York	3	.430
North Carolina	18	.238
North Dakota	47	.112
Ohio	6	.384
Oklahoma	22	.229
Oregon	23	.214
Pennsylvania	4	.417
Rhode Island	28	.200

(Continued)

State	2015 Rank	2015 Score[a]
South Carolina	39	.156
South Dakota	48	.103
Tennessee	44	.136
Texas	19	.234
Utah	46	.115
Vermont	33	.178
Virginia	32	.178
Washington	11	.272
West Virginia	38	.157
Wisconsin	26	.204
Wyoming	49	.081
Mean		.225
Median		.203

[a] A state legislature's professionalism score is based on its member pay, number of days in session, and staff per member, all compared with those characteristics in Congress during the same year.

Source: Adapted from Peverill Squire, "A Squire Index Update," *State Politics & Policy Quarterly* 17 (2017): 361–71.

TABLE A.4 State Legislative Salaries as of June 2018 (from Highest to Lowest)

State	Legislative Salary	Estimated Legislative Salary with Expenses Included[a]	Median Household Income in State, 2016
California	**$107,241**	**$142,953**	$66,637
Pennsylvania	**$87,180**	**$100,905**	$60,979
New York	**$79,500**	**$91,158**	$61,437
Michigan	**$71,685**	**$82,485**	$57,091
Illinois	**$67,836**	**$75,884**	$55,137
Hawaii	$62,604	**$76,104**	$72,133
Massachusetts	$62,548	No per diem	$72,266
Ohio	**$60,584**	No per diem	$53,985
Wisconsin	$50,950	$54,055 (S) $55,189 (A)	$59,817
Alaska	$50,400	$75,150	$75,723
Maryland	$50,330	$64,370	$73,760
New Jersey	$49,000	No per diem	$68,468
Washington	$48,731	$56,051	$70,310
Alabama	$46,257	No per diem	$47,221
Delaware	$45,291	No per diem	$58,046
Minnesota	$45,000	$49,472 (S) $48,432 (H)	$70,218
Arkansas	$40,188	$47,163	$45,907
Oklahoma	$38,400	$48,256	$50,943
Missouri	$35,915	$44,325	$55,016
Colorado	$30,000	$41,160	$70,566
Florida	$29,697	$38,817	$51,176
Connecticut	$28,000	No per diem	$75,923
Indiana	$25,945	$33,730	$56,094
Iowa	$25,000	$42,640	$59,094
Oregon	$24,216	$38,328	$59,135
Arizona	$24,000	$29,970	$57,100
Mississippi	$23,500	$37,765	$41,099
Louisiana	$22,800	$31,492	$42,196
Tennessee	$22,667	$30,224	$51,344
West Virginia	$20,000	$25,764	$44,354
Virginia	$18,000 (S) $17,640 (H)	$26,120 (S) $25,760 (H)	$66,451
Idaho	$17,358	$27,678	$56,564
Georgia	$17,342	$24,262	$53,527

(Continued)

State	Legislative Salary	Estimated Legislative Salary with Expenses Included[a]	Median Household Income in State, 2016
Rhode Island	$15,630	No per diem	$61,528
North Carolina	$13,951	$22,375	$53,764
Maine[c]	$12,215	$16,135	$50,856
Nebraska	$12,000	$22,800	$59,374
South Carolina	$10,400	$21,512	$54,336
Vermont[c]	$10,126	$19,126	$60,837
Nevada[b]	$9,043	$17,563	$55,431
Utah[b]	$9,009	$13,695	$67,481
Kentucky[b]	$8,470	$15,580	$45,369
Texas	$7,200	$15,180	$58,146
Kansas[b]	$7,093	$18,613	$56,810
North Dakota[b]	$7,080	$13,808	$60,184
South Dakota	$6,000	$11,472	$57,450
Wyoming[b]	$4,200	$7,252	$57,829
Montana[b]	$4,079	$9,209	$57,075
New Hampshire	$100	No per diem	$76,260
New Mexico	$0	$7,245	$48,451
Median	$24,108	$32,611	$59,039

[a] Expenses are calculated for the maximum regular session. Salaries in bold are greater than the state's median household income.
[b] The legislature is paid on a daily, weekly, or monthly basis. Annual salary is an estimate. In Nevada, the per diem is only paid for the first sixty days of the legislative session.
[c] Maine pays more for the longer session year than for the shorter session year. The pay for the two years calculated here was $14,271 (2017) and $10,158 (2018).
Sources: Salary data were calculated by the authors from National Conference of State Legislatures data, http://www.ncsl.org/research/about-state-legislatures/legislator-compensation-2018.aspx, *The Book of the States* for various years, and legislative websites. Median household income data are from the U.S. Census Bureau, 2017 Current Population Survey, Annual Social and Economic Supplements Data Tables, Table H-8. Median Household Income by State: 1984 to 2016.

Notes

Chapter 1: Ninety-Nine Chambers and Why They Matter

1. *St. Louis Post-Dispatch*, "Timeline of Events Leading to Greiten's Resignation," May 30, 2018.
2. Jason Hancock, Allison Kite, and Tessa Weinberg, "GOP Lawmakers Mark Victories in 2018 Session Despite Cloud Cast by Greitens' Scandals," *Kansas City Star*, May 19, 2018.
3. Peverill Squire, *The Evolution of American Legislatures: Colonies, Territories, and States, 1619–2009* (Ann Arbor: University of Michigan Press, 2012); Peverill Squire, *The Rise of the Representative: Lawmakers and Constituents in Colonial America* (Ann Arbor: University of Michigan Press, 2017).
4. Squire, *The Evolution of American Legislatures*, 87.
5. Peverill Squire and Keith E. Hamm, *101 Chambers: Congress, State Legislatures, and the Future of Legislative Studies* (Columbus: Ohio State University Press, 2005), 19.
6. William H. Riker, "The Heresthetics of Constitution-Making: The Presidency in 1787, with Comments on Determinism and Rational Choice," *American Political Science Review* 78 (1984): 1–16.
7. Squire and Hamm, *101 Chambers*, 29.
8. Nelson W. Polsby, "The Institutionalization of the U.S. House of Representatives," *American Political Science Review* 62 (1968): 144–68; Peverill Squire, "Electoral Career Movements and the Flow of Political Power in the American Federal System," *State Politics & Policy Quarterly* 14 (2014): 72–89.
9. Alvin W. Johnson, *The Unicameral Legislature* (Minneapolis: University of Minnesota Press, 1938), 32–33.
10. Squire, *The Evolution of American Legislatures*.
11. The discussion in this section is based on Squire, *The Evolution of American Legislatures*, chapters 4 and 5.
12. Squire and Hamm, *101 Chambers*, 35–39.
13. Laura J. Scalia, *America's Jeffersonian Experiment: Remaking State Constitutions, 1820–1850* (DeKalb: Northern Illinois University Press, 1999), 107.
14. Squire, *The Evolution of American Legislatures*, chapter 6.
15. *Connecticut Courant*, "Extract of a Letter from a Gentleman at Little Rock, Arkansas, to His Friend in Louisville, Kentucky Dated December 10, 1837," December 30, 1837; *Niles' Weekly Register*, "Murder in Arkansas," June 23, 1838.
16. See Charles Albro Barker, ed., *Memoirs of Elisha Oscar Crosby* (San Marino, CA: Huntington Library, 1945), 59; *Daily Alta California*, "Liberality," July 2, 1850; *Daily Alta California*, "Legislative Intelligence," April 2, 1852.
17. William H. Ellison, *A Self-Governing Dominion: California, 1849–1860* (Berkeley: University of California Press, 1950), 76.

18 Ralph Volney Harlow, *The History of Legislative Methods in the Period before 1825* (New Haven, CT: Yale University Press, 1917), 66.

19 Justin E. Walsh, *The Centennial History of the Indiana General Assembly 1816–1878* (Indianapolis: The Select Committee on the Centennial History of the Indiana General Assembly, 1987), 92.

20 Squire, *The Evolution of American Legislatures*, 221–25.

21 Squire, *The Evolution of American Legislatures*, 286–91; Squire and Hamm, *101 Chambers*, 81–86.

22 James D. King, "Changes in Professionalism in U.S. State Legislatures," *Legislative Studies Quarterly* 25 (2000): 327–43; Christopher Z. Mooney, "Citizens, Structures, and Sister States: Influences on State Legislative Professionalism," *Legislative Studies Quarterly* 20 (1995): 47–67; Peverill Squire, "Legislative Professionalization and Membership Diversity in State Legislatures," *Legislative Studies Quarterly* 17 (1992): 69–79; Peverill Squire, "Uncontested Seats in State Legislative Elections," *Legislative Studies Quarterly* 25 (2000): 131–46; Peverill Squire, "Measuring Legislative Professionalism: The Squire Index Revisited," *State Politics & Policy Quarterly* 7 (2007): 211–27; Peverill Squire, "A Squire Index Update," *State Politics & Policy Quarterly* 17 (2017): 361–71; Squire, *The Evolution of American Legislatures*, 291–312.

23 Simeon E. Baldwin, "Legislative Divorces and the Fourteenth Amendment," *Harvard Law Review* 27 (1914): 699–700; Doris Jonas Freed and Henry H. Foster Jr., "Divorce American Style," *Annals of the American Academy of Political and Social Science* 383 (1969): 73–75; Glenda Riley, "Legislative Divorce in Virginia, 1803–1850," *Journal of the Early Republic* 11 (1991): 51–67.

24 Alexei Koseff, "In California's Democrat-Dominated Capitol, It's Senate vs. Assembly," *Sacramento Bee*, August 24, 2016.

25 Kevin Landrigan, "NH Lawmakers Kill Internet Sales-Tax Bill," *New Hampshire Union Leader*, July 25, 2018.

26 John Frank, "In Leaked Meeting, Republican State Senator Blasts Pat McCrory and House Lawmakers on Puppy Mill Bill," *Charlotte Observer*, January 27, 2014.

27 John Baer, "Two Pa. House and Senate Leaders (Sorta) Defend Our Lackluster Legislature," philly.com, July 1, 2018, http://www.philly.com/philly/columnists/john_baer/pennsylvania -legislature-gerrymandering-redistricting-20180702.html.

28 J. Michael Medina, "The Origination Clause in the American Constitution: A Comparative Survey," *Tulsa Law Review* 23 (1987): 165–234, 166.

29 Malcolm E. Jewell and Samuel C. Patterson, *The Legislative Process in the United States*, 4th ed. (New York: Random House, 1986), 170; James R. Rogers, "An Informational Rationale for Congruent Bicameralism," *Journal of Theoretical Politics* 13 (2001): 123–52; Squire and Hamm, *101 Chambers*, 114–15.

30 Daphne Psaledakis, "Differences between the House and Senate Go Beyond the Surface," *Columbia Missourian*, April 23, 2018.

31 *Bismarck Tribune*, "Burgum Kicked Off Senate Floor for Wearing Jeans," February 16, 2017.

32 See the discussion in Charlyne Berens, *One House* (Lincoln: University of Nebraska Press, 2005), 36–41.

33 Jack Rodgers, Robert Sittig, and Susan Welch, "The Legislature," in *Nebraska Government and Politics*, ed. Robert D. Miewald (Lincoln: University of Nebraska Press, 1984); Tom Todd, "Nebraska's Unicameral Legislature: A Description and Some Comparisons with Minnesota's Bicameral Legislature," *Journal of the American Society of Legislative Clerks and Secretaries* 4 (1988); Senator Tom Brewer, "Nebraska Should Abandon Unicameral System," *Chadron Record*, April 15, 2018.

34 Barry Bedlan, "Ventura Sends Scouts to Nebraska's 'Unicameral,'" *Minneapolis Star-Tribune*, April 16, 1999; Mario F. Cattabiani, "Toward a Smaller Harrisburg," *Philadelphia Inquirer*, May 9, 2007; Robb Douglas, "Going Nebraska's Way," in *State Government 1993–94*, ed. Thad L. Beyle (Washington, DC: CQ Press, 1993); Richard Emery, "Abolish the State Legislature: Focus a State Constitutional Convention on Addressing the Root Cause of New York's State's Dysfunction," *New York Daily News*, July 31, 2017; Jon Geeting, "The Argument for Turning the PA Legislature into a Unicameral Body," *City &*

State PA, June 29, 2018, https://www.cityandstatepa.com/content/argument-turning-pa-legisl ature-unicameral-body; Michael Kelly, "Kelly: 'The Unicameral'—Nebraska-Born, Though Not Spread," *Omaha World-Herald*, http://m.omaha.com/news/kelly-the-unicameral-nebraska -born-though-not-spread/article_3f376661-9189-59f4-884b-ef44b2b0f911.html?mode=jqm; Joe Mathews and Mark Paul, *California Crackup: How Reform Broke the Golden State and How We Can Fix It* (Berkeley, University of California Press, 2010); Bob Mercer, "Reforms Mulled for Legislature," *Rapid City Journal*, August 14, 1996; Keith M. Phaneuf, "Connecticut Legislators in 13th Year without a Raise," CTmirror.org, June 19, 2014; Stacey Range, "New Grassroots Efforts Focus on Eliminating State Senate," *Lansing State Journal*, April 16, 2005; Maine Legislature, http://www.mainelegislature.org/legis/bills/bills_125th/ billtexts/HP059901.asp.; "Should Michigan Go the Way of Nebraska and Adopt Unicameral Legislature?" June 5, 2017, WDET.com, https://wdet.org/posts/2017/06/05/85290-shoul d-michigan-go-the-way-of-nebraska-and-adopt-unicameral-legislature; Thomas Suddes, "The Ohio General Assembly Needs to Engage in Real Reform: Thomas Suddes," Cleveland.com, September 16, 2017, https://www.cleveland.com/opinion/index.ssf/2017/09/the_ohio_general _assembly_need.html

[35] See https://www.leg.state.mn.us/lrl/history/caucus_table.

[36] John H. Aldrich and James S. Coleman Battista, "Conditional Party Government in the States," *American Journal of Political Science* 46 (2002): 164–72; Brian F. Schaffner, "Political Parties and the Representativeness of Legislative Committees," *Legislative Studies Quarterly* 32 (2011): 475–97; Gerald C. Wright and Brian F. Schaffner, "The Influence of Party: Evidence from the State Legislatures," *American Political Science Review* 96 (2002): 367–79. On recent developments, see Seth E. Masket and Boris Shor, "Polarization without Parties: Term Limits and Legislative Partisanship in Nebraska's Unicameral Legislature," *State Politics & Policy Quarterly* 15 (2015): 67–90.

[37] Robert Luce, *Legislative Assemblies* (Boston: Houghton Mifflin, 1924), 23.

[38] Don W. Driggs and Leonard E. Goodall, *Nevada Government and Politics* (Lincoln: University of Nebraska Press, 1996), 66; James D. Driscoll, *California's Legislature* (Sacramento: Center for California Studies, 1986), 8; Frederic L. Paxson, "A Constitution of Democracy—Wisconsin, 1847," *Mississippi Valley Historical Review* 2 (1915): 3–24, 9.

[39] Luce, *Legislative Assemblies*, 21.

[40] Luce, *Legislative Assemblies*, 21–22.

[41] Squire and Hamm, *101 Chambers*, 48.

[42] Squire and Hamm, *101 Chambers*, 46–48.

[43] Reynolds v. Sims, 377 U.S. 533 (1964).

[44] Rhode Island Constitution, Article 7, Section 1, and Article 8, Section 1.

[45] North Dakota, for example, downsized both chambers of its legislature in 2003 as a result of its redistricting process, going to forty-seven Senate districts and ninety-four House districts from forty-nine Senate districts and ninety-eight House districts the decade before. Cost savings to the state were given as the rationale behind the reduction in the number of seats. See Janet Cole, "N.D. Legislative Districts Set, but Not without Problems," *The Forum* (Fargo), December 1, 2001, and Joel Heitkamp, "Fewer Districts Is the Right Way," *Bismarck Tribune*, December 19, 2001. Redistricting also prompted New York to add a seat to its upper house in 2003, bringing the total number to sixty-two. This time, the explanation was party politics. Adding a seat allowed the GOP Senate majority to avoid eliminating a district upstate that they held and to create several districts in New York City that improved their party's prospects to win there. See Richard Perez-Pena, "Questions from Justice Department Delay Plan to Add District to New York Senate," *New York Times*, June 4, 2002. A similar rationale explains the decision to add another Senate district in 2012: Jimmy Vielkind, "State's Highest Court Upholds State Senate Upsize," TimesUnion.com, http://blog.timesunion.com/capitol/ archives/129451/states-highest -court-upholds-state-senate-upsize/.

[46] This count through 2017 was taken from the National Conference of State Legislatures, http:// www.ncsl.org/research/about-state-legislatures/incaseofatie.aspx.

[47] David Postman, "Senators Take Aim at the Tie That Binds the State House," *Seattle Times*, June 12, 2001.

48 Francis Quinn, "Mellow (Mostly) in Maine," *State Legislatures Magazine* (July/August 2001): 24–26.

49 Wayne L. Francis, "Leadership, Party Caucuses, and Committees in U.S. State Legislatures," *Legislative Studies Quarterly* 10 (1985): 243–57.

50 Justin H. Kirkland, "Chamber Size Effects on the Collaborative Structure of Legislatures," *Legislative Studies Quarterly* 39 (2014): 169–98.

51 Alan Rosenthal, *Legislative Life* (New York: Harper & Row, 1981), 132–34.

52 Ross K. Baker, *House and Senate*, 3rd ed. (New York: Norton, 2001), 72; Roger H. Davidson, Walter J. Oleszek, and Frances E. Lee, *Congress and Its Members*, 11th ed. (Washington, DC: CQ Press, 2008), 28; Lewis A. Froman Jr., *The Congressional Process* (Boston: Little, Brown, 1967), 7–15.

53 Andrew J. Taylor, "Size, Power, and Electoral Systems: Exogenous Determinants of Legislative Procedural Choice," *Legislative Studies Quarterly* 31 (2006): 323–45.

54 James R. Rogers, "Bicameral Sequence: Theory and State Legislative Evidence," *American Journal of Political Science* 42 (1998): 1025–60.

55 Arleen Leibowitz and Robert Tollison, "A Theory of Legislative Organization: Making the Most of Your Majority," *Quarterly Journal of Economics* 94 (1980): 261–77.

56 Jowei Chen and Neil Malhotra, "The Law of k/n: The Effect of Chamber Size on Government Spending in Bicameral Legislatures," *American Political Science Review* 101 (2007): 657–76.

57 Dongwon Lee, "Supermajority Rules and Bicameral Bargaining," *Public Choice* 169 (2016):53–75.

58 *Boston Globe*, "Giving the State Senate Its Due," April 6, 2015; Robert A. Deleo, "Mass. Committee Structure Is Successful, *Boston Globe*, April 13, 2015; Avi Green, "On Beacon Hill, a Backroom Battle that Matters, wbur.org, April 29, 2015, http://www.wbur.org/cognoscenti/201 5/04/29/on-beacon-hill-a-backroom-battle-that-matters. See also http://www.ncsl.org/Portals/1/ HTML_LargeReports/Partisanship_1.htm.

59 Luce, *Legislative Assemblies*, 113; Michael J. Dubin, *Party Affiliations in the State Legislatures: A Year by Year Summary, 1796–2006* (Jefferson, NC: McFarland, 2007).

60 Luce, *Legislative Assemblies*, 119.

61 Squire and Hamm, *101 Chambers*, 62–63.

62 See a June 11, 2014, press release from New York senator Tony Avella, http:// www.nysenate .gov/press-release/release-state-senate-passes-senator-avella-s-good- government-legislation.

63 Fanny Seiler, "House Panel Passes Term Extension for Lawmakers," *Charleston Gazette*, February 26, 2003.

64 William D. Berry, Michael B. Berkman, and Stuart Schneiderman, "Legislative Professionalism and Incumbent Reelection: The Development of Institutional Boundaries," *American Political Science Review* 94 (2000): 859–74; John M. Carey, Richard G. Niemi, and Lynda W. Powell, "Incumbency and the Probability of Reelection in State Legislative Elections," *Journal of Politics* 62 (2000): 671–700.

65 Brian J. Gaines, Timothy P. Nokken, and Collin Groebe, "Is Four Twice as Nice as Two? A Natural Experiment on the Electoral Effects of Legislative Term Length," *State Politics & Policy Quarterly* 12 (2012): 43–57.

66 Rocío Titiunik and Andrew Feher, "Legislative Behaviour Absent Re-election Incentives: Findings from a Natural Experiment in the Arkansas Senate," *Journal of the Royal Statistical Society Statistics in Society Series A* 181 (2018): 321–78.

67 The Congress under the Articles of Confederation operated under similar term limits with three annual terms out of six years.

68 See Edwin L. Cobb, "Representation and the Rotation Agreement: The Case of Tennessee," *Western Political Quarterly* 23 (1970): 516–29; Malcolm E. Jewell, "State Legislatures in Southern Politics," *Journal of Politics* 26 (1964): 177–96.

69 See Jennie Drage Bowser and Gary Moncrief, "Term Limits in State Legislatures," in *Institutional Change in American Politics: The Case of Term Limits*, ed. Karl T. Kurtz, Bruce Cain, and Richard G. Niemi (Ann Arbor: University of Michigan Press, 2007).

70 See Daniel A. Smith, "Overturning Term Limits: The Legislature's Own Private Idaho?" *PS: Political Science & Politics* 36 (2003): 215–20.

71 See, for example, Susan M. Miller, Jill Nicholson-Crotty, and Sean Nicholson Crotty, "Reexamining the Institutional Effects of Term Limits in U.S. State Legislatures," *Legislative Studies Quarterly* 36 (2011): 71–97.

[72] See, for example, Karl T. Kurtz, Bruce Cain, and Richard G. Niemi, eds., *Institutional Change in American Politics: The Case of Term Limits* (Ann Arbor: University of Michigan Press, 2007).

[73] Gary Moncrief, Richard G. Niemi, and Lynda W. Powell, "Time, Term Limits, and Turnover: Membership Stability in U.S. State Legislatures," *Legislative Studies Quarterly* 29 (2004): 357–81.

[74] Bruce Cain and Gerald Wright, "Committees," in *Institutional Change in American Politics: The Case of Term Limits*, ed. Karl T. Kurtz, Bruce Cain, and Richard G. Niemi (Ann Arbor: University of Michigan Press, 2007), 89.

[75] Susan M. Miller, Jill Nicholson-Crotty, and Sean Nicholson-Crotty, "The Consequences of Term Limits for Policy Diffusion," *Political Science Quarterly* 71 (2018): 573–85.

[76] Richard Powell, "Executive-Legislative Relations," in *Institutional Change in American Politics: The Case of Term Limits*, ed. Karl T. Kurtz, Bruce Cain, and Richard G. Niemi (Ann Arbor: University of Michigan Press, 2007). But note the variation in these relationships across term-limited states in Travis J. Baker and David M. Hedge, "Term Limits and Legislative-Executive Conflict in the American States," *Legislative Studies Quarterly* 38 (2013): 237–58.

[77] Marjorie Sarbaugh-Thompson, John Strate, Kelly LeRoux, Richard C. Elling, Lyke Thompson, and Charles D. Elder, "Legislators and Administrators: Complex Relationships Complicated by Term Limits," *Legislative Studies Quarterly* 35 (2010): 57–89.

[78] Luke Keele, Neil Malhotra, and Colin H. McCubbins, "Do Term Limits Restrain State Fiscal Policy? Approaches for Causal Inference in Assessing the Effects of Legislative Institutions," *Legislative Studies Quarterly* 38 (2013): 291–326. For a contrary finding, see Jeff Cummins, "The Effects of Legislative Term Limits on State Fiscal Conditions," *American Politics Research* 41 (2013): 417–42.

[79] Daniel Lewis, "Legislative Term Limits and Fiscal Policy Performance," *Legislative Studies Quarterly* 37 (2012): 305–28.

[80] John Myers, "California's New Legislature Will Look a Lot Like the Old One—and That's Just What Voters Ordered," *Los Angeles Times*, December 2, 2018.

[81] Norma Love, "Traditional Campaigns a Memory," *Concord Monitor*, October 21, 2002.

[82] Peverill Squire, "Professionalization and Public Opinion of State Legislatures," *Journal of Politics* 55 (1993): 479–91.

[83] Bill McAllister, "Alaska Senate District Tests Candidates' Stamina," Stateline.org, October 17, 2002.

[84] Marty Trillhaase, "Wanted: Pilots to Fly a Helicopter District," *Lewiston Tribune*, February 3, 2012.

[85] State of Rhode Island and Providence Plantations, *Journal of the House of Representatives*, May 31, 2000.

[86] Stephen Calabrese, "Multimember District Congressional Elections," *Legislative Studies Quarterly* 25 (2000): 611–43.

[87] Richard G. Niemi, Jeffrey S. Hill, and Bernard Grofman, "The Impact of Multimember Districts on Party Representation in U.S. State Legislatures," *Legislative Studies Quarterly* 10 (1985): 441–55.

[88] Josh Goodman, "The Disappearance of Multi-Member Constituencies," Stateline.org, July 7, 2011, http://www.governing.com/blogs/politics/The-Disappearance-of-Multi-Member -Constituencies.html.

[89] Christopher A. Cooper and Lilliard E. Richardson Jr., "Institutions and Representational Roles in American State Legislatures," *State Politics & Policy Quarterly* 6 (2006): 174–94.

[90] Patricia K. Freeman and Lilliard E. Richardson Jr., "Explaining Variation in Casework among State Legislators," *Legislative Studies Quarterly* 21 (1996): 41–56.

[91] Justin H. Kirkland, "Multimember Districts' Effect on Collaboration between U.S. State Legislators," *Legislative Studies Quarterly* 37 (2012): 329–53.

[92] Jeffrey A. Taylor, Paul S. Herrnson, James M. Curry, "The Impact of District Magnitude on the Legislative Behavior of State Representatives," *Political Research Quarterly* 71 (2018): 302–17.

[93] James M. Snyder Jr. and Michiko Ueda, "Do Multimember Districts Lead to Free-Riding?" *Legislative Studies Quarterly* 32 (2007): 649–79.

[94] Greg D. Adams, "Legislative Effects of Single-Member vs. Multi-Member Districts," *American Journal of Political Science* 40 (1996): 129–44.

Chapter 2: State Legislative Campaigns and Elections

[1] Emily Tillett, "Virginia Election Results 2017: Republican David Yancey Wins Virginia House Seat," *CBS News*, January 4, 2018, https://www.cbsnews.com/news/virginia-election -results-lottery-drawing-house-of-delegates-david-yancy-winner-virginia-house-seat/.

[2] This account of the 2017 Virginia House elections relies on the following sources: Will Houp, "15 Flipped House Seats Cost $19 Million in Virginia's Most Expensive Elections in 20 Years," *The (Norfolk) Virginian-Pilot*, January 29, 2018; Jack Moore, "Dems Unseat GOP in Slew of Va. Delegate Races; Roem Will Become 1st Transgender House Member," WTOP, November 7, 2017, https://wtop.com/virginia/2017/11/virginia-house-delegates-results-democrats-republic ans/slide/1/; Fenit Nirapill, "Why Democrats Care about Virginia's Normally Sleepy House of Delegates Races," *Washington Post*, November 1, 2017; Tillett, "Virginia election results 2017; Katie Ziegler, "In Virginia, Women Ran and Women Won," National Conference of State Legislatures, November 8, 2017, http://www.ncsl.org/blog/2017/11/08/in-virginia-women-ran-an d-women-won.aspx.

[3] Alex Samuels, "Hey, Texplainer: How Much Does It Cost to Run for Office in Texas?" *Texas Tribune*, November 10, 2017, https://www.texastribune.org/2017/11/10/hey-texplainer-how-m uch-does-it-cost-run-office-texas/.

[4] Christopher Placek, "McAuliffe Wins Country's Most Expensive Legislative Race," *Daily Herald*, November 8, 2016.

[5] See Alan Greenblatt, "This Could Be the Most Expensive State Legislative Race in History: Here Is Why It Is a Waste of Money," *Governing*, November 6, 2017, http://www.governing.com/ topics/politics/gov-new-jersey-state-senate-president.html.

[6] Calculations made by the authors from data reported by Chris Essig, Aditi Bhandari, and Jolie McCullough, "Here's How Much Texas Candidates Spent per Vote in the November Election," *Texas Tribune*, March 1, 2017, https://www.texastribune.org/2017/03/01/heres-how-much -texas-candidates-spent-vote-general-election/.

[7] Michael Dresser, "Google No Longer Accepting State, Local Election Ads in Maryland as Result of New Law," *Baltimore Sun*, June 29, 2018.

[8] The projections are from Borrell Associates, *2018 Local Political Advertising Outlook*, https:// www.newsmediaalliance.org/wp-content/uploads/2018/01/Borrell-Political-Ad-Spending-Webi nar_1-9-18.pdf.

[9] Personal communication with the authors, July 23, 2014.

[10] These figures are estimates by the authors, based on data from the National Institute on Money in State Politics, https://www.followthemoney.org/tools/election-overview?s=MT&y=2016. The site indicates that in 2016 the total amount of money raised by all legislative candidates in the 2016 election was $1.5 million. There are one hundred House districts in Montana, so the average raised by all candidates in a district was just over $15,173. This calculation includes candidates who lost in the primary.

[11] The report identifies all the legislative races in each state in which the two main candidates were "relatively equal" or "competitive" in their fundraising. The study defines "monetary competitiveness" to mean that neither candidate received more than twice the amount her opponent did. For each of these races in a state, the authors identify the candidate who raised the most money, and take the average of all those "top-funded candidates." The assumption is that this average figure represents the amount a candidate needs to raise to have a competitive edge in a highly contested race. One drawback to this study is that it does not distinguish between House and Senate races. See J. T. Stepleton, "Monetary Competitiveness in State Legislative Races, 2015–2016." FollowTheMoney.org, November 2017, https://www.followthemoney.org/rese arch/institute-reports/monetary-competitiveness-in-2015-and-2016-state-legislative-races.

[12] Zach Holden, *Overview of Campaign Finances 2011–2012 Elections* (Helena, MT: National Institute on Money in State Politics, May 2014).

[13] Nicholas Seabrook, "Money and State Legislative Elections: The Conditional Impact of Political Context," *American Politics Research* 38 (2010): 399–424.

[14] Louis Jacobson, "2014 Elections Where Third-Party Candidates Could Make a Big Difference," *Governing*, August 2014, http://www.governing.com/topics/ elections/gov-2014-elections -third-party.html.

[15] Gary Cox and Scott Morgenstern, "The Incumbency Advantage in Multimember Districts: Evidence from the U.S. States," *Legislative Studies Quarterly* 20 (1995): 329–49.

[16] James Curry, Paul Herrnson, and Jeffrey Taylor, "The Impact of District Magnitude on Campaign Fundraising," *Legislative Studies Quarterly* 38 (2013): 517–43.

[17] James M. Snyder Jr. and Michiko Ueda, "Do Multimember Districts Lead to Free-Riding?" *Legislative Studies Quarterly* 32 (2007): 649–79.

[18] See Peverill Squire and Keith E. Hamm, *101 Chambers: Congress, State Legislatures, and the Future of Legislative Studies* (Columbus: Ohio State University Press, 2005), 49–54.

[19] See *The Book of the States, 2018 Edition* (Lexington, KY: Council of State Governments, 2018), 34–36.

[20] Brinley Hineman, "Judge Upholds Candidate Disqualification over Citizenship," *Brunswick News*, July 18, 2018. See Constitution of the State of Georgia, Article III, Section II, Paragraph III.

[21] Courtney Teague, "Lack of US Citizenship Trips up GOP State House Candidate," *Honolulu Civil Beat*, August 1, 2018, https://www.civilbeat.org/2018/08/lack-of-us-citizenship-trips-up-gop-state -house-candidate/. See also Constitution of the State of Hawaii, Article III, Section 6.

[22] Dustin Gardiner, "Judge Tosses Lawsuit Challenging Arizona State Rep.-Elect Raquel Terán's Citizenship," *Arizona Republic*, November 14, 2018.

[23] "Arkansas Has Nation's Highest Filing Fees," KARK.com, February 23, 2018, accessed at: https ://www.kark.com/news/local-news/arkansas-has-nations-highest-filing-fees/988784323.

[24] On the impact of filing fees on state legislative elections, see Thomas Stratmann, "Ballot Access Restrictions and Candidate Entry in Elections," *European Journal of Political Economy* 21 (2005): 59–71.

[25] Trapper Byrne and Melody Gutierrez, "Jerry Brown Pardons Ex-California Lawmaker Roderick Wright for Perjury and Voter Fraud," *San Francisco Chronicle*, November 21, 2018; Jean Merl, "California Sen. Rod Wright Convicted of Perjury, Voter Fraud," *Los Angeles Times*, January 28, 2014.

[26] Alexei Koseff, "California Makes it Easier for Lawmakers to Live Outside of Their Districts," *Sacramento Bee*, September 29, 2018.

[27] Michael Van Sickler, "It's Official: Florida Lawmakers Really Must Live in Their District," *Miami Herald*, March 4, 2014.

[28] Patricia Mazzei, "Miami Lawmaker to Resign, Plead Guilty in Criminal Case over Residency," *Miami Herald*, October 31, 2017.

[29] Sarah Blaskey and David Smiley, "Where Does She Live? A Miami Lawmaker's Bizarre Attempt to Reside in Her District," *Miami Herald*, July 3, 2018.

[30] National Conference of State Legislatures, "Primary Runoffs," http://www.ncsl.org/research/e lections-and-campaigns/primary-runoffs.aspx.

[31] Mike Hashimoto, "As Bob Deuell Feared, Low Turnout Cost Him in Senate Runoff," *Dallas Morning News*, May 28, 2014, accessed July 23, 2014, http://dallas morningviewsblog .dallasnews.com/2014/05/as-bob-deuell-feared-low-turnout-cost-him-in-senate-runoff.html/. For more on this race, see Brandi Grissom, "Tea Party Conservatives Win Top GOP Runoff Contests," *Texas Tribune*, May 28, 2014, http:// www.texastribune.org/2014/05/28/tea-party -conservatives-win-top-gop-runoff-con test/; and Forrest Wilder, "Meet Bob Hall, the Tea Party True Believer Headed to the Senate," *Texas Observer*, May 30, 2014, http://www.texasobserver .org/meet-bob-hall-tea-party-true-believer-headed-texas-senate/.

[32] Randy Krehbiel, "Six More House Incumbents Ousted in GOP Runoff Elections," *Tulsa World*, August 29, 2018. Also see Eric Levitz, "Oklahoma Teachers Just Purged the Statehouse of the Their Enemies," *New York Magazine*, August 2018.

[33] Michael P. MacDonald, "A Comparative Analysis of Redistricting Institutions in the United States, 2001–2002," *State Politics & Policy Quarterly* 4 (2004): 371–95. See table 3 for MacDonald's assessment of the redistricting outcome in each state.

[34] Brennan Center for Justice, "Gill v. Whitford," October 26, 2018, https://www.brennancenter .org/legal-work/whitford-v-gill.

[35] Dylan Brogan, "No Contest," *Isthmus*, November 15, 2018, https://isthmus.com/news/news/dems-sweep-statewide-offices-in-midterms-but-remain-underrepresented-in-assembly/.

[36] MacDonald, "A Comparative Analysis of Redistricting Institutions."

[37] Tim Storey, "GOP Makes Historic State Legislative Gains in 2010," *The Rasmussen Report*, http://www.rasmussenreports.com/public_content/political_commentary/commentary_by_tim_storey/gop_makes_historic_state_legislative_gains_in_2010.

[38] The quote is from Catharine Vaughan, CEO of Flippable, a nonprofit working to elect more Democrats at the state legislative level. See, Charlotte Alder, "Never Mind Congress: These Democrats Want to Win State Legislatures," *Time Magazine*, August 16, 2018, http://time.com/5368460/flippable-democrats-state-legislature/.

[39] See, for example, Seth Masket, Jonathan Winburn, and Gerald Wright, "The Gerrymanderers Are Coming! Legislative Redistricting Won't Affect Competition or Polarization Much, No Matter Who Does It," *PS: Political Science & Politics* 45 (2012): 39–43; Richard Forgette, Andrew Garner, and John Winkle, "Do Redistricting Principles and Practices Affect U.S. State Legislative Electoral Competition?" *State Politics & Policy Quarterly* 9 (2009): 151–75.

[40] See Todd Makse, "Strategic Constituency Manipulation in State Legislative Redistricting," *Legislative Studies Quarterly* 37 (2012): 225–50. Also see Justin Levitt, "Redistricting and the West: The Legal Context," in *Reapportionment and Redistricting in the West*, ed. Gary Moncrief (Lanham, MD: Lexington Books, 2011), 15–38.

[41] Brogan, "No Contest."

[42] Barry Edwards, Michael Crespin, Ryan Williamson, and Maxwell Palmer, "Institutional Control of Redistricting and the Geography of Representation," *Journal of Politics* 79 (2017): 722–26.

[43] John Sides, "What Comes Next in the Fight against Partisan Gerrymandering?" The Monkey Cage, *Washington Post*, October 13, 2018, https://www.washingtonpost.com/news/monkey-cage/wp/2018/10/13/what-comes-next-in-the-fight-against-partisan-gerrymandering/?utm_term=.b84a91be8fc4.

[44] The actual number depends on one's interpretation of "outside the immediate control of the legislature"; as of this writing there are at least sixteen states using commissions, plus the unusual case of Iowa, described in the text. But there are other procedures as well, such as in Maryland, where the governor submits a plan to which the legislature responds. See MacDonald, "A Comparative Analysis of Redistricting Institutions," or the National Conference of State Legislature's (NCSL) website for a discussion of the specifics in each state.

[45] Tim Storey, "Redistricting Commissions and Alternatives to the Legislature Conducting Redistricting," NCSL website, accessed July 23, 2007, http://www.ncsl.org/programs/legismgt/redistrict/com&alter.htm. See also Jonathan Winburn, "Does It Matter If Legislatures or Commissions Draw the Lines?," in Moncrief, *Reapportionment and Redistricting in the West*.

[46] See Peverill Squire, "What the West Can Learn from Iowa," in Moncrief, *Reapportionment and Redistricting in the West*, 161–75.

[47] For a detailed description of the Iowa redistricting process, see Squire, "What the West Can Learn from Iowa."

[48] Lynn Okamoto, "Redistricting Gives Legislators Opportunities, Tough Choices," *Des Moines Register*, June 21, 2001.

[49] This assumes we are dealing with SMDs only. MMDs must have the same population *per seat* as SMDs. Thus, if an SMD in a state has a twenty-five-thousand population, a three-person MMD in the same state should have a population of seventy-five thousand.

[50] Reynolds v. Sims, 377 U.S. 533 (1964).

[51] White v. Regester, 412 U.S. 755 (1973).

[52] Citizens United v. Federal Election Commission, 558 U.S. 310 (2010).

[53] See, for example, Nicholas Confessore, "A National Strategy Funds State Political Monopolies," *New York Times*, January 11, 2014, http://www.nytimes.com/2014/01/12/us/politics/a-national-strategy-funds-state-political-monopolies.html?_r=0.

[54] Peter Jensen, "Napa Assembly Race Ranks 3rd in Independent Spending in California," *Napa Valley Register*, May 31, 2014, http://napavalleyregister.com/news/local/napa-assembly-race-ranks-rd-in-independent-spending-in-california/article_0fb5eb71-c66d-5095-9f0e-d4d0ae1d8d99.html; and Jim Miller, "Independent Spending in California's Statewide, Legislative Races the Highest in Years," *Sacramento Bee*, June 1, 2014.

[55] Michael Malbin, Charles Hunt, Jaclyn Kettler, Brendan Glavin, and Keith Hamm, "Independent Spending in State Elections, 2006–2016," paper presented at the American Political Science Association annual meeting, Boston, 2018.

[56] Andrew Kenney, "Colorado Senate: Democrats Set to Retake Control of State Government," *Denver Post*, November 6, 2011.

[57] Steven Rogers, "Term Limits: Keeping Incumbents in Office," paper presented at the 2014 State Politics and Policy Conference, Indiana University, May 2014.

[58] Gary Moncrief, Peverill Squire, and Malcolm F. Jewell, *Who Runs for the Legislature?* (Upper Saddle River, NJ: Prentice Hall, 2001), 4.

[59] Peverill Squire, "Uncontested Seats in State Legislative Elections," *Legislative Studies Quarterly* 25 (2000): 131–46; see also Erin Madigan, "Scores of Statehouse Candidates Lack Challengers," Stateline.org, October 29, 2004; John McGlennon and Cory Kaufman, "Expanding the Playing Field," *Report from the Thomas Jefferson Program in Public Policy* (Williamsburg, VA: The College of William & Mary, 2007); and Steven Rogers, "Accountability in a Federal System" (PhD dissertation, Princeton University, 2013), 13–14.

[60] Rogers, "Accountability in a Federal System," 13.

[61] David Konisky and Michiko Ueda, "The Effects of Uncontested Elections on Legislator Performance," *Legislative Studies Quarterly* 36 (2011): 199–229. See also Kyle Dropp and Zachary Peskowitz, "Electoral Security and the Provision of Constituency Service," *Journal of Politics* 74 (2012): 220–34.

[62] Jason Rosenbaum, "Candidate for Graham's Seat Changes Mind," *Columbia Daily Tribune*, May 19, 2008.

[63] Grant Reeher, *First Person Political: Legislative Life and the Meaning of Public Service* (New York: New York University Press, 2006), 94.

[64] Reeher, *First Person Political*, 95.

[65] Briana Bierschbach, "Is There a Doctor in the (State) House?" MPR News, July 9, 2018, https://www.mprnews.org/story/2018/07/09/no-doctor-serving-in-minnesota-house-politics.

[66] James Q. Lynch, "New Districts Create More Interest," *Iowa City Gazette*, July 10, 2001.

[67] Pamela Ban, Elena Llaudet, and James M. Snyder Jr., "Challenger Quality and the Incumbency Advantage," *Legislative Studies Quarterly* 41 (2016): 153–79. Also see Thomas Carsey, Jonathan Winburn, and William D. Berry, "Rethinking the Normal Vote, the Personal Vote, and the Impact of Legislative Professionalism in U.S. State Legislative Elections." *State Politics & Policy Quarterly* 17(2017): 465–88.

[68] Thomas M. Carsey, Richard G. Niemi, William D. Berry, Lynda W. Powell, and James M. Snyder Jr., "State Legislative Elections, 1967–2003: Announcing the Completion of a Cleaned and Updated Dataset," *State Politics & Policy Quarterly* 8, no. 4 (2008): 430–43; FollowTheMoney .org: https://www.followthemoney.org/research/institute-reports/money-incumbency-in-2015-and-2016-state-legislative-races.

[69] Nathaniel Birkhead, "The Role of Ideology in State Legislative Elections," *Legislative Studies Quarterly* 40 (2015): 55–82.

[70] Katy Barnitz, "Rep. Youngblood found guilty of DWI," *Albuquerque Journal*, September 25 2018.

[71] Associated Press, "State Senator charged with domestic violence loses seat." November 7, 2018, https://poststar.com/news/national/govt-and-politics/state-senator-charged-with-domestic-violence-loses-seat/article_f69f972b-4028-53e0-bec5-cff0cdfd4e1f.html.

[72] Steven Rogers, "Strategic Challenger Entry in a Federal System: The Role of Economic and Political Conditions in State Legislative Competition,' *Legislative Studies Quarterly* 40 (2015): 539–70. Also see Joshua Zingher and Jesse Richman, "Polarization and the Nationalization of State Legislative Elections," *American Politics Research* (2018): 1–19.

[73] Rogers, "Accountability in a Federal System."

[74] Masket, Seth E., *No Middle Ground: How Informal Party Organizations Control Nominations and Polarize Legislatures.* Ann Arbor: University of Michigan Press, 2009.

[75] The survey was of nonincumbent legislative candidates and was conducted by the authors in 1998 and 2002. Overall, more than one thousand candidates in eleven states responded. Details on the methodology appear in Moncrief, Squire, and Jewell, *Who Runs for the Legislature?* which includes data from the first (1998) survey.

[76] Michael Dresser, "Two Baltimore State Senators Defeated in Maryland General Assembly Races; Conway Trails in Tight Contest," *Baltimore Sun*, June 26, 2018; Vivian Wang, "Democratic Insurgents Topple 6 New York Senate Incumbents," *New York Times*, September 14, 2018.

[77] See National Conference of State Legislatures, "Who We Elect: An Interactive Graph," accessed at: http://www.ncsl.org/research/about-state-legislatures/who-we-elect-an-interactive-graphic.aspx.

[78] http://www.cawp.rutgers.edu/women-state-legislature-2018.

[79] See Susan Carroll and Kira Sanbonmatsu, *More Women Can Run: Gender and Pathways to the State Legislatures* (New York: Oxford University Press, 2013). See also Kira Sanbonmatsu, *Where Women Run: Gender and Party in American States* (Ann Arbor: University of Michigan Press, 2006); Richard Fox and Jennifer Lawless, "Entering the Arena? Gender and the Decision to Run for Office," *American Journal of Political Science* 48, no. 2 (2004): 264–80; David Niven, *The Missing Majority: The Recruitment of Women as State Legislative Candidates* (Westport, CT: Praeger, 1998); and Moncrief, Squire, and Jewell, *Who Runs for the Legislature?* especially chapter 4.

[80] Sanbonmatsu, *Where Women Run*; Carroll and Sanbonmatsu, *More Women Can Run*; Tracy Osborn, *How Women Represent Women: Political Parties, Gender, and Representation in the State Legislatures* (New York: Oxford University Press, 2012); and Laurel Elder, "The Partisan Gap among Women State Legislators," *Journal of Women, Politics & Policy* 33 (2012): 65–85.

[81] Center for Women in American Politics, "Results: Record Number of Women Elected to State Legislatures Nationwide," November 30, 2018.

[82] See, for example, Susan Carroll, *Women as Candidates in American Politics*, 2nd ed. (Bloomington: Indiana University Press, 1994); Moncrief, Squire, and Jewell, *Who Runs for the Legislature?* and Fox and Lawless, "Entering the Arena?"

[83] Peter Slevin, "After Adopting Term Limits, States Lose Female Legislators," *Washington Post*, April 22, 2007.

[84] See Peverill Squire and Gary Moncrief, *State Legislatures Today* (Boston: Longman, 2010), 57; and Carroll and Sanbonmatsu, *More Women Can Run*, 49.

[85] Samantha Pettey, "Female Candidate Emergence and Term Limits: A State-Level Analysis," *Political Research Quarterly* 71 (2018): 318–29.

[86] Sanbonmatsu, *Where Women Run*.

[87] Audrey Carlson and Denise Lu, "More Women Than Men: State Legislatures Could Shift for the First Time," *New York Times*. June 30 2018.

[88] This discussion of campaign techniques is based, in part, on Gary Moncrief and Peverill Squire, "State House and Local Office Campaigns," in *Guide to Political Campaigns in America*, ed. Paul Herrnson (Washington, DC: CQ Press, 2005).

[89] Michael G. Miller, "The Power of an Hour: Effects of Candidate Time Expenditure in State Legislative Elections," *Legislative Studies Quarterly* 41 (2016): 327–59.

[90] Susan Sharon, "There are More Women Serving in the Maine Legislature Than Ever Before," Maine Public Radio, November 9, 2018, accessed at: http://www.mainepublic.org/post/there-are-more-women-serving-maine-legislature-ever#stream/0.

[91] Jonathan Smith, "Professionalization of State Legislative Campaigns in South Carolina, North Carolina and Georgia," paper presented at the annual meeting of the Southern Political Science Association, Atlanta, Georgia, November 2001. See also Robert Hogan, "Voter Contact Techniques in State Legislative Campaigns: The Prevalence of Mass Media Advertising," *Legislative Studies Quarterly* 22 (1997): 551–71; and Owen Abbe and Paul S. Herrnson, "Campaign Professionalism in State Legislative Elections," *State Politics & Policy Quarterly* 3 (2003): 223–45.

[92] Michael McNamara, *The Political Campaign Desk Reference*, 2nd ed. (Denver: Outskirts Press, 2012), 177.

[93] Lindsey Erdody, "Political Campaigns Boost Investment in Social Media Ads," *Indiana Business Journal*, September 21, 2018, https://www.ibj.com/articles/70545-political-campaigns-boost-investment-in-social-media-ads.

[94] The quote is from Brandon Evans, as reported in Erdody, "Political Campaigns Boost Investment in Social Media Ads."

[95] Jeff Chester and Kathryn Montgomery, "The Role of Digital Marketing in Political Campaigns," *Internet Policy Review* 6 (2017), https://policyreview.info/articles/analysis/role-digital-marketing-political-campaigns.

[96] Dresser, "Google No Longer Accepting State, Local Election Ads in Maryland."

[97] Hogan, "Voter Contact Techniques in State Legislative Campaigns."

[98] Moncrief, Squire, and Jewell, *Who Runs for the Legislature?*, 76.

[99] William March, "Most Expensive Florida Legislative Race Ever?" *Tampa Bay Times*, November 19, 2018.

[100] Ronald Keith Gaddie, *Born to Run: Origins of the Political Career* (Lanham, MD: Rowman & Littlefield, 2004), 7.

[101] Gaddie, *Born to Run*, 8.

[102] Richard Niemi, Lynda Powell, William Berry, Thomas Carsey, and James Snyder Jr., "Competition in State Legislative Elections," in *The Marketplace of Democracy*, ed. Michael P. McDonald and John Samples (Washington, DC: Brookings Institution and Cato Press, 2006), 56. By "median," the authors refer to the incumbency rate in the median state. See also FollowTheMoney.org: https://www.followthemoney.org/research/institute-reports/money -incumbency-in-2015-and-2016-state-legislative-races.

[103] For a more detailed analysis and explanation of the effect of term limits on turnover, see Gary F. Moncrief, Richard G. Niemi, and Lynda W. Powell, "Time, Term Limits and Turnover: Trends in Membership Stability in U.S. State Legislatures," *Legislative Studies Quarterly* 29 (2004): 357–81.

[104] The figures total forty-nine because the Nebraska legislature is nonpartisan.

[105] These figures are based on data from the National Conference of State Legislatures as of June 2012.

[106] Campaign donors are well aware of this phenomenon. A recent study finds that unified government yields a substantial advantage to the governing party in corporate campaign contributions. See Erik Engstrom and William Ewell, "The Impact of Unified Party Government on Campaign Contributions," *Legislative Studies Quarterly* 35 (2010): 543–69.

[107] David Lublin, *The Republican South* (Princeton, NJ: Princeton University Press, 2004), 47.

[108] *The Book of the States, 1962–1963* (Chicago: Council of State Governments, 1962), 41.

[109] Adam S. Myers, "Changing Patterns of Uncontested Seats in Southern State Legislative Elections," *Social Science Quarterly* 99 (2018): 583–98.

[110] Charles Bullock III, Donna Hoffman, and Ronald Keith Gaddie, "Regional Variations in the Realignment of American Politics, 1944–2004," *Social Science Quarterly* 87 (2006): 494–512.

[111] Eric R. A. N. Smith and Peverill Squire, "State and National Politics in the Mountain West," in *The Politics of Realignment*, ed. Peter F. Galderisi, Michael S. Lyons, Randy T. Simmons, and John G. Francis (Boulder: Westview, 1987), 44–45.

[112] Bullock, Hoffman, and Gaddie, "Regional Variations in the Realignment of American Politics," 513–17.

Chapter 3: The Changing Job of State Legislator

[1] http://www.wyoleg.gov/Legislators/2018/S/2021; Legislative Handbook, April 2018.

[2] CA.gov, http://www.calhr.ca.gov/cccc/Pages/cccc-resolutions-20180626.aspx.

[3] This information was gleaned from payroll data provided by the California Senate for October 31, 2017, https://www.senate.ca.gov/sites/senate.ca.gov/files/senatepayrollbg_103117.pdf.

[4] Michael B. Berkman, "Former State Legislators in the U.S. House of Representatives: Institutional and Policy Mastery," *Legislative Studies Quarterly* 18 (1993): 77–104; William D. Berry, Michael B. Berkman, and Stuart Schneiderman, "Legislative Professionalism and Incumbent Reelection: The Development of Institutional Boundaries," *American Political Science Review* 94 (2000): 859–74; Ann O'M. Bowman and Richard C. Kearney, "Dimensions of State Government Capability," *Western Political Quarterly* 41 (1988): 341–62; John M. Carey, Richard G. Niemi, and Lynda W. Powell, "Incumbency and the Probability of Reelection in State Legislative Elections," *Journal of Politics* 62 (2000): 671–700; James D. King, "Changes in Professionalism in U.S. State Legislatures," *Legislative Studies Quarterly* 25 (2000): 327–43; Gary F. Moncrief, "Dimensions of the Concept of Professionalism in State Legislatures: A Research Note," *State & Local Government Review* 20 (1988): 128–32; Peverill Squire, "Legislative Professionalization and Membership Diversity in State Legislatures," *Legislative Studies Quarterly* 17 (1992):

69–79; Peverill Squire, "Uncontested Seats in State Legislative Elections," *Legislative Studies Quarterly* 25 (2000): 131–46; Peverill Squire, "Measuring State Legislative Professionalism: The Squire Index Revisited," *State Politics & Policy Quarterly* 7 (2007): 211–27; Peverill Squire, "A Squire Index Update," *State Politics & Policy Quarterly* 17 (2017): 361–71.

[5] See Wayne L. Francis, "Costs and Benefits of Legislative Service in the American States," *American Journal of Political Science* 29 (1985): 626–42.

[6] Peverill Squire, "Career Opportunities and Membership Stability in Legislatures," *Legislative Studies Quarterly* 13 (1988): 65–82.

[7] Alan Rosenthal, "State Legislative Development: Observations from Three Perspectives," *Legislative Studies Quarterly* 21 (1996): 169–98.

[8] Rosenthal, "State Legislative Development," 171–72.

[9] William D. Berry, Michael B. Berkman, and Stuart Schneiderman, "Legislative Professionalism and Incumbent Reelection: The Development of Institutional Boundaries," *American Political Science Review* 94 (2000): 859–74; Gary Moncrief, Richard G. Niemi, and Lynda W. Powell, "Time, Term Limits, and Turnover: Membership Stability in U.S. State Legislatures," *Legislative Studies Quarterly* 29 (2004): 357–81; Joel F. Turner, Scott Lasley, and Jeffrey P. Kash, "Changes in Latitudes, Differences in Attitudes: Assessing the Distinctiveness of Southern State Legislators," *American Review of Politics* 36 (2018): 38–57.

[10] James M. Cook, "Twitter Adoption and Activity in U.S. Legislatures: A 50-State Study," *American Behavioral Scientist* 61 (2017): 724–40; Jeffrey J. Harden, "Multidimensional Responsiveness: The Determinants of Legislators' Representational Priorities," *Legislative Studies Quarterly* 38 (2013): 155–84; Jeffrey R. Lax and Justin H. Phillips, "Gay Rights in the States: Public Opinion and Policy Responsiveness," *American Political Science Review* 103 (2009): 367–86; Jeffrey R. Lax and Justin H. Phillips, "The Democratic Deficit in the States," *American Journal of Political Science* 56 (2012): 148–66; Cherie Maestas, "The Incentive to Listen: Progressive Ambition, Resources, and Opinion Monitoring among State Legislators," *Journal of Politics* 65 (2003): 439–56; Susan M. Miller, "Administering Representation: The Role of Elected Administrators in Translating Citizens' Preferences into Public Policy," *Journal of Public Administration Research and Theory* 23 (2013): 865–97; Peverill Squire, "Professionalism and Public Opinion of State Legislatures," *Journal of Politics* 55 (1993): 479–91; and Gerald Wright, "Do Term Limits Affect Legislative Roll Call Voting? Representation, Polarization, and Participation," *State Politics & Policy Quarterly* 7 (2007): 256–80.

[11] Adam R. Brown, and Jay Goodliffe, "Why Do Legislators Skip Votes? Position Taking versus Policy Influence," *Political Behavior* 39 (2017): 425–55; David Fortunato and Tessa Provins, "Compensation, Opportunity, and Information: A Comparative Analysis of Legislative Nonresponse in the American States," *Political Research Quarterly* 70 (2017): 644–56; Shannon Jenkins, "Examining the Influences over Roll Call Voting in Multiple Issue Areas: A Comparative US State Analysis," *Journal of Legislative Studies* 16 (2010): 14–31.

[12] Clint S. Swift and Kathryn A. VanderMolen, "Term Limits and Collaboration across the Aisle: An Analysis of Bipartisan Cosponsorship in Term Limited and Non-Term Limited State Legislatures," *State Politics & Policy Quarterly* 16 (2016):198–226.

[13] Josh Ryan, "Conference Committee Proposal Rights and Policy Outcomes in the States," *Journal of Politics* 76 (2014):1059–73; Peverill Squire, "Membership Turnover and the Efficient Processing of Legislation," *Legislative Studies Quarterly* 23 (1998): 23–32.

[14] Sarah E. Anderson, Daniel M. Butler, and Laurel Harbridge, "Legislative Institutions as a Source of Party Leaders' Influence," *Legislative Studies Quarterly* 41 (2016): 605–31; Jesse Richman, "The Logic of Legislative Leadership: Preferences, Challenges, and the Speaker's Powers," *Legislative Studies Quarterly* 35 (2010): 211–33.

[15] Kyle T. Kattelman, "Legislative Professionalism and Interest Group Concentration: The ESA Model Revisited," *Interest Groups and Advocacy* 4 (2015): 165–84; Turner, Lasley and Kash, "Changes in Latitudes."

[16] Frederick J. Boehmke and Charles R. Shipan, "Oversight Capabilities in the States: Are Professionalized Legislatures Better at Getting What They Want?" *State Politics & Policy Quarterly* 15 (2015): 366–86; John D. Huber, Charles R. Shipan, and Madelaine Pfahler, "Legislatures and Statutory Control of Bureaucracy," *American Journal of Political Science* 45 (2001): 330–45;

Robert J. McGrath, "Legislatures, Courts, and Statutory Control of the Bureaucracy across the U.S. States," *State Politics & Policy Quarterly* 13 (2013): 373–97; Jill Nicholson-Crotty and Susan M. Miller, "Bureaucratic Effectiveness and Influence in the Legislature," *Journal of Public Administration Research and Theory* 22 (2012): 347–71; Michael Thom and Brian An, "Fade to Black? Exploring Policy Enactment and Termination through the Rise and Fall of State Tax Incentives for the Motion Picture Industry." *American Politics Research* 45 (2017): 85–108.

[17] Travis J. Baker and David M. Hedge, "Term Limits and Legislative-Executive Conflict in the American States," *Legislative Studies Quarterly* 38 (2013): 237–58; Thad Kousser and Justin H. Phillips, *The Power of American Governors: Winning on Budgets and Losing on Policy* (New York: Cambridge University Press, 2012); Daniel C. Lewis, Saundra K. Schneider, and William G. Jacoby, "Institutional Characteristics and State Policy Priorities: The Impact of Legislatures and Governors," *State Politics & Policy Quarterly* 15 (2015): 447–75.

[18] Jerrell D. Coggburn, "Exploring Differences in the American States' Procurement Practices," *Journal of Public Procurement* 3 (2003): 3–28; Sangjoon Ka and Paul Teske, "Ideology and Professionalism: Electricity Regulation and Deregulation over Time in the American States," *American Politics Research* 30 (2002): 323–43; J. E. Kellough and S. C. Selden, "The Reinvention of Public Personnel Administration: An Analysis of the Diffusion of Personnel Management Reforms in the States," *Public Administration Review* 63 (2003): 165–76; Edward Alan Miller, Lili Wang, Zhanlian Feng, and Vincent Mor, "Improving Direct-Care Compensation in Nursing Homes: Medicaid Wage Pass-Through Adoption, 1999–2004," *Journal of Health Politics, Policy and Law* 37 (2012): 469–512; Matthew C. Nattinger and Brian Kaskie, "Determinants of the Rigor of State Protection Policies for Persons with Dementia in Assisted Living," *Journal of Aging & Social Policy*, 29 (2017): 123–42; Mary Schmeida and Ramona McNeil, "Children's Mental-Health Language Access Laws: State Factors Influence Policy Adoption," *Administration and Policy in Mental Health and Mental Health Services Research* 40 (2013): 364–70.

[19] Vincent Arel-Bundock and Srinivas Parinandi, "Conditional Tax Competition in American States," *Journal of Public Policy* 38 (2018): 191–220; Joel Slemrod, "The Etiology of Tax Complexity: Evidence from U.S. State Income Tax Systems," *Public Finance Review* 33 (2005): 279–99.

[20] Troy D. Abel, Debra J. Salazar, and Patricia Robert, "States of Environmental Justice: Redistributive Politics across the United States, 1993–2004," *Review of Policy Research* 32 (2015): 200–225; Graeme Boushey and Adam Luedtke, "Immigrants across the U.S. Federal Laboratory: Explaining State-Level Innovation in Immigration Policy," *State Politics & Policy Quarterly* 11 (2011): 390–414; Timothy Marquez and Scot Schraufnagel, "Hispanic Population Growth and State Immigration Policy: An Analysis of Restriction (2008–2012)," *Publius* 43 (2013): 347–67; James E. Monogan, III, "The Politics of Immigration Policy in the 50 US States, 2005–2011." *Journal of Public Policy* 33 (2013): 35–64; Vivian E. Thomson and Vicki Arroyo, "Upside-Down Cooperative Federalism: Climate Change Policymaking and the States," *Virginia Environmental Law Journal* 29 (2011): 3–61; Caroline J. Tolbert, Karen Mossberger, and Ramona McNeal, "Institutions, Policy Innovation, and E-Government in the American States," *Public Administration Review* 68 (2008): 549–63; Neal D. Woods, "The Policy Consequences of Political Corruption: Evidence from State Environmental Programs," *Social Science Quarterly* 89 (2008): 258–71; Hongtao Yi, "Network Structure and Governance Performance: What Makes a Difference?" *Public Administration Review* 78 (2018):195–205; Hongtao Yi and Richard C. Feiock, "Renewable Energy Politics: Policy Typologies, Policy Tools, and State Deployment of Renewables," *Policy Studies Journal* 42 (2014): 391–415.

[21] Kathleen Marchetti, "Consider the Context: How State Policy Environments Shape Interest Group Advocacy," *State and Local Government Review* 47 (2015):155–69.

[22] Jerrell D. Coggburn and Richard C. Kearney, "Trouble Keeping Promises? An Analysis of Underfunding in State Retiree Benefits," *Public Administration Review* 70 (2010): 97–108; James C. Hearn, Michael K. McLendon, and T. Austin Lacy, "State Funded 'Eminent Scholars' Programs: University Faculty Recruitment as an Emerging Policy Instrument," *Journal of Higher Education* 84 (2013): 601–39; Michael K. McLendon, James C. Hearn, and Christine G. Mokher, "Partisans, Professionals, and Power: The Role of Political Factors in State Higher Education Funding," *Journal of Higher Education* 80 (2009): 686–713; Michael K. McLendon, David A.

Tandberg, and Nicholas W. Hillman, "Financing College Opportunity: Factors Influencing State Spending on Student Financial Aid and Campus Appropriations, 1990 through 2010," *Annals of the American Academy of Political and Social Science* 655 (2014): 143–62; David A. Tandberg, "The Conditioning Role of State Higher Education Governance Structures," *Journal of Higher Education* 84 (2013): 506–43; A. Y. Yi, "Covet Thy Neighbor or 'Reverse Policy Diffusion'? State Adoption of Performance Funding 2.0," *Research in Higher Education* 58 (2017):746–71.

23 Frederick J. Boehmke, "Sources of Variation in the Frequency of Statewide Initiatives: The Role of Interest Group Populations," *Political Research Quarterly* 58 (2005): 565–75.

24 Derek A. Epp, *The Structure of Policy Change* (Chicago: University of Chicago Press, 2018), 109–111; Thad Kousser, *Term Limits and the Dismantling of State Legislative Professionalism* (New York: Cambridge University Press, 2005), 197–98; Pamela J. Clouser McCann, Charles R. Shipan, and Craig Volden, "Top-Down Federalism: State Policy Responses to National Government Discussions," *Publius* 45 (2015):495–525; Charles R. Shipan and Craig Volden, "When the Smoke Clears: Expertise, Learning and Policy Diffusion," *Journal of Public Policy* 34 (2014): 357–87.

25 Joshua M. Jansa, Eric R. Hansen, and Virginia H. Gray, "Copy and Paste Lawmaking: Legislative Professionalism and Policy Reinvention in the States," *American Politics Research*, https://doi.org/10.1177/1532673X18776628.

26 David Fortunato and Ian R. Turner, "Legislative Capacity and Credit Risk," *American Journal of Political Science* 62 (2018): 623–36.

27 Bryan M. Black and Laine P. Shay, "States Testing the Legal Limits: The Effect of Electoral Competition on the Constitutionality of State Statutes," *State Politics & Policy Quarterly* 18 (2018): 246–70; Susan M. Miller, Eve M. Ringsmuth, and Joshua M. Little, "Pushing Constitutional Limits in the U.S. States: Legislative Professionalism and Judicial Review of State Laws by the U.S. Supreme Court," *State Politics & Policy Quarterly* 15 (2015): 476–91.

28 Peverill Squire, "Professionalism and Public Opinion of State Legislatures," *Journal of Politics* 55 (1993): 479–91; Christine A. Kelleher and Jennifer Wolak, "Explaining Public Confidence in the Branches of State Government," *Political Research Quarterly* 60 (2007): 707–21.

29 Lilliard E. Richardson Jr., David M. Konisky, and Jeffrey Milyo, "Public Approval of U.S. State Legislatures," *Legislative Studies Quarterly* 37 (2012): 99–116.

30 See Bill Boyarsky, *Big Daddy: Jesse Unruh and the Art of Power Politics* (Berkeley: University of California Press, 2008), 163–72; Citizens Conference on State Legislatures, *State Legislatures: An Evaluation of Their Effectiveness* (New York: Praeger, 1971); Donald G. Herzberg, and Alan Rosenthal, *Strengthening the States: Essays on Legislative Reform* (Garden City, NY: Doubleday, 1971); Peverill Squire, *The Evolution of American Legislatures: Colonies, Territories and States, 1619–2009* (Ann Arbor: University of Michigan Press, 2012), 297–301; Jesse Unruh, "Science in Law-Making," *National Civic Review* 54 (1965): 466–72; Alan Wyner, "Legislative Reform and Politics in California: What Happened, Why, and So What?," in *State Legislative Innovation*, ed. James A. Robinson (New York: Praeger, 1973).

31 Squire, "A Squire Index Update;" Squire, "Measuring State Legislative Professionalism: The Squire Index Revisited;" Squire, *The Evolution of American Legislatures*, 307–10; and Peverill Squire and Keith E. Hamm, *101 Chambers: Congress, State Legislatures, and the Future of Legislative Studies* (Columbus: Ohio State University Press, 2005), chapter 3.

32 A detailed explanation of how this measure is calculated can be found in Squire, "Measuring State Legislative Professionalism: The Squire Index Revisited."

33 Tyler Whitley, "This Is Not Something You Do for the Money," *Richmond Times-Dispatch*, February 11, 2007.

34 Jack Penchoff, "Legislative Pay Daze," *State News*, February 2007. The longitudinal salary study discussed in the article was conducted by the Council on State Governments.

35 Peverill Squire, "The State Wealth-Legislative Compensation Effect," *Canadian Journal of Political Science* 41 (2008): 1–18.

36 For slightly earlier salary figures, see the Pew Charitable Trusts, Philadelphia Research Initiative, "City Councils in Philadelphia and Other Major Cities: Who Holds Office, How Long They Serve, and How Much It All Costs," February 2, 2011.

37 Patrick Condon, "Minnesota Legislators Swap Capitol Careers for Lucrative County Paychecks," *Minneapolis Star Tribune*, June 15, 2014.

38 Laurie Roberts, "Roberts: Arizona Legislator Proposes Tripling Pay . . . for Legislators," *Arizona Republic*, January 22, 2018.

39 Tom Rafferty, "Informal Poll: Lawmakers Paying Part of Lodging," *Bismarck Tribune*, April 5, 2005.

40 Associated Press, "California Lawmakers Collect Per Diem Pay Even When Absent," September 20, 2016, https://www.nbclosangeles.com/news/california/California-Lawmakers -Collect-Per-Diem-Pay-Even-When-Absent-394198951.html.

41 Conrad Defiebre, "State Legislators Get Healthy Expense Raises," *Minneapolis Star Tribune*, January 10, 2007.

42 Roberts, "Roberts: Arizona Legislator Proposes Tripling Pay . . . for Legislators."

43 The favorable tax treatment can be found in the Internal Revenue Code, Title 26, Subtitle A, Chapter 1, Subchapter B, Part VI, Section 162 (h).

44 Jon Campbell, "Per Diems Help Pay for Lawmakers' Real Estate," *Poughkeepsie Journal*, November 29, 2017.

45 See *The Book of the States, 2017* (Lexington, KY: Council of State Governments, 2017), 67–72.

46 Barry Massey, "NM Legislators Receive Pensions, But No Salary," *Idaho Statesman*, May 8, 2013.

47 Ross Ramsey, "How Lawmakers' Pensions Would Grow under Budget," *Texas Tribune*, May 17, 2013.

48 Scott Canon, "Kansas Legislators Amass Full-Time Government Pensions from Part-Time Jobs," *Kansas City Star*, May 28, 2016.

49 John Klingner and Ted Dabrowski, "The Cost of Illinois' Lawmakers," *Illinois Policy*, Summer 2016, https://www.illinoispolicy.org/reports/the-cost-of-illinois-lawmakers/.

50 Christopher Cousins, "How Much Does Each Lawmaker Cost Maine," *Bangor Daily News*, March 26, 2018.

51 Klingner and Dabrowski, "The Cost of Illinois' Lawmakers."

52 *Des Moines Register*, "Being a Lawmaker: It's the Best Part-Time Job in Iowa," October 9, 2011.

53 Jan Murphy, "Want Health Insurance for Life? Dental and Vision Too? Become a State Lawmaker or a Judge," PennLive.com, June 20, 2018, https://www.pennlive.com/politics/index.ssf/2 018/06/retiree_health_benefits_fallin.html.

54 Brian Joseph, "Capitalizing on Cars," *Orange County Register*, August 1, 2006; Alexei Koseff, "Getting Rid of California Lawmakers' Cars Actually Did Save Some Money," *Sacramento Bee*, August 7, 2017; Patrick McGreevy, "Mileage Plan for California Lawmakers Is Pricier Than Providing Cars," *Los Angeles Times*, November 25, 2011; Kevin Yamamura and Jim Sanders, "Senate, Assembly Get Deals on Wheels," *Sacramento Bee*, December 19, 2002.

55 Virginia Young, "Missouri Legislators Can Go to School on the State's Dime," *St. Louis Post-Dispatch*, March 28, 2018.

56 Melissa Maynard, "One Last Freebie Splurge in Alabama," *Stateline.org*, December 29, 2010; Jon Solomon, "Iron Bowl 75: Crusader Jim Metrock Seeks to End Free-Ticket Tradition for Alabama Legislature," *Birmingham News*, November 23, 2010; Jon Solomon, "Which Alabama Public Officials Bought Auburn Football Tickets in 2013?" *Birmingham News*, March 4, 2014.

57 *Houston Chronicle*, "Thrifty Lawmakers Get Prison Bargains," February 8, 2006; Patricia Kilday Hart, "Patricia Kilday Hart: Gifts for Fundraiser Don't Pass Smell Test," *Houston Chronicle*, August 22, 2011; Eva Ruth Moravec, "Strong-Armed Texas State Lawmaker Leaves Gavels in Pieces," June 2, 2015, *Prison Legal News*, https://www.prisonlegalnews.org/in-the-news/2015/a rticle-tx-prison-industry-programs-quotes-pln/.

58 Wes Allison, "Infusion of Lawmakers/Perquisites, Parties on Assembly's Agenda," *Richmond Times-Dispatch*, January 13, 1999; Jackie Kruszewski, "Does Downtown Richmond Have a Parking Problem?" *Style Weekly*, August 8, 2017, https://www.styleweekly.com/richmond/doe s-downtown-richmond-have-a-parking-problem/Content?oid=4142364.

59 Alexei Koseff and Bryan Anderson, "Secret DMV Office Near California Capitol Serves Lawmakers and Their Staff," *Sacramento Bee*, August 9, 2018.

[60] Rachel Leingang, "Law Enforcement: We Can't Ticket Legislators for Speeding in Arizona," *Arizona Republic*, July 19, 2018; Rachel Leingang, "Ducey Signs Executive Order Saying Arizona Lawmakers Can Get Speeding Tickets," *Arizona Republic*, July 20, 2018.

[61] Matt Volz, 'Montana Lawmakers Consider Raising Their Own Pay 69 Percent," *Helena Independent Record*, September 11, 2018.

[62] *Grand Island Independent*, "Senators Don't Get Paycheck Due to Higher Insurance Costs," February 1, 2006.

[63] Tara Jeffries, "Low Pay Limits Who Serves in General Assembly," May 29, 2014, http://www.wral.com/low-pay-limits-who-serves-in-general-assembly/13681551/.

[64] James Salzer, "Ralston: Georgia Lawmakers Pay Raise Proposal an Easy Political Target," *Atlanta Journal-Constitution*, December 18, 2017.

[65] Amendment 57 to the 1901 constitution.

[66] See Alabama Constitution, Amendment 871.

[67] See the New Hampshire Constitution, Part Second, Article 15, as amended in 1889.

[68] See New Mexico Constitution, Article 4, Section 10.

[69] See the Texas Constitution, Article 3, Section 24(a), "Members of the Legislature shall receive from the Public Treasury a salary of Six Hundred Dollars ($600) per month, unless a greater amount is recommended by the Texas Ethics Commission and approved by the voters of this State in which case the salary is that amount." The procedure involving the Ethics Commission recommendation followed by a public vote, placed in the constitution by the voters in 1991, has never been used.

[70] Rhode Island Constitution, Article 6, Section 3: "Commencing in January 1995, senators and representatives shall be compensated at an annual rate of ten thousand dollars ($10,000). Commencing in 1996, the rate of compensation shall be adjusted annually to reflect changes in the cost of living, as determined by the United States government, during a twelve (12) month period ending in the immediately preceding year."

[71] These data are from Joan Barron, "Barron: Legislative Compensation Commissions Can Help," *Casper Star-Tribune*, August 4, 2017; *The Book of the States, 2017*, 61–62.

[72] Alan Greenblatt, "Election Brings Change to How Minnesota Lawmakers Are Paid," *Governing*, November 9, 2016, http://www.governing.com/topics/elections/gov-minnesota-legislative-pay-ballot-measure.html.

[73] Johanna Donlin, "Compensation Commissions," *Legisbrief* 7 (November–December 1999).

[74] See, for example, Andrew Garber, "State Lawmakers Object, Get Raises Anyway," *Seattle Times*, May 20, 2003.

[75] Austin Huguelet, "Missouri Senators Reject Raises for Themselves, Statewide Officials," *St. Louis Post-Dispatch*, January 31, 2017; David C. Valentine, "Citizens' Commission on Compensation for Elected Officials," Missouri Legislative Academy, Report 16-2006, November 2006; *Kansas City Star*, "Editorial: Eric Greitens' Confrontational Style Is No Way to Govern," February 13, 2017.

[76] Salzer, "Ralston: Georgia Lawmakers Pay Raise Proposal an Easy Political Target."

[77] Tom Loftus, "Lawmakers' Pay Disparity Prompts Review," Louisville *Courier Journal*, May 30, 2014.

[78] Amy Lester, "Do Oklahoma Legislators Make Too Much Money?" July 14, 2011, http://wnow.dua1.worldnow.com/story/15081983/tonight-at-10-oklahoma-lawmakers-among-best-paid-in-nation.

[79] Letter to New York State Commission on Legislative, Judicial, and Executive Compensation from Carl E. Heastie, Speaker, New York Assembly, October 5, 2016.

[80] Morgan Cullen, "Pay Problem: January 2011," http://www.ncsl.org/research/about-state-legislatures/pay-problem.aspx.

[81] Jeffries, "Low Pay Limits Who Serves in General Assembly."

[82] Lester, "Do Oklahoma Legislators Make Too Much Money?"

[83] Jim McLean, "House Votes Against Pay Increase," *Topeka Capital-Journal*, March 13, 2001.

[84] Michele McNeil Solida, "159% Lawmaker Pay Hike Urged," *Indianapolis Star*, August 27, 2004.

[85] See, for example, Pat Kessler, "Reality Check: Pay Hikes at the Capitol," CBS Minnesota, August 22, 2018, https://minnesota.cbslocal.com/2018/08/22/rc-capitol-pay-hike/.

86 Niki Kelly, "Daniels OKs Legislative Pay Raises," *Fort Wayne Journal Gazette*, April 25, 2007; Mary Beth Schneider, "Plan Doubles Lawmaker Pay, Ensures Raises," *Indianapolis Star*, February 21, 2007.

87 See Florida Statutes 2007, Title III, Chapter 11.13: "Compensation of members, (b)."

88 David Abel, "Romney OK's Pay Increases for Lawmakers," *Boston Globe*, January 4, 2007; Rick Klein, "Legislative Pay Raise a Political Hot Potato," *Boston Globe*, December 26, 2002; Matt Murphy, "Mass. Lawmakers Taking Pay Cut," *Lowell Sun*, January 4, 2103.

89 Jan Murphy, "Pennsylvania Lawmakers Get Automatic 2% Pay Raises to $83,802/Year," *Harrisburg Patriot-News*, November 19, 2012.

90 Morgan Cullen, "The Politically Perilous Pay Problem," October 13, 2017, http://www.ncsl.org/bookstore/state-legislatures-magazine/legislator-salary-commissions.aspx.

91 Ben Brachfeld, "Commission Recommends Pay Increases and Ethics Reforms for State Legislators," *Gotham Gazette*, December 7, 2018, http://www.gothamgazette.com/state/8125-commission-recommends-pay-increases-and-ethics-reforms-for-state-legislators; David Lombardo, "Panel Approves 63 Percent Raise for State Legislators," *Times Union*, December 6, 2018.

92 *Topeka Capital-Journal*, "Alldritt Expects to Resign House Seat," November 28, 2001.

93 Melissa Santos, "Can Average People Still Serve in the Legislature When Sessions Go Months Beyond Schedule?" *News Tribune*, July 19, 2017.

94 Jeff Mapes, "Several Oregon Legislators Use Campaign Money So They Can Pocket State Expense Money," *The Oregonian*, July 22, 2013.

95 *Walla Walla Union-Bulletin*, "Legislature Demographics Don't Reflect Washington Population," February 18, 2014.

96 Angela Evancie and Peter Hirschfeld, "Low Pay, Weird Schedule: Who Exactly Can Pull Off the Legislator Lifestyle?" *Brave Little State*, Vermont Public Radio, August 4, 2017, http://digital.vpr.net/post/low-pay-weird-schedule-who-exactly-can-pull-legislator-lifestyle#stream/0.

97 Andrea Fanta, "Bill Would Raise Lawmaker Pay, But Plan Stalls in Election Year," *St. Petersburg Times*, April 9, 2006.

98 Squire, *The Evolution of American Legislatures*, 243–48, 270–73; Alabama did not change to biennial sessions until 1939. See Alden J. Powell, "Constitutional Growth and Revision in the South," *Journal of Politics* 10 (1948): 354–84.

99 See National Conference of State Legislatures, Legislative Sessions with Limited Scope, http://www.ncsl.org/research/about-state-legislatures/legislative-sessions-with-limited-scope.aspx.

100 Laura Hancock, "Wyoming Lawmaker Decries Legislating through the Budget," *Casper Star-Tribune*, May 29, 2014.

101 Rosenthal, "State Legislative Development," 192.

102 Manny Fernandez, "In Texas, Resistance to a Renewed Call for an Annual Roundup of Legislators," *New York Times*, January 5, 2013.

103 See NCSL, http://www.ncsl.org/research/about-state-legislatures/legislative-session-length.aspx.

104 See Article III, Section IV, Paragraph I.

105 These data were calculated by the authors from the Utah State Legislature, Legislative Calendar, https://le.utah.gov/.

106 These data were calculated by the authors from the Michigan Legislature's calendars, http://www.legislature.mi.gov/(S(5rvl2go0bjef0tqkrx0estxv))/mileg.aspx?page=sessionschedules.

107 Emily Lawler, "Michigan Lawmakers to Meet Fewer Days Than Average in 2018," *MLive.com*, November 24, 2018, https://articles.mlive.com/news/index.ssf/2018/11/michigan_lawmakers_to_meet_few.amp.

108 Karl T. Kurtz, Gary Moncrief, Richard G. Niemi, and Lynda W. Powell, "Full-Time, Part-Time, and Real Time: Explaining State Legislators' Perceptions of Time on the Job," *State Politics & Policy Quarterly* 6 (2006): 322–38. See also Alan Rosenthal, *Heavy Lifting: The Job of the American Legislature* (Washington, DC: CQ Press, 2004), 22.

109 Kurtz, Moncrief, Niemi, and Powell, "Full-Time, Part-Time, and Real Time."

110 *Black Hills Pioneer*, "South Dakota Lawmakers Say Duties Amount to Half-Time Job," July 7, 2003.

111 Evancie and Hirschfeld, "Low Pay, Weird Schedule."

[112] Squire, *The Evolution of American Legislatures*, 291–97.

[113] Alan Rosenthal, *Legislative Life* (New York: Harper & Row, 1981), 206–7; Squire, *The Evolution of American Legislatures*, 297–307.

[114] See *The Book of the States 2017*, 105–8, and National Conference of State Legislatures, "Summary of Personal Staff Survey," January 2010.

[115] Nicholas Pugliese, "Murphy, Lawmakers Quietly Approve Millions in Raises for Legislative Aides," northjersey.com, October 8, 2018, https://www.northjersey.com/story/news/watchdog/2018/10/08/nj-lawmakers-quietly-approved-millions-raises-legislative-aides/1534117002/.

[116] Doug Finke, "Office Allowance Helps Legislators Work with Constituents," *Springfield State Journal-Register*, December 2, 2012.

[117] Robert Swift, "NEPA State Lawmakers Spend $706,000 on District Office Leases," *Scranton Times-Tribune*, May 4, 2014.

[118] Finke, "Office Allowance Helps Legislators Work with Constituents."

[119] Matthew Hamilton, "Legislature's Efficiency Is Measured by Many Metrics," *Times Union*, January 3, 2018.

[120] Mike Maciag, "Louisiana's Budget Crisis Empowers an Unusual Group," *Governing*, July 2016, http://www.governing.com/topics/politics/gov-louisiana-budget.html.

[121] Summer Ballentine, "Estimated Cost of Missouri Corporate Tax Break Questioned," *St. Louis Post Dispatch*, March 13, 2017.

[122] Allie Morris, "N.H. Fetal Homicide Bill Unintentionally Gives Pregnant Women Impunity to Murder," *Concord Monitor*, June 12, 2017.

[123] These data are from Karl Kurtz, "Who We Elect: The Demographics of State Legislatures," http://www.ncsl.org/research/about-state-legislatures/who-we-elect.aspx.

[124] Molly Beck, "At 19, Kalan Heywood Will be the Youngest Lawmaker in Wisconsin—And Likely in the Nation," *Milwaukee Journal Sentinel*, September 28, 2018.

[125] Hayley Miller, "West Virginia Lawmaker Caught on Camera Singing N-Word in Lil' Wayne Song," *Huffington Post*, March 7, 2018, https://www.huffingtonpost.com/entry/saira-blair-west-virginia-racial-slur_us_5a9fed6de4b0e9381c142956; Kurtz, "Who We Elect"; Jim Workman, "Starting Young: Young Lawmakers Taking Their Place in W.Va. Politics," *State Journal*, January 23, 2017.

[126] Elizabeth M. Cox, *Women, State and Territorial Legislatures, 1895–1995: A State-by-State Analysis, with Rosters of 6,000 Women* (Jefferson, NC: McFarland, 1996), 329.

[127] These data are taken from the Center for American Women in Politics, "Results: Record Number of Women Elected to State Legislatures Nationwide," November 30, 2018.

[128] See Center for American Women in Politics, "Women State Legislative Committee Chairs 2017"; R. Darcy, "Women in the State Legislative Power Structure: Committee Chairs," *Social Science Quarterly* 77 (1996): 888–911; Thomas H. Little, Dana Dunn, and Rebecca E. Dean, "A View from the Top: Gender Differences in Leadership Priorities among State Legislative Leaders," *Women and Politics* 22 (2001): 29–50; Donald E. Whistler and Mark C. Ellickson, "The Incorporation of Women in State Legislatures: A Description," *Women and Politics* 20 (1999): 81–97.

[129] Squire and Hamm, *101 Chambers*, 138.

[130] Race and Ethnicity data reported here are from National Conference of State Legislatures "Legislatures at a Glance," http://www.ncsl.org/research/about-state-legislatures/legislatures-at-a-glance.aspx.

[131] Jack E. Holmes, *Politics in New Mexico* (Albuquerque: University of New Mexico Press, 1967), 230.

[132] Christina E. Bejarano, *The Latina Advantage* (Austin: University of Texas Press, 2013), 78–84, 108–12. On the history of the caucuses see, for California, California Latino Legislative Caucus, "Our Story," https://latinocaucus.legislature.ca.gov/our-story; and for Texas see Cynthia E. Orozco, "Mexican American Legislative Caucus," http://www.tshaonline.org/handbook/online/articles/wem04.

[133] See National Caucus of Native American State Legislators, http://www.ncsl.org/research/state-tribal-institute/national-caucus-native-american-state-legislators.aspx.

[134] See S. Glenn Starbird Jr., "A Brief History of Indian Legislative Representations," as updated, https://legislature.maine.gov/lawlibrary/history-of-tribal-representation-in-maine/9261; Marina

Villeneuve, "Only 1 Tribal Representative Bound for Maine State House," *Portland Press Herald*, December 9, 2018.

[135] Jean Reith Schroedel and Artour Aslanian, "A Case Study of Descriptive Representation: The Experience of Native American Elected Officials in South Dakota," *American Indian Quarterly* 41 (2017): 250–86.

[136] Squire, "Legislative Professionalization and Membership Diversity in State Legislatures."

[137] A negative relationship is reported by Christina E. Bejarano, "New Expectations for Latina State Legislative Representation," in *Distinct Identities*, ed. Nadia E. Brown and Sarah Allen Gershon (New York: Routledge, 2016), 194–95 and Beth Reingold, Kerry L. Haynie, and Kathleen A. Bratton, "Gender, Race, Ethnicity and the Political Geography of Descriptive Representation in U.S. State Legislatures," paper presented at the Women in Politics Workshop, University of Tennessee, Knoxville, April 11, 2014, 56. For no relationship, see the first edition of this book, Peverill Squire and Gary Moncrief, *State Legislatures Today: Politics under the Domes* (Boston: Longman, 2010), 98–99; Barbara Norrander and Clyde Wilcox, "Trends in the Geography of Women in U.S. State Legislatures," in *Women and Elective Office*, 3rd edition, ed. Sue Thomas and Clyde Wilcox (New York: Oxford University Press, 2014), 283–85; and Becki Scola, *Gender, Race and Office Holding in the United States* (New York: Routledge, 2014), 106–15.

[138] See Squire and Moncrief, *State Legislatures Today: Politics under the Domes*, 1st ed., 98–99.

[139] Jason P. Casellas, "The Institutional and Demographic Determinants of Latino Representation," *Legislative Studies Quarterly* 34 (2009): 399–426; Scola, *Gender, Race and Office Holding in the United States*, 112–13. Bejarano, "New Expectations for Latina State Legislative Representation," reports no relationship.

[140] Bejarano, "New Expectations for Latina State Legislative Representation," 194–95; Reingold, Haynie, and Bratton, "Gender, Race, Ethnicity and the Political Geography of Descriptive Representation in U.S. State Legislatures," 57; Scola, *Gender, Race and Office Holding in the United States*, 106–115.

[141] Bejarano, "New Expectations for Latina State Legislative Representation," 194–95; Scola, *Gender, Race and Office Holding in the United States*, 106–15.

[142] Laurel Elder, "The Partisan Gap among Women State Legislators," *Journal of Women, Politics, and Policy* 33 (2012): 65–85; Norrander and Wilcox, "Trends in the Geography of Women in U.S. State Legislatures," 283–85.

[143] Bejarano, *The Latina Advantage*, 131–35. The claim on disparate political experience is challenged by Ricardo Ramírez and Carmen Burlingame, "The Unique Career Path of Latina Legislators, 1990–2010," in *Distinct Identities*, ed. Nadia E. Brown and Sarah Allen Gershon (New York: Routledge, 2016), 215.

[144] Donald E. Whistler and Mark C. Ellickson, "A Rational Choice Approach to Explaining Policy Preferences and Concern for Representing Women among State Legislators," *Politics & Policy* 38 (2010): 25–51.

[145] Anna Mitchell Mahoney, *Women Take Their Place in State Legislatures* (Philadelphia: Temple University Press, 2018), 18; Tracy L. Osborn, *How Women Represent Women: Political Parties, Gender, and Representation in the State Legislatures* (New York: Oxford University Press, 2012). Also see Susan Carroll and Kira Sanbonmatsu, *More Women Can Run* (New York: Oxford University Press, 2013).

[146] Bailey Sanders, "Partisan Bridges to Bipartisanship: The Case of Contraceptive Coverage," *Legislative Studies Quarterly* 43 (2018): 521–46.

[147] Kathleen Bratton, "The Effect of Legislative Diversity on Agenda Setting," *American Politics Research* 30 (2002): 115–42; Tracy Osborn, "Women's State Legislators and Representation: The Role of Political Parties and Institutions," *State and Local Government Review* 46 (2014): 146–55; Caroline Tolbert and Gertrude Steuernagel, "Women Lawmakers, State Mandates, and Women's Health," *Women and Politics* 22 (2001): 1–39.

[148] Marie Courtemanche and Joanne Connor Green, "The Influence of Women Legislators on State Health Care Spending for the Poor," *Social Sciences* 2017 6(2), 40; doi:10.3390/socsci6020040; Kimberly Cowell-Myers and Laura Langbein, "Linking Women's Descriptive and Substantive Representation in the United States," *Politics & Gender* 5 (2009): 491–518.

[149] Byron D'Andra Orey, L. Marvin Overby, and Christopher W. Larimer, "African-American Committee Chairs in U.S. State Legislatures," *Social Science Quarterly* 88 (2007): 619–39.

[150] Kerry L. Haynie, *African American Legislators in the American States* (New York: Columbia University Press, 2001).

[151] David E. Broockman, "Black Politicians Are More Intrinsically Motivated to Advance Blacks' Interests: A Field Experiment Manipulating Political Incentives," *American Journal of Political Science* 57 (2013): 521–36; Jeffrey J. Harden, "Multidimensional Responsiveness: The Determinants of Legislators' Representational Priorities," *Legislative Studies Quarterly* 38 (2013): 155–84.

[152] Chris T. Owens, "Black Substantive Representation in State Legislatures from 1971–1994," *Social Science Quarterly* 86 (2005): 779–91.

[153] Irene Browne, Beth Reingold, and Anne Kronberg, "Race Relations, Black Elites, and Immigration Politics: Conflict, Commonalities, and Context," *Social Forces* (2018): 1691–1720; Tamelyn Tucker-Worgs, and Donn C. Worgs, "Black Morality Politics: Preachers, Politicians, and Voters in the Battle Over Same-Sex Marriage in Maryland." *Journal of Black Studies* 45 (2014): 338–62.

[154] Kathleen A. Bratton, "The Behavior and Success of Latino State Legislators: Evidence from the States," *Social Science Quarterly* 87 (2006): 1136–57.

[155] Robert R. Preuhs, "Descriptive Representation as a Mechanism to Mitigate Policy Backlash," *Political Research Quarterly* 60 (2007): 277–92.

[156] Eric Gonzalez Juenke and Robert R. Preuhs, "Irreplaceable Legislators? Rethinking Minority Representatives in the New Century," *American Journal of Political Science* 56 (2012): 705–15; Renita Miller, "Minority Voices: The Representational Roles of African American and Latino Legislators during State Legislative Deliberations" (Doctoral thesis, Rice University, 2013, http://hdl.handle.net/1911/72075).

[157] Richard C. Witmer, Joshua Johnson, Frederick J. Boehmke, "American Indian Policy in the States," *Social Science Quarterly* 95 (2015): 1043–63.

[158] Danielle Casarez Lemi, "Identity and Coalitions in a Multiracial Era: How State Legislators Navigate Race and Ethnicity," *Politics, Groups, and Identities* 6 (2018): 725–42.

[159] Kathleen Bratton, Kerry L. Haynie, and Beth Reingold, "Agenda Setting and African American Women Legislators in State Legislatures," *Journal of Women, Politics, and Policy* 28 (2006): 71–96; and Byron D'Andrá Orey, Wendy Smooth, Kimberly S. Adams, and Kisha Harris-Clark, "Race *and* Gender Matter: Refining Models of Legislative Policy Making in State Legislatures," *Journal of Women, Politics, and Policy* 28 (2006): 97–119.

[160] Beth Reingold and Adrienne R. Smith, "Welfare Policymaking and Intersections of Race, Ethnicity, and Gender in U.S. State Legislatures," *American Journal of Political Science* 56 (2012): 131–47.

[161] Wendy Smooth, "Standing for Women? Which Women? The Substantive Representation of Women's Interests and the Research Imperative of Intersectionality," *Politics & Gender* 7 (2011): 436–41.

[162] Nadia Brown and Kira Hudson Banks, "Black Women's Agenda Setting in the Maryland State Legislature," *Journal of African American Studies* 18 (2014): 164–80. See also Philip J. Welch, Joseph A. Dake, James H. Price, Amy J. Thompson, and Sunday E. Ubokudom, "State Legislators' Support for Evidence-Based Obesity Reduction Policies," *Preventive Medicine* 55 (2012): 427–29.

[163] Nadia Brown, "Employing Intersectionality: The Impact of Generation on Black Women Maryland State Legislators Views on Anti-Domestic Violence Legislation," *Journal of Race and Policy* 9 (2013): 47–70.

[164] Tonya M. Williams, "Why Are You Under the Skirts of Women? Race, Gender, and Abortion Policy in the Georgia State Legislature," in *Distinct Identities*, ed. Nadia E. Brown and Sarah Allen Gershon (New York: Routledge, 2016).

[165] Jessie Balmert, "'You Don't Look Like a Legislator': Security Stops Black, Female Lawmaker Going to Work," *Cincinnati Enquirer*, May 31, 2018.

[166] Liam Stack, "Black Female Lawmaker in Vermont Resigns after Racial Harassment," *New York Times*, September 26, 2018; Jim Therrien, "AG, State Police in Investigate Online Threats to Rep. Kiah Morris," *Bennington Banner*, August 27, 2018.

[167] Ben Giles and Paulina Pineda, "Legislative Staffers Say Pro-Trump Supporters Called them 'Illegal' for Being Dark Skinned," *Arizona Capitol Times*, January 26, 2018.

[168] Patrick Marley, Molly Beck, and Daniel Bice, "Wisconsin Assembly Republican Leader Apologizes for Making Racial, Sexual Comments to Female Lawmakers," *Milwaukee Journal-Sentinel*, September 26, 2018.

[169] These data are from the Victory Institute: https://victoryfund.org/our-candidates/?candidate-category=winning-candidates&office_level=state-legislature. See also Alan Greenblatt, "'Rainbow Wave' Hits Statehouses," *Governing*, November 21, 2018, http://www.governing.com/topics/politics/gov-rainbow-wave-lgbt-candidate-2018-midterm-election.html.

[170] These data are from the Victory Institute: https://outforamerica.org/?office-level=State%20 Legislature.

[171] John Kennedy, "Florida's First Openly Gay State Lawmakers Say Equality Just Part of Their Priority List," *Palm Beach Post*, December 24, 2012.

[172] Howard Koplowitz, "Jefferson County Election Results: Sheriff Mike Hale Concedes to Democrat Mark Pettway," al.com, November 7, 2018, https://www.al.com/news/birmingham/2018/11/jefferson-county-election-results-sheriff-mike-hale-down-by-19-points-against-democrat-mark-pettway.html; Hannah Wiley, "In Texas, the 'Rainbow Wave' Outpaces the Blue One," *Texas Tribune*, November 7, 2018, https://www.texastribune.org/2018/11/07/texas-midterm-election-rainbow-wave-lgbtq-candidates.

[173] Andrew Kenney, "Colorado's First Transgender Legislator: How Brianna Titone Flipped a Republican District," *Denver Post*, November 10, 2018; *Washington Blade*, "Two Transgender Women Elected to N.H. House," November 7, 2018.

[174] See Louis Jacobson, "Being a Gay or Lesbian State Lawmaker Is Now So Common It Is No Longer an Issue," *State Legislatures Magazine*, July–August 2014, http://www.ncsl.org/research/about-state-legislatures/the-power-of-pride.aspx.

[175] Donald Haider-Markel, "Representation and Backlash: The Positive and Negative Influence of Descriptive Representation," *Legislative Studies Quarterly* 32 (2007): 107–33; Lori Riverstone-Newell, "The Rise of State Preemption Laws in Response to Local Policy Innovation," *Publius* 47 (2017): 403–25.

[176] Greenblatt, "'Rainbow Wave' Hits Statehouses."

[177] Ann Morse, "Oath of Citizenship to Oath of Office," *State Legislatures*, May 2006, 29–30.

[178] Nicole Filler and Pei-te Lien, "Asian Pacific Americans in U.S. Politics," in *Distinct Identities*, ed. Nadia E. Brown and Sarah Allen Gershon (New York: Routledge, 2016), 222–23.

[179] Morse, "Oath of Citizenship to Oath of Office."

[180] Alan Greenblatt, "'That's Me. Trump's Banning Me.' What Motivates Refugees to Run for Office in America," *Governing*, December 27, 2017, http://www.governing.com/topics/politics/gov-refugees-running-for-office-2017-2017-elections.html. See also Katharine Q. Seelye, "She Was a Refugee from Afghanistan. She May Soon Enter the New Hampshire Legislature," *New York Times*, September 13, 2018.

[181] Caitlin Andrews, "Election Highlights Diversity in Politics," *Concord Monitor*, November 11, 2018.

[182] Karl Kurtz, "Who We Elect"; Scott Smallwood and Alex Richards, "How Educated Are State Legislators?" *Chronicle of Higher Education*, June 12, 2011. See http://chronicle.com/article/Degrees-in-the-Statehouse/127797/.

[183] Eric Kelderman, "For Love of Alma Mater: Does a Degree Influence Decision Making?" *Chronicle of Higher Education*, June 12, 2011.

[184] Aaron K. Chatterji, Joowon Kim, and Ryan C. McDevitt, "School Spirit: Legislator School Ties and State Funding for Higher Education," *Journal of Public Finance* 164 (2018): 254–69; Megan Thiele, Kristen Shorette, and Catherine Bolzendahl, "Returns to Education: Exploring the Link between Legislators' Public School Degrees and State Spending on Higher Education," *Sociological Inquiry* 82 (2012): 305–28.

[185] Squire and Hamm, *101 Chambers*, 131–33.

[186] The 2015 data are from Kurtz, "Who We Elect"

[187] William Yardley, "Some Rural Lawmakers Defy Power Erosion," *New York Times*, July 13, 2011.

[188] Squire and Hamm, *101 Chambers*, 134–35; and data from the National Conference of State Legislatures, http://www.ncsl.org/research/about-state-legislatures/ legislator-occupations -national-data.aspx.

[189] See Heinz Eulau and David Koff, "Occupational Mobility and Political Career," *Western Political Quarterly* 15 (1962): 507–21; and Charles Hyneman, "Who Makes Our Laws?" *Political Science Quarterly* 55 (1940): 556–81.

[190] Beth Bazar, *State Legislators' Occupations: A Decade of Change* (Denver: National Conference of State Legislatures, 1987), 4; Alan Rosenthal, "The Legislative Institution: Transformed and at Risk," in *The State of the States*, ed. Carl E. Van Horn (Washington, DC: CQ Press, 1989), 72.

[191] David R. Derge, "The Lawyer as Decision-Maker in the American State Legislature," *Journal of Politics* 21 (1959): 408–33; David R. Derge, "The Lawyer in the Indiana General Assembly," *Midwest Journal of Political Science* 6 (1962): 19–53; Gerard Padró I. Miquel and James M. Snyder Jr., "Legislative Effectiveness and Legislative Careers," *Legislative Studies Quarterly* 31 (2006): 347–81.

[192] Mary Clarkin, "Kansas Lawmaking Body Won't Have any Licensed Lawyers in 2017 Session," *Hutchinson News*, December 9, 2016.

[193] Nicholas Carnes, "Why Are So Few Working-Class People in Political Office? Evidence from State Legislatures," *Politics, Groups and Identities* 4 (2016): 84–109; Nicholas Carnes and Eric R. Hansen, "Does Paying Politicians More Promote Economic Diversity in Legislatures?" *American Political Science Review* 110 (2016): 699–716.

[194] Evancie and Hirschfeld, "Low Pay, Weird Schedule."

[195] Taken from the entries for March 11, 2007, "A Week in the Life, Part One," and March 10, 2007, "A Week in the Life, Part Two," http://www.politicalparlor.net/wp/posts-from -the-legislature/page/8/.

[196] Chris Camire, "Commute Stipend Boosts Legislators' Pay, But Not All Take It," *Lowell Sun*, January 6, 2013.

[197] Jane Carroll Andrade, "Keeping in Touch," *State Legislatures*, February 2006.

[198] Andrade, "Keeping in Touch."

[199] Tom Gorman, "Part-Time Legislature Suits Most Nevadans Just Fine," *Los Angeles Times*, February 5, 2001.

[200] Andrade, "Keeping in Touch."

[201] Danny Hakim and Trymaine Lee, "New York Legislators Pushing to Raise Their Pay," *New York Times*, February 10, 2008.

[202] Taryn Luna, "When Jerry Hill Gets Ticked Off, You Might Get a New Law," *Sacramento Bee*, May 16, 2017

[203] Stacy Forster, "Legislative Expenses Drive Up the Price of Government," *Milwaukee Journal Sentinel*, October 16, 2004.

[204] Elizabeth Pierce, "Legislators Give Up Weekends for Cracker Barrels," *Yankton Daily Press & Dakotan*, January 12, 2002.

[205] Kirsten Stewart, "Extend Session for Two Weeks? Thanks but No Thanks, Legislators Decide," *Salt Lake Tribune*, January 31, 2003.

[206] David Montero, "Two Democrats to Retire from Legislature," *Salt Lake Tribune*, March 5, 2012.

[207] Alan Greenblatt, "Low Pay and Time Away Drive Some Lawmakers to Call It Quits," *Governing*, February 2017, http://www.governing.com/topics/mgmt/gov-legislative-pay-salaries.html.

[208] Amie Van Overmeer, "Women Advised to Be Candidates," *Des Moines Register*, October 7, 2001.

[209] Kyle Roerink, "2013 Look Back: 'I Had Butterflies': Wyoming Freshmen Lawmakers Recount First Year on Floor," *Casper Star-Tribune*, December 30, 2013.

[210] Both quotes are from Morgan C. Matthews and Kathryn J. Lively, "Making Volunteer-based Democracy 'Work': Gendered Coping Strategies in a Citizen Legislature," *Socius* 3 (2017): Article first published online: April 21, 2017; Issue published: January 1, 2017 https://doi.org /10.1177/2378023117705535.

[211] Brianne Pfannenstiel, "Baby in the House: Iowa Legislature Welcomes Its Newest (and Smallest) Member," *Des Moines Register*, February 22, 2018.

212 *Terre Haute Tribune Star*, "Battles Resigns as 45th District State Rep; Says He Won't Seek Re-Election," May 16, 2014.

213 James Q. Lynch, "Freshman Legislators Learn Tough Lessons," *Cedar Rapids Gazette*, May 14, 2001.

214 Roerink, "2013 Look Back: 'I Had Butterflies': Wyoming Freshmen Lawmakers Recount First Year on Floor."

215 Chris McGann, "Legislature: We've Had an Awful Session," *Seattle Post Intelligencer*, April 14, 2005.

216 Aurelio Rojas, "Illness under Control, Firebaugh Fights Back," *Sacramento Bee*, March 29, 2004.

217 Cara Buckley, "Tallahassee Politicking Hasn't Shed Frat-House Reputation," *Miami Herald*, May 5, 2005.

218 Eric R. Hansen, Nicholas Carnes, and Virginia Gray, "What Happens When Insurers Make Insurance Laws? State Legislative Agendas and the Occupational Makeup of Government, *State Politics & Policy Quarterly*, https://doi.org/10.1177/1532440018813013.

219 Kristian Hernández, "Michigan Lawmakers Voted on Bills Even after Admitting Conflicts of Interest," Center for Public Integrity, April 25, 2018, https://www.publicintegrity.org/2018/04/25/21697/michigan-lawmakers-voted-bills-even-after-admitting-conflicts-interest.

220 Kevin McDermott, "Missouri Republicans' Push to Limit Lawsuits Could Have Unexpected Beneficiaries: Themselves." *St. Louis Post-Dispatch*, February 13, 2017.

221 Fenit Nirappil, "Del. Dan Morhaim Faces Legislative Inquiry over Dual Marijuana Roles," *Washington Post*, September 23, 2016.

222 Tim Novak, "2 Chicago Cop-Legislators Changed Law to Benefit 2 People: Themselves," *Chicago Sun-Times*, October 22, 2017.

223 Matthew Tully, "Matthew Tully: Conflicts of Interest Rampant at Indiana Statehouse," *Indianapolis Star*, March 22, 2013.

224 Liz Essley Whyte and Ryan J. Foley, "State Lawmakers Blur Line between Public, Personal Interests," *Des Moines Register*, December 6, 2017.

225 Michele McNeil Solida and Jennifer Wagner, "Lawmakers' Job Conflicts are Obscured, Defended," *Indianapolis Star*, January 22, 2002.

226 Forrest Wilder, "Loan-Shark Attack at the Lege!!!" *Texas Observer*, June 9, 2011, http://www.texasobserver.org/loan-shark-attack-at-the-lege/.

227 Jeff Stensland, "Potential Conflicts of Interest Rife in S.C.," *The State* [Columbia], July 3, 2005.

228 Janie Har and Dave Hogan, "Bill Aims to Reveal Legislators' Outside Income," *The Oregonian*, February 21, 2007.

229 Beth A. Rosenson, "The Impact of Ethics Laws on Legislative Recruitment and the Occupational Composition of State Legislatures," *Political Research Quarterly* 59 (2006): 619–27.

230 Brianne Pfannenstiel, "Special Interest Groups Spend Big at Iowa Capitol," *Des Moines Register*, August 24, 2017.

231 J. Taylor Rushing, "Recovering Davis Files Film Bill," *Florida Times-Union*, March 11, 2007.

232 David McGrath Schwartz, "Incoming Legislative Leaders Impart Advice to Freshmen Lawmakers," *Las Vegas Sun*, November 29, 2012.

233 Karen Brooks Harper, "Huge Crop of Texas House Freshmen Learning the Ropes at the Capitol, Sometimes Painfully," *Dallas Morning News*, February 6, 2013.

234 Patrick Anderson, "R.I. Lawmaker Changes Tune on Drinking at State House," *Providence Journal*, March 7, 2017.

235 Alexei Koseff and Taryn Luna, "Booze Fuels Business—and Bad Behavior—at California Capitol," *Sacramento Bee*, August 30, 2018.

236 John Wright, "Our Million-Dollar Legislature," *St. Louis Post-Dispatch*, March 23, 2014.

237 Ed Vogel, "Poll: Public Disapproves of Lawmaker Gifts," *Las Vegas Review Journal*, April 11, 2006.

238 Benjamin Weiser, "Sheldon Silver Is Convicted in 2nd Corruption Trial," *New York Times*, May 11, 2018.

[239] Brian Lyman, "Appeals Court Upholds Most Mike Hubbard Felony Ethics Convictions," *Montgomery Advertiser*, August 27, 2018; Milton J. Valencia, "DiMasi Found Guilty on 7 of 9 Counts in Kickback Scheme," *Boston Globe*, June 16, 2011.

[240] Alan Greenblatt, "Are South Carolina Voters Too Tolerant of Corruption?" *Governing*, March 2017, http://www.governing.com/topics/politics/gov-south-carolina-ethics.html; Andy Shain and Joseph Cranney, "Veteran Senator Resigns after Pleading Guilty in South Carolina Statehouse Corruption Probe," *Post and Courier*, June 5, 2018.

[241] United States District Attorney's Office, Eastern District of Arkansas, "Former Arkansas State Senator and Representative Pleads Guilty to Conspiracy and Bribery," April 30, 2018, https://www.justice.gov/usao-edar/pr/former-arkansas-state-senator-and-representative-pleads-guilty-conspiracy-and-bribery.

[242] Department of Justice, Office of Public Affairs, "Arkansas State Representative Pleads Guilty to Bribe Conspiracy," January 4, 2017; https://www.justice.gov/opa/pr/arkansas-state-representative-pleads-guilty-bribe-conspiracy; https://5newsonline.com/2018/04/11/ex-state-lawmaker-testifies-he-and-ex-senator-took-kickbacks/.

[243] Craig R. McCoy, "State Rep. Vanessa Brown Guilty on All Counts; Took $4,000 Bribe in Sting," *Philadelphia Inquirer*, October 31, 2018.

[244] Lisa Demer, Don Hunter, and Sabra Ayres, "Kohring Also Charged with Bribery, Extortion," *Anchorage Daily News*, May 4, 2007.

[245] See the *Anchorage Daily News* web summary of the investigation, David Hulen and Rich Mauer, "The Alaska Political Corruption Investigation," October 29, 2007; Dan Joling, "Kohring Corruption Trial Sent to Jurors," *Juneau Empire*, November 1, 2007.

[246] Karl Vick, "I'll Sell My Soul to the Devil," *Washington Post*, November 12, 2007.

[247] Chris Frates, "Senator Recall, DA Probe Afoot," *Denver Post*, March 7, 2006.

[248] Matt Dinger, "Former Oklahoma Rep. Randy Terrill Sentenced in Bribery Trial," *The Oklahoman*, December 20, 2013.

[249] See Alan Rosenthal, *The Decline of Representative Democracy* (Washington, DC: CQ Press, 1998), 92–93; "Tennessee Waltz: The Dance Is Over," FBI.gov, http://www.fbi.gov/news/stories/2008/may/tennesseewaltz_050208.

[250] Oguzhan Dincer and Michael Johnston, "Measuring Illegal and Legal Corruption in American States: Some Results from 2017 Corruption in America Survey," Institute for Corruption Studies, http://greasethewheels.org/cpi/.

[251] See Beth A. Rosenson, *The Shadowlands of Conduct* (Washington, DC: Georgetown University Press, 2005).

[252] Leah Rush and David Jimenez, "States Outpace Congress in Upgrading Lobbying Laws," The Center for Public Integrity, March 1, 2006, http://projects.publicintegrity.org/hiredguns/report.aspx?aid=781. See also NCSL, http://www.ncsl.org/research/ethics/50-state-legislative-ethics-and-lobbying-laws.aspx.

[253] Cynthia Opheim, "Explaining the Differences in State Lobby Regulation," *Western Political Quarterly* 44 (1991): 405–21; Joshua Ozymy, "Keepin on the Sunny Side: Scandals, Organized Interests and the Passage of Legislative Lobbying Laws in the American States," *American Politics Research* 41 (2013): 3–23. For a caveat, see James Strickland, "A Paradox of Political Reform: Shadow Interests in the U.S. States," *American Politics Research* (2018): https://doi.org/10.1177/1532673X18788049.

[254] Christopher Witko, "Explaining Increases in the Stringency of State Campaign Finance Regulation, 1993–2002," *State Politics & Policy Quarterly* 7 (2007): 369–93.

[255] John Moritz and Michael R. Wickline, "Arkansas Governor Calls for Legislator to Resign," *Northwest Arkansas Democrat Gazette*, July 18, 2018.

[256] Monique Garcia and Rick Pearson, "Republican State Lawmaker Resigns after Ex-Girlfriend's Accusations; Rauner Calls It 'Right Thing to Do'," *Chicago Tribune*, August 2, 2018.

[257] Joel Ebert, "Sexual Harassment Troubles Mount in Statehouses around the Country," *USA Today*, November 20, 2017; Jen Fifield, "Statehouse Sexual Harassment Tally: 18 Lawmakers Gone or Punished," *Stateline.org*, December 26, 2017, http://www.pewtrusts.org/en/research-and-analysis/blogs/stateline/2017/12/26/statehouse-sexual-harassment-tally-at-least-18-lawmakers-gone-or-punished.

258 *Boston Herald*, "Sexual Misconduct Claims in State Legislatures since 2017," August 26, 2018.

259 *Sun Sentinel*, "Let a Cultural Reboot Be Sen. Jack Latvala's Legacy," December 20, 2017.

260 Taryn Luna, "California Senator Resigns Amid Harassment Allegations," *Sacramento Bee*, February 22, 2018.

261 Taryn Luna, "It's 'Boys Club' at the California Capitol, Say Women Working There," *Sacramento Bee*, October 23, 2017; Adam Nagourney and Jennifer Medina, "Women Denounce Harassment in California's Capital," *New York Times*, October 17, 2017.

262 J. Patrick Coolican, "One in Five Minnesota House Members, Staff Have Been Harassed or Witnessed It," *Star Tribune*, December 10, 2018.

263 See, for example, the discussion in http://radio.wosu.org/post/toxic-statehouse-culture-goes-beyond-inappropriate-behavior-women-say#stream/0.

264 Rachel Leingang and Yvonne Wingett Sanchez, "Arizona Rep. Paul Mosley Accused of Inappropriate Comments Involving Women, Religion," *Arizona Republic*, July 16, 2018.

265 Melanie Mason, "As the Legislative Year Ends, the #MeToo Movement Shows Its Influence," *Los Angeles Times*, September 3, 2018.

266 David Lieb, "Legislatures Lack Public Records on Harassment," *Columbia Missourian*, April 16, 2018.

267 Jen Fifield, "Sexual Harassment Training Is Hard to Find in Statehouses, *Governing*, November 15, 2017, http://www.governing.com/topics/mgmt/sl-sexual-harassment-training-statehouses.html; Jen Fifield, "Lawmakers Have Left, but the Harassment Culture in Statehouses Remains," *Governing*, May 14, 2018, http://www.governing.com/topics/politics/sl-harassment-statehouse-metoo.html; David A. Lieb, "States Split in Taking Action to Combat Sexual Harassment in Government," *St. Louis Post-Dispatch*, August 26, 2018.

268 Tony Cook, "For the First Time, Indiana Lawmakers Will be Subject to a Sexual Harassment Policy," *Indianapolis Star*, March 22, 2018.

269 Dana Ferguson, "Lawmakers Train to Avoid Sex Harassment, Some Lament Effort as Unnecessary," *Argus Leader*, January 18, 2018.

270 Tony Cook, Kaitlin Lange, and Ryan Martin, "Former Intern Says Brian Bosma Tried to Intimidate Her over Alleged Sexual Encounter," *Indianapolis Star*, October 10, 2018; Dirk VanderHart, "Oregon Legislature Pushes Back against Sexual Harassment Investigation," OPB, August 24, 2018, https://www.opb.org/news/article/oregon-legislature-sexual-harassment-investigation/; *Journal News*, "NY Senate Fails with Its Real-Time #MeToo Reaction: Editorial," January 12, 2018.

271 John Frank, "#MeToo Dominated Colorado's 2018 Legislative Session. But Advocates Ask: Did Anything Change?" *Denver Post*, May 13, 2018.

272 Mattie Quinn, "Her Accusations Ended His Political Career. Here's What She Wants You to Know," *Governing*, May 22, 2018, http://www.governing.com/23-percent-podcast/gov-faith-winter.html.

273 Mason, "As the Legislative Year Ends, the #MeToo Movement Shows Its Influence."

274 Christina A. Cassidy, "Many State Lawmakers Accused of Sexual Misconduct Run Again," *San Francisco Chronicle*, July 18, 2018; Candice Norwood, "Does #MeToo Matter? Of 19 State Candidates Facing Accusations, Only 1 Lost," *Governing*, November 7, 2018, http://www.governing.com/topics/politics/gov-sexual-misconduct-lawmakers-midterms-2018.html; Samantha Schmidt, "More Than a Dozen State Lawmakers Accused of Sexual Misconduct Are Running for Office Today. Will They Win?" *Washington Post*, November 6, 2018; Julie Turkewitz and Alan Blinder, "Accused of Harassment, and Seeking Redemption at the Ballot Box," *New York Times*, August 5, 2018.

275 Mary Jo Pitzl, "Arizona Primary Voters Show Disdain for Incumbents, Tossing Three in Major Races," *Arizona Republic*, August 29, 2018.

276 Squire, "Career Opportunities and Membership Stability in Legislatures," and Peverill Squire, "Member Career Opportunities and the Internal Organization of Legislatures," *Journal of Politics* 50 (1988): 726–44.

277 See the first edition of this book, Squire and Moncrief, *State Legislatures Today: Politics under the Domes*, 109–14.

[278] Squire, "Career Opportunities and Membership Stability in Legislatures," and Squire, "Member Career Opportunities and the Internal Organization of Legislatures."

[279] Cherie Maestas, "Professional Legislatures and Ambitious Politicians: Policy Responsiveness of State Institutions," *Legislative Studies Quarterly* 25 (2000): 663–90.

[280] Richard A. Clucas, "Principal-Agent Theory and the Power of State House Speakers," *Legislative Studies Quarterly* 26 (2001): 319–38; and Squire, "Career Opportunities and Membership Stability in Legislatures."

Chapter 4: Legislative Organization across the States

[1] For Connecticut, see https://www.cga.ct.gov/asp/menu/rules.asp. For Mississippi, see http://billstatus.ls.state.ms.us/htms/h_rules.pdf.

[2] See Douglas G. Feig, "The State Legislature: Representative of the People or the Powerful?" in *Mississippi Government and Politics: Modernizers versus Traditionalists*, ed. Dale Krane and Stephen Shaffer (Lincoln: University of Nebraska Press, 1992), 121.

[3] Feig, "The State Legislature: Representative of the People or the Powerful?" 121.

[4] The list of Connecticut leadership positions is taken from http://www.housedems.ct.gov/leadership for the majority party Democrats, and http://www.cthousegop.com/leadership-team/ for the minority party Republicans

[5] Malcolm E. Jewell and Samuel C. Patterson, *The Legislative Process in the United States*, 3rd ed. (New York: Random House, 1977), 178.

[6] Alan Rosenthal, *The Decline of Representative Democracy* (Washington, DC: CQ Press, 1998), 133.

[7] Alan Rosenthal, *Engines of Democracy* (Washington, DC: CQ Press, 2009), 430.

[8] Keith E. Hamm and Ronald D. Hedlund, "Political Parties in State Legislatures," in *The Encyclopedia of the American Legislative System*, ed. Joel J. Silbey (New York: Scribner's, 1994).

[9] Bruce Cain and Gerald Wright, "Committees," in *Institutional Change in American Politics: The Case of Term Limits*, ed. Karl T. Kurtz, Bruce Cain, and Richard Niemi (Ann Arbor: University of Michigan Press, 2007).

[10] Malcolm E. Jewell and Samuel C. Patterson, *The Legislative Process in the United States*, 4th ed. (New York: Random House, 1986), 119.

[11] See Mike Baker, "2 Dems to Work with GOP to Control State Senate," *Seattle Times*, December 10, 2012; Terry Baquet, "Tucker Gets Nod as House Speaker," *Times-Picayune*, November 20, 2007; Mario Cattabiani, Angela Couloumbis, and Amy Worden, "Gavel Passes from Perzel," *Philadelphia Inquirer*, January 3, 2007; Mike Dennison, "Big Skies, Big Leaders," *State Legislatures* 31, no. 7 (2005), 46–50; Jessica Fender, "Wilder's Ouster Spells End of Era," *The Tennessean*, January 10, 2007; Karen Hansen, "Are Coalitions Really on the Rise?" *State Legislatures* 15, no. 4 (1989): 11–12; Nathaniel Herz, "Alaska House Will be Run by Coalition," *Bristol Bay Times*, November 25, 2016; Jewell and Patterson, *The Legislative Process in the United States*, 155–56; Thomas Kaplan, "Top Breakaway Democrat Favors G.O.P. Coalition in State Senate," *New York Times*, November 27, 2012; Karl Kurtz, "Coalition Chooses New Mexico Senate Leader," http://ncsl.typepad.com/the_thicket/2009/01/coalition-chooses-new-mexico-senate-leader.html; Karl Kurtz, "Surprise New Texas House Speaker, http://ncsl.typepad.com/the_thicket/2009/01/surprise-new-texas-house-speaker.html; and Alan Rosenthal, *The Decline of Representative Democracy: Process, Participation, and Power in State Legislatures* (Washington, DC: CQ Press 1998), 248.

[12] Theo Emery, "In the Tennessee Senate, a Historic Shift of Power," *New York Times*, January 27, 2007.

[13] Tom Humphrey, "Williams Elected as House Speaker," *Knoxville News Sentinel*, January 14, 2009.

[14] Herz, "Alaska House Will be Run by Coalition."

15 Sarah D. Wire, "Some House Members Call for the Removal of Speaker," *Columbia Missourian*, May 14, 2008.

16 Michele Jacklin, "Conservative Democrats Are Victorious in Connecticut House," *State Legislatures* 15 (1989): 13–15.

17 See James Richardson, *Willie Brown* (Berkeley: University of California Press, 1996), 261–71, 358. See also Thad Kousser, *Term Limits and the Dismantling of State Legislative Professionalism* (New York: Cambridge University Press, 2005), 33.

18 Nancy Martorano, Bruce Anderson, and Keith E. Hamm, "A Transforming South: Exploring Patterns of State House Contestation," *American Review of Politics* 21 (2000): 179–200.

19 Keith E. Hamm and Robert Harmel, "Legislative Party Development and the Speaker System: The Case of the Texas House," *Journal of Politics* 55 (1993): 1140–51; Robert Harmel, "Minority Partisanship in One-Party Predominant Legislatures: A Five-State Study," *Journal of Politics* 48 (1986): 729–40; Robert Harmel and Keith E. Hamm, "Development of a Party Role in a No-Party Legislature," *Western Political Quarterly* 39 (1986): 79–92.

20 Rosenthal, *The Decline of Representative Democracy*, 281.

21 Hamm and Hedlund, "Political Parties in State Legislatures," 968.

22 John A. Straayer, *The Colorado General Assembly*, 2nd ed. (Boulder: University Press of Colorado, 2000), 142, 231; Rosenthal, *The Decline of Representative Democracy*, 77.

23 Wayne L. Francis, *The Legislative Committee Game: A Comparative Analysis of 50 States* (Columbus: Ohio State University Press, 1989), 45.

24 Anthony Gierzynski, *Legislative Party Campaign Committees in the American States* (Lexington: University Press of Kentucky, 1992), 48–50; Cindy Simon Rosenthal, "New Party or Campaign Bank Account? Explaining the Rise of State Legislative Campaign Committees," *Legislative Studies Quarterly* 20 (1995): 249–68; Daniel M. Shea, *Transforming Democracy: Legislative Campaign Committees and Political Parties* (Albany: State University of New York Press, 1995).

25 Jeffrey M. Stonecash and Amy Widestrom, "Political Parties and Elections," in *Governing New York State*, 5th ed., ed. Robert F. Pecorella and Jeffrey M. Stonecash (Albany: State University Press of New York, 2006), 65.

26 Scott Mooneyham, "House May Limit Length of Session," *Charlotte Observer*, September 3, 2002.

27 See *The Book of the States 2017 edition* (Lexington, KY: Council of State Governments, 2017), 56–60, and state legislative web pages.

28 There were negotiations to split control of the two positions in late 2008, but ultimately the decision was made to give both titles to the new Democratic leader. See Danny Hakim, "Democrats Reach Pact to Lead the Senate," *New York Times*, January 6, 2009. During the summer of 2009 an attempted coup left control of the chamber tied between Democrats and Republicans. The Republicans who claimed to be in charge of the senate operated with a separate president and majority leader. Following the 2012 elections a coalition took control of the senate, and it operated with co-presidents who also served as their party's leader.

29 Gary M. Halter, *Government & Politics of Texas* (Madison, WI: Brown & Benchmark, 1997), 104–5; Rosenthal, *The Decline of Representative Democracy*, 248.

30 Dana Beyerle, "Mitchem Elected President Pro Tem of the Senate," *Tuscaloosa News*, January 10, 2007; David Firestone, "In Alabama, Senate Ends Bitter Rift over Leader," *New York Times*, March 31, 1999; Buster Kantrow, "Deal Ends Political Row That Tied Alabama Senate in Knots," Stateline.org, April 6, 1999; Kevin Sack, "Tug-of-War over Power Roils Senate in Alabama," *New York Times*, March 4, 1999; David White, "Boycott Shuts Down Senate," *Birmingham News*, March 4, 1999; David White, "Distrust Keeps Senate in Limbo," *Birmingham News*, March 11, 1999; David White, "New Rules Reduce Windom's Authority," *Birmingham News*, March 31, 1999; David White, "Senate Adjourns to Allow Cool-Off," *Birmingham News*, March 12, 1999; David White, "Senate Erupts into Renewed Chaos; Senate Talks Dissolve into Chaos," *Birmingham News*, March 29, 1999; David White, "Senate Frozen for 4th Straight Day," *Birmingham News*, March 8, 1999; David White, "Senators to Learn If New Rules Will Work," *Birmingham News*, April 6, 1999; David White, "Siegelman Wins Praise for Session," *Birmingham News*, June 13, 1999. See the discussion in Peverill Squire and Gary Moncrief, *State Legislatures Today*, 2nd ed. (Lanham, MD: Rowman & Littlefield, 2015), 110–13.

[31] Jewell and Patterson, *The Legislative Process in the United States*, 119.

[32] On this point, see Peverill Squire, "Changing State Legislative Leadership Careers," in *Changing Patterns in State Legislative Careers*, ed. Gary F. Moncrief and Joel A. Thompson (Ann Arbor: University of Michigan Press, 1992), 180–85. See also Patricia K. Freeman, "A Comparative Analysis of Speaker Career Patterns in U.S. State Legislatures," *Legislative Studies Quarterly* 20 (1995): 365–76.

[33] James D. Driscoll, *California's Legislature* (Sacramento: Center for California Studies, 1986), 199–200.

[34] Shane Goldmacher, "For Bass, Budget Gets Top Billing," *Capitol Alert*, May 12, 2008, http://www.sacbee.com/static/weblogs/capitolalertlatest/012494.html.

[35] Jewell and Patterson, *The Legislative Process in the United States*, 119. See also Malcolm E. Jewell, "Survey on Selection of State Legislative Leaders," *Comparative State Politics Newsletter* 1 (1980): 10.

[36] Thad L. Beyle, "Political Change in North Carolina: A Legislative Coup D'Etat," *Comparative State Politics Newsletter* 10 (1989): 4.

[37] *Evansville Courier & Press*, "Stumbo Tops Salary List for Kentucky Legislators," June 25, 2012.

[38] Rosenthal, *The Decline of Representative Democracy*, 254–60.

[39] On bill referrals, see Peverill Squire and Keith E. Hamm, *101 Chambers: Congress, State Legislatures and the Future of Legislative Studies* (Columbus: Ohio State University Press, 2005), 120.

[40] Chris Church and Derek Gomes, "Dickinson Resigns from Lone Committee Assignment," *South County Independent*, January 17, 2014.

[41] Barb Berggoetz and Tony Cook, "Senate Leader Punishes Mike Delph over Tweet," *Indianapolis Star*, February 21, 2014.

[42] Alisa Ulferts, "Ire from Top Not New for Senator," *St. Petersburg Times*, July 14, 2003.

[43] Steven Harmon, "Senate Leader Flexes Muscle in Warning to Lawmakers," *San Jose Mercury*, March 13, 2007; Brian Joseph, "Spitzer Sent to 'the Doghouse,'" *Orange County Register*, May 11, 2007; E. J. Schultz, "Democratic Assemblywoman Banished from Capitol for Withholding Budget Vote," *Sacramento Bee*, August 19, 2008.

[44] Steve Wiegand, "Assembly Civility Is a Bit Fleeting," *Sacramento Bee*, December 7, 2006.

[45] Barry Edwards, "Formal Authority, Persuasive Power, and Effectiveness in State Legislatures," *State Politics & Policy Quarterly* 18 (2018): 324–46.

[46] Richard A. Clucas, "Principal-Agent Theory and the Power of State House Speakers," *Legislative Studies Quarterly* 26 (2001): 319–38; Christopher Z. Mooney, "Measuring State House Speakers' Formal Powers, 1981–2010," *State Politics & Policy Quarterly* 13 (2013): 262–73. See also James Coleman Battista, "Formal and Perceived Leadership Power in U.S. State Legislatures," *State Politics & Policy Quarterly* 11 (2011): 102–18; and Jennifer Hayes Clark, *Minority Parties in U.S. Legislatures* (Ann Arbor: University of Michigan Press, 2015), 38–43.

[47] Clucas, "Principal-Agent Theory and the Power of State House Speakers"; Richard A. Clucas, "Legislative Professionalism and the Power of State House Leaders," *State Politics & Policy Quarterly* 7 (2007): 1–19.

[48] Gary F. Moncrief, Joel A. Thompson, and Karl T. Kurtz, "The Old Statehouse, It Ain't What It Used to Be," *Legislative Studies Quarterly* 21 (1996): 57–72; William Pound, "State Legislative Careers: Twenty-Five Years of Reform," in *Changing Patterns in State Legislative Careers*, ed. Gary F. Moncrief and Joel A. Thompson (Ann Arbor: University of Michigan Press, 1992), 20–21; Jesse Richman, "The Logic of Legislative Leadership: Preferences, Challenges, and the Speaker's Powers," *Legislative Studies Quarterly* 35 (2010): 211–33.

[49] Thomas H. Little and Rick Farmer, "Legislative Leadership," in *Institutional Change in American Politics: The Case of Term Limits*, ed. Karl T. Kurtz, Bruce Cain, and Richard G. Niemi (Ann Arbor: University of Michigan Press, 2007), 71.

[50] Mark Pazniokas, "House Speaker Talks the Talk," *Hartford Courant*, May 4, 2005.

[51] Richard A. Clucas, *The Speaker's Electoral Connection: Willie Brown and the California Assembly* (Berkeley, CA: Institute of Governmental Studies, 1995), 19–27.

[52] Former Idaho House speaker Bruce Newcomb, quoted at "Behind the Scenes in the Idaho Legislature," a workshop conducted by Carl Bianchi, Gary Moncrief, and Bruce Newcomb, Boise State University, February 2, 2008.

[53] Ralph G. Wright, *Inside the Statehouse: Lessons from the Speaker* (Washington, DC: CQ Press, 2005), 89.

[54] See Squire and Hamm, *101 Chambers*, 118–20.

[55] See Clark, *Minority Parties in U.S.*, 38–45.

[56] Brian Bakst, "Senate GOP Back in Charge; DFL Awaits Walz Picks," *Capitol View*, December 11, 2018, https://blogs.mprnews.org/capitol-view/2018/12/senate-gop-back-in-charge-dfl-awaits-walz-picks/.

[57] William L. Spence, "Just Another Day on the Mountain: House Minority Leader Mat Epelding Faces Challenge of Literal and Figurative Heights," *Spokesman-Review*, February 12, 2018.

[58] Keith E. Hamm, Ronald D. Hedlund, and Nancy Martorano, "Measuring State Legislative Committee Power: Change and Chamber Differences in the 20th Century," *State Politics & Policy Quarterly* 6 (2006): 88–111.

[59] Jack R. Van Der Slik and Kent D. Redfield, *Lawmaking in Illinois* (Springfield, IL: Office of Public Affairs Communication, 1986), 139.

[60] See Bruce E. Cain and Thad Kousser, *Adapting to Term Limits: Recent Experiences and New Directions* (San Francisco: Public Policy Institute of California, 2004), 31–32.

[61] See Matthew C. Moen, Kenneth T. Palmer, and Richard J. Powell, *Changing Members: The Maine Legislature in the Era of Term Limits* (Lanham, MD: Lexington Books, 2005), 94; Belle Zeller, ed., *American State Legislatures* (New York: Crowell, 1954), 260.

[62] Robert Luce, *Legislative Procedure* (Boston: Houghton Mifflin, 1922), 137.

[63] Tim Groseclose and David C. King, "Committee Theories Reconsidered," in *Congress Reconsidered*, 7th ed., ed. Lawrence C. Dodd and Bruce I. Oppenheimer (Washington, DC: CQ Press, 2001), 207–8.

[64] Todd Makse, "Majority Party Change and Committee Jurisdictions in State Legislatures," *Legislative Studies Quarterly* 39 (2014): 387–405.

[65] Briana Bierschbach, "House Democrats Signal Policy Priorities in New Committee Structure," *Minnesota Public Radio*, November 21, 2018, https://blogs.mprnews.org/capitol-view/2018/11/house-democrats-signal-priorities-in-new-committee-structure/.

[66] Todd Makse, "The Retention of Expertise and Productivity in State Legislative Committees," *State Politics & Policy Quarterly* 17 (2017): 418–40.

[67] American Society of Legislative Clerks and Secretaries in cooperation with the National Conference of State Legislatures, *Inside the Legislative Process* (Denver, CO: National Conference of State Legislatures, 1998), 4. See also Ronald D. Hedlund and Keith E. Hamm, "Political Parties as Vehicles for Organizing U.S. State Legislative Committees," *Legislative Studies Quarterly* 21 (1996): 383–408.

[68] Legislative Affairs Agency, "Alaska State Legislature Uniform Rules," 1.

[69] Ronald D. Hedlund, Kevin Coombs, Nancy Martorano, and Keith E. Hamm, "Partisan Stacking on Legislative Committees," *Legislative Studies Quarterly* 34 (2009): 175–91.

[70] Jim Nolan, "Bolling's Vote Gives GOP Control of Senate," *Richmond Times Dispatch*, January 12, 2012.

[71] See Georgia House of Representatives, "Rules, Ethics, and Decorum of the House of Representatives," Rule 11.8.

[72] Jim Tharpe, Nancy Badertscher, and Sonji Jacobs, "Legislature '05: Republicans Write Rules; New GOP Majority Locks in Power as Democratic Unity Noticeably Erodes," *Atlanta Journal-Constitution*, January 11, 2005.

[73] Tom Baxter and Jim Galloway, "Legislature 2005: Democrat Denied Ceremonial Role," *Atlanta Journal-Constitution*, January 13, 2005. See also Kamal Ghali, "A Procedural Rule and a Substantive Problem: Rule 11.8, Legislative Hawks, and the Concentration of Power in Georgia's Speaker of the House," *Yale Law Journal* 117, Pocket Part 210 (2008), http://www.yalelawjournal.org/forum/a-procedural-rule-and-a-substantive-problem-legislative-hawks-and-the-concentration-of-power-in-georgias-speaker-of-the-house.

[74] http://www.ilga.gov/house/rules.asp. See Rule 10b; Ted Dabrowski and Joe Tabor, "Madigan's Rules: How Illinois Gives Its House Speaker Power to Manipulate and Control the Legislative Process," Illinois Policy Institute, Winter 2017, 9.

[75] Clark, *Minority Parties in U.S. Legislatures*, 61–92.

[76] Blake Aued, "Endangered 'Hawks': Former Speaker's Lieutenants," *Athens Banner-Herald*, December 17, 2009.

[77] See Hawaii House of Representatives, "Rules of the House of Representatives, State of Hawaii, The Twenty-Ninth State Legislature, 2017–2018," Rule 11.2 (2).

[78] Arkansas House of Representatives, "House Rules as Amended by HR 1031 of 2007," Rule 52 (a) (1); Rules of the House of Representatives, Committee Chairperson's Manual and Committee Rules, and Joint Rules of the House and Senate of the State of Arkansas, Ninety-First General Assembly," Rule 54 (a) (1).

[79] American Society of Legislative Clerks and Secretaries, *Inside the Legislative Process*, 4.8.

[80] http://www.ilga.gov/house/rules.asp. See Rule 5b.

[81] General Assembly of North Carolina Session 2017, "House Resolution 114," Rule 26 (c).

[82] Clark, *Minority Parties in U.S. Legislatures*, 90–91.

[83] Michigan House of Representatives, "Standing Rules of the House of Representatives in Accordance with the Michigan Constitution, Article 4, Section 16," House Resolution No. 283, Adopted January 12, 2017, Rule 8.

[84] Kristin Kanthak, "U.S. State Legislative Committee Assignments and Encouragement of Party Loyalty: An Exploratory Analysis," *State Politics & Policy Quarterly* 9 (2009): 284–303.

[85] Nancy Martorano, Keith E. Hamm, and Ronald D. Hedlund, "Examining Committee Structures, Procedures, and Powers in U.S. State Legislatures," paper presented at the 2000 Annual Meeting of the Midwest Political Science Association.

[86] See Parliamentary Manual of the Senate, Ninety-First General Assembly, Rule 7.01 (b) (2), www.arkansas.gov/senate/docs/2017-SenateRules.pdf.

[87] Rules of the Senate of South Carolina, Adopted December 6, 2016, Rule 19 (D), https://www.scstatehouse.gov/senatepage/senrule.php.

[88] For Mississippi, see http://billstatus.ls.state.ms.us/htms/h_rules.pdf, Rule 60 (3); For Texas see Texas House Rules, 85th Legislature, 2017, Rule 4, Section 1

[89] See Roger H. Davidson, Walter J. Oleszek, Frances E. Lee, and Eric Schickler, *Congress and Its Members*, 16th ed. (Thousand Oaks, CA: CQ Press, 2018), 193.

[90] Alabama House of Representatives, "House Rules," Rule 63, http://www.legislature.state.al.us/aliswww/ISD/House/ALHouseRules_Presiding.aspx.

[91] Minnesota House of Representatives, "Permanent Rules of the House of Representatives 2017–2018," Article 6, 6.02, https://www.house.leg.state.mn.us/cco/rules/permrule/hrule.htm.

[92] Keith E. Hamm, Ronald D. Hedlund, and Stephanie Shirley Post, "Committee Specialization in U.S. State Legislatures during the 20th Century: Do Legislatures Tap the Talents of Their Members?" *State Politics & Policy Quarterly* 11 (2011): 299–324.

[93] California State Assembly, "Standing Rules of the Assembly 2017–18 Regular Session," Rule 12, https://leginfo.legislature.ca.gov/faces/publicationsTemplate.xhtml.

[94] Clark, *Minority Parties in U.S. Legislatures*, 90–91; Ronald D. Hedlund, "Entering the Committee System: State Committee Assignments," *Western Political Quarterly* 42 (1989): 597–625; Ronald Hedlund, "Accommodating Member Requests in Committee Assignments: Individual-Level Explanations," in *Changing Patterns in State Legislative Careers*, ed. Gary F. Moncrief and Joel A. Thompson (Ann Arbor: University of Michigan Press, 1992); and Ronald D. Hedlund and Samuel C. Patterson, "The Electoral Antecedents of State Legislative Committee Assignments," *Legislative Studies Quarterly* 17 (1992): 539–59.

[95] Wright, *Inside the Statehouse*, 105.

[96] See James Coleman Battista, "Re-examining Legislative Committee Representativeness in the States," *State Politics & Policy Quarterly* 4 (2004): 161–80; L. Marvin Overby and Thomas A. Kazee, "Outlying Committees in the Statehouse: An Examination of the Prevalence of Committee Outliers in State Legislatures," *Journal of Politics* 62 (2000): 701–28; L. Marvin Overby, Thomas A. Kazee, and David W. Prince, "Committee Outliers in State Legislatures," *Legislative Studies Quarterly* 29 (2004): 81–107; David W. Prince and L. Marvin Overby, "Legislative Organization Theory and Committee Preference Outliers in State Senates," *State Politics & Policy Quarterly* 5 (2005): 68–87.

[97] Jesse Richman, "Uncertainty and the Prevalence of Committee Outliers," *Legislative Studies Quarterly* 33 (2008): 323–47.

[98] http://blog.chron.com/bigjolly/2013/02/speaker-joe-straus-setting-the- agenda-for-texas-and-moving-republicans-forward/; http://www.texasgopvote.com/ regions/texas/2013-texas-legislature-house-committee-assignments-005081.

[99] Dick Aldrich, "Missouri House Speaker-to-Be Tilley Selects Three Democrats for Committee Chairs," December 5, 2010, http://m.semissourian.com/ story/1685364.html.

[100] Rules of the Senate of South Carolina, Adopted December 6, 2016, Rule 19 (E),

[101] State of Arkansas, "Parliamentary Manual of the Senate, Ninety-First General Assembly," Rule 7.01 (b) (2) and Rule 7.05 (a); For Virginia, Rules of the Senate, Adopted January 13, 2016, Rule 18 and 20 (a).

[102] Angela Delli Santi, "New Jersey Legislative Leaders Shuffle Committees," *The Press of Atlantic City*, January 12, 2012.

[103] Peverill Squire, "Career Opportunities and Membership Stability in Legislatures," *Legislative Studies Quarterly* 13 (1988): 65–82; Peverill Squire, "Member Career Opportunities and the Internal Organization of Legislatures," *Journal of Politics* 50 (1988): 726–44; Peverill Squire, "The Theory of Legislative Institutionalization and the California Assembly," *Journal of Politics* 54 (1992): 1026–54.

[104] Charles G. Bell and Charles M. Price, *The First Term* (Beverly Hills, CA: Sage, 1975).

[105] Karen Brooks Harper, "Huge Crop of Texas House Freshmen Learning the Ropes at the Capitol, Sometimes Painfully," *Dallas Morning News*, February 6, 2013.

[106] Mike Maciag, "Louisiana's Budget Crisis Empowers an Unusual Group," *Governing*, July 2016, http://www.governing.com/topics/politics/gov-louisiana-budget.html.

[107] Angela Evancie and Peter Hirschfeld, "Low Pay, Weird Schedule: Who Exactly Can Pull Off the Legislator Lifestyle?" *Brave Little State*, Vermont Public Radio, August 4, 2017, http://digital.vpr.net/post/low-pay-weird-schedule-who-exactly-can-pull-legislator-lifestyle#stream/0.

[108] Mattie Quinn, "A Cautionary Tale for the Newly Elected," *Governing.com*, December 11, 2018, http://www.governing.com/23-percent-podcast/gov-lauren-matsumoto-hawaii.html.

[109] Steve Bousquet, "Freshmen Get First Taste of Life at Capitol," *St. Petersburg Times*, November 22, 2004.

[110] Diane Brooks, "Politics, Personalities, Populism: Wide Range of Experience and Ideas in the 39th," *Seattle Times*, October 25, 2000.

[111] James Q. Lynch, "Freshman Legislators Learn Tough Lessons," *Cedar Rapids Gazette*, May 14, 2001.

[112] Mike Klein, "New Kid on the Block," *Des Moines Register*, January 26, 2003.

[113] Andy Kanengiser, "Lawmaker Learns the Ropes," *Clarion-Ledger*, March 19, 2004.

[114] Mike Billips, "Staton Leads Legislature's Freshman Class," *Macon Telegraph*, April 4, 2005; Dan Gearino, "Freshman Legislators Make Themselves Heard," *Waterloo/Cedar Falls Courier*, May 15, 2005.

[115] Kolten Parker, "Freshman Sen. Campbell Passes First Bill amid Hazing," *Houston Chronicle*, http://blog.chron.com/texaspolitics/2013/04/freshman-sen-campbell-passes-first-bill-amid-hazing/.

[116] NCSL, http://www.ncsl.org/ncsl-in-dc/standing-committees/legislative-effectiveness/sample-agendas-from-various-states.aspx; see also Alan Rosenthal, "Education and Training of Legislators," in Kurtz, Cain, and Niemi, *Institutional Change in American Politics*.

[117] See, for example, the discussion in William K. Muir Jr., *Legislature: California's School for Politics* (Berkeley: University of California Press, 1982), 120–37.

[118] George Skelton, "First-Day Advice for Newcomers to the Legislature," *Los Angeles Times*, December 4, 2000.

[119] Edward Fitzpatrick, "Getting Elected: The Easy Part," *Providence Journal*, December 6, 2000.

[120] David McGrath Schwartz, "Incoming Legislative Leaders Impart Advice to Freshmen Lawmakers," *Las Vegas Sun*, November 29, 2012.

[121] Herb Jackson, "Voting Record Belies Kean's 'Independent' Claim," *(Hackensack) Record*, October 2, 2006.

Chapter 5: The Legislative Process in the States

1 Shannon Jenkins, *The Context of Legislating* (New York: Routledge, 2016), 123.
2 Except for the omission of Utah, this list of states is identical to the one found in the second edition of this book, based on data from 2011 and 2012, and is similar to the list of "high passage" states in the first edition, based on data from 2005 and 2006. In other words, there is substantial consistency in bill passage rates by state over time.
3 Brenda Erickson, "LegisBrief: Limiting Bill Introductions," National Conference of State Legislatures, June 2017, 2–3.
4 Edward Schneier, John Brian Murtaugh, and Antoinette Pole, *New York Politics* (Armonk, NY: M. E. Sharpe, 2001), 245–46.
5 FiscalNote, "Three Legislative Factors That Lead to Efficient Bill Passage." March 2, 2016, accessed at: https://fiscalnote.com/2016/03/02/three-legislative-factors-that-lead-to-efficient-bill-passage/
6 Alan Rosenthal, *Heavy Lifting* (Washington, DC: CQ Politics, 2004), 60. Also see Massachusetts Department of Education, "Student Day Government Handbook," April 2018, 8.
7 Carol Kozma, "Yes, Citizen. You, Too, Can File Your Own Bill," *Lowell Sun*, November 16, 2013.
8 These county local committees are in addition to the more generic "Local Legislation Committee" and the "County and Municipal Government Committee."
9 *Birmingham News*, "Let Local School Systems Set Their Own Schedules," April 12, 2008.
10 Tanya Bagashka and Jennifer Hayes Clark, "Electoral Rules and Legislative Particularism: Evidence from U.S. State Legislatures," *American Political Science Review* 110 (2016): 44–56.
11 Senator John Marty, "'Garbage Bills': Public Pressure Can Halt Meltdown of the Legislative Process." *Minnpost* at https://www.minnpost.com/community-voices/2018/09/garbage-bills-public-pressure-can-halt-meltdown-of-the-legislative-process/.
12 "Frequently Asked Questions about the Minnesota Legislature." See the answer to question 5 under "bills" at https://www.leg.state.mn.us/leg/faq/faqtoc?subject=2
13 Ashley Hupfl, "The Big Ugly," *City & State New York*, May 26, 2015.
14 Ann Dermody, "Watching State Legislatures 'Carry-Over' Bills," October18, 2017 at https://info.cq.com/resources/watching-state-legislatures-carry-effect/ (accessed September 7, 2018).
15 Peverill Squire, "Membership Turnover and the Efficient Processing of Legislation," *Legislative Studies Quarterly* 23 (1998): 23–32.
16 Jenkins, *The Context of Legislating*, 59 and 127.
17 Alan Rosenthal discussed the sausage-making metaphor and why it was no longer appropriate in "The Legislature as Sausage Factory: It's About Time We Examine This Metaphor," *State Legislatures* (September 2001): 12–15. Spawning fish is from Frank Smallwood, *Free & Independent* (Brattleboro, VT: The Stephen Greene Press, 1976), 85. The casino metaphor is from John Straayer, *The Colorado General Assembly*, 2nd ed. (Boulder: University of Colorado Press, 2000), 7. The jazz band is from Burdett Loomis, *Time, Politics, and Policies* (Lawrence: University of Kansas Press, 1994), 172.
18 We are not the only legislative observers to use the "train analogy." See Alan Rosenthal, *The Engines of Democracy* (Washington, DC: CQ Press, 2009).
19 Smallwood, *Free & Independent*, 81.
20 See 149th Delaware General Assembly, at https://legis.delaware.gov/BillDetail?legislationId=26921.
21 Dave Rees, "Killed Bills: An Itemized Inventory of the General Assembly Floor," *Hampton Roads Daily Press*, March 16, 2018.
22 See, for example, the discussion in John G. Van Laningham, "The Making of the 1986 Florida Safety Belt Law: Issues and Insight," *Florida State University Law Review* 14 (1986): 685–717.
23 National Association of State Budget Officers, *Budget Processes in the States* (Washington DC, 2015), 8–15
24 Tommy Neal, "Learning the Game: How the Legislative Process Works," National Conference of State Legislatures, 2005, 34.

[25] The following discussion is based on box 6.1 in Keith Hamm and Gary Moncrief, "Legislative Politics in the States," in *Politics in the American States*, ed. Virginia Gray, Russell L. Hanson, and Thad Kousser, 10th ed. (Washington, DC: CQ Press, 2013).

[26] Tommy Neal, *Lawmaking and the Legislative Process* (Phoenix, AZ: Oryx Press, 1996), 48–49.

[27] See Joint Committee on Legislative Management, Legislative Commissioners Office, Connecticut General Assembly, *This Is Your General Assembly, 2013–2014*, http://www.cga.ct.gov/asp/cont ent/This_is_Your_General_Assembly.pdf.

[28] Peverill Squire and Keith E. Hamm, *101 Chambers: Congress, State Legislatures, and the Future of Legislative Studies* (Columbus: Ohio State University Press, 2005), 120.

[29] Barb Berggoetz and Tony Cook, "Bosma Moves Gay Marriage Ban to New Committee," *Indianapolis Star*, January 21, 2014; Barb Berggoetz and Tony Cook, "Elections Committee Advances HJR-3 to Full House," *Indianapolis Star*, January 23, 2014.

[30] Ralph G. Wright, *Inside the Statehouse* (Washington, DC: CQ Press, 2005), 109.

[31] Neal, *Lawmaking and the Legislative Process*, 53–54.

[32] Sean Collins Walsh, "After Hundreds Opposed 'Sanctuary' Bill, Committee Approves It," *Austin American-Statesman*, February 2, 2017.

[33] Alejandro Lazo, "In Hawaii, 'Citizens' Filibuster' Targets Gay-Marriage Bill," *Wall Street Journal*, November 9–10, 2013.

[34] Denton Darrington, longtime chair of the Idaho Senate Judiciary Committee, as quoted in Heath Druzin, "As End of Session Nears, It's Fighting Time," Idaho *Statesman*, March 26, 2008.

[35] National Conference of State Legislatures, "Inside the Legislative Process," 4-87 and 4-89. Also see Henry Kim and Justin Phillips, "Dividing the Spoils of Power: How Are the Benefits of Majority Party Status Distributed in U.S. State Legislatures," *State Politics & Policy Quarterly* 9 (2009): 125–50.

[36] Neal reports that twenty-one legislative chambers require all bills to be reported out. Neal, *Lawmaking and the Legislative Process*.

[37] Jenkins, *The Context of Legislating*, 101.

[38] Squire and Hamm, *101 Chambers*, 124–26; Jennifer Hayes Clark, *Minority Parties in U.S. Legislatures* (Ann Arbor: University of Michigan Press, 2015), 43.

[39] Ted Dabrowski and Joe Tabor, "Madigan's Rules: How Illinois Gives Its House Speaker Power to Manipulate and Control the Legislative Process, Illinois Policy Institute, Winter 2017, 12.

[40] See the example discussed in Bill White, "Pennsylvania Rep. Daryl Metcalfe's Action on Redistricting Proves He's Shameless," *Morning Call*, May 2, 2018.

[41] Jeremy M. Creelan and Laura M. Moultan, *The New York State Legislative Process: An Evaluation and Blueprint for Reform* (New York: Brennan Center for Justice at NYU School of Law, 2004).

[42] Dabrowski and Tabor, "Madigan's Rules," 10.

[43] *Jefferson City News Tribune*, "Few Bills Defeated on Floor Votes," May 21, 2001.

[44] See Indiana Chamber of Commerce, "How a Bill Becomes a Law," 2008, 4.

[45] Jesse McKinley, "What Is a Majority Vote in the State Senate? The Answer Goes beyond Simple Math," *New York Times*, February 24, 2014.

[46] Peverill Squire, "Quorum Exploitation in the American Legislative Experience," *Studies in American Political Development* 27 (2013): 142–64.

[47] Nancy Martorano, Keith E. Hamm, and Ronald D. Hedlund, "Examining Committee Structures, Procedures, and Powers in U.S. State Legislatures," paper presented at the 2000 Annual Meeting of the Midwest Political Science Association. See also Scott Matthew Cody, "The Causes and Consequences of Restrictive Rules of Debate in State Senates" (PhD dissertation, University of Iowa, 2006).

[48] Squire and Hamm, *101 Chambers*, 122–23.

[49] Kavita Kumar and Matthew Franck, "UM Gets Caught in Political Crossfire," *St. Louis Post-Dispatch*, April 20, 2007; David A. Lieb, "Democrats Block Blunt's Higher Education Plan," *Jefferson City News Tribune*, March 14, 2007; Kit Wagar, "Missouri Senate Tradition at Stake," *Kansas City Star*, April 19, 2007; Kelly Wiese, "MOHELA All-Nighter Ends after 15 Hours," *St. Louis Post-Dispatch*, March 13, 2007.

50 Avery G. Wilks, "SC Democrats Kill Senate GOP's Abortion Ban with Days-Long Filibuster," *The State*, May 4, 2018.

51 Kurt Erickson, "After 24 Hour Filibuster, Missouri Senate Endorses Electricity Rate Deal Sought by Ameren," *St. Louis Post-Dispatch*, February 8, 2018.

52 See Legislative Reference Library of Texas, http://www.lrl.state.tx.us/whatsNew/ client/index.cf m/2011/5/23/Filibusters-and-Chubbing; Clark, Minority Parties in U.S. Legislatures, 132.

53 Brandi Grissom and Lauren McGaughy, "What Happens When a Small Band of Angry Legislators Takes Control of the Texas House? We're About to Learn," *Dallas News*, May 18, 2017.

54 Noelle Crombie, "Oregon House Spends Hours Reading Aloud Marijuana Bill before Vote," *The Oregonian*, February 15, 2016.

55 Sara Catania, "The Importance of Being Ernie," *Mother Jones* (January/February 2006), accessed at http://www.motherjones.com/politics/2006/01/importance-being-ernie. Also see Fred Knapp, "Tempers Flare over Filibuster Tactics; Election Compromise, Help after Foster Care Debated," Nebraska Educational Telecommunications, April 4, 2013, accessed at netnebraska.org/article/news/termpers-flare-over-filibuster-tactics-election-compromise-help -after-foster-care.

56 Ashton Pittman, "Updated: House Passes Lottery Bill, Sends to Governor's Desk," *Jackson Free Press*, August 28, 2018, http://www.jacksonfreepress.com/news/2018/aug/28/democrats -renege-lottery-bill-after-leaders-scrap-/.

57 StateScape, "Bill Crossover Deadlines," http://statescape.com/resources/legislative/bill-crossover -deadlines.aspx.

58 Squire and Hamm, *101 Chambers*, 114.

59 Josh Ryan, "Conference Committee Proposal Rights and Policy Outcomes in the States," *Journal of Politics* 76 (2014):1059–73.

60 Neal, *Learning the Game*, 28.

61 Edward V. Schneier, John Brian Murtaugh, and Antoinette Pole, *New York Politics: A Tale of Two States*, 2nd ed. (Armonk, NY: M. E. Sharpe, 2010), 275; Squire and Hamm, *101 Chambers*, 113–14.

62 Creelan and Moultan, *The New York State Legislative Process.*

63 Jo Ingles, "Kasich Let Concealed Carry Bill Become Law without His Signature," http://radio .wosu.org/post/kasich-let-concealed-carry-bill-become-law-without-his-signature#stream/0.

64 Bryan Anderson, "What You Missed from Jerry Brown's Busy Weekend + Veto Rates" *Sacramento Bee*, October 1, 2018.

65 Scott Thistle, "Voters Put Democrats in Charge at State House with Majorities in House and Senate," *Press Herald*, November 8, 2018. See also Darren Fishell, "LePage has Vetoed More Bills Than All Maine Governors Since 1917, Combined," *Bangor Daily News*, July 16, 2018.

66 Calculated by the authors from *The Book of the States, 2017* (Lexington, KY: Council of State Governments, 2017), 101–2.

67 Kevin Miller, "Lawmakers Overturn 20 of the Governor's 43 Vetoes," *Press Herald*, July 9, 2018.

68 Four states did not hold regular session in 2018. Of the remaining forty-six states, thirty-one held sessions of four months or less. See http://www.ncsl.org/documents/ncsl/2018_Session _Calendar.pdf

69 Harvey J. Tucker, "Legislative Logjams: A Comparative State Analysis," *Western Political Quarterly* 38, (1987): 432–46.

70 Burdett A. Loomis, *Time, Politics, and Policies* (Lawrence: University Press of Kansas, 1994), 7.

71 Sky Chadde, "A Duet of 'Kumbaya' on the Senate Floor," *Columbia Missourian*, May 3, 2017.

72 Susan M. Cover, "Lawmakers Face Music—Literally—as Term Draws to Close," *Kennebec Journal*, June 16, 2003.

73 Cover, "Lawmakers Face Music."

74 Colin Campbell, "At 3 A.M., NC Senate GOP Strips Education Funding from Democrats' Districts," *News & Observer*, May 13, 2017; Terry Ganey, "Late-Night Senate Action on Economic Development Stalls," *Columbia Daily Tribune*, May 15, 2009.

75 Micaela Massimino, "AM Alert: It's Time for Sausage-Making—and Legislative Bingo," *Sacramento Bee Capitol Alert*, August 31, 2012; Jeremy B. White, "'Daisy Dukes,' 'Free OJ'—It's Legislative Bingo Time," *Sacramento Bee*, September 10, 2015.

[76] Rod Boshart, "Game Over: Senators Urged to Stay Professional," Cedar Rapids *Gazette*, April 20, 2007.

[77] Ed Fletcher, "Season of the Stealth Bill," *Sacramento Bee*, September 1, 2003; Jeremy B. White, "Gut and Amend: A List of Last-Minute Bills Changes," *Sacramento Bee Capitol Alert*, September 9, 2013.

[78] Madalyn Gunnell, "Utah Lawmakers Filed a Record 1,359 Bills This Year—One of Them to Shame Lawmakers Who Create Too Many," *Salt Lake Tribune*, March 5, 2018.

[79] Jon Davis, "Gut and Go, Other Legislative Practices Scrutinized in Kansas During 2018 Session," CSG Midwest, *Stateline.org*, April 2018. Accessed at: https://www.csgmidwest.org/policyresearch/0418-gut-go-legislation.aspx. Also see *Grand Forks Herald*, "Keep Hog house Oil-Tax Cut in Barn," March 2, 2011.

[80] Nathan Eagle, "Nonprofits Sue Hawaii over 'Deceptive' Gut-and-Replace Legislative Practice." September 5, 2018, https://www.civilbeat.org/2018/09/nonprofits-sue-hawaii-over-deceptive-gut-and-replace-legislative-practice/.

[81] Julie Hauserman, "Chaos Leaves Lawmakers Unsure What They Did," *St. Petersburg Times*, May 13, 2003.

[82] Jim Carlton, "If You Paid Half Price for That New SUV, You Must Be in Arizona," *Wall Street Journal*, October 26, 2000.

[83] Carlton, "If You Paid Half Price for That New SUV, You Must Be in Arizona."

[84] John Wagner and Anita Kumar, "Budget Cuts Are Focus for Md., Va.," *Washington Post*, January 11, 2009.

[85] See Glenn Abney and Thomas P. Lauth, "The End of Executive Dominance in State Appropriations," *Public Administration Review* 58 (1998): 388–94.

[86] Thad Kousser and Justin H. Phillips, "Who Blinks First? Legislative Patience and Bargaining with Governors," *Legislative Studies Quarterly* 34 (2009): 55–86.

[87] Elizabeth Hill, "Legislative Analyst's Office," *California Regulatory Law Reporter* 17 (2001): 381–85; Paul Sabatier and David Whiteman, "Legislative Decision Making and Substantive Policy Information: Models of Information Flow," *Legislative Studies Quarterly* 10 (1985): 395–421.

[88] Carl Klarner, Justin Phillips and Matt Muckler, "Overcoming Fiscal Gridlock: Institutions and Budget Bargaining," *Journal of Politics*, 74 (2012): 992-1009.

[89] Dan Krassner, "Alaskans Made Government Accountable to the People," *Mat-Su Valley Frontiersman*, July 23, 2018.

[90] Elaine S. Povich, "Earmarks May Make a Comeback in Congress. In Some States, They Never Went Away," *Stateline.org*, February 12, 2018, http://www.governing.com/topics/finance/sl-earmarks-states-congress.html. See also Joel A. Thompson, "Bringing Home the Bacon: The Politics of Pork Barrel in the North Carolina Legislature," *Legislative Studies Quarterly* 11 (1986): 91–108; and Joel A. Thompson and Gary Moncrief, "Pursuing the Pork in a State Legislature," *Legislative Studies Quarterly* 13 (1988): 393–401.

[91] The Empire Center for Public Policy, "More Capital Pork Flowing from Albany," June 14, 2018. See also Tom Precious, "To Understand the State's Pork Projects, You Have to Meet SAM," *Buffalo News*, April 4, 2018.

[92] Tom Precious, "Local Lawmakers Celebrate Their Pork, without Apology," *Buffalo News*, April 4, 2018.

[93] Precious, "To Understand the State's Pork Projects."

[94] Dan Morain, "Legislative 'Pork' OKd in Boom Leaves Bad Taste in Lean Times," *Los Angeles Times*, December 30, 2004.

[95] Povich, "Earmarks May Make a Comeback in Congress. In Some States, They Never Went Away."

[96] Michael C. Herron and Brett A. Theodos, "Government Redistribution in the Shadow of Legislative Elections: A Study of the Illinois Member Initiative Grants Program," *Legislative Studies Quarterly* 29, no. 2 (2004): 287–311.

[97] Smallwood, *Free & Independent*, 91.

[98] David A. Lieb, "Missouri Governor Candidate Steelman Calls Senators 'Cowards,'" *Jefferson City News Tribune*, May 15, 2008.

[99] Jim Sanders, "Assembly Vote 'Disappears,'" *Sacramento Bee Capitol Alert*, January 29, 2008.

[100] Jennifer Hayes Clark, "Examining Parties as Procedural Cartels: Evidence from the U.S. States," *Legislative Studies Quarterly* 37 (2012): 491–507.

[101] Gerald C. Wright and Brian F. Schaffner, "The Influence of Party: Evidence from the State Legislature," *American Political Science Review* 96 (2002): 367–79. See also Brian Schaffner, "Political Parties and the Representativeness of Legislative Committees," *Legislative Studies Quarterly* 32 (2007): 475–97.

[102] Christopher Mooney, "Explaining Legislative Leadership Influence: Simple Collective Action or Conditional Explanations?" *Political Research Quarterly* 66, no. 3 (2012): 559–71. Also see Jesse Richman, "The Logic of Legislative Leadership: Preferences, Challenges, and the Speaker's Powers," *Legislative Studies Quarterly* 35 (2010): 211–34.

[103] Gary Cox, Thad Kousser, and Matthew McCubbins, "Party Power or Preferences? Quasi-Experimental Evidence from American State Legislatures," *Journal of Politics* 72 (2010): 799–811; John Aldrich and James S. Coleman Battista, "Conditional Party Government in the States," *American Journal of Political Science* 46 (2000): 164–72.

[104] Richard Clucas, "Principle-Agent Theory and the Power of State House Speakers," *Legislative Studies Quarterly* 26, no. 2 (2001): 319–38.

[105] Sarah Anzia and Molly Jackman, "Legislative Organization and the Second Face of Power: Evidence from U.S. State Legislatures," *Journal of Politics* 75 (2013): 210–24. Also see Cox, Kousser, and McCubbins "Party Power or Preferences?"

[106] Boris Shor, "Polarization in American State Legislatures," in *American Gridlock*, ed. James A. Thurber and Antoine Yoshinaka (New York: Cambridge University Press, 2015); Boris Shor and Nolan McCarty, "The Ideological Mapping of American Legislatures," *American Political Science Review* 105 (2011): 530–41; Aldrich and Battista, "Conditional Party Government in the States." For the most current data, see https://americanlegislatures.com/category/polarization/.

[107] Alan Rosenthal, *Heavy Lifting: The Job of the American Legislature* (Washington, DC: CQ Press, 2004), 49.

[108] Ryan Tracy, "Green-Energy Mandates Find Improbable Allies," *Wall Street Journal*, July 18, 2013.

[109] Alexandra Berzon, "West Virginia Tightens Oversight after Spill," *Wall Street Journal*, March 10, 2014.

[110] See the classic discussion in Richard F. Fenno Jr., *Home Style: House Members in Their Districts* (Boston: Little, Brown, 1978), 18–24.

[111] *Sacramento Bee Capitol Alert*, "AM Alert: 'Hope for the Best and Ignore the Obvious,'" November 20, 2008.

[112] Shannon Jenkins, "The Impact of Party and Ideology on Roll-Call Voting in State Legislatures," *Legislative Studies Quarterly* 31 (2006): 235–57. On party leaders getting members to change their minds on a bill, see Jeffrey J. Harden and Justin H. Kirkland, *Indecision in American Legislatures* (Ann Arbor: University of Michigan Press, 2018).

[113] David Yamane and Elizabeth Oldmixon, "Religion in the Legislative Arena: Affiliation, Salience, Advocacy, and Public Policymaking," *Legislative Studies Quarterly* 31 (2006): 433–60.

[114] Clayton D. Peoples, "Interlegislator Relations and Policy Making: A Sociological Study of Roll-Call Voting in a State Legislature," *Sociological Forum* 23 (2008): 455–80. See also Eric Uslaner and Ronald Weber, *Patterns of Decision Making in State Legislatures* (New York: Praeger, 1981), 33–41.

[115] Marwa Eltagouri, "A Cyclist's Widow Asked a Lawmaker Why She Opposed a Distracted-Driving Bill. The Answer: Spite," *Washington Post*, February 23, 2018.

[116] Seth E. Masket, "Where You Sit Is Where You Stand: The Impact of Seating Proximity on Legislative Cue-Taking," *Quarterly Journal of Political Science* 3 (2008): 301–11. See also Samuel C. Patterson, "Party Opposition in the Legislature: The Ecology of Legislative Institutionalization," *Polity* 4 (1972): 344–66.

[117] See, for example, Anzia and Jackman, "Legislative Organization and the Second Face of Power;" Clark, "Examining Parties as Procedural Cartels"; Cox, Kousser, and McCubbins, "Party Power of Preferences"; and Asya Magazinnik and Sepehr Shahshahani, "Strategic Abstention, Missing Data, and Ideal Point Estimation," paper presented at the 2016 American Political Science

Association, Philadelphia. Also see Jenkins, *The Context of Legislating*, and Clark, *Minority Parties in U.S. Legislatures*.

[118] Sarah Anderson, Daniel Butler and Laurel Harbridge, "Legislative Institutions as a Source of Party Leaders' Influence." *Legislative Studies Quarterly* 41(2016): 605–31.

Chapter 6: The Legislative Context

[1] See, for example, Devin Caughey and Christopher Warshaw, "Policy Preferences and Policy Change: Dynamic Responsiveness in the American States, 1936–2014," *American Political Science Review* 112 (2018): 249–66; Jeffrey Lax and Justin Phillips, "The Democratic Deficit in the States," *American Journal of Political Science* 56 (2012): 148–66; Barbara Norrander and Clyde Wilcox, "Public Opinion and Policymaking in the States: The Case of Post-*Roe* Abortion Policy," *Policy Studies Journal* 27 (1999): 707–22.

[2] Robert S. Erikson, Gerald C. Wright, and John P. McIver, *Statehouse Democracy: Public Opinion and Policy in the American States* (New York: Cambridge University Press, 1993).

[3] Lax and Phillips, "The Democratic Deficit in the States." Also see Caughey and Warshaw, "Policy Preferences and Policy Change"; Justin Phillips, "Public Opinion and Morality," in *Politics in the American States*, 11th ed., ed. Virginia Gray, Russell L. Hanson and Thad Kousser (Los Angeles: Sage/CQ Press, 2018).

[4] Gerald Wright, "Do Term Limits Affect Legislative Roll Call Voting? Representation, Polarization, and Participation," *State Politics & Policy Quarterly* 7 (2007): 256–80; Gerald C. Wright and Jon Winburn, "Patterns of Constituency-Legislator Policy Congruence in the States," paper presented at the annual meeting of the State Politics and Policy Conference, Milwaukee, Wisconsin, 2002.

[5] For a recent, comprehensive examination of the role of these various activities, see Jeffrey Harden, *Multidimensional Democracy: A Supply and Demand Theory of Representation in American Legislatures* (New York: Cambridge University Press, 2016).

[6] For a detailed discussion of the concept of representation, see Hannah Pitkin, *The Concept of Representation* (Berkeley: University of California Press, 1967). Also see Michael Mezey, *Representative Democracy: Legislators and Their Constituents* (Lanham, MD: Rowman & Littlefield, 2008); for a discussion of representation specific to state legislatures, see Alan Rosenthal, *Heavy Lifting: The Job of the American Legislature* (Washington, DC: CQ Press, 2004), chapters 2 and 3; on its development in America, see Peverill Squire, *The Rise of the Representative: Lawmakers and Constituents in Colonial America* (Ann Arbor: University of Michigan Press, 2017).

[7] Ring v. Arizona, 536 U.S. 584 (2002).

[8] Dan Popkey, "Legislator Laments His Own Vote against Principles," *Idaho Statesman*, January 26, 2003, 1A.

[9] Popkey, "Legislator Laments His Own Vote against Principles."

[10] Popkey, "Legislator Laments His Own Vote against Principles."

[11] Squire, *The Evolution of American Legislatures*, 27–28; Squire, *The Rise of the Representative*, 5–7.

[12] Popkey, "Legislator Laments His Own Vote against Principles."

[13] Rosenthal, *Heavy Lifting*, 40, table 3.2.

[14] Rosenthal, *Heavy Lifting*, 41, table 3.3.

[15] David Broockman and Christopher Skovron, "Bias in Perceptions of Public Opinion among Political Elites." *American Political Science Review* 112 (2018), 542

[16] Richard Fenno, *Home Style: House Members in Their Districts* (Boston: Little, Brown, 1978), 1.

[17] Fenno, *Home Style*, especially chapter 1, 1–29; Malcolm E. Jewell, *Representation in State Legislatures* (Lexington: University of Kentucky Press, 1982), and Michael A. Smith, *Bringing Representation Home* (Columbia: University of Missouri Press, 2003).

[18] Steven Rogers, "Electoral Accountability for State Legislative Roll Calls and Ideological Representation," *American Political Science Review* 111 (2017): 555–71.

[19] Nathan Grasse and Brianne Heidbreder, "The Influence of Lobbying Activity in State Legislatures: Evidence from Wisconsin," *Legislative Studies Quarterly* 36 (2011): 567–89.

20 https://www.ethics.state.tx.us/dfs/loblistsREG.htm#R2016.

21 Anthony Nownes, Clive Thomas, and Ronald Hrebenar, "Interest Groups in the States," in *Politics in the American States*, ed. Virginia Gray, Russell L. Hanson, and Thad Kousser, 9th ed. (Washington, DC: CQ Press, 2008), 111.

22 James M. Strickland and Jesse M. Crosson, "K Street on Main? How Political Institutions Cultivate a Professional Lobbying Elite," paper presented at the American Political Science Association annual meeting, Philadelphia, PA, August 2016. Also see Christopher Mooney, "Lobbyists and Interest Groups." In Karl T. Kurtz, Bruce Cain, and Richard Niemi, eds. *Institutional Change in American Politics: The Case of Term Limits* (Ann Arbor: University of Michigan Press, 2007).

23 Strickland and Crosson, 27.

24 We are grateful to James Strickland for calculating and sharing these figures. It should be pointed out that some single-client lobbyists may, in fact, be contract lobbyists who simply contract to represent one client. Nonetheless, these figures represent the best estimate of the number of multi-client lobbyists.

25 These figures are from the most recent lists (usually 2017 or 2018) of registered lobbyists available on various state Secretary of State or Ethics Commission websites.

26 Rosenthal, *Heavy Lifting*, 108.

27 The Joint Legislative Ethics Committee, Office of the Legislative Inspector General, *2017 Ohio Lobbying Statistics Report* (Columbus, OH: The 132nd Ohio General Assembly, March 15, 2018), 9.

28 Alan Rosenthal, *The Third House: Lobbyists and Lobbying in the States*, 2nd ed. (Washington, DC: CQ Press, 2001), 83.

29 Nownes, Thomas, and Hrebenar, "Interest Groups in the States," 107.

30 John Straayer, *The Colorado General Assembly*, 2nd ed. (Boulder: University Press of Colorado, 2000), 194–95.

31 Allison Kite and Jason Hancock, "Buying Influence: Do Dark Money, Lobbyist Gifts Affect Missouri Legislators' Policy?" *Kansas City Star*, August 27, 2018.

32 Rosenthal, *The Third House*, 137.

33 *St. Petersburg Times*, "Rookie Content with Nibbling Start," March 8, 2005.

34 Wilson Ring, "New Lawmakers Told to Succeed They Must Work Together, Be Humble," *Boston Globe*, November 30, 2000.

35 Anthony Nownes and Patricia Freeman, "Interest Group Activity in the States," *Journal of Politics* 60 (1998): 86–112, 92.

36 Katharine W. V. Bradley and Jake Haselswerdt, "Who Lobbies the Lobbyists? State Medicaid Bureaucrats' Engagement in the Legislative Process," *Journal of Public Policy* 38 (2018): 83–111.

37 John Cluverius, "How the Flattened Costs of Grassroots Lobbying Affect Legislator Responsiveness," *Political Research Quarterly* 70 (2017): 279–90.

38 Alexander Fouirnaies, "When Are Agenda Setters Valuable?" *American Journal of Political Science*, 62 (2018): 176–91; Alexander Fouirnaies and Andrew B. Hall, "How Do Interest Groups Seek Access to Committees?" *American Journal of Political Science* 62 (2018): 132–47.

39 Lynda Powell, *The Influence of Campaign Contributions in State Legislatures* (Ann Arbor: University of Michigan Press, 2012).

40 Rosenthal, *The Third House*, 138.

41 Jeffrey Stinson, "Money Pours into State Races as Stakes Rise," *Stateline.org*, August 29, 2014.

42 Noel Gallagher, "Money from Outside Groups Pours into Maine Statehouse Campaigns," *Portland Press-Herald*, September 12, 2018.

43 Jim Miller, "Spending in California's 2016 election hit $680 million," *Sacramento Bee*, February 7, 2017.

44 William March, "Most Expensive Florida Legislative Race Ever?" *Tampa Bay Times*, November 19, 2018.

45 Greta Kaul and Peter Callaghan, "As DFL Groups Spend Big on the Guv Race, Republicans Dig In on the Minnesota House," *MinnPost*, November 2, 2018, https://www.minnpost.com/state-government/2018/11/as-dfl-groups-spend-big-on-the-guv-race-republicans-dig-in-on-the-minnesota-house/.

46 Susan M. Miller, Jill Nicholson-Crotty, and Sean Nicholson-Crotty, "Reexamining the Institutional Effects of Term Limits in U.S. State Legislatures," *Legislative Studies Quarterly* 36 (2011): 71–97.

47 Kristin Garrett and Joshua Jansa, "Interest Group Influence in Policy Diffusion Networks," *State Politics & Policy Quarterly* 15 (2015), 411; Susan M. Miller, Jill Nicholson-Crotty and Sean Nicholson-Crotty, "The Consequences of Legislative Term Limits for Policy Diffusion," *Political Research Quarterly* 71 (2018), 573.

48 Dorie E. Apollonio, Stanton A. Glantz, and Lisa A. Bero, "Corrigendum to 'Term Limits and the Tobacco Industry,'" *Social Science & Medicine* 104 (2014): 1–5.

49 See Christopher Z. Mooney, "Lobbyists and Interest Groups," in *Institutional Change in American Politics: The Case of Term Limits*, ed. Karl T. Kurtz, Bruce Cain, and Richard G. Niemi (Ann Arbor: University of Michigan Press, 2007).

50 Rita Flórez, "Limits of Limitations," University of Missouri *Illumination* 15 (2012): 16–19.

51 Mike Maciag, "Louisiana's Budget Crisis Empowers an Unusual Group," *Governing*, July 2016, http://www.governing.com/topics/politics/gov-louisiana-budget.html.

52 Amending the U.S. Constitution potentially involves a referendum because Article 5 stipulates that one of the two amendment procedures is to hold ratifying conventions in each state subsequent to approval of the proposed amendment by Congress. A convention, however, is not the same as a vote of the public.

53 Todd Donovan, Christopher Z. Mooney, and Michael A. Smith, *State and Local Politics: Institutions and Reform* (Belmont, CA: Wadsworth Cengage, 2009), 100–101.

54 For detail on recall election procedures by state, see https://ballotpedia.org/State_legislative _recalls.

55 Steve Mitchell, quoted in Pete Nichols, "Tax Hike Opponents Lecture on Recall Rights," *The State News*, July 20, 2007.

56 Kevin McGill, "Recall Petitions Filed against Legislators," Associated Press, June 25, 2008.

57 Steve Mitchell, quoted in Pete Nichols, "Tax Hike Opponents Lecture on Recall Rights," *The State News*, July 20, 2007.

58 In Delaware, constitutional amendments are not subject to referendum vote, but the legislature may, if it chooses, place statutes on the ballot for approval or rejection. For details about the way the various instruments of direct democracy operate in the different states, see the Initiative and Referendum Institute website, http://www.iandrinstitute.org.

59 Shaun Bowler and Todd Donovan, "The Initiative Process," in *Politics in the American States*, ed. Virginia Gray, Russell L. Hanson, and Thad Kousser, 9th ed. (Washington, DC: CQ Press, 2008), 130. We cite thirty-five states here because we are focusing only on the recall, the initiative, and the specific type of referendum known as the "popular referendum." If we include the instrument of "legislative referendum" as well, then all fifty states have at least one instrument of direct democracy.

60 Vladimir Kogan, "When Voters Pull the Trigger: Can Direct Democracy Restrain Legislative Excesses?" *Legislative Studies Quarterly* 41 (2016): 297–325.

61 Technically, this is not quite true because the legislature could always begin a new constitutional amendment to overturn the one passed by initiative. This would be political folly and therefore not likely to happen.

62 Virginia Young, "Compromise Dog Breeding Measure Is Rushed into Law," *St. Louis Post-Dispatch*, April 28, 2011.

63 Elisabeth R. Gerber, Arthur Lupia, Mathew D. McCubbins, and D. Roderick Kiewiet, *Stealing the Initiative: How State Government Responds to Direct Democracy* (Upper Saddle River, NJ: Prentice-Hall, 2001).

64 Eric Morath, "Republicans Warming to Higher Wage Floor," *Wall Street Journal*, May 29, 2014.

65 Dan Krassner, "Alaskans Made Government Accountable to the People," *Mat-Su Valley Frontiersman*, July 23, 2018.

66 Colin Lecher, "California Just Passed One of the Toughest Data Privacy Laws in the Country," theverge.com, June 28, 2018, https://www.theverge.com/2018/6/28/17509720/california-consumer-privacy-act-legislation-law-vote; Anahad O'Connor and Margot Sanger-Katz,

"California, of All Places, Has Banned Soda Taxes. How A New Industry Strategy Is Succeeding," *New York Times*, June 27, 2018.

67 Nick Evans, "Amending the Amendment Process: Ohio May Raise the Bar for Ballot Issues," WOSU Public Media, November 21, 2018, http://radio.wosu.org/post/amending-amendment-process-ohio-may-raise-bar-ballot-issues#stream/0.

68 John Matusaka, *For the Many or the Few: The Initiative, Public Policy, and American Democracy* (Chicago: University of Chicago Press, 2004).

69 Mark Baldassare, Dean Bonner, Sonja Petek, and Nicole Wilcoxon, "Californians and their Government," Public Policy Institute of California, March 2013, 6.

70 Wisconsin Watch, "After Gov. Scott Walker Took Office, Bills Moved Faster through the Wisconsin Legislature." Accessed at: https://www.wisconsinwatch.org/2018/08/after-gov-scott-walker-took-office-bills-moved-faster-through-the-wisconsin-legislature/amp/.

71 Gary Moncrief and Peverill Squire, *Why States Matter*, 2nd ed. (Lanham, MD: Rowman & Littlefield), 14.

72 See, for example, Alan Ehrenhalt, "Butch's Battle," *Governing Magazine*, June 2009, http://www.governing.com/hidden/Butchs-Battle.html.

73 Lee Davidson and Taylor Anderson, "Utah Legislature Overrides Vetoes in Balance-of-Powers Battle with Gov. Gary Herbert," *Salt Lake Tribune*, April 18, 2018.

74 Alan Rosenthal, *Heavy Lifting*, 165–79. See also Margaret Ferguson, "Governors and the Executive Branch," in Gray, Hanson, and Kousser, *Politics in the American States*, 10th edition; Thad Kousser and Justin Phillips, *The Power of American Governors* (New York: Cambridge University Press, 2012); and Alan Rosenthal, *The Best Job in Politics* (Los Angeles: Sage/CQ Press, 2013).

75 Kousser and Phillips, *The Power of American Governors*, 220.

76 Brianne Heidbreder, "Agenda Setting in the States: How Politics and Policy Needs Shape Gubernatorial Agendas," *Politics & Policy* 40 (2012): 296–319.

77 The notion of the governor as "chief legislator" dates back to the beginning of the twentieth century. See Leslie Lipson, "Influence of the Governor upon Legislation," *Annals of the American Academy of Political and Social Science* 195 (1938): 72–78.

78 Daniel Lewis, Saundra Schneider, and William Jacoby, "Institutional Characteristics and State Policy Priorities: The Impact of Legislatures and Governors," *State Politics & Policy Quarterly* 15 (2015): 1–29.

79 Straayer, *The Colorado General Assembly*, 214.

80 Ring, "New Lawmakers Told to Succeed They Must Work Together, Be Humble."

81 Robert McGrath, Jon Rogowski, and Josh Ryan, "Gubernatorial Veto Powers and the Size of the Legislative Coalition," *Legislative Studies Quarterly* 40: 571–98 and Robert McGrath, Jon Rogowski, and Josh Ryan, "Veto Override Requirements and Executive Success," *Political Science Research and Methods* 6 (2018) 153–79.

82 Sarah McCally Morehouse and Malcolm E. Jewell, *State Politics, Parties and Policy*, 2nd ed. (Lanham, MD: Rowman & Littlefield, 2003), 179.

83 Joseph F. Zimmerman, *The Government and Politics of New York State* (New York: New York University Press, 1981), 200–204.

84 Eugene J. Gleason and Joseph Zimmerman, "The Strong Governorship: Status and Problems—New York," *Public Administration Review* 36 (1976): 92–95.

85 Alex Stuckey and Virginia Young, "Battle over Money Anticipated during Missouri Veto Session," *St. Louis Post-Dispatch*, September 7, 2014.

86 Glenn Abney and Thomas P. Lauth, "The Line-Item Veto in the States: An Instrument for Fiscal Restraint or an Instrument of Partisanship?" *Public Administration Review* 45 (1985): 372–77; Thomas P. Lauth and Catherine C. Reese, "The Line-Item Veto in Georgia: Fiscal Restraint or Inter-Branch Politics?" *Public Budgeting & Finance* 26 (2006): 1–19.

87 "Governor Vetoes 40 Projects in Louisiana Construction Budget," NOLA.com, June 6, 2018, https://www.nola.com/politics/index.ssf/2018/06/governor_vetoes_40_projects_in.html.

88 Jeff Stensland, "Veto Overrides Prompt Scolding," *The State*, May 27, 2005.

89 Stensland, "Veto Overrides Prompt Scolding."

90 Tim Smith, "Sanford's Joke on Terrorism at Statehouse Draws Criticism," *The Greenville News*, October 10, 2007.

[91] Lisa Sandberg, "Sessions Upend Legislators' Lives," San Antonio *Express-News*, July 31, 2005.

[92] This discussion is based on the following media accounts: Joseph O'Sullivan, "Washington Governor Convenes Special Session Vetoes 27 Bill," *Tacoma Tribune* News Service, March 11, 2016; accessed at: http://www.governing.com/topics/politics/tns-washington-inslee -vetoes.html and Jim Camden, "Washington Lawmakers Pass Budget, Adjourn," *Spokane Spokesman-Review*, March 29, 2016.

[93] Morehouse and Jewell, *State Politics, Parties and Policy*, 188.

[94] Mary Beth Schneider, "Job Offers to 2 Lawmakers Questionable, Dems Say," *Indianapolis Star*, March 2, 2006.

[95] Mississippi HB 509 was accessed through the Mississippi State Legislature's website, http://bil lstatus.ls.state.ms.us/documents/2008/html/HB/0500-0599/ HB0509SG.htm.

[96] Mordecai Lee, "Political-Administrative Relations in State Government: A Legislative Perspective," *International Journal of Public Administration* 29 (2006): 1021–47.

[97] Brian Gerber, Cherie Maestas, and Nelson Dometrius, "State Legislative Influence over Agency Rulemaking: The Utility of Ex Ante Review," *State Politics & Policy Quarterly* 5 (2005): 24–46; Neal D. Woods, "Separation of Powers and the Politics of Administrative Rule Review," *State Politics & Policy Quarterly* 15 (2015): 345–65.

[98] Christopher Reenock and Sarah Poggione, "Agency Design as an Ongoing Tool of Bureaucratic Influence," *Legislative Studies Quarterly* 29 (2004): 383–406. But see also Edward H. Stiglitz, "Unitary Innovations and Political Accountability," *Cornell Law Review* 99 (2014): 1133–84.

[99] Frederick Boehmke and Charles Shipan, "Oversight Capabilities in the States: Are Professionalized Legislatures Better at Getting What They Want?" *State Politics & Policy Quarterly* 15 (2015): 366–86.

[100] Jeffrey Harden, "Multidimensional Responsiveness: The Determinants of Legislators' Representational Priorities," *Legislative Studies Quarterly* 38 (2013): 155–84.

[101] Adam Belz, "Dying Lundby Recalls Political Career," *Cedar Rapids Gazette*, January 1, 2009.

[102] Grant Reeher, *First Person Political* (New York: New York University Press, 2006), 63.

[103] George Serra and Neil Pinney, "Casework, Issues and Voting in State Legislative Elections," *Journal of Legislative Studies* 10 (2004): 32–46.

[104] Patricia Freeman and Lillard Richardson Jr., "Exploring Variation in Casework among State Legislators," *Legislative Studies Quarterly* 21 (1996): 41–56; Karl Kurtz, Gary Moncrief, Richard Niemi, and Lynda Powell, "Full-Time, Part-Time, and Real Time: Explaining State Legislators' Perceptions of Time on the Job," *State Politics & Policy Quarterly* 6 (2006): 322–38; Gary Moncrief, Joel A. Thompson, and Karl T. Kurtz, "The Old Statehouse, It Ain't What It Used to Be," *Legislative Studies Quarterly* 21 (1996): 57–72.

[105] Rosenthal, *Heavy Lifting*, 27.

[106] On this point, see Michael B. Miller, "Comment: The Justiciability of Legislative Rules and the 'Political' Political Question Doctrine," *California Law Review* 78 (1990): 1341–74. See also the discussion in Peverill Squire and Keith E. Hamm, *101 Chambers: Congress, State Legislatures and the Future of Legislative Studies* (Columbus: Ohio State University Press, 2005), 157, note 38.

[107] These data were gathered by the authors from the American Judicature Society's web page on judicial selection, http://www.judicialselection.us/.

[108] Melinda Gann Hall, "State Courts: Politics and the Judicial Process," in Gray, Hanson, and Kousser, *Politics in the American States* (Los Angeles: Sage/CQ Press, 2018).

[109] Matthew H. Bosworth, "Legislative Responses to Unconstitutionality: A View from the States," *Journal of Law and Courts* 5 (2017): 243–66.

[110] Joshua Miller, "Legislature Gives Swift Approval to Voyeurism Measure," *Boston Globe*, March 7, 2014.

[111] Teena Wilhelm, "The Policymaking Role of State Supreme Courts in Education Policy," *Legislative Studies Quarterly* 32 (2007): 309–33; Teena Wilhelm, "Strange Bedfellows," *American Politics Research* 37 (2009): 3–29.

[112] Laura Langer and Paul Brace, "The Preemptive Power of State Supreme Courts: Adoption of Abortion and Death Penalty Legislation," *Policy Studies Journal* 33 (2005): 317–40.

[113] Chris Moon, "Lawmakers May Spurn Court," *Topeka Capitol-Journal*, June 8, 2005.

[114] Moon, "Lawmakers May Spurn Court."

[115] David Klepper, "Spoiling for a Fight in Kansas," *Kansas City Star*, June 8, 2005.

[116] Klepper, "Spoiling for a Fight in Kansas."

[117] Klepper, "Spoiling for a Fight in Kansas."

[118] *Kansas City Star*, "Obstinacy, Pettiness Won't End Problems," March 22, 2006.

[119] Scott Rothschild, "After 7 Years, Litigation Is Dismissed," Lawrence *Journal-World*, July 29, 2006.

[120] The discussion of the 2014 case and the quotations are from Trevor Graff and John Eligon, "Court Orders Kansas Legislature to Spend More on Schools," *New York Times,* March 7, 2014.

[121] David Ramsey, "Kansas GOP Leaders Seek to Block State Supreme Court from Enforcing Educating Adequacy Requirements." *Arkansas Times*, April 7, 2018.

[122] Dion Lefler, Hunter Woodall, Katy Bergen, and Suzanne Tobias, "Kansas School Funding Still Inadequate, Supreme Court Says," *Kansas City Star* June 25, 2018.

[123] Peter Hancock, "Ahead of Kansas Primaries, Conservatives Renew Push for Constitutional Amendment on School Finance," *Lawrence World-Journal*, June 26, 2018.

[124] Brian M. Rosenthal, "Baumgartner Uses Bill to Mock State Supreme Court," *Seattle Times*, February 17, 2014.

[125] "What's Next? Will the Iowa Legislature Declare Eminent Domain over the Courts?" *Des Moines Register*, February 12, 2018.

[126] Michael Wines, "Judges Say Throw Out the Map. Lawmakers Say Throw Out the Judges," *New York Times*, February 14, 2018.

[127] Lacie Pierson, "Legislators Pass Impeachment Articles against All Supreme Court Justices," *Charleston Gazette-Mail*, August 13, 2018.

[128] Tina Sfondeles, "'D-Day' Spells Defeat for Rauner's Term Limits Referendum," *Chicago Sun-Times*, August 22, 2014.

[129] Robert Lowry, "Fiscal Policy in the American States," in *Politics in the American States*, ed. Virginia Gray, Russell L. Hanson, and Thad Kousser, 9th ed. (Washington, DC: CQ Press, 2008), 293.

[130] Lowry, "Fiscal Policy in the American States."

[131] Tracy Gordon, *State and Local Budgets and the Great Recession* (Stanford, CA: Stanford Center on Poverty and Inequality, 2012).

[132] Nicholas Johnson, Catherine Collins, and Ashali Singham, "State Tax Changes in Response to the Recession," Center on Budget and Policy Priorities, March 8, 2010, accessed September 8, 2014, at http://www.cbpp.org/cms/?fa=view&id=3108.

[133] These data are from the California Department of Finance, http://www.dof.ca.gov/budget/C A_budget_information/budget_faq/index.html.

[134] Larry Gerston, *American Federalism: A Concise Introduction* (Armonk, NY: M. E. Sharpe, 2007), 94–98.

[135] Erik Schelzig, "New Drunk Driving Law Endangers Federal Road Funding," *Tennessean*, August 25, 2016.

[136] John Kincaid, "State-Federal Relations: A Policy Tug of War," *The Book of the States, 2007 Edition* (Lexington, KY: Council of State Governments, 2007); Dale Krane, "The Middle Tier in American Federalism: State Government Policy Activism During the Bush Administration," *Publius: The Journal of Federalism* 37 (2007): 453–77.

[137] Boris Shor, "Ideology, Party, and Opinion: Explaining Individual Legislator ACA Implementation Votes in the States," *State Politics & Policy Quarterly* 18 (2018): 371–94.

[138] Alex Garlick, "National Policies, Agendas, and Polarization in American State Legislatures: 2011 to 2014." *American Politics Research* 45 (2017): 939–79.

[139] 545 U.S. 469 (2005).

[140] Marion Massaron Ross and Kristen Tolan, "Legislative Responses to *Kelo v. City of New London* and Subsequent Court Decisions—One Year Later," *Journal of Affordable Housing and Community Development Law* 16 (2006): 52–85.

[141] Elizabeth Fredericksen, Stephanie Witt, and David Nice, *The Politics of Intergovernmental Relations*, 3rd ed. (San Diego: Birkdale Publishers, 2016), chapter 6.

[142] Fredericksen, Witt, and Nice, *The Politics of Intergovernmental Relations*, 204.

[143] Tim Henderson, "Age Gap Fuels City-State Clashes," *Stateline*, July 12, 2016. http://www
.pewtrusts.org/en/research-and-analysis/blogs/stateline/2016/07/12/age-gap-fuels-city-state-
clashes.

[144] Alan Blinder, "When a State Balks at a City's Minimum Wage," *New York Times*, February
21, 2016. Data taken from U.C. Berkeley Labor Center, "Inventory of US City and County
Minimum Wage Ordinances," as of June 20, 2018, http://laborcenter.berkeley.edu/minimum
-wage-living-wage-resources/inventory-of-us-city-and-county-minimum-wage-ordinances/.

[145] Blinder, "When a State Balks at a City's Minimum Wage."

[146] U.C. Berkeley Labor Center, "Inventory of US City and County Minimum Wage Ordinances."

[147] Lauren E. Phillips, "Impeding Innovation: State Preemption of Progressive Local Regulations,"
Columbia Law Review 117 (2017): 2225–63; Lori Riverstone-Newell, "The Rise of State Preemption Laws in Response to Local Policy Innovation," *Publius: The Journal of Federalism*
47 (2017): 403–25. See also William D. Hicks, and Carol Weissert "Home Rule Be Damned:
Exploring Policy Conflicts between the Statehouse and City Hall," *PS: Political Science & Politics* 51 (2018): 26–38.

[148] Arian Campo-Flores, "States Block Gun Curbs by Cities," *Wall Street Journal*, May 10, 2018.

[149] Joel Ebert, "Legislation in Response to Memphis' Confederate Statue Removal Signed by Gov.
Haslem," *Tennessean*, May 22, 2018.

[150] *Arizona Daily Sun*, "Ducey Signs Bill Barring Cities from Taxing Sugary Drinks," March
17, 2018.

[151] Jack Suntrup, "Columbia City Council Members Take On State Lawmakers' Proposals,"
Columbia Missourian, April 20, 2015.

[152] Valerie Bauerlein and Jon Kamp, "Cities, States Clash on Social Policy," *Wall Street Journal*,
July 8, 2016.

Chapter 7: Are State Legislatures Representative Institutions?

[1] Data from FollowTheMoney.org: https://www.followthemoney.org/research/institute-reports/
money-incumbency-in-2015-and-2016-state-legislative-races.

[2] Linda Casey, "The Role of Money and Incumbency in 2009–2010 State Elections," National
Institute on Money in State Politics, July 3, 2012.

[3] Quinnipiac University New York State Poll, "November 27, 2013—New York State Voters Back
De Blasio Tax Plan 2–1, Quinnipiac University Poll Finds: State Government Dysfunctional, Voters Say," November 27, 2013.

[4] These data are taken from Rasmussen Reports, *Illinois Toplines*, December 19, 2007.

[5] Alan Greenblatt, "Why Attempts to Recall State Lawmakers Are Rare," *Governing*, November
2017, http://www.governing.com/topics/politics/gov-state-recalls-rare.html.

[6] National Center for State Courts, "How the Public Views the State Courts," May 14, 1999.

[7] Peverill Squire, "Professionalization and Public Opinion of State Legislatures," *Journal of Politics*
55 (1993): 479–91. See also Christine A. Kelleher and Jennifer Wolak, "Explaining Public Confidence in the Branches of State Government," *Political Research Quarterly* 60 (2007): 707–21.

[8] In particular, see Squire, "Professionalization and Public Opinion of State Legislatures," and
Cherie Maestas, "The Incentive to Listen: Progressive Ambition, Resources, and Opinion Monitoring among State Legislators," *Journal of Politics* 65 (2003): 439–56.

[9] For examples of skeptical columnists, see Jeff Jacoby, "Short Live the Legislature!" *Boston
Globe*, August 12, 2018; and Errol Louis, "The Full-Time Legislature Fraud," *New York Daily
News*, January 12, 2016. On California and Michigan, see Kathleen Gray, "Push for Part-Time
Legislature Proposal for November Ballot Halted," *Lansing State Journal*, June 18, 2014; Dan
Turner, "Running California Isn't Part-Time Job," *Los Angeles Times*, June 5, 2012.

[10] Johns Hopkins University, "JHU Survey: Americans Don't Know Much about State Government," December 11, 2018.

[11] Michigan State University, Institute for Public Policy and Social Research, "State of the State
Survey Winter 2018."

12 Franklin & Marshall College, Center for Opinion Research, Floyd Institute for Public Policy, "June 2018 Franklin & Marshall College Poll."

13 Common Cause, "New Mexico Public Opinion Survey February 2018."

14 Siena College, "Small Majority Says Gov's Ethics Package Would Reduce Corruption," February 24, 2015.

15 Lilliard E. Richardson Jr., David M. Konisky, and Jeffrey Milyo, "Public Approval of U.S. State Legislatures," *Legislative Studies Quarterly* 37 (2012): 99–116.

16 Lilliard Richardson and Jeffrey Milyo, "Giving the People What They Want? Legislative Polarization and Public Approval of State Legislatures," *State and Local Government Review* 48 (2016): 270–81.

17 Berkeley IGS Poll, "Californians Remain Much More Optimistic about the Overall Direction of the State Than the Nation. Views of the Job Performance of the Governor and the State Legislature at Near Record Highs," April 5, 2017.

18 Bob Bernick Jr., "Utahns Fail Quiz on Own Legislators," *Deseret News*, March 20, 2006. Similar results were obtained in a 1988 statewide survey in Ohio and a 1981 poll in Oklahoma. See Samuel C. Patterson, Randall B. Ripley, and Stephen V. Quinlan, "Citizens' Orientations toward Legislatures: Congress and the State Legislature," *Western Political Quarterly* 45 (1992): 315–38; Donald Songer, "Government Closest to the People: Constituent Knowledge in State & National Politics," *Polity* 17 (1984): 387–95.

19 Elon Poll, "The State of Political Knowledge in North Carolina," February 12–15, 2018.

20 Johns Hopkins University, "JHU Survey: American Don't Know Much About State Government."

21 Quinnipiac University New York State Poll, November 27, 2013.

22 Siena College, "Small Majority Says Gov's Ethics Package Would Reduce Corruption."

23 DHM Research, "Oregon Public Broadcasting Omnibus Survey," February 2, 2018.

24 These data are from questions qkn9a and qkn9b of the Rutgers-Eagleton Poll of February 1998.

25 Elon Poll, "The State of Political Knowledge in North Carolina."

26 Johns Hopkins University, "JHU Survey: American Don't Know Much about State Government."

27 Vanderbilt University, Center for the Study of Democratic Institutions, "Vanderbilt University Poll," April 28–May 13, 2014.

28 Rutgers-Eagleton Poll, "Cranky Electorate Gives Democrats the Edge in Legislative Campaign," October 25, 2007. See question AE1.

29 Elon Poll, "The State of Political Knowledge in North Carolina."

30 See, for example, Charles Layton and Mary Walton, "State of the American Newspaper, Missing the Story at the Statehouse," *American Journalism Review*, July/August 1998; Charles Layton and Jennifer Dorroh, "Sad State," *American Journalism Review*, June 2002; Jennifer Dorroh, "Statehouse Exodus," *American Journalism Review*, April/May 2009.

31 Paul Starr, "Goodbye to the Age of Newspapers (Hello to a New Age of Corruption)," *The New Republic*, March 4, 2009; see also David W. Chen, "In New Jersey, Only a Few Media Watchdogs are Left," *New York Times*, January 3, 2017.

32 See Erik Smith, "A Fond Farewell to Legislative Life," Washington State Wire, http://washingtonstatewire.com/blog/a-fond-farewell-to-the-legislative-life/.

33 Tara McClellan McAndrew, "The Vanishing Statehouse Press Corps," *Illinois Times*, March 2, 2017, http://illinoistimes.com/article-18344-the-vanishing-statehouse-press-corps.html.

34 Anna Marum, "Oregon's Dwindling Statehouse Reporters Are 'Treading Water," *Columbia Journalism Review*, June 13, 2018, https://www.cjr.org/united_states_project/oregon-capitol-press-corps.php.

35 Alan Ehrenhalt, "Is Statehouse News Actually Declining, or Just Different?" *Governing.com*, December 2018, http://www.governing.com/columns/assessments/gov-statehouse-reporting-news-coverage.html.

36 Joni Enda, Katerina Eva Matsa, and Jan Lauren Boyles, "America's Shifting Statehouse Press," Pew Research Center, July 2014; see also *American Journalism Review*, "AJR's 2009 Count of Statehouse Reporters," April/May 2009.

37 See Alan Greenblatt, "5 Reasons State House Speakers May Be Prone to Corruption," *Governing*, January 26, 2015, http://www.governing.com/topics/politics/gov-speakers-indicted-new-york-rhode-island-south-carolina-alabama.html; Steve LeBlanc, "A Tale of 3 Speakers—Sal-

vatore DiMasi, Thomas Finneran and Charles Flaherty," *MassLive*, July 4, 2011, https://www
.masslive.com/news/index.ssf/2011/07/a_tale_of_3_speakers_--_salvat.html.

38 Steve Bousquet, "We're Losing a Leash on Legislators," *St. Petersburg Times*, February 9, 2008.

39 Jon Marcus, "Animal Statehouse," *American Journalism Review*, June 2000.

40 Marcus, "Animal Statehouse."

41 Patrick Anderson, "R. I. Lawmaker Changes Tune on Drinking at State House," *Providence Journal*, March 7, 2017.

42 Michael X. Delli Carpini, Scott Keeter, and J. David Kennamer, "Effects of the News Media on Citizen Knowledge of State Politics and Government," *Journalism Quarterly* 71 (1994): 443–56.

43 Project for Excellence in Journalism, "The Changing Newsroom: What Is Being Gained and What Is Being Lost in America's Daily Newspapers?" July 21, 2008. See the response to survey question 19.

44 Ehrenhalt, "Is Statehouse News Actually Declining, or Just Different;" Mark Lisheron, "Reloading at the Statehouse," *American Journalism Review*, September 2010. See also Paul W. Taylor, "Can Online News Outlets Help Fill Statehouse Reporting's Void?" http://www.governing.com/columns/dispatch/col-can-online-news-fill-statehouse-reporters-void.html.

45 Enda, Matsa, and Boyles, "America's Shifting Statehouse Press."

46 On access issues, see Christopher Cadelago, "Huff, Steinberg Tangle over Press Access to Chambers," *Sacramento Bee Capitol Alert*, July 3, 2014.

47 Ehrenhalt, "Is Statehouse News Actually Declining, or Just Different." See also the discussion in https://www.bettergov.org/news/as-statehouse-press-corps-dwindles-other-reliable-news-sources-needed.

48 See https://twitter.com/danvock/lists/statehouse-reporters/members.

49 Paul Ferber, Franz Foltz, and Rudy Pugliese, "Demographics and Political Characteristics Affecting State Legislative Websites: The Quality and Digital Divides," *Journal of Political Marketing* 7 (2008). These relationships are generally true for e-government in general. See Caroline J. Tolbert, Karen Mossberger, and Ramona McNeal, "Institutions, Policy Innovation, and E-Government in the American States," *Public Administration Review* 68 (2008): 549–63.

50 See Jodie Condit Fagan and Bryan Fagan, "An Accessibility Study of State Legislative Web Sites," *Government Information Quarterly* 21 (2004): 61–81; Paul Ferber, Franz Foltz, and Rudy Pugliese, "State Legislature Web Sites and Public Participation: Designing a Civic Resource," *Atlantic Journal of Communication* 14 (2006): 229–46; Paul Ferber, Franz Foltz, and Rudy Pugliese, "The Internet and Public Participation: State Legislature Web Sites and the Many Definitions of Interactivity," *Bulletin of Science, Technology & Society* 25 (2005): 85–93.

51 Lilliard E. Richardson Jr. and Christopher A. Cooper, "E-mail Communication and the Policy Process in the State Legislature," *Policy Studies Journal* 34 (2006): 113–29.

52 David Rice and David Ingram, "Smothering Legislators with E-Mail Is More Effective When Less Transparent," *Winston-Salem Journal*, June 12, 2005.

53 John Miller, "Idaho Lawmaker Turns Off Mass Committee E-Mails after Deluge," *Idaho Statesman*, March 6, 2007.

54 Daniel Victor, "Here's Why You Should Call, Not Email, Your Legislators," *New York Times*, November 22, 2016.

55 See http://www.ncsl.org/research/telecommunications-and-information-technology/legislative-social-media.

56 Seanna Adcox, "Lawmakers Connect through Video Logs," *Charleston Post and Courier*, January 14, 2007; Nancy Hicks, "Some Senators Use Blogs to Keep in Touch," *Lincoln Journal Star*, March 29, 2005.

57 Bryan Anderson, "This Lawmaker Blocked Anti-Vaccine Activists on Twitter. Now He's Facing a Lawsuit," *Sacramento Bee*, July 31, 2018; Max Brantley, Public Officials Who Block Social Media Accounts May Be Running Afoul of the Law," *Arkansas Times*, March 17, 2017; Jerry Iannelli, "Miami State Sen. Frank Artiles Has Blocked More Than 400 People on Facebook," *Miami New Times*, March 15, 2017; Rachel Leingang, "Politicians Block Constituents' Speech on Social Media," *Arizona Capitol Times*, March 16, 2018; Roger McKinney, "Reisch Unblocks Constituent on Twitter, Calls Lawsuit "Frivolous," *Columbia Daily Tribune*, July 16, 2018;

Joseph O'Sullivan, "Facing Pressure, Washington State Lawmaker Unblocks Constituents from His Facebook Page," *Seattle Times*, July 22, 2018. See also NPR, "When Politicians Block Critics on Social Media," October 29, 2017, https://www.npr.org/2017/10/29/560660157/when-poli ticians-block-critics-on-social-media,

58 Tod Newcombe, "Are State Ethics Rules Keeping Up with Social Media?" *Governing*, May 2017, http://www.governing.com/columns/tech-talk/gov-social-media-states-ethics.html.

59 Mattie Quinn, "A Cautionary Tale for the Newly Elected," *Governing.com*, December 11, 2018, http://www.governing.com/23-percent-podcast/gov-lauren-matsumoto-hawaii.html.

60 These data are from http://www.ncsl.org/research/telecommunications-and-information -technology/legislative-webcasts-and-broadcasts.aspx.

61 These numbers are reported in Pam Greenberg, "Is Anybody Watching?" The Thicket at State Legislatures, January 29, 2008, http://ncsl.typepad.com/the_ thicket/2008/01/is-anybody -watc.html.

62 Brian Stelter, "From Texas Statehouse to YouTube, a Filibuster Is a Hit," *New York Times*, June 30, 2013.

63 Christopher A. Cooper and Lilliard E. Richardson Jr., "Institutions and Representational Roles in American State Legislatures," *State Politics & Policy Quarterly* 6 (2006): 174–94.

64 Daniel M. Butler, Christopher F. Karpowitz, and Jeremy C. Pope, "A Field Experiment on Legislators' Home Styles: Service versus Policy," *Journal of Politics* 74 (2012): 474–86; Jeffrey J. Harden, "Multidimensional Responsiveness: The Determinants of Legislators' Representational Priorities," *Legislative Studies Quarterly* 38 (2013): 155–84.

65 Jennifer Wolak, "Public Expectations of State Legislators," *Legislative Studies Quarterly* 42 (2017): 175–209.

66 Gerald Wright, "Do Term Limits Affect Legislative Roll Call Voting? Representation, Polarization, and Participation," *State Politics & Policy Quarterly* 7 (2007): 256–80.

67 Michael A. Smith, *Bringing Representation Home: State Legislators among Their Constituencies* (Columbia: University of Missouri Press, 2003).

68 Alan Rosenthal, *Heavy Lifting: The Job of the American Legislature* (Washington, DC: CQ Press, 2004), 233–41.

69 Paul Eakins, "How Constituents Can Compete with Lobbyists for Legislators' Time," *Topeka Capital-Journal*, January 7, 2001.

70 Eakins, "How Constituents Can Compete with Lobbyists for Legislators' Time."

71 Terry Ganey, "Missouri Plan Bill Spurs 'Robo-Calls,'" *Columbia Daily Tribune*, April 9, 2009.

72 Daniel M. Butler and David W. Nickerson, "Can Learning Constituency Opinion Affect How Legislators Vote? Results from a Field Experiment," *Quarterly Journal of Political Science* 6 (2011): 55–83; Rebekah Herrick, "Listening and Representation," *State Politics & Policy Quarterly* 13 (2013): 88–106. See also Elizabeth A. Dodson, Katherine A. Stamatakis, Stephanie Chalifour, Debra Haire-Joshu, Timothy McBride, and Ross C. Brownson, "State Legislators' Work on Public Health-Related Issues: What Influences Priorities?" *Journal of Public Health Management and Practice* 19 (2013): 25–29.

73 Steven Rogers, "Electoral Accountability for State Legislative Roll Calls and Ideological Representation," *American Political Science Review* 111 (2017): 555–71.

74 David E. Broockman and Daniel M. Butler, "The Causal Effects of Elite Position-Taking on Voter Attitudes: Field Experiments with Elite Communication," *American Journal of Political Science* 61 (2017): 208–21.

75 David E. Broockman and Christopher Skovron, "Bias in Perceptions of Public Opinion among Political Elites," *American Political Science Review* 112 (2018): 542–63.

76 Katie Edwards and Sidney Bennett, "Legislators' Attitudes, Knowledge, and Progressive Policy Endorsement Related to Domestic and Sexual Violence: A Pilot Study," *Human Service Organizations: Management, Leadership & Governance* 41 (2017): 503–14.

77 Justin H. Kirkland and Jeffrey J. Harden Representation, "Competing Principals, and Waffling on Bills in US Legislatures" *Legislative Studies Quarterly* 41 (2016): 657–86.

78 Patrick Flavin and William W. Franko, "Government's Unequal Attentiveness to Citizens' Political Priorities," *Policy Studies Journal* 45 (2017): 659–87.

[79] The classic statement is Richard Fenno, "If, As Ralph Nader Says, Congress Is 'the Broken Branch,' How Come We Love Our Congressmen So Much?" in *Congress in Change: Evolution and Reform*, ed. Norman Ornstein (New York: Praeger, 1975).

[80] Hanna Pitkin, *The Concept of Representation* (Berkeley: University of California Press, 1967); Heinz Eulau and Paul Karps, "The Puzzle of Representation: Specifying the Components of Responsiveness," in *The Politics of Representation: Continuities in Theory and Research*, ed. Heinz Eulau and John C. Wahlke (Beverly Hills, CA: Sage, 1978); Malcolm Jewell, *Representation in State Legislatures* (Lexington: University Press of Kentucky, 1982).

[81] Alan Rosenthal, *The Decline of Representative Government* (Washington, DC: CQ Press, 1998), 15.

[82] As quoted in Grant Reeher, *First Person Political: Legislative Life and the Meaning of Public Service* (New York: New York University Press, 2006), 104.

[83] Michael Mezey, *Representative Democracy* (Lanham, MD: Rowman & Littlefield, 2008), 87.

[84] Rosenthal, *Heavy Lifting*, 30–31.

[85] Betsy Z. Russell, "ITD Board Passes Over Dover Bridge Project," *Spokesman-Review*, January 8, 2009.

[86] As quoted in Rosenthal, *Heavy Lifting*, 24.

[87] Harden, "Multidimensional Responsiveness: The Determinants of Legislators' Representational Priorities."

[88] As quoted in Reeher, *First Person Political*, 81.

[89] Gary F. Moncrief, Joel A. Thompson, and Karl T. Kurtz, "The Old Statehouse, It Ain't What It Used to Be," *Legislative Studies Quarterly* 21 (1996): 57–72.

[90] Rosenthal, *Heavy Lifting*, 22.

[91] Karl T. Kurtz, Gary Moncrief, Richard G. Niemi, and Lynda W. Powell, "Full-Time, Part-Time, and Real Time: Explaining State Legislators' Perceptions of Time on the Job," *State Politics & Policy Quarterly* 6 (2006): 322–38.

[92] Grant Reeher, *First Person Political*, 75. The study asked "which is the most important thing" legislators should do—pass bills, committee work, constituent service, try to cause the chamber to move in a particular direction, or "other." A plurality (38 percent in Connecticut; 46 percent in New York) chose constituent service. Legislators in the third state surveyed (Vermont) ranked constituent service third.

[93] Annie Baxter, "Who to Blame? Parade Provides Few Answers," Minnesota Public Radio, July 5, 2005.

[94] Robert E. Hogan, "Policy Responsiveness and Incumbent Reelection in State Legislatures," *American Journal of Political Science* 52 (2008): 858–73. An argument that this relationship raises damning doubts about the representativeness of state legislatures is given in Eric Prier, *The Myth of Representation and the Florida Legislature: A House of Competing Loyalties, 1927–2000* (Gainesville: University Press of Florida, 2003).

[95] These data are from a Democracy Corps survey conducted from February 14 to February 19, 2007, by Greenberg Quinlan Research.

Index

About the Authors

Peverill Squire is a professor of political science and holds the Hicks and Martha Griffiths Chair in American Political Institutions at the University of Missouri. Among the books he has authored are *The Rise of the Representative: Lawmakers and Constituents in Colonial America* (2017) and *The Evolution of American Legislatures: Colonies, Territories and States, 1619–2009* (2012). He has served as senior editor of *Legislative Studies Quarterly*, chair of the American Political Science Association's Legislative Studies Section and cochair of the International Political Science Association's Research Committee of Legislative Specialists. In 2018 he was given the Career Achievement Award by the American Political Science Association's State Politics and Policy Section.

Gary Moncrief is University Foundation Professor of Political Science at Boise State University. He received his undergraduate degree in political science from the University of California, Santa Barbara and his PhD degree from the University of Kentucky. He is the coauthor or editor of six books, including *Who Runs for the Legislature?* (2001); *Reapportionment and Redistricting in the West* (2012); and *Why States Matter* (second edition, 2017). He has worked with the Council of State Governments, the National Conference of State Legislatures, and the State Legislative Leaders Foundation, and was a consulting scholar with the Eagleton Institute of Politics, Rutgers University.